POVERTY AND FOOD SECURITY IN INDIA
Problems and Policies

POVERTY AND FOOD SECURITY IN INDIA

Problems and Policies

Edited by

M.S. BHATT

DEPARTMENT OF ECONOMICS
Jamia Millia Islamia
New Delhi

AAKAR BOOKS

POVERTY AND FOOD SECURITY IN INDIA
Problems and Policies

First Published, 2004

ISBN 81-87879-37-8

Published by
AAKAR BOOKS
28-E Pocket-IV, Mayur Vihar Phase-I, Delhi-110 091
Phone : 011-22795505 Telefax : 011-22795641
E-mail : aakarb@del2.vsnl.net.in

Typeset at
Nidhi Laser Point, Shahdara, Delhi-110 032

Printed in India on behalf of M/s Aakar Books by
Mudrak, 30 A, Patparganj, Delhi-110 091

Acknowledgements

The present book is a collection of revised versions of the articles presented in a two-day national seminar on: 'Poverty and Food Security – Problems and Policies' organised by the Department of Economics, Jamia Millia Islamia, New Delhi in February, 2003. Many people and organisations generously rendered their assistance and cooperation first in the seminar arrangements and then in processing the proceedings in the form of a book. But for their help it would have been difficult to translate promise into performance. I would like to place on record my gratitude to all these persons and institutions. In particular, the following deserve a special mention:

My wife for her unbounded love and care. She generously lent her precious time and cheerfully bore all inconveniences;

My daughter whose similing face was a source of inspiration and joy;

Shri Syed Shahid Mahdi, former Vice-Chancellor, Jamia Millia Islamia, for his keen interest, encouragement and excellent leadership at various stages of the seminar and publication of the book;

All participants in the above-referred national seminar, particularly the contributors to the present volume who took lot of pains to revise their papers as per our requirements;

Professor Naushad Ali Azad, Dean, Faculty of Social Sciences, Jamia Millia Islamia, for his total involvement and dedication both with the organisation of the seminar and publication of the book. The groundwork was in fact completed under his leadership;

Professor Khan Masood Ahmad, Chairman, Department of Economics, Jamia Millia Islamia, for forewording the present volume and providing all logistic facilities to the editorial staff. His involvement and interest acted as a source of great encouragement;

All my colleagues in the Department of Economics, Jamia Millia Islamia, New Delhi, for their unflattering support and conferring on me the honour of being the Editor of the book. Dr Shahid Ashraf, Dr Shahid Ahmed, S.K. Mathur and Asheref Illiyan, in particular, deserve special thanks;

My research staff and students at the department, particularly Mr Brajesh Kumar, Mr Zakir Hussain, Mr A.K.M. Nazrul Islam and Mr Madan Pal Singh for their valuable support and assistance;

Ministerial staff of the Department of Economics – Abida Begum, Shamsad Khan, Arif Ali and Nazim for their back-up services. In particular Shamsad Khan who diligently processed various drafts of the book;

Mr K.K. Saxena of 'Aakar Books', for his commendable work in getting the book printed in an excellent way;

Last but not the least, Indian Council of Social Science Research (ICSSR), New Delhi and Jamia Cooperative Bank for their financial help.

M.S. BHATT

Foreword

The Department of Economics, Jamia Millia Islamia, New Delhi organised a two-days national seminar on: 'Poverty and Food Security – Problems and Policies' in February 2003. The organisers of this seminar had made a commitment to the participants and sponsors that the papers presented in the seminar would be published. I am indeed happy to know that the organisers have kept their promise. I am honoured to Foreword the book. The Department has always been conscious of its social responsibilities as a centre of higher learning and research. We contribute, in our own humble way, to socio-economic transformation of the society at large. Through debates, seminars and conferences, we provide a platform to people of different persuations for frank and informed debates and discussions. We plan to enlarge the scope and coverage of these activities on more systematic and meaningful lines. The present book is a step in this direction.

Poverty alleviation and achieving food security (both at the national and household levels) have been among the major objectives of development planning in India. Numerous programmes have been put in place to achieve these objective. These include both 'growth-oriented' and 'direct-effect' related programmes of various hues and nomenclatures. A number of steps to improve the nutritional status of the population have been initiated. These include: improving food distribution (mainly through public distribution system); improving household food security; food supplementation through programmes like Integrated Child Development Services (ICDS); nutritional education; efforts to tackle adverse effects of undernutrition, infections and micro-nutrient deficiency. Achieving food self sufficiency has remained the cornerstone of our agricultural policy. Approaches to achieve it have, of course, varied in their orientation, focus and structure but the basic objectives continue to remain the same.

Billions of rupees have been expended in various poverty alleviation and rural development programmes. The government currently spends approximately Rs 24,000 crore per year on food subsidy alone. India has accumulated the largest food stocks in its history. Millions of tonnes of rice and wheat lie in the FCI godowns. Poverty and agriculture-related programmes have been widely evaluated and analysed, both by the official and non-official researchers. This evaluation suggests that both our achievements and failures are graphic. Much has been achieved and much remains to be achieved. Improvements in the life expectancy, literacy, availability of food, and percapita income are accompanied by poverty, hunger, malnutrition and intra-household inequalities in the distribution of food.

Social problems like poverty and hunger cannot be appreciated only in a static framework. The complexity of the issues demand perpetual debates and dialogues among the stockholders. Well informed debates on poverty, hunger, famines, starvation, food-security and food-self sufficiency have taken place. These debates have greatly influenced the evolution of policies and enriched our understanding of the issues involved. With changing context, new problems and issues surface. At times old issues persist in a vicious manner. Future shape and gravity of the present societal concerns need to be assessed objectively. All these demand free and frank debates and dialogue on a regular basis. In case of poverty and food security these assume added significance. Both these problems have persisted for long . Academicians have tried to understand and analyse the roots of these problems. Seminal studies are available which deal with the different facets of poverty and food security. I am happy to say that this spirit has guided and shaped the publication of the present volume. The book, according to my understanding, covers major aspects of poverty and food security. Both macro and regional facets get reflected through its various chapters.

Realisation of the right to food, removal of poverty, hunger and starvation are the primary responsibilities of the state; yet all these goals cannot be achieved entirely by the state. All concerned have to share their responsibilities. Poverty, hunger and malnutrition cannot be wiped-off merely by redistributive food-based programmes alone. The long-term sustainable solution lies in the more imaginative rural development policies that attempt to improve the productive capacities of the poorest in the poorer regions. This is easy said than done. There is an urgent need for more pragmatic policies and programmes. I am sure that the collections of papers in this volume and introduction by the Editor will in its own way help the formulation of these programmes and policies in times to come. I would like to strike a note of caution. We should not be over-ambitious and unrealistic while developing answers and responses to challenges of poverty and food security. The context in which policies are ultimately to be implemented must be analysed objectively. A lot of literature is now available dealing with the inter-linked nature of rural markets in India. This literature suggests that reforms or institutional changes in our market may not yield desired results if other markets are neglected or not properly accounted for. For example, considerable attention is directed at rural credit markets in our poverty alleviation programmes without regard to other markets, like: land, irrigation, labour, extension, insurance and commodity markets. Some rural markets are highly skewed, some are characterised by lot of market imperfections and still others are missing. The rural poor have either no access/control over these markets or have highly rationed access only. This, in turn, denies them the benefits of agricultural growth and overall economic development. The existing nature of rural markets, according to me, acts a barrier to growth and neutralises the impact of poverty alleviation programmes. We must identify the missing links and find appropriate solutions so that growth flows down instead of trickling down. Poverty and food security are too complex problems to be left only to the state to solve. Markets and civil society institutions have to play a role. By ensuring access to and control over production resources such as land, water, improved seeds, appropriate technology, credit, extension services, the poor can become active participants in the process of growth and benefit from it. It is hoped that the present volume will prove a useful addition to the literature on theory and policy of poverty and food security.

Khan Masood Ahmad
Professor and Head
Department of Economics
Jamia Millia Islamia
New Delhi – 110025

Contents

Contributors

Agrawal, Rashmi, Chief, Gender Studies Division, Institute of Applied Manpower Research, Plot No. – 25, Sector 7-A, Narela Institutional Area Delhi – 110040 (India)

Ahmed, Shahid, Lecturer, Department of Economics, Jamia Millia Islamia, Jamia Nagar, New Delhi – 110025 (India)

Ashraf, Shahid, Reader, Department of Economics, Jamia Millia Islamia, Jamia Nagar, New Delhi – 110025 (India)

Azad, N.A., Professor, Department of Economics, Jamia Millia Islamia, Jamia Nagar, New Delhi – 110025 (India)
E-mail: azad_jmi@yahoo.com

Bhat, R.L., Professor, Department of Economics, University of Jammu, New Campus, Jammu – 180004, Jammu & Kashmir (India)

Bhatt, M.S., Professor, Department of Economics, Jamia Millia Islamia Jamia Nagar, New Delhi – 110025 (India)
E-Mail: ab1sul2@yahoo.com

Bilgrami, S.A.R., Professor, Department of Economics, Jamia Millia Islamia, Jamia Nagar, New Delhi – 110025 (India)

Ciamarra, Ugo Pica, Research Fellow, Department of Public Economics, University of Rome, 'La Sapienza' Via der castro Laurenzia No, 900161 Roma, Italy

Dastidar, A.G., Research Associate, Delhi School of Economics, University of Delhi, University Enclave, Delhi – 110007 (India)

Farooqui, T.A., Lecturer, Department of Economics Jamia Millia Islamia, Jamia Nagar, New Delhi – 110025 (India)

Gokarn, Subir, Credit Rating Information Services of India Limited (CRISIL), Hindustan Times Building, 9th Floor, 18–20 Kasturba Gandhi Marg, New Delhi – 110001 (India)

Goldar, B., Professor, Indian Council For Research on International Economic Relations, Indian Habitat Centre, Lodhi Road, New Delhi – 110003 (India)

Gonsalves, Colin, Senior Supreme Court Lawyer and Social Activist, Society for Legal Information Centre (SLIC) Delhi (India) E-mail: slicdelhi@vsnl.net

Illiyan, Asheref, Lecturer, Department of Economics, Jamia Millia Islamia, Jamia Nagar, New Delhi – 110025 (India)

Jaffer, P.C., Indian Administrative Services and Research Scholar, Faculty of Education, Jamia Millia Islamia, Jamia Nagar, New Delhi – 110025 (India)

Joshi, D., Credit Rating Information Services of India Limited (CRISIL) Hindustan Times Building, 9th Floor, 18-20 Kasturba Gandhi Marg, New Delhi – 110001 (India)

Khan, M.A., Professor, Department of Commerce and Business Studies, Jamia Millia Islamia, Jamia Nagar, New Delhi – 110025 (India)

Krishnakumar, S., Department of Economics, College of Vocational Studies, University of Delhi, Sheikh Sarai, New Delhi (India)

Kumar, Arun, Professor, Centre For Economic Studies and Planning, Jawaharlal Nehru University, New Delhi – 110067 (India) E-mail: chaircesp@mail.jnu.ac.in

Kumar, Brajesh, Research Assistant, Department of Economics, Jamia Millia Islamia, Jamia Nagar, New Delhi – 110025 (India) E-mail: Brajesh_Kumar@mail.com

Mathur, S.K., Lecturer, Department of Economics, Jamia Millia Islamia, Jamia Nagar, New Delhi – 110025 (India) E-mail: som@del3.vsnl.net.in

Medrano, P., Country Director and WFP Representative in India, World Food Programme, 2-Poorvi Marg, Vasant Vihar, New Delhi - 110057 (India)

Rao, B.V.L.N. (Retd.), Deputy Advisor, L.E.M. Division, Planning Commission, Yojana Bhavan, New Delhi – 110001 (India)

Rao, K.S., Research Officer, Institute of Applied Manpower Research, Plot No. – 25, Sector 7 – A, Narela Institutional Area, New Delhi – 110040 (India)

Shakthivel, S., Research Associate, Institute of Economics Growth, Delhi University Enclave, Delhi – 110007 (India)

Shariff, A., Chief Economist and Head, Human Resource Division, National Council of Applied Economic Research (NCAER), New Delhi - 110002 (India)

Sharma, K.R., Research Scholar, Department of Economics, University of Jammu, New Campus, Jammu – 180004, Jammu and Kashmir (India)

Yazdani, G., Lecturer, Faculty of Law, Jamia Millia Islamia, Jamia Nagar, New Delhi – 110025 (India)

Introduction

I

Poverty and food security are complex and multi-dimensional issues. Both are interlinked. Poverty encompasses a variety of historical, economic, social, cultural, psychological, spatial, national, international and environmental dimensions. It is not amenable to straightforward procedures of conceptualisation, characterisation, aggregation, identification and alleviation. Given this complexity, an easy way to explain poverty is to focus on its effects. From this angle *Poverty is what poverty does*. It breeds malnutrition, hunger, starvation, illiteracy, marginalisation, lower life expectancy and violence against the weak and social unrest. In 1901, Seebohm Rowntree defined 'families as being in *primary poverty*, if their total earnings are insufficient to obtain minimum necessities for the maintenance of merely physical efficiency'.[1] Amazingly, mainstream policy definitions of poverty continue to replicate Rowntree. Roughly 100 years after his definition, the United Nations Development Programme (UNDP) describes poverty as, *being unable to obtain good food and other items that are essential to everyday life.*

Food is basic to survival. Its insecurity is pregnant with serious ramifications for socio-economic development of a society and its sustainability. No civilised society can afford to ignore them. Pangs associated with an empty stomach are defined as hunger. *Everything else can wait, but not hunger.*[2] *A hungry person listens neither to religion nor reasons, nor is bent by prayers,* rightly remarks the Roman philosopher Seneca.[3] Death due to starvation is the logical culmination of persistence of these pangs. Right to food from this perspective is understood as the right to have two square meals. This is critical but not sufficient. A broader construction encompasses hidden hunger. Besides food, this would include basic needs. Nutrition security is thus broader than food security. Moreover, availability of food at the macro level cannot be equated with availability at the individual/household level or vice versa. Availability, access, utilisation and vulnerability are important determinants of food insecurity at various levels of aggregation. Availability, in turn, is determined by quantum and quality of sources of food. Access hinges on purchasing power. Dietary patterns, preferences, nutritional knowledge and caring practices directly influence utilisation of food. Vulnerability encompasses exchange entitlement failures resulting into starvation and at times starvation deaths.

Food insecurity affects people discriminately. For example, when families are subject to starvation, children and women suffer the most due to their greater vulnerability or need for higher nutrition requirements. Growing infants, adolescent girls, pregnant or lactating mothers face far greater risk to their survival and physical/intellectual growth from nutrition depletion. Damage thus beset is irreversible. Similarly, people with labour-based exchange entitlements are subject to greater risks compared to people with production-based exchange entitlements.

Though causality between poverty and food security is obvious, yet its direction is not definite. On balance, the relationship appears interactive. Direction of this causality may or may not be definite but the consequences of poverty and food insecurity are stark and telling. Economic history is full of instances which suggest that the opportunity cost of persistent poverty and food insecurity is heavy and invariably irreversible. The tragedy of hunger in the midst of plenty is a stark reality in today's world. *Across the world there are people who cannot realise their full human potential, either because their diets are inadequate or because of sickness their bodies are unable to benefit fully from the food they consume. In the poorest countries the majority of people are affected by hunger, greatly magnifying the dimensions of other correctable defects in efforts to meet basic human needs. Whenever and wherever people face food insecurity, they and their nations pay a heavy price through reduced survival capabilities, lost productivity and social development.*[4]

Literature on poverty, hunger, starvation and destitution has indeed mushroomed since the days of Rowntree. Path-breaking contributions by Myrdal, Pyaatt, Atkinson, Sen, Bliss, Harriss, Lipton, Desai, Streeten, Bardhan, Morris, Rawls, Dréze, Dasgupta, Ravallion and Chambers (to name a few) in areas of theory and measurement of poverty, hunger, destitution, inequality, justice and positive freedoms have brought poverty and food/nutrition security to the centrestage of research and policy. This in turn has influenced evolution of new strategies. International funding agencies have attempted to redesign their programmes in the light of these theoretical developments. Some voluntary organisations have also played a critical role by representing the voices of millions of deprived people all over the world and common concerns like poverty, food security and environment degradation.

Despite informed understanding, commitments, policies, programmes and achievements, poverty and food insecurity continue to be among the most critical and pressing economic and social issues of our times. Failures outmatch achievements. If official data are to be trusted, then globally the proportion of people living in poverty declined from 29 per cent in 1987 to 26 per cent in 1998, although the total number of poor remained almost unchanged at around 1.2 billion. In Sub-Saharan Africa, an additional 74 million people joined the ranks of the poor reaching a total of 291 million in 1998. In Latin America, the figure increased from 64 to 78 million (This figure rises to 183 million if a poverty line of $ 2 per day is used. Using this poverty line for all regions yields a number of poor people equal to 2.8 billion, with the largest concentration of poor still in South Asia). In South Asia, a total of 522 million people live in poverty. Countries in Eastern Europe and Central Asia experienced an increase in both incidence of poverty and number of people living below the international poverty line. Here incidence of poverty rose from 2 to 5 per cent, translating into 24 million people in poverty.[5] According to FAO, 830 million human beings suffer from malnutrition and hunger. The world produces more than enough food to feed its entire population. Yet an estimated 35,000 people die of hunger each day in the majority world.[6] Throughout the developed world, farming industry is characterised by subsidies and protection. *True, more food than ever before is being grown, but it is the wrong food at wrong places while much of the world still goes hungry. This bizarre combination of over-production and malnutrition does not even reflect efficiency, however, measured.*

Over the past decade, the total number of chronically undernourished in the developing world has fallen by approximately 40 million but the average rate of decline has continued to slow, reaching only 6 million a year, compared with 8 million reduction rate target. Consequently, the annual reduction required to reach the target by 2015 has grown from 20 to 22 million people per year. Hence, the gap between reductions realised and reductions needed is widening. Continuing at the current rate, it would take more than 60 years to reach the target. Income inequality within countries has not changed significantly in most regions over the years. Average income of the 20 richest countries is now 30 times that of the 20 poorest countries, as compared to 15 times 40 years ago. Industrial countries account for 24 per cent of world's population but they manage to use 48 per cent of its grain and 61 per cent of its meat.[7] Life expectancy in developing countries rose from 55 years in 1970 to 65 years in 1998 but is still far below that of 78 years in OECD countries. Infant mortality rates have fallen from 107 per 1,000 live births in 1970, to 59 in 1998. Net primary school enrolments improved from 78 per cent in 1980 to 84 per cent in 1998 and adult literacy rose from 53 per cent in 1970 to 74 per cent in 1998. However, because of population growth, today there are 41 million more illiterate adults than in 1970.[8] Not surprisingly, the poor generally fare the worst in terms of social indicators, such as illiteracy, malnutrition, ill health (incidence of communicable diseases such as tuberculosis and HIV/AIDS) and mortality and morbidity rates. Among this group, women and girls are often the most severely disadvantaged, as is evidenced by low school enrolment rates and higher incidence of maternal mortality rates. Thus it is obvious even from an optimistic prospective that:

> Freedom from colonisation, science and technology notwithstanding, the spectre of starvation continues to haunt most developing nations. South Asia, in spite of being endowed with rich natural resources and reaching peak agricultural productivity with green revolution, accounts for the highest proportion (40 per cent) of food insecure people (294 million people) in the world.[9]

II

Removal of poverty and achieving food self-sufficiency has been among the basic objectives of development planning in India right from 1951-52. Strategies to achieve these objectives, however, have differed widely. Policy shifts have also taken place in response to the experiences accumulated over time. Changes in approach have been particularly sharp since the *mid-sixties and seventies*.

In the initial phase (1951–65), it was believed that structural and institutional reforms through direct state intervention would generate an in-built mechanism to ensure sustained and self-reliant economic growth on the one hand and the gradual removal of poverty on the other. Poverty was perceived to be a consequence of lack of economic growth and an inegalitarian agrarian structure. Industrialisation of the economy was, therefore, viewed as an indispensable means to accelerate the tempo of economic growth and removal of poverty. Agrarian restructuring was considered as a necessary pre-condition to unleash productive forces from the shackles of predatory landlordism. However, experience in the first decade of development planning (1951–60) demonstrated that the planner's optimism about the country's ability to achieve higher rates of growth, reduce poverty and eliminate hunger was not justified. Subsequent Five-Year Plans, however, did not make any specific departure from the earlier two plans in tackling the problem of mass poverty directly.

A direct interventionist strategy at the macro level was evolved during the Fifth Five-Year Plan to combat absolute poverty. The contents of the anti-poverty programme consisted of: *(i)* provision of employment opportunities; *(ii)* gearing the pattern of investment and composition of output to the consumption pattern of the poor; *(iii)* ensuring availability of basic elements of consumption at stable prices; and *(iv)* provision of social consumption, i.e. education, health, nutrition, etc. Minimum Needs Programme (MNP) was initiated during this period.

It was in the background of this experience that a target group-oriented approach was launched during Sixth Five-Year Plan (1980–85). A number of programmes were launched to alleviate poverty. These plans became integral parts of Seventh and Eighth Five-Year Plan strategies with little variations here and there. Billions of rupees have been pumped through these programmes into the economy. Ensuring food security of late has received added attention as an anti-poverty strategy. Public Distribution System (PDS) restructured into the Targeted Public Distribution System (TPDS) in 1997. TPDS included a 2-tiered subsidised pricing structure for families below (BPL) and above the poverty line (APL). BPL families were supplied foodgrains at a lower price. APL families were supplied at a higher price. Later on, allocation of foodgrains for BPL families was increased. In addition to TPDS, the Government of India operates a number of rural poverty programmes, most of these include a food distribution component. Integrated Rural Development Programme (IRDP), like Community Development Programme of the early fifties, was originally conceived as overall rural development programme. However, it was introduced in selected blocks in 1978-79 and universalised since 02, October 1980 as a major programme of direct attack on rural poverty. Training of Rural Youth for Self-employment (TRYSEM), Development of Women and Children in Rural Areas (DWCRA), Supply of Improved Tool

Kits to Rural Artisans (SITRA), Ganga Kalyan Yojana (GKY) and Million Wells Scheme (MWS) were introduced as adjuncts to IRDP to take care of specific needs of the target groups. These schemes, in actual practice, were implemented as *stand-alone* programmes by the respective line departments. There was little vertical and horizontal coordination. Mid-term Appraisal of the Ninth Five-Year Plan concluded that these programmes, 'presented a matrix of multiple programmes without desired linkages'. These programmes were basically subsidy driven. Their limitations and impacts have been widely reported (See Chapters 8, 9, 19 and 20). Planning Commission (Government of India) appointed an expert committee in 1997 for a thorough review of self-employment and wage-employment programmes. The Committee in its report recommended: *(i)* merger of all self-employment programmes for rural poor; *(ii)* shift from individual beneficiary approach to group-based approach; *(iii)* identification of 'activity clusters' in specific areas, and *(iv)* strong training and market linkages. The government accepted these recommendations and on 1 April 1999 IRDP and allied programmes were merged into a single programme known as Swarnjayanti Gram Swarozgar Yojna (SGSY). SGSY is purported as a holistic programme of micro enterprise development in rural areas with special focus on: *organising the rural poor into self-help groups; capacity building; planning of activity of clusters;* infrastructure support, technology, credit and market linkages. It is predominantly a credit driven programme. All employment programmes were similarly merged into one programme called *Sampoorna Gramin Rozgar Yojna* (SGRY).

Like poverty alleviation, policy attempts to achieve food self-sufficiency at the macro level can be captured through the evolution of post-independent agricultural policy. Broadly this policy can be described in three distinct phases, viz., *(i)* agrarian reform phase, *(ii)* technology phase, and *(iii)* subsidies and incentive phase. These phases significantly correlate with the different stages of poverty alleviation policy as mentioned above.

Grow more food was the catchword of all attempts to achieve self-sufficiency in the first phase. Operationally this was to be achieved by extensive agricultural practices, i.e. by bringing more and more land under cultivation. Among other factors land reforms (as mentioned earlier) were considered as a key requirement to achieve the goal of *grow more food*. Between 1951-52, a number of reform measures were initiated to change the feudal agrarian system.

Some of the significant steps initiated during this phase included: agrarian reforms like abolition of intermediaries in land and conferring the right of tenure to the tiller; building up rural infrastructure like irrigation, water, electrification; arrangement of institutional credit for agricultural purposes; rural marketing networks and setting up extension services. Agricultural research centres of national importance were established during this phase. In addition to these measures, the Community Development Programme (CDP) was launched which aimed at overall development of rural India with people's participation as a critical input. Similarly Cooperative Credit Societies at various levels of administration were established to meet the credit requirements of the agricultural sector. Although this phase did not see a significant success towards food self-sufficiency, it certainly provided the initial momentum.

The second phase started from the mid-sixties. It marked a dramatic shift of focus on agriculture. This shift was warranted by a number of developments on the food front. Chief among these was failure of the first phase measures to enable the country to grow enough food and reduce country's dependency on food imports. The situation was further aggravated by natural disasters like droughts and external factors like 1962 and 1965 wars with China and Pakistan. Institutional solutions to the problems of agriculture were replaced by a technology-led approach. Green Revolution transformed Indian agriculture from a deficit scenario to a surplus one. Application of high yielding varieties of seeds, use of chemical fertilisers and pesticides, assured irrigation, marketing facilities, etc., were the salient focal areas of this phase. It had also seen a rare rural to rural migration in India. People migrated from low productive states to newly grown-up agricultural states in search of better livelihood. The government had initiated a national food buffer system to intervene in the market at minimum prices. This phase is considered the golden period of Indian agriculture. Green Revolution was started in the selected regions/districts having certain initial advantages like assured irrigation. It mainly concentrated in the northwest and a few river valleys in peninsular regions of India. The bulk of the areas of central, western, eastern and northeastern states of India remained out of the preview of the Green Revolution. These regions witnessed massive improvements in agricultural production, which in turn helped the country overcome the looming crisis on the agricultural front.

This agricultural transformation had a profound impact on the socio-economic life of the people in these regions. Studies after studies have reported these impacts. Impressive gains in cereal production were accompanied by inequalities in the overall agricultural growth across the regions, income inequalities within the Green Revolution belts, regional imbalances and serious environmental problems like soil degradation. Emergence of a new powerful class of prosperous farmers (described by some as *KULAKS*/capitalist farmers) was yet another important development. This class gradually became very influential in policy making. Due to its strong influence, the land distribution was badly affected. Large subsidies and guarantees to purchase surplus products were underwritten. At the state level, the reduction of power and water rates led to a disastrous fallout. For example, the Food Corporation of India (FCI) was forced to buy around 70 to 80 per cent of the marketable produce of some states, causing huge storage and management problems. The Government of India had to modify its policy on export of cereal commodities. By the late '90s, India emerged as a major rice exporter. These developments are typed as the *subsidy and incentive phase*. With economic reforms and trade liberalisation, commercialisation of agriculture has led to some major developments of far-reaching consequences. These developments threaten to undermine the very rationale of food self-sufficiency. Policy makers and academicians in times to come have to provide appropriate answers to the following questions related to poverty eradication and agricultural growth:

(i) How to sustain agricultural growth in those areas where the Green Revolution has succeeded in raising the yields and added strength to the overall process of economic growth?

(ii) How to spread the Green Revolution in those areas which have not been so far covered by it but promise lot of potential?

(iii) How to evolve more efficient and vibrant factors and commodity markets necessary for achieving objective numbers *(i)* and *(ii)* above?

(iv) How to integrate poor with the agricultural growth process so that they not only benefit from it but also facilitate its further consolidation?

(v) How to implement more effectively, various poverty alleviation programmes?

(vi) What sorts of changes/reforms are needed in rural markets which can facilitate both agricultural growth and poverty alleviation?

(vii) How to identify an appropriate combination of the government, market and civil society roles in the eradication of poverty?

(viii) How to use science and technology both for realising the full potential of agricultural growth and poverty alleviation?

In retrospect, both our achievements and failures on poverty and food security fronts are glaring. Plenty and poverty, starvation and surplus co-exist. Four decades ago, the country could not produce enough to feed its 440 million population. Today it is able to feed itself without having to wait for the next shipload of PL480 wheat and the shame associated with it. Thanks to the Green Revolution, today our warehouses are filled with surplus of foodgrains. This has ensured food security at the national level. Net availability of foodgrains has increased from 394.9 gram per day in 1951 to 491 gram per day in 2002. We produced 50 million of metric tonne of foodgrains in 1951. Today it is more than 206 million metric tonne. Per capita availability has recorded impressive gains.

As a result, dietary energy availability from cereals, millets, and pulses alone (excluding oilseeds, sugar, roots, and tubers) has gone up from 1,180 calories per capita daily to 1,650 calories. In some regions agricultural growth has also accelerated the overall growth. Official estimates suggest that the incidence of poverty has come down from 53.84 per cent in September 1957–May 1958 to 26 per cent in 2002. Despite these achievements there is enough evidence to suggest that food security at the national level does not mean no one goes hungry. In absolute numbers, about 260 million people are still below the officially defined poverty line, which means one out of every four Indians not having enough purchasing power to meet his/her daily food requirements. Overall poverty figures disguise persistent poverty and food access problems of certain segments of population. In recent years, for example, poverty rates among scheduled castes and scheduled tribes have been reported as high as 55 per cent and 49 per cent respectively, higher than the rates among all other castes. Similarly, intra-household distribution of food is highly skewed with damaging effects on women and children. Recent data indicate that about 36 per cent of women suffer chronic energy deficiency, a third of all babies are born underweight, and 47 per cent of children under three are underweight (with 18 per cent severely underweight).

According to World Food Programme:

> About one fifth of Indians experience all four dimensions of food insecurity (deficiency, inaccessibility, poor utilisation of food and disaster proneness). These are people whom analysts may choose to catalogue as suffering varyingly from chronic food insecurity, nutritional insecurity and transitory food insecurity but the fact remains that they represent the unfilled belly of India.[10]
>
> Above 6 per cent economic growth is accompanied by staggering 208 million undernourished. Forty million Indians are exposed to natural disasters every year. One out of every four chronically food insecure people lives in India. In every five Indians, one suffers from overt or covert hunger. About 50 per cent of India's children are undernourished and stunted, 33 per cent have low birth weight, 69 out of 1,000 die before the age

> of one year. Almost 36 per cent women are malnourished and 52 per cent suffer from anaemia and other micronutrient deficiencies resulting into shocking a high maternal mortality rate of 540 per 1,00,000 live births.[11]

Production gains have not been uniform across the crops. Failure of pulse production is a telling example. Following a 50 per cent increase between 1951 and 1961, there has been virtually no change over the last two decades. As a consequence, the per capita availability of pulses, which stood at 70 gram per day in 1961, has now dropped sharply to about 45 gram per day. With an increase in cereal-millet availability, the pulse-cereal ratio has shown a marked deterioration, falling from about 20 per cent to half that figure at present. Inclusion of pulses in cereal-millet-based diets is critical not only in increasing the protein content, but also in improving the nutritional quality of the protein. A balanced diet recommended by the Indian Council of Medical Research in 1968 contained 70 gram of pulses for an adult subject. A 25 per cent higher production level is needed to support availability at the individual level since allowances have to be made for losses, wastage, and seed purposes. At no time during the last three decades could the production level permit inclusion of 70 gram of pulses daily. This is indeed a disturbing situation.

> Skewed distribution of food is yet another disturbing phenomenon. Many households do not get enough food because of poor purchasing power. A large proportion of such households do not get enough protein either. Impressive buffer stocks of foodgrains held in recent years are a reflection of this low consumption. Current levels of production obviously under such circumstances would not be enough to build reserves.

Be that as it may, availability of food is only one of the components of the consumption. Non-food items, quality of food and intra-household distribution of food are equally important. Unfortunately these issues have not received the desired attention. Persistence of poverty, hunger and starvation along with growing availability of food has rendered the rationale of both poverty alleviation and food self-sufficiency policies suspect and created a paradoxical situation. Policies and programmes have systematically failed with a huge opportunity cost. There is a consensus among policy makers, planners and economists that the problems of poverty, hunger and malnutrition have not been solved satisfactorily. It is also acknowledged that persistence of these problems has the potential of undermining the very process of democratic governance.

There is need for fresh answers to these questions. Available solutions have outlived their utility. Time has come to recast and redefine the agenda for poverty and food insecurity eradication. This is easier said than done. There is a need for a dispassionate debate, discussion and meaningful action. This challenging task cannot be solved by state intervention alone. It is against this backdrop that the Department of Economics, Jamia Millia Islamia, organised a two-day National Seminar on 'Poverty and Food Security in India—Problems and Policies' from 18-19 February 2003. The main objective of this seminar was to involve academicians, policy makers and NGOs for free and informed answers to the above-mentioned issues. How far we succeeded shall partly be reflected through the pages of the present volume, which is a collection of the revised articles presented in this seminar. We are conscious that many crucial theoretical and policy issues could not find a place in this volume. With all humility, we do accept the primacy of these issues. But due to obvious reasons, these could not be accommodated. Whatever we have presented is expected to prove a useful addition to the literature on poverty and food security. It is hoped that it will serve, in some way, as a fruitful guide to formulation of effective policies for poverty and food insecurity eradication. The volume has been organised in two sections. Section I deals with the macro issues and Section II presents some illustrations of the issues at the regional / micro level. A chapter-wise resume of these sections is presented in the following pages.

III

Poverty and hunger alleviation strategies have often been

formulated and implemented in isolation by different agencies with lop-sided coordination at the grassroot level. These have also been premised on ill-conceived formulations. This obviously causes replication, waste and mushrooming of programmes. Moreover, expenditure on these strategies is invariably treated as consumption. Consequences are not far to seek. Pedro Medrano's paper (Chapter 1) provides evidence and argument to understand the limitations and consequences of mainstream approaches and policies, which have informed poverty and hunger alleviation efforts. Medrano pleads for a paradigm shift in our approach to *targeted food interventions*. He argues: 'money spent on them should be treated as investment in human resource development.' Medrano' offers very appealing and intuitive policy options for India to manage its food security efficiently and justly. He argues that:

> Economics of hunger is simple and straightforward: direct and integrated food-based interventions are not only an investment but also savings, with very high returns. Social policy is a productive factor; it should not be regarded as a choice between economic efficiency and social equity when investing in a social programme. While overarching goal of development at the global level is the reduction and elimination of poverty, policy and planning have often overlooked the intrinsic causal relationship between poverty and hunger, their linkages and their repercussions. As the world, particularly the developing countries, grapple with stark and depressing realities of hunger, malnutrition and low basic human development indicators like low birth weight (LBW), etc., question arises why mammoth investments in employment, education, skills and training have not filtered down to the pockets of intense hunger and suffering throughout the world. What is the missing link, the elusive gap? In a fresh beginning, the concept of poverty must be re-defined in order to illuminate its true connotations. Neither 'growth-mediated-security' nor 'support-led-security' which respectively emphasise economic development and welfare strategies has solved poverty and hunger related problems completely or permanently. Denial of access to a minimum quality of life required by every individual to achieve his/her full potential is a broader view of poverty. This entails a closer scrutiny of the 'minimum quality of life' uncontested basic needs or

> entitlements of every individual have a healthy productive life, namely sufficient food, nutrition, safe drinking water, shelter.

Professor Arun Kumar (Chapter 2) very ably and dispassionately relates the issues and challenges of food insecurity to vital and wider issues of sovereignty, national security and globalisation. For him food self-sufficiency is linked with the independence of nation to pursue its own goals. The type of globalisation, which we have pursued, poses a serious thereat to this independence. Prof. Kumar argues:

> Food security does not just stand for availability of food to the population, as would be the case with the availability of other goods. Clearly, it is more basic than most other goods and its reduced availability causes severe problems for society. It may be imported, but as happened in the mid-sixties when the USA extracted a heavy price from the Indian economy for the food it exported to India. This may entail a heavy political and economic price, which may not be in the nation's wider interest. The issue of food self-sufficiency is then linked up with the independence of the nation to pursue its own goals. That the present Indian ruling classes have not been protecting the wider national interest is obvious. Our farmers' interest, an important part of the national interest, has been compromised. These aspects need to be fully analysed and understood. Responsibility of society to individual and of state to citizen needs to be reasserted. Immorality and amorality of the markets needs to be understood. The issue then is what should have priority, 'Man' or 'Market'? The answer should be obvious. But how this is to be brought about in the contemporary situation is a major intellectual challenge.

Environment-economy-poverty linkages have become serious issues of theory, research and policy. The end of eighties saw a concerted reappraisal of the concerns about uses of resources and their availability, environmental consequences of overexploitation of natural resources, and interface among environment, economy and poverty. This has given birth to a new approach to economic development that seeks to reconcile human needs and capacity of the environment to cope with the consequences of economic development. This new approach is described as sustainable development. Equity and caring for the needs of the last are central to it. This calls for meeting the survival needs of the world's poorest as a first goal and striving for a standard of living which ensures security and dignity for all. Obviously, there is need for new form of decision-making and policy instruments. Against this backdrop, Prof. Azad in his paper on *Poverty and Sustainable Development* (Chapter 3) tries to explore salient dimensions of poverty, sustainable development and the relationship between the two. The paper identifies some policy inputs for poverty alleviation and sustainable development. According to Prof Azad:

> Poverty and sustainable development (SD) are two socio-economic phenomena drawing global attention of academics, researchers, policy makers as well as human activists. Traditionally the issues of poverty and SD have been treated separately and singularly but during the last one decade there have been conceptual developments and paradigm shifts in these areas. They are now viewed as concepts that are multi-dimensional and more comprehensive. Also, there is some degree of convergence within and between the two in that the issue of poverty and food security (as well as many other issues of human deprivation and social welfare) are now considered an integral part of the bigger challenge known as SD. Further, most of the remedial aspects of poverty and SD require direct action and a pro-active involvement on part of the government, the private sector, the civil society and the NGOs at all levels–local, national and global... We conclude by saying that enhanced public investment in physical and social infrastructure of the rural areas is the key to a successful long-term SD in India. The focus has to be on productivity improvements in on-farm activities and, at the same time, strengthening the possibilities of income and employment generation in the non-farm and off-farm activities of the rural areas. How these resources will be mobilised and how the various programmes for the alleviation of income and human poverty will be organised and implemented remains the million dollar question.

Gunnar Myrdal once remarked, *It is in the agricultural sector that the battle for long-term economic development will be won or lost*. No industry is more indispensable to our present and future wellbeing than agriculture. Though 'Agriculture is truly one of the triumphs of human civilisation yet throughout the modern world there is soil erosion, water pollution, increasing pests and diseases, falling yields and collapsing agricultural economics.' The manner in which Third World agricultural trade is being liberalised has added yet another dimension to the battle for long-term economic development in the developing countries like India. There is need for a passionate understanding of the issues involved. Dr Krishna Kumar's paper (Chapter 4) on *Agricultural Trade Liberalisation and Food Security* is timely and full of theoretical and empirical insights. Implications of agricultural trade liberalisation on food security have been delineated. Dr Kumar argues:

> The nineties have witnessed the rise to the dominance of neo-liberalism in the international economy. The period was also witness to new steps in trade liberalisation starting with the Uruguay Round. As against the previous rounds, the decade witnessed agriculture being brought under the purview of trade negotiations. This marks a departure from the history of world food regimes till date where domestic national food policies had autonomy over international considerations. Ever since, production for the global market started regaining currency amidst the policy makers, despite lessons from the Mexican experience. The same is not without consequences due to manifold reasons: secular deterioration in the relative terms of trade of primary commodities, the presence of well-entrenched international marketing groups for commodities in the world markets that negates the chances of any price increases being transferred to the less developed countries and the growing concerns of the declining per capita availability of foodgrains. The third of which is made even more complicated by the erratic fluctuations of the prices in the world grain market. There have been two streams of arguments with regard to agricultural trade liberalisation: one which argues for a system that counts on the neoclassical logic of 'getting prices right', so as to disallow the 'plundering of agriculture' for the sake of industrial development. The other school looks at food as a wage-good in the classical political economy tradition and considers agricultural surplus to be necessary component to facilitate the process of industrialisation. In the structuralist scheme of things, the price of foodgrains turns out to be an important determinant

of industrial performance in the country. The latter group also gives due focus on issues relating to food security.

Poverty and unemployment in India have often been studied at *All India* and *All States* levels using mostly data sets made available by the National Sample Organisation. This context is indeed vital but not adequate. Some aspects of poverty-employment relationship can only be better appreciated if analysed in a decentralised frame of reference. In view of the debates on poverty, food security and economic growth, this type of research has assumed added significance. Prof. Goldar and Dr Sakthivel's paper (Chapter 5) on *Employment and Poverty in Rural India—A Study of NSS Regions*" is an interesting addition to the literature on poverty and employment. The authors try to study changes in the incidence of rural poverty and growth-employment across the NSS regions with special reference to the 1990s. Specific objectives of this study were:

(i) To find out whether observed changes in the rural poverty ratios hold true across the NSS regions;

(ii) Whether inter-regional variations in the decline of poverty is correlated by employment growth.

The study concludes:

> There has been a general reduction in rural poverty in India in the 1990s. However, inter-regional dispersion in poverty has not come down, and in a significant proportion of regions, there has been either an increase or only a marginal decline in poverty. A moderate growth has taken place in rural employment in the primary sector, with somewhat better performance in secondary and tertiary sectors. Estimates on rural employment suggest that growth of male employment has been fairly distributed across all regions while growth of female employment does not follow this trend. In a majority of regions, rural employment has grown. But female employment, witnessed mixed results wherein 50 out of 74 regions displayed positive growth while the rest had slipped into the negative growth territory. On an average there has been a moderate growth of women employment in rural areas. An analysis of association between employment growth and poverty reduction suggest that there is no significant relationship. It appears that even with a significant growth in

> employment, some regions have failed to make any dent on poverty. And, on the other hand, without any significant growth in employment in some regions, poverty reduction has been possible. A significant negative relationship is found between poverty ratio and the share of secondary and tertiary sectors in rural employment. Based on estimates, it seems that there was about 2.5 percentage point increase in the share of secondary and tertiary sectors in rural employment and this has made a part of contribution to the total reduction in rural poverty in India in the 1990s.

Empirical studies suggest that poverty and food insecurity hurt women more than men. According to the UN, 70 per cent of the world's poor are women. Nobel Laureate Amartya Sen says: *Within each community, nationality and class, the burden of hardship falls disproportionately on women.* Even among women, poverty and food insecurity are discriminatory. For example, predominantly self-employed women in the rural informal sector belonging to lower social strata are severely affected by poverty and food insecurity. Low and irregular wages aggravate the problem of food insecurity during lean agricultural operations. Relative share of women in workforce has increased over the years. It has also been observed that the poorer the family, the higher is women's labour participation. But their access to and control over critical resources is marginal. The United Nation's Millennium Development Goals (UNMDG) have identified women's empowerment, as a goal in its own right and declared, 'If this goal is to be reached, it is critical that feminisation of poverty (increasingly recognised by the government as well as international documents) receive *systematic attention*, especially in the era of globalisation. Dr Shahid Ashraf and T.A. Farooqui (Chapter 6) outline the recipe of this *systematic attention* with reference to rural female workforce. Citing from the empirical studies, the authors opine:

> *Poverty and food security are inter-linked and the roadmap towards decreasing poverty and improving food security, specifically of the rural women is through their access to employment. For the vast majority of rural females the most viable strategy is the sustained self-employment for their individual and household food security.*

The paper suggests that developing gender specific institutions for increasing rural female employment is an important and viable strategy.

Dr Rashmi Agrawal and B.V.L. Rao (Chapter 10) arguing from a macro perspective describe various facets of gender discrimination. The strength of this article lies in its macro and micro empirical basis. The authors rightly conclude that:

> Empowerment of 'self' is an essential pre-requisite to socio-economic and political empowerment of women. This, of necessity, has to be taken up in a phased manner. There should be a national plan of personality development of women. Implementation of the programme may be in a phased manner to cover all women gradually with special focus on the most needy women or where some kinds of empowerment strategies have been adopted.

Seen in the context of development as 'process of expending real freedoms that people enjoy', the 'rights approach' to food security is quite appealing. Right to food is interpreted as freedom from hunger (both open and hidden). The main objective of this approach is to fix responsibility and accountability. Citizen's organisations like People's Union for Civil Liberties (PUCL) have filed public interest litigations invoking right to food. Apex courts have in turn issued landmark directions/interim orders that have imparted vitality to *right to food campaign*. Developments at the international level have also added strength to this campaign. The campaign is still in its embryonic stage. Lot more needs to be done in order to ensure that it does not remain a pipe dream. Dr Shahid Ahmed and Dr Gulam Yazdani reviewed these developments in their article entitled *Human Rights, Agricultural Deregulation and Food Security* (Chapter 7). They argue:

> Food Security and Food Sovereignty are essential conditions for life with dignity. Liberalisation of agriculture under the Agreement on Agriculture (AoA) is threatening the livelihoods of millions, especially the most vulnerable rural population in the poorest countries. Globalisation of food trade is leaving behind those who are unable to participate for lack of assets, skills, technology and ethnic-gender-based discrimination.

> Reality is that the economic policies of most governments have widened the gap between wealthy and poor countries and have accentuated the unequal distribution of earnings within countries... First and most important right of all human beings is the right to food.

Distribution of the incidence of food insecurity across occupations, gender, households, age, consumption pattern and socio-religious milieus are fundamental to policy formulation. Article 47 of the Constitution of India states that 'the state shall regard raising the level of nutrition and standard of living of its people and improvements in the public health as one of its primary duty.' Successive Five-Year Plans laid down policies and strategies to improve micro and macro nutrient nutritional status of the people. As a result of these interventions there has been a substantial reduction in sever energy deficiency and improvements in nutritional status of all segments of the population. But gray areas are still there. Poverty is considered one of the major causes of low dietary intake. Professor Abusaleh Shariff's paper *Nutritional Food Security in India* (Chapter 8) outlines various dimensions of nutritional food insecurity with special reference to its distribution. Various policies have also been reviewed. Prof Shariff opines:

> Strategies to augment just the income levels are not adequate to eliminate undernutrition. Employment generation, as an empowering strategy, needs to be strengthened. Any amount of safety net will be inadequate due to resource constraint. State policies and programmes relating to nutrition and health are too weak to make the desired impact...Sustainability of our agriculture is the crucial issue. Increase in production in the future will come not from area expansion, but from enhanced productivity through improved and sustainable agricultural practices. Innovative packages are needed which will harness our traditional skills and strengths. In view of the fact that large areas of the country are becoming prone to soil degradation community based programmes for conservation and enhancement of land, water resources combined with sustainable systems of use, need to be developed through micro-planning. Realities of the agriculture scenario today underscore

> the importance of diversification. Availability of animal protein in Indian diet needs to be increased at least twofold from the present level of ten gram with special emphasis on maintaining the nutritional levels of growing children and nursing mothers.

Evaluation of poverty alleviation programmes is a favorite hunting ground of empirical researchers in India. Studies after studies are available. These have been conducted at almost all possible levels of aggregation by researchers, official agencies, NGOs, and international organisations. The central message from most of these studies is that despite achievements poverty still persists. To review these studies needs both expertise and patience to sift fact from fiction. This is a difficult task. But Ananya Ghosh Dastidar's paper entitled *Poverty Alleviation Programme in India: Issues and Concerns* (Chapter 9) shows how this difficult task can be made easy and meaningful. This paper dissects various poverty alleviation programmes and available literature. On the basis of this dissection suggestions have been put forth which should serve as a basis for improving the effectiveness of poverty alleviation programmes. She aptly remarks:

> Redesigning of the Poverty Alleviation Programmes (PAP), with a view to improving the targeting aspect should be a top priority of the government, in particular the attempt must be to enhance the coverage of the poor population. Also, administrative procedures related to funds disbursal should be simplified and made more transparent. Alongside these measures, the institution of the Gram Sabha should be made functional and Panchayats made more accountable to them. There is need to draw attention, at the same time, to some serious lacunae in the literature that focuses on the design and implementation of PAPs in the Indian context. First of these relate to government's stance regarding the role of NGOs in alleviating poverty. There is no indication in the existing literature as to how the government should go about framing a 'NGOs-policy' that incorporates role these agencies could play in making PAPs a success. It is also widely recognised that one of the most serious problems faced at the implementation stage is that of widespread mis-targeting which in turn stems largely from rampant corruption encountered at each level. Yet the following questions are not

> clearly raised in the existing literature: 'What incentive do programme officials have, to implement the programmes effectively?' 'Is there a proper system of accountability built into the programme-administration system itself, which attempts to take care of the problem of corruption?' There is an urgent need to analyse these questions.'

Micro illustrations of the problems and prospects are provided by Dr Srinavasa Rao and Prof. M. Altaf Khan through their case studies of Bahraich District of Uttar Pradesh and Orissa, respectively. Incidence of poverty in Orissa has persistently remained one of the highest in the country. Despite much promise and potential the state continues to be one of the least developed Indian states. Recently the state has come to limelight for wrong reason, i.e. starvation deaths. Independent sources have confirmed that people have died due to starvation despite food being available at block headquarters. This is a classical case of criminal mismanagement of food distribution. Prof. Altaf's paper (Chapter 20) assumes significance in this context. His main argument is:

> *No poor, No hunger, No violence is our Kalma.* To achieve this noble purpose, there is a need for setting up a centre for poverty eradication programme where a Tailor-made Management Programme (TMP) for poverty eradication programmes will develop. State and district level centres are required to conduct overall studies of poverty problems of various states of India. Poverty problem are quite different from state to state and district to district. Coordination of all these should be made at a state as well as district level. These centres will cater the different needs like awareness programmes, coordination programmes and credit programms.

K. Srinivassa Rao's impact study (Chapter 19) analyses various operational aspects of rural development programmes such as: guidelines, survival of assets created, targeting, identification impact on productivity, functioning of *Panchayati Raj Institutions* and their role in poverty alleviation, role of women *Panchas* and *Sarpanchas*, etc. The study has been conducted by the Institute of Applied Manpower Research, New Delhi under the auspices of Ministry of Rural

Development (Government of India), Current Evaluation Programme. The study buttresses the main inferences of Dr Ananya Ghosh Dastidar and Prof. Altaf. Rao concludes:

> On the strength of the survey results we believe a holistic approach is needed to implement various programmes at the grassroots level and to tackle issues ranging from socio-economic to local level administration. In spite of continuous efforts made by the government, chronic problems are rampant in the studied villages. Our study reveals that the required infrastructure facilities are not available in the desired quantity and quality in the sampled district. If at all some facilities exist, their working condition is very poor. For anti-poverty programmes, being aimed at the most disadvantaged group with low income and low level of literacy, need for a locally effective delivery system is of critical importance. Assistance has to reach the doorstep of the beneficiary. Such a function can be best performed only by the local Panchayats. The Gram Sabha can play a key role.

An influential school of thought believes that growth in general and agricultural growth in particular is the most appropriate strategy to remove rural poverty. A number of studies have been conducted to elucidate the validity of this argument. These studies promise that there is significant positive correlation between persistence of poverty and low growth. Therefore, all barriers to higher growth must go. Trade liberalisation and economic reforms, seen from this angle are considered as necessary pre-conditions for higher growth. Analyses of sectoral and spatial distribution of growth are available which surmise that reforms, in particular trade liberalisation, have a very strong positive impact on growth. An implicit implication of argument is that with higher growth incidence of poverty is bound to reduce. Premising their argument on this formulation, Subir Gokaran and D. Joshi (Chapter 11) examine spatial and sectoral pattern of growth between 1980s and 1990s. They suggest that reforms have helped but all states were not equally equipped to harvest the benefits of reforms. They argue:

> Most states have witnessed acceleration in both industry and services. Since the reforms of the 1990s were oriented primarily

> towards these two sectors, it may be reasonable to conclude that these states were, by and large, able to take advantage of the increased opportunities offered by the reforms. However, the full benefits of reforms were denied to them, because of the negative trend in the mostly unreformed agricultural sector. Most states experienced a deceleration in growth in this sector, which obviously detracted from their achievements in industrial and services sectors. It would thus be unfair to conclude that reforms have not resulted in faster growth. If anything, this decomposition only reinforces the link between reforms and growth.

Somesh Kumar Mathur (Chapter 12) examines the impact of trade liberalisation on economic growth and poor with special reference to some Asian countries. Trade, according to Somesh, is likely to make impact on the poor through higher growth. Regression analysis employed by the author shows that trade openness is one of significant factors in explaining variations in growth of per capita gross domestic product in the sampled South Asian countries. Economic growth, in turn, has a significant positive impact on poverty. He explores possible caveats and pre-conditions for this to materialise both in the short and long run. The author concludes:

> There is unambiguous empirical evidence from economies around the globe and for some of the Asian economies that trade openness promotes economic growth. Raising economic growth in a sustained manner reduces poverty. However, most of the poor in the developing economies are in the agricultural sector, therefore, raising growth in the agricultural sector is an essential ingredient for making the reform process successful. There is no convincing evidence that economic growth per se could lower income and wealth inequalities. Policies, like fully government-funded public and social services with land reforms, may be the key for promoting distribution of incomes in the countries. Impact of trade reform on the poor in the short run will critically depend on their location in terms of consumption and production (income). The best outcome is when the poor are employed primarily in the exportable sector and consume importable goods. And the worst outcome occurs if the poor are primarily employed in the importable sector and consume primarily exportable goods. Long-run effects of trade reform are beneficial

> to the poor if labour market functions efficiently. Labour market segmentation dampens the positive effect. A combination of slower output growth in agriculture with deteriorating terms of trade is the major reason why rural incomes in South Asia have tended to lag behind urban incomes. Globalisation and trade reform would have had greater positive effect if agricultural growth would not have lagged due to falling terms of trade, low technology diffusion and cuts in public investment including investment in rural infrastructure, public irrigation, roads and power. Appropriate mix of trade policies with complementary macro and microeconomic policies are needed to benefit from interaction with the global economy. Safety nets are absolutely essential to alleviate and minimise pains of adjustment at least in the short run.

While Gokaran, Joshi and Somesh view growth and economic reforms as *poverty reducing*, Colin Gonsalves and Prof. S.A.R. Bilgrami (Chapter 13 and 14 respectively) suspect this line of argument. Gonsalves focuses on the type of reforms initiated on behest of international funding agencies like World Bank and IMF. He laments the manner in which structures, organisations institutions, (built over the years spending millions of public money) are being systematically destroyed in the name of reforms. Gonsalves believes that this is fraught with serious ramifications for our sovereignty and economic independence. In this respect he illustrates the manner in which government appointed high-level committees seem to implement the agenda set by the international funding agencies. Gonsalves elaborates this point by citing the specific example of 'High Level Committee on long-term grain policy'. He concludes:

> Built up painstakingly over the last 3 decades it is an incredible structure for the maintenance of national food security. It rests on three pillars: (a) a reasonable price paid to farmers so that production levels of cereals are kept up; (b) The FCI system for large scale and efficient procurement, storage and transportation of grain, and (c) a public distribution system (PDS) for the transfer of subsidised grain to the poor. It is essential to maintain cereal self-sufficiency because the devious policies of rich countries and the highly volatile nature of international cereal prices make

> the import of cereals a very dangerous policy. Surplus production of a few advanced countries accounts for four fifth of the global trade in cereals. US farm subsidy is expected to be about 50 billion dollars a year. Once the US grain exporters get a monopoly on the basis of highly subsidised grain exports, prices will be pushed up leading to a grave crisis.

Professor Bilgrami on the other hand discusses the impact of economic reforms on the poor. He shares the widely held view that economic reforms are anti-poor. Gradual retreat of government from critical areas and curtailment of government expenditure on welfare programmes is bound to hurt the poor further. According to him, reform programmes per se is not undesirable provided it takes care of the welfare of the weaker sections of the society. Professor Bilgrami avers:

> Since the initiation of economic reforms in 1991, one widely discussed issue has been its impact on the poor. Popular notion that has emerged is that the on-going reform measures are 'anti-poor.' It is argued that these do not envisage welfare-based support to economically weaker sections of the society. Five decades of our 'planned' development present extreme divergences. Equity-based approach of our plans remained unsuccessful in reducing the struggles of the poor. But succeeded, from all angles, in multiplying the comforts of the rich. The gist of our achievements is that we have given too little to the poor and too much to the rich. Instead of paying more attention on reforming our own policies to make them more effective and useful for the poor, we have introduced an unbalanced reform policy, which is bound to aggravate poverty. When the role of government is gradually reducing and the markets are dominating, the emergence of frustration amongst the poor is quite natural. The 'human face' of economic reforms or its 'swadeshi texture' proposes to take care of this critical dimension.

Poverty debate in India has centred round such issues as: definition of poverty line, nutrition and undernutrition, deflators to be used to update/down-date the normatively defined national poverty line, identification, aggregation of characteristics of poverty, determinants of poverty, quality of the data utilised in particularly, National Sample Survey

Consumption Expenditure Data (NSS data) official strategies for poverty alleviation, and evaluation. Number of studies have been conducted on these aspects of the debate. Most of these studies deal with the issues in an aggregated framework. This context is important but not sufficient. It is in this context that Prof. Bhatt and B. Kumar's paper on *Rural Poverty and Agrarian Power: Village-level Evidence from Bihar* (Chapter 15) assumes significance. Bhatt and Kumar explore and explain the causality between rural poverty and agrarian power and land concentration with special reference to Bihar. They have tested the following hypothesis:

> There is significant causal relationship between rural poverty as dependent variable, and land concentration and agrarian power as predictors.

Results of logistic regression employed in the study have confirmed the proposed relationship between dependent variable and the explanatory variables. The authors opine that land distribution alone cannot achieve the objective of providing command-over food thereby alleviate poverty and reduce inequality. Increasing output or productivity of land/labour in the reformed sector demands more than the celebrated remark by Arthur Young, *The magic of property turns sand into gold*. In Bihar, prevailing agrarian power and institutions, which sustains it, breed rural underdevelopment. For poverty removal, achieving higher growth is a critical requirement. Along with reforms in the agrarian power structures, there is need for major reforms in the size, quality and direction of state intervention. Restructuring of factor and commodity markets is warranted both from efficiency and equity considerations. Basic question is *Can this be done through state interventions*? There is no reason why it cannot be done. Alternative is anarchy.

Agrarian reforms have invariably been considered necessary for tapping the potentialities of men and material and overcome rural underdevelopment. Decadent and exploitative land ownership pattern breed underdevelopment. Agrarian reforms have been justified both on equity and efficiency grounds. Theory and practice lend credence to the view that reforming such agrarian systems posters social equity and triggers efficiency in resource allocation. Contrasting views are available about the way this restructuring should be initiated. For example, some favour state-led land reforms while others believe that market-assisted voluntary reforms are more effective. Agrarian history tells us that no single solution transcends all contexts. All these options are supplemented by success stories in the past. Ugopica Ciamara's paper entitled *State-led and Market Assisted Land Reforms: History Theory and Insights from Philippines* (Chapter 16) very ably steers clear of the misconcepts about these contrasting arguments. He believes that in theory both state-led or market–assisted land reforms can do well if associated with high quality institutions and placing of resources with the poor. Ciamara elucidates his thesis by analysing the Philippines experience with land reforms. He addresses that:

> Philippine agrarian reform experience of 1988 shows that state-led and market-assisted land reform approaches to land reallocation can be successful complement policies. The Philippine agrarian reform programme is both coercive state-led and voluntary market-driven. The Philippine experience indicates that possibilities exist for the process of land acquisition and distribution to be successfully carried out under a joint state-led/market-assisted approach, challenging the disagreement between state-led and market-assisted land reform proponents. Of course the Philippine programme is very innovative and worth monitoring carefully and subject to rigorous and independent scrutiny in order to extract lessons for better applications in other contexts.

This study thus offers important policy messages for India. There is an urgent need for recasting the issues relating to agrarian reforms and their link with rural poverty and food security. These issues have been sidetracked for long.

People's Participation via democratic decentralisation has always been treated as a critical input for rural development and poverty alleviation. Exceptions apart, India's experience with this form of development administration has been far from satisfactory. Despite constitutional mandates the progress on this front has been lop-sided to say the least. Constitutional 73rd and 74th amendment acts were, indeed, landmark developments in the legislative history of India. Following from these amendments almost all India states have created the *Panchayati Raj Institutions* in place. However, much needs to done to make this system vibrant and sustainable. This is a difficult task. Kerala provides example of how to make difficult goals easy to achieve. Asheref Illiyan and P.C. Jaffer recast Kerala's experiences and experiments with people's participation in their paper *People's Participation in Poverty Alleviation and Rural Development Programme—A Case of Kerala's People's Plan Experience (PPP)* (Chapter 17). Kerala's PPP is a unique exercise in democratic governance and people's participation. With all its limitations it has proved an effective strategy of poverty eradication. The authors conclude that:

> People's Plan Programme launched by Government of Kerala was indeed a major innovation carried out in this field so far. It has made a major impact on planning and rural development in the state. Enthusiasm generated among masses is a reflection of the positive impact this new approach has made. Our analysis makes it clear that people's participation in rural development and poverty alleviation schemes makes a significant difference in terms of better allocation of resources, completion of projects in time and space, formulating projects suitable to local resource endowment, proper identification of beneficiaries, proper monitoring and social audit, etc. A new culture of participative development has developed. Of course this model is not free of limitations as common people who do not have any experience are asked to prepare complex plan documents. These have to be looked upon as aberrations that are bound to take place while the system moves into a new phase. It is to be noted that other states have to learn lessons and take inspirations from this unique experience, Kerala's experiment in decentralisation could serve as a role model for other states.

Small and hinterland states and regions have often been left out in studies on poverty, hunger, nutrition and food security under the pretext of non-availability of data or their relative small size. This has led to a lot of randomisation about the nature, magnitude and roots of the above-mentioned problems of these regions/states. This highlights the need for context-specific studies. These studies are bound to supplement our understanding of the issues involved. These aspects have not received due attention in the approach to poverty and food security. Against this backdrop Prof. R.L. Bhatt and Kuldeep Raj Sharma highlight the repercussions of inadequate food intake on the physical and mental development of human body citing evidence from Khour block of Jammu District of Jammu & Kashmir state (Chapter 19). Data have been collected from 214 sampled primary school children who were studying in class II–VI and were between 6–12 years of age. Some interesting conclusions of this study in the words of authors are:

> Mother's and father's education are also positively correlated with each other. Both the variables have a positive correlation with all the nutrient intake variables and outcome measures, a reasonable positive correlation with the productivity of a child and a negative correlation with the health of the child.

NOTES

1. Education for All – The Year 2000 Assessment, UNESCO, Paris.
2. *Human Development in South Asia, 2002, Agricultural and Rural Development,* Mahbub-ul-Haq Human Development Centre, (Pakistan, 2003), pp.96-97, 101.
3. Lang, T. and Hines, 1993, Colin, 'The New Protection', *Earthscan,* London.
4. Medrano, P., 2002, *Tackling Hunger: United Nations World Food Programme's Effort to Help Food Insecurity in India, A Review of Strategic Action, New Delhi, pp.* 2. http://www.newint.org/issue267/267facts.html.
5. National Family Health Survey (NFHS-2), 1998-99, India.
6. *Poverty Reduction and the World Bank: Progress in Fiscal 1999.* World Bank, Washington, 2000.
7. Sarin, Rita, 2003, 'Food Security Through Women's Leadership in the Village Panchayats', Paper Presented in 'International Gender Poverty Summit', Vigyan Bhawan, New Delhi, India, 9–11, November, 2003.

8. Sen, A.K., 1981, *Poverty and Famines: An Essay on Entitlement and Deprivation*, Chapter 3, Oxford University Press, Delhi.

REFERENCES

1. Sen, A.K., 1981, "Poverty and Famines: An Essay on Entitlement and Deprivation", Chapter 3, Oxford University Press, Delhi.
2. Sarin Rita, 2003, 'Food Security Through Women's Leadership in the Village Panchayats", Paper Presented in 'International Gender Poverty Summit', Vigyan Bhawan, New Delhi, India, November 9–11, 2003.
3. Medrano, P, 2002, *Tackling Hunger: United Nations World Food Programme's Effort to Help Eliminate Food Insecurity in India*, New Delhi, India.
4. Medrano, P., 2002, *Tackling Hunger: United Nations World Food Programme's Effort to Help Food Insecurity in India, A Review of Strategic Action*, New Delhi, pp. 2.
5. *Poverty Reduction and the World Bank: Progress in Fiscal 1999*, World Bank, Washington, 2000.
6. Medrano, P, 2002, *Tackling Hunger: United Nations World Food Programme's Effort to Help Eliminate Food Insecurity in India*, New Delhi, India. (http://www.newint.org/issue267/267facts.html)
7. Lang, T. and Hines Colin, 1993, 'The New Protection', *Earthscan*, London.
8. Education for All – The Year 2000 Assessment, UNESCO, Paris.
9. 'Human Development in South Asia', 2002, *Agricultural and Rural Development*, Mahbub-ul- Haq Human Development Centre (2003, Pakistan), pp.96-97, 101.
10. Medrano, P., *Tackling Hunger: United Nations World Food Programme's Effort to Help Food Insecurity in India, A Review of Strategic Action*, New Delhi, 2002, pp. 2.
11. National Family Health Survey (NFHS-2), 1998-99, India.

MACRO PERSPECTIVE

Chapter 1

Mainstreaming Food and Nutrition Issues into Poverty Alleviation Efforts*

Pedro Medrano

Why Mainstream Food and Nutrition Issues—making a Case for Hunger? There are mainly two strands to this argument. On the one hand, poverty eradication approaches which do not prioritise food and nutrition issues have never been and can never be entirely successful; and on the other, programmes to directly address hunger and undernutrition can prove to be the fastest track to poverty alleviation and economic development, as opposed to employment generation schemes or cash transfers. There is no doubt that it is imperative to construct a coherent framework which would encompass agricultural and rural development, removal of trade barriers and incentives for local production, natural resource and eco-management, technical assistance, access to land, credit and technology to farmers, and beyond-farm investments such as health, education, infrastructure, and private investment. However, we will not go far if we do not begin at point zero: that is, empty stomachs, hunger pangs of a stunted child, a

* Transcribed version of a recorded lecture. A revised version of the paper was presented at the National Food Security Submit, New Delhi, February 4-5, 2004 Usual disclaimers apply.

starving mother, a lethargic farmer, or a diseased elderly. Macroeconomic and growth-led policies are often premised on some misconceptions that people are physically and psychologically equipped and ready to participate in vigorous economic activity and add further momentum to the externally boosted process. It is also presumed that if they are excluded from the economic process, somehow the dynamic results of economic growth will filter down to them, solve their problems and make them ready. We are of the view that strategies for poverty eradication must factor in strategies for direct relief from hunger and malnutrition on a priority basis.

Success stories of countries such as Sri Lanka, Chile, etc., show that direct social spending and investment in human capital leads to rapid and lasting improvements in human development indicators thus preparing population for full participation in the economy and ensuring a positive head start for the country in the race toward development. Sri Lanka, despite its low per capita income, has been cited a model of success for achieving high levels of human development. It embarked on a fight against hunger as early as 1942, with schemes such as free or subsidised rice for all, public health measures, etc. Fruits of this expansion were also reaped early and by the end of the 1950s, Sri Lanka was altogether exceptional in having an astonishingly higher life expectancy at birth than any other country among the low-income developing countries.[1] Between 1940 and 1960, death rate fell from 20.6 to 8.6. Chile, with one of the most comprehensive nutrition and health services in the world, is another success story. The system monitors all young children, provides supplementation, primary care and nutritional rehabilitation. Government's commitment to nutritional programmes has been sustained even during times of social expenditure cuts. Roughly between 1973 and 1985, 'infant mortality rates dropped sharply from 66 to 19 per thousand live births while the percentage of undernourished children below five years dropped from 15.5 to 8.7.'[2]

Different Dimensions of Hunger

There is hard evidence and overwhelming indication that links hunger and malnutrition to economic development, peace and social stability of current and future generations. And this holds true for not only the poor countries but for the welfare of all—because our futures are connected, and we cannot live or even expect to live in isolation. Following are some challenging aspects of hunger.

Hunger Trap

Families facing chronic food insecurity are caught in a hunger trap. The very inadequacy and uncertainty of their food supply make it difficult for them to improve their situation. Development opportunities may exist, but poor families often cannot take advantage of them. For them, there is no long-term solution without a short-term solution. Vicious cycle of hunger begins with low-birth weight babies born in food deficient homes, who remain undernourished throughout childhood and are unable to develop their mental and physical capacities to even average levels. Upon reaching adulthood, stunted, wasted and with inadequate skills, they are forced to sell their only asset, physical labour, at any available wage rate. As may be expected, market would pay only the lowest possible wages for such inefficient labour thus extending the initial food shortage-poverty scenario into a lifelong one.

Inter-generational Cycle of Hunger

In order to address food insecurity in the long run, it is imperative to break the inter-generational cycle of hunger. The curse of hunger trap continues beyond the lifetime of an individual spilling into forthcoming generations. Women from 'hunger-trapped' households marry young, put in enormous amounts of physical labour, and suffer near starvation while fighting to survive. Thus caught in the trap of undernourishment and anaemia, they give birth to small, weak and vulnerable infants perpetuating the cycle of hunger forever. Sixty per cent of women in their childbearing years are stunted as a result of inadequate nutrition during their own childhood.

During pregnancy their anaemic condition is further aggravated. A malnourished anaemic woman is likely to deliver a baby with low birth weight. A baby thus born will carry the handicap throughout its life-span, and so on. Resources and actions must be prioritised towards those for whom any delay in addressing hunger will have fatal results. Amongst the highest priorities is greater attention to the special problems of women and children.[3]

Risk-vulnerability Dimension

Poor people are more vulnerable than other population groups because they are more exposed to risk and have little access to appropriate interventions. Being poor and hence vulnerable makes individuals very risk-averse. Therefore, unwilling or unable to engage in high return activities. Moreover, the coping strategies available to them during a shock are likely to further reduce their human capital.

Ethical Dimension

'Hunger, above all, is a fundamental violation of human rights' (World Food Day and Tele Food, 2001). This concerns the right to food as a basic and inherent birth right of every individual. Right to food is possibly most delicate, ethically significant component of the entire gamut of human rights. "Participatory exercises conducted by IFAD[4] missions elsewhere in Asia also reveal that the poor see poverty as shame, humiliation, and powerlessness.'[5] Value and meaning of food in human life transcends social, economic or political concerns. Food sustains life and thus food is a moral right of every human being. Fight against hunger is much more than a political or economic struggle; it is a battle to uphold the causes of humanity and civilisation. Intrinsic moral and ethical dimension of food is accordingly upheld and recognised by all religions in the world, particularly in India. This deep reverence held for food as the basic foundation of life, sacredness of food, are clearly conveyed in numerous religious texts. Just as Mahatma Gandhi, at Naokhali in 1946, said, 'God is bread' for those who are hungry.

Gender Dimension of Hunger

For entire families caught in the vicious cycle of hunger and malnutrition, a breakthrough into a stage where basic needs are satisfied seems to be a distant dream. For women and girls in these deprived households, situation is even more bleak and full of despair. In terms of access to food and nutrition, deep-seated intra-household inequalities and disparities divide women from men. In India and other parts of South Asia, women will traditionally eat only after men and children have been fed. It is culturally accepted that men of the household, the customary breadwinners, are entitled to the lion's share of the available food, both in terms of quality as well as quantity. Women must make do with the leftovers, whether their needs are sufficed or not. This tradition is perpetuated in most rural areas, despite the fact that women labour in field alongside men and additionally burdened with collection of fuel, fodder, water, caring for the sick and food preparation. 'Growing empirical evidence, mainly drawn from India, suggests that allocation of household resources favours males over females. Disparities in nutritional intake and medical care favour boys and have a direct impact on lower survival chances of girls in South Asia. Related to this point, Rosenzweig and Shultz (1982) use an econometric study based on ICRISAT data in rural India to show that boys, because they are expected to be more economically productive as adults, receive a larger share of family resources and have a greater chance to survive.'[6] Although women's needs are greater and more urgent during adolescence, pregnancy and breast-feeding, this pattern of discrimination continues throughout the life.

Costs of Hunger

Not only does hunger conclusively exclude a large segment of the population from availing of their fair share of benefits or of contributing to economic growth, but it also leads to substantial economic losses in terms of lowered productivity and higher health and welfare costs. At the global level. Food and Agriculture Organisation (FAO) estimates that 'each year hunger robs 46 million years of productive disability-free life from people valued at over $ 16 billion.' Further, 'apart from contributing to global stability, hunger reduction should reduce the world's expenditure on conflict prevention and rehabilitation of war-torn areas. A study by the United States Agency for International Development (USAID) found that meeting the World Food Summit (WFS) target would lower the cost of peacekeeping and humanitarian operations by about US $ 2.5 billion per year' (FAO, World Food Summit: Five Years Later 2001). Similar calculations in the World Health Organization (WHO) Commission on Macroeconomics and health suggest that improved nutrition and health indicators can lead to gains of hundreds of billions of dollars per year.

Poverty-hunger Linkages—Two Sides of the Coin

Hunger is the poverty of the worst kind, as it tends to rob one of physical, mental and psychological wellbeing, opportunity, dignity and moral strength. In some ways it is more devastating than economic impoverishment because it cannot be treated with an immediate dose of welfare or cash transfer and it threatens not only the present and future outcome of the affected person's life but that of his/her progeny as well. Yet it is more silent, more invisible than any other social malady (as it spreads over age and gender groups); to reverse its fearful trends may take lifetimes and cost us enormously in terms of human life and capital. Question of priority is not about hunger versus income poverty, but rather about the removal of hunger as a pre-investment to better livelihoods and productive capacity. This, then, is the heart of the argument. Our battle strategy should be to 'eliminate' by attacking hunger directly and to simultaneously 'mitigate' through risk management and coping mechanisms, and finally, to 'prevent' by addressing income, economic growth, employment, etc. This can constitute a fuller, broader framework for the concept of poverty alleviation.

In many countries poverty and undernutrition are closely related with each other, because the definition of the poverty line often relies on the expenditure necessary to obtain a certain minimum food or nutrient basket. Lipton has argued that using a calorie-based poverty line, or food adequacy standard, is an appropriate way to measure moderate or extreme levels of poverty in developing countries. Evidence indicates a direct and strong correlation between poverty and nutritional trends. Because undernutrition affects capacity to work, it affects functioning of labour markets in a central way. A worker's current nutritional status, and thus his/her ability to carry out sustained work, depends not only on his current consumption of nutrients, but also on the history of that consumption. Hence, while low incomes certainly create low nutrition, low nutrition in turn creates low incomes.

Traditional versus New Approaches Toward Poverty Eradication

Largely prevailing wisdom of economic growth and welfare-oriented approaches to poverty has lately been challenged and re-examined by many researchers. We know now that these approaches often do not work. Even economic superpowers like America, have experienced calorie and nutrition deprivation among children. According to the US Third National Health and Nutrition Examination Survey (NHANES III), which was conducted from 1988 to 1994, employment is not a guarantee of being well fed (more than half of the Americans, who say they are sometimes or often hungry due to lack of income, live in households in which at least one person has a job). The survey found that people most at risk for not having enough to eat were children and the poor.

Hunger thus needs to be addressed directly and immediately—a twin track approach might be more practical. As of late, the World Food Summit and other major global fora have begun to recognise and articulate these issues. As the FAO Report at the World Food Summit: Five Years Later (WFS+5) suggests, 'A twin-track approach is required for quick success in reducing hunger and poverty. One track would create opportunities for the hungry to improve their livelihoods by promoting development, particularly agricultural and rural development, through policy reform and investments in agriculture. Another track would involve direct and immediate action to fight hunger through programmes to enhance immediate access to food by the hungry, thereby increasing their productive potential and allowing them to take advantage of the opportunities offered by development. . .'

Economics of hunger is simple and straightforward: direct and integrated food-based interventions are not only an investment but also savings, with very high returns! 'Food assistance can become a win-win event. Apart from targeted households and individuals, food assistance can benefit governments, agriculture producers, private sector entrepreneurs and the nation as a whole. By ending inheritance of hunger, a stronger human capital base is created while saving future health and welfare costs.'[7] Premised on the notion of hunger as a structural problem that needs direct intervention, we as the World Food Programme (WFP) deal with the aspect of food, the most direct and basic answer to hunger and malnutrition. In our experience this basic instrument of development has proven to be often a strongest resource in bringing about positive changes in recipient or beneficiary's life. Food programmes ensure an effective and fast track to sustainable development by committing to removal of hunger on a priority basis. Adoption of food security as a goal can help re-focus poverty alleviation programmes on the more micro aspects such as vulnerability, seasonality, coping mechanisms and intra-household distribution of resources. Benefits of food programmes are varied and numerous. For example, 'A well-designed and implemented school feeding programme can go a long way towards increasing school enrolment, attendance and retention of working children and allow them to gain greater benefit from teaching. Food as an incentive, as compared to other types of income transfers, is particularly appropriate in areas of high food insecurity. Such a programme is also justified by the prevalence of hunger and undernutrition in these areas.'[8] Another study on food consumption patterns (in India) shows that 'The current level of per capita consumption of cereals and pulses shows a positive and significant association with the long-term nutrition achievements, as expected, and this is stronger for girls. The effect is not significant for young children, but it is large and significant among children 6–12 years of age. This suggests that there is a direct association between a higher level of consumption of calories and improvement in height-for-age. Consequently, the relationship is absent among children less than two years of age who would consume relatively small amounts of cereals and pulses in their normal diet.'[9] These indicate diverse ways in which food and nutritional interventions can become powerful engines for building human capital and thus for economic growth.

Thus improvements in nutrition are a prerequisite for the poor to take full advantage of the opportunities created by development. This is not to deny the importance of measures to increase capital – human, financial, physical, natural and social – available to poor. It is simply to say that improving nutrition comes first, not merely in order of importance but in temporal sequence.

International Agendas for Poverty Alleviation

World Food Summit has stressed that world leaders recognise hunger as central to the experience of poor people, and establish food security as a primary goal within their national poverty reduction strategies. In the declaration of the WFS+5, it is stated: 'We stress the inherent linkage between rapid progress towards (the targets of the World Food Summit Plan of Action, as reaffirmed by the United Nations Millennium Declaration, and the size, direction and efficient use of investment in distribution. As we agreed in the Monterrey Consensus, mobilising domestic and international resources to reach those objectives, is contingent on several factors, inter alia: (*i*) an enabling environment for savings and investment in rural areas within the framework of a sound national macroeconomic system, (*ii*) a broad-based national poverty reduction strategy aiming at improving access to food including through increasing food production and distribution, (*iii*) promoting opportunities for internal and external private investment, (*iv*) trade, (*v*) adequate attention in the national budget towards social-economic development, (*vi*) complementing national efforts with ODA[10] in critical areas of social infrastructure and human development, and (*vii*) transparent and effective management of public resources.'[11]

This provides a general basis and a common global framework for leaders and policy makers to draw on. Broad issues are universal, while each country and region may need to tailor their national strategy to fit their unique needs in the most appropriate manner. For example, African nations have formulated the New Partnership for Africa's Development (NEPAD), a broad-based initiative that includes agriculture and food security as significant components, in response to the vast development challenges in their region.

Social protection, safety nets and risk management are another major area, which national and international policy makers and planners heavily focus on. World Bank's risk management theory, European Union's (EU) social protection approach, etc., are such examples. These concepts have some overlap with the life cycle approach advocated by WFP and other food aid organisations. World Bank in a redefined approach to combating poverty has formulated a 'social risk management strategy', premised on incorporating risk management activities in all aspects of development (fiscal, financial, social, etc.). This approach builds on the existing social protection framework, which is geared towards enabling people-at-risk to cope better (namely the poor). Key assumption here is that poverty puts people at greater risk during natural or man-made crisis. And also makes them risk-averse toward undertaking productive ventures in fear of further impoverishment. Poverty, however, is already in a state of ongoing crisis and deprivation or state of long-term emergency. And hence any broad-based definition of poverty which would duly recognise hunger as both a cause and symptom, would lead to the conclusion that a hungry and poor person is not merely at risk or risk-averse but is already victimised and has already suffered losses in physical and mental capacity to perform within a normal economic environment, let alone emergencies or disasters. This intrinsic and automatic recognition of hunger relief as the necessary first step towards development is essential.

A recent European Union (EU) study has developed a 'Capabilities' approach that aims to combat social exclusion, beyond traditional welfare approaches. Albeit income-oriented, this approach recognises need for an effective marriage between macroeconomic policy and 'social inclusion' objectives, which echoes WFS twin track approach. It is further stressed that 'social policy' is a productive factor; thus it should not be regarded as a choice between economic efficiency and social equity when investing in social programmes. In fact this is the best solution for achieving a healthy, competent labour force capable of participating in a productive economy. EU report states '. . .income poverty, tackled by traditional social policy, does not fully capture resource deprivation which is arguably a more relevant indicator of individuals' capability to participate in social life . . .' and further, 'Plainly, minimum levels of . . . primary goods, that is goods which are useful to anybody . . . are needed. Such goods include money, but they also encompass goods such as health and the social bases for self-respect.'[12] One can imagine dire situation and sheer challenges facing the developing world, if even the egalitarian welfare states are revamping their traditional approaches to social policy.

New Millennium Development Goal explicitly links hunger target to that of poverty and seeks to halve both extreme hunger and poverty by 2015. Persistent hunger on one hand, and economic disparities on the other can only breed resentment and instigate violence, putting the social fabric of a country at risk. As stated in FAO papers prepared for World Food Summit: Five Years Later, 'Getting rid of hunger is an essential first step in the quest for poverty alleviation and sustainable economic growth. We all do ourselves a favour by facing the fact that widespread hunger can only breed hopelessness, desperation and conflict, which know no boundaries. It is in everyone's self-interest to banish hunger from the world.'

While recommendations and pledges in WFS report (International Alliance against Hunger) may range from social protection to animal and plant health protection to school feeding schemes, we must consider and weigh the priorities in each country-specific context. India for instance, home to about 35 per cent of the world's undernourished children, cannot afford to wait indefinitely for extensive growth-led programmes to hit their targets and for the benefits to trickle down to these children. Such skewed policies in general enhance risk of depleting the most valuable and inexhaustible resource any country can have – its population and particularly the young. This is certainly true for India with one of the fastest growing labour forces.

Towards a Hunger Free India: India's approach to food and nutrition security for all the population, particularly the most vulnerable, has been constantly developed and fine-tuned during consecutive Five-Year Plans. Naturally, poverty alleviation programmes have been an integral part of India's planned economic development for decades. Plans spanned economic growth-led policies, to strategies of entitlements (through self-employment and wage-employment schemes, food security and social security), building up of capabilities (through basic minimum services like education, health and housing), to issues of governance as the most effective delivery mechanism for poverty reduction (through Panchayati Raj Institutions). There has been a decline in income poverty as seen by the 55th Round Survey (July 1999–June 2000, NSSO). Though poverty ratio declined the number of poor remained stable at around 320 million for a period of two decades.

Furthermore, if we examine the extent to which poverty alleviation has 'alleviated' hunger and malnutrition, we encounter a mixed picture. In a recent article 'Calorie Deprivation in Rural India, 1983–1999-2000' in the *Economic and Political Weekly* (January 25, 2003:369–376) Meenakshi and Vishwanathan have stated that there has been a secular decline in calorie intakes in rural areas, amounting to approximately 70 calories per capita over the period 1983 to 1999-2000. This decrease can be discerned in virtually all states and has translated into corresponding increases in head count ratios of calorie deprivation. Thus, while magnitude of income poverty has declined that of calorie deprivation has increased. In a recent study, I chose five states with highest levels of poverty and followed trends between poverty ratios and nutrition levels. Among the states with the worst poverty levels, levels of undernutrition were understandably very high. What is interesting is that even the states with the lowest levels of poverty ratios also had high levels of undernutrition. All this points to the need for a wider and different approach to addressing malnutrition and hunger in India. Employment/ income generating programmes are not the direct channels to food and nutritional security.

Tenth Five-Year Plan, states 'Data from research studies and clinical experience shows that social and economic deprivation lead to undernutrition and poor health. In spite of huge buffer stocks and anti-poverty programmes which generate income in the hands of the poor, 8 per cent Indians do not get two square meals a day and there are pockets where severe undernutrition takes its toll even today. During the Tenth Plan there will be focused and comprehensive interventions aimed at improving the nutritional and health status of individuals.' These strategies are accompanied by a shift in focus from household to the family and individual and also to universal and targeted coverage of the screened/ identified vulnerable groups. Government of India has adequate resources and full commitment to these goals. Tenth Five-Year Plan aptly and adequately addresses relevant issues for a strong agenda against hunger and malnutrition. To achieve the goal of substantially reducing hunger by 2015 and to realise the vision of a hunger-free India by 2020, all development practitioners and stakeholders must accelerate their efforts in pinpointing immediate and exact interventions, upscale and expand the positive experiences, and focus on specific time-bound goals. Streamlining the various inter-ministerial and inter-departmental lines would also be a crucial step.

'Hunger Mainstreaming' – An Action Plan

Vision of ensuring/promotion access to, availability and absorption of adequate, nutritious food has been central to WFP's organisational 'mantra' over the years. This goal, which places three dimensions of food security, access, availability and absorption, at the core of any strategy, should not be in the sidelines of an agenda or at the bottom of any list. Its place is on the same platform with any other development initiative. It is true that launching a comprehensive anti-hunger programme such as the one proposed by FAO with an investment of 24 billion dollars would require full-fledged international and national commitment, a conducive policy environment and substantive political will. In the context of Indian realities, investments in a comprehensive campaign against hunger might span following basic elements.

Greater Investment in and Consolidation of Food Programmes

'Food aid can make a difference – both in emergencies and in situations of chronic hunger. Direct nutritional support to pregnant and nursing women helps their babies grow into healthy adults. School feeding programmes not only feed hungry children but also help increase school attendance. Studies show that educated people are best able to break out of the cycle of poverty and hunger.'[13] As discussed earlier, food-based interventions would be at the helm of a broad-based twin-track approach to elimination of hunger. Strengthening and expansion of and coordination among various programmes, would be a major determinant of success.

Basic Needs Prioritisation

Focus must be on the provision of a comprehensive package of minimum basic needs. Sufficient food and nutrient intake must be accompanied by safe drinking water and proper sanitation.

Food Supplementation

While investments are being made in food assistance programmes, it is important to have a focused approach towards resolving stark nutritional problems. For example, the incidence of low birth weight (LBW) in India stands at 33 per cent (with sampling limitations). This phenomenon is strongly associated with the undernutrition of mothers. Food supplements that provide more energy can significantly improve birth weight. In India the benefits of food supplementation have not been studied to a great extent. But a study in Gambia shows that locally produced biscuits providing 1,017 Kcal and 22 g protein per day have reduced LBW prevalence by 39 per cent. Such improvements in pregnancy outcome can be obtained by providing food supplements through programmes such as ICDS.

Enhancing the National Capacity for Delivery of Assistance

Programmes to provide direct assistance to the hungry can only succeed when national governments establish effective capacity for delivery of such assistance. This requires a supportive national policy environment for development of social safety nets, which can be provided in cooperation with civic society organisations. Social safety net policies specifically targeted at hunger reduction should give recognition to the special vulnerability that women and children are exposed at critical times in their lives and should support creation and implementation of programmes such as mother-child feeding, related health and nutritional education and school feeding.

Identifying and Scaling up Small-scale Interventions

Utilising food reserves to dovetail with and to scale up replicable interventions can yield rich dividends e.g. Indiamix promoted by WFP. World Food Programme has evolved a blended food, which can locally produced. It is a nutritionally balanced product, fortified with micronutrients. India has surplus food reserves of 32.4 million tonnes much above the minimum buffer stock norms. What is required is a small portion of this surplus. Indiamix can be made from local wheat in the ratio of 1 : 2 and can effectively be used for the eligible pregnant women. Similarly other major problems such as stunting, wasting, being underweight and various micronutrient deficiencies can be addressed through a realistic combination of interventions.

Making Social Protection More 'Hunger-Sensitive'

Provision of a better safety net would be an effective approach during economic downturns. India has built the most extensive food assistance programmes in the developing world, with three largest schemes (ICDS, Mid-Day Meal Schemes, etc.) together cover about a third of India's population. Yet we must explore new avenues of streamlining and converging this assistance in ways that would yield higher levels of consumption of poor women and children, greater coverage, greater and intensified targeting throughout the life cycle of individuals and families. Only a sustained and fierce attack on nutritional vulnerability of the hungry poor bring about a 'positive shock' that will enable them to manage risk better and climb out of poverty.

Making the Notion of Poverty more Sensitive to Hunger and Malnutrition

Redefining poverty line to reflect current ground realities would be an appropriate start and would add fresh angles and insights to ongoing research. As asserted by Meenakshi and Vishwanathan in their article, normative basis of the official (income) poverty line also needs to be re-examined. Notions of minimum standards of living have changed substantially since the time when first attempts to define a poverty line were made several decades ago. Focus on an adequate food basket needs to give way to a more comprehensive view – one that includes access to adequate shelter, a safe living environment and good health.

Prioritising the Interventions

Geographic targeting and hunger mapping can help prioritise focused interventions. The fight can only begin when we have identified who the hungry are, where they are located, and why they are hungry. We need to know food-insecure areas with high incidence of malnutrition, areas with low productivity, areas prone to recurring natural disasters, etc. WFP in collaboration with the MS Swaminathan Research Foundation have come up with the Food Insecurity Atlases of both rural and urban India which provide information on three crucial dimensions of food insecurity: availability (defined by food deficits, instability of production, disaster proneness, etc.), access (defined by calorie consumption, poverty levels, female literacy, proportion of vulnerable groups in the population, etc.) and absorption (defined by life expectancy, infant mortality rate, chronic energy deficiency, proportion of severely stunted and wasted children, etc.). Indicators do of course vary for rural and urban areas.

Giving Hunger a Human Face

It is important for implementers, planners and policy makers to be aware that they are dealing with hungry people, not hunger. Some of the essential directions would be: implementing the life cycle approach, decentralised delivery of services, stepping up support mechanisms and safety net programmes, forward and backward linkages, and extension services, etc. While hunger is the entry point to poverty alleviation, hungry people are, no doubt, the entry point to hunger alleviation. Answer to hunger and malnutrition is not transfer of a single commodity or service: it is a task of empowering the hungry person of building human resource and human capital, of enriching his life with dignity and self-respect, and of enabling him to realise his innate and genetic potential to the fullest. This demands a substantive investment in a range of goods and services that can serve as minimum requirements for a healthy life. His Excellency the President of India on the occasion of the release of the Urban Atlas stressed how the human resources of India should be considered 'a blessing, not a burden'. He prioritised elimination of hunger and thirst as overriding objectives – to achieve a hunger-free and drinking water-secure India by 2007. If this dream is realised, there will be a dramatic and positive change in the quality of life of vulnerable poor.

Horizontal Convergence and Integration among Diverse Initiatives

A synergy among parallel programmes in order to address all basic needs through a prudent mix of policy and actions must be realised with immediate effect. There has been much dialogue about the concepts of 'complementarity', 'convergence' and 'synergy' in areas of hunger and food insecurity. While concrete measures have been few and far apart. I propose here some basic models for convergence at the grassroots level that could potentially lead to multiple benefits for the community. For example Department of Women and Child (DWCD)/Integrated Child Development Services (ICDS) initiatives could converge with Food-for-Work (FFW) programmes in building infrastructure, such as the construction of Anganwadi Centres (AWC). In a strategic alliance between Department of Women and Child and other line ministry such as Rural Development, a scheme such as Food-for-Social Work could be developed. Within this scheme, women community members would support the work of Anganwadi Workers (AWW) and other community level workers, through participation joint ICDS-FFW initiatives such as: (*i*) construction and building of sanitation facilities, kitchens, etc., near the AWC, (*ii*) cooking for the AWC and/or the primary school, (*iii*) AWC and school gardening, (*iv*) water supply to the AWC (*v*) support to AWW and school staff in vaccination, pre-school activities, hygiene/sanitation (*vi*) running community kitchens or food distribution facilities for the old and the infirm, (*vii*) running creches, (*viii*) managing community food banks, and (*ix*) expanding outreach of AWC services to below three year olds. Further, there could be schemes for adolescent girls through food-for-education, or for older women through food-for-training where they would participate in skills development and other training workshops. Programmes like these would promote the participation of women, ensure better nutrition for them and their children, support ongoing work by government workers, enhance community ownership and leadership, reduce risk of seasonal shocks during lean periods and lower chances of migration for participating families. These are just a few of countless ways of effective coordination of inter-sectoral efforts that could serve multiple objectives for community and hence intensify the dual campaign against hunger and poverty.

Concluding remarks

While the overarching goal of development at the global level is the reduction and elimination of poverty, policy and planning have often overlooked the intrinsic causal relationship between poverty and hunger, their linkages and their repercussions. As the world, particularly the developing countries, grapple with stark and depressing realities of hunger, malnutrition and low basic human development indicators like LBW, etc., the question arises why mammoth investments in employment, education, skills and training have not filtered down to the pockets of intense hunger and suffering throughout the world. What is the missing link, the elusive gap? In a fresh beginning, the concept of poverty must be redefined in order to illuminate its true connotations. Neither 'growth-mediated security' nor 'support-led security' approaches, which respectively emphasise economic development and welfare strategies have solved poverty and hunger-related problems completely or permanently. Denial of access to minimum quality of life required by every individual to achieve his/her full potential is thus a broader view of poverty. This entails a closer scrutiny of the 'minimum quality of life' – which brings us to the uncontested basic needs or entitlements of every individual in this world in order to have a healthy productive life, namely sufficient food, nutrition, safe drinking water, shelter.

NOTES

1. Dreze, Jean and Sen, Amartya, 1989, *Hunger and Public Action*, Oxford University Press.
2. Dreze and Sen, Ibid.
3. Regional Office for South Asia, World Food Programme, 2001, *Enabling Development Food Assistance in South Asia*, Oxford University Press, New Delhi, India, p. 190.

4. International Fund for Agricultural Development
5. Asia and the Pacific Division, Programme Management Department, 2002. *Assessment of Rural Poverty*, IFAD, Rome, p. 1.
6. Asia and the Pacific Division - Programme Management Department, 2002. *Assessment of Rural Poverty*. IFAD, Rome, p. 25.
7. Regional Office for South Asia, World Food Programme, 2001, *Enabling Development Food Assistance in South Asia*, Oxford University Press, New Delhi, India, p. 191.
8. Ute Meir, 2002. 'The Role of Food Assistance Programmes in Promoting Education and Reducing Child Work in Rural India,' in Ramachandran Nira and Lionel Massun *Coming to Grips with Rural Child Work – A Food Security Approach*, United Nations World Food Programme and Institute for Human Development, India, p. 369.
9. Abusaleh Shariff, 1999, 'Women's Status and Child Health,' in Krishnaraj, Maithreyi, Ratna M. Sudarshan and Abusaleh Shariff, *Gender Population & Development*, Oxford University Press, New Delhi, India.
10. Abbreviation for Official Development Assistance
11. Declaration of the World Food Summit: Five-Years Later, Appendix, 10-13 June 2002, Part One, International Alliance against Hunger.
12. EXSPRO-"Social Exclusion and Social Protection: The Future Role for the EU Draft Report South Bank University, European Institute, 2001.
13. Annan, Kofi, Address to the World Food Summit: Five Years Later, 10-13 June, 2002, Rome.

Chapter 2

Globalisation and India's Food Security
Issues and Challenges*

Arun Kumar

There are several aspects of the title. First, Globalisation, second, food security in India, third, inter-linkage between them and fourth, the challenges that lie ahead. One can see good and bad in almost anything and that also applies to globalisation. The question should be, what is the dominant effect or in the net, what is the effect, positive or negative?[1] Whether one sees things in a positive or negative light depends on the framework one adopts. As is often said, whether one sees the glass half full or half empty depends on one's perspective.

Today in India, *there is little agreement on what is in the national interest,* whether in the short run or the long run. This has led to poor governance, ad hoc measures by policy makers and to sectarianism amongst those who constitute the ruling groups. Absence of a wider national perspective has roots in the way our ruling class formed/emerged before independence. The ruling class's current attitude to globalisation, its acceptance of a junior role in the process and the feeling that India's position cannot be any different and that it cannot pose an alternative can only be understood in a longer timeframe than a decade or two.[2] There would be no reason to worry if the

* Published in *Bhartiya Samajik Chintan*, Vol. II, No. 4, January 2004, pp. 20 – 38. Usual disclaimers apply.

ruling classes in India had an independent national perspective. Why is this missing?

Food security does not just stand for availability of food to the population as would be the case with the availability of other goods. Clearly, it is more basic than most other goods and its reduced availability causes severe problems for society. It may be imported, but as happened in the mid-sixties when the USA extracted a heavy price from the Indian economy for the food it exported to India.[3] This may entail a heavy political and economic price which may not be in the nation's wider interest. *The issue of food self-sufficiency is then linked up with the independence of the nation to pursue its own goals.* That the present Indian ruling classes have not been protecting the wider national interest is obvious. In the Uruguay Round of negotiations, they allowed the advanced nations to retain the subsidies they give to their farmers but accepted lowering of subsidies we pay our farmers.[5] Thus, our farmers' interest, an important part of the national interest, was compromised. These aspects need to be fully analysed and understood.

This paper is divided into five sections. The first looks at the current globalisation of the Indian economy as a link in a chain that stretches back at least 250 years. During this period, the country has experienced a one-way process of globalisation with influences coming from the West and denting India's dynamism. At the economic level, globalisation has meant a process of marketisation. In the second section, the strategic retreat of the state and the rise to dominance of the markets the world over and specifically in India are discussed. Market failure and the role of government and the consequences of the process of marketization in India are presented here. In the next section, link of this process with the growth of the black economy (therefore, illegality) in India is presented. This has weakened Indian capital and, therefore, has not been able to take an independent stance in economy policy. The fourth section deals with the impact of this kind of globalisation since 1991 on food security in India. Elements relating to changing technology and the developments in WTO are discussed. Finally, the concluding section presents a summary of the arguments and highlights the challenges for the Indian economy in this century.

Globalisation

Globalisation is a vast and complex issue both in space and over time. It affects society at various levels and in its various dimensions – social, political, economic and cultural. To focus and simplify, *only the economic aspect is being considered* here which is not to argue that the other dimensions are less important. They are not specifically have addressed.

Here globalisation is being taken *in the sense of greater integration of the Indian economy with the global economy.* It involves the easier flow of capital, technology and goods and services across the borders.[6] It is not that the Indian economy was closed before 1991 but the above-mentioned flows have become easier after 1991. Laws governing their flow have become less restrictive. For instance, Foreign Exchange Regulation Act (FERA) has been greatly diluted and the laws replacing it, FERA and Money Laundering Act have been made much less strict. Kumar (1994)[7] lists that large number of changes that were immediately introduced between 1991 and 1994.

The Long View: One-Way Globalisation

Actually, the Indian economy has been globalising for a long time and certainly much before 1991 when New Economic Policy (NEP) was introduced or 1, January, 1995 when WTO came into being. These dates, undoubtedly important, *mark the beginning of another phase of globalisation of the Indian economy.* However, they cannot be understood in themselves. They are one link (the most recent one) in a chain that stretches back in time to perhaps the middle of the eighteenth century. This is not to say that India was not interacting with other parts of the world before then. Indian traders have been going to Arabia, Africa and the South East Asia for a long time.

What separates the last 250 years from the earlier period is that *increasingly there has been a one-way globalisation of India.* Earlier there was a two-way flow of ideas and goods. There can hardly be any objection to a two-way process. In the last

250 years, life has changed and dramatically so in the last 100 years. New ideas, new goods and new ways of doing things have come into day-to-day life but it has all originated in the West with the developing world making little contribution. This represents a *lack of dynamism in developing societies, like, India.* In 1750, India and China dominated manufacturing output in the World (contributing 57.3 per cent). By 1900, USA and Europe replaced them contributing 23.6 per cent and 62 per cent respectively to the World's manufacturing output.[8]

British rulers introduced 'modern' institutions and technology into India in the nineteenth century. For instance, universities, bureaucracy, Railways, etc. Universities have undoubtedly helped promoting education but have been critical for the hegemony of Western thought in the Indian subcontinent. *Indian intellectuals strive to be 'derived' intellectuals, recycling models from the West.* Railways enabled development but also helped open the Indian subcontinent for exploitation by British capital. Bureaucracy and the police became the instruments of control of the Indian population by a handful of British rulers based in India.

At the time of independence, the Indian ruling elite which took over the reins of power was substantially influenced by notions of Western modernity and did not see a different (independent) path for itself. It voluntarily accepted this path and placed the country on this road to development. The Bombay Plan drawn up in 1946 by an influential group of industrialists was one such blueprint for independent India. Mahatma Gandhi who suggested an indigenous path of development based on decentralised economic structures and non-market based solutions to India's problems, was quickly marginalised by the elite. Not just the communists but also the nationalists saw Mahatma Gandhi's call to base our approach on our past and not on the notions emerging from the West as undesirable archaic if not reactionary.[10] Planning approach adopted by India was *a path of development evolved by the West.* However, based on the experiences of the national movement, *certain innovations were introduced on this basic theme,* like, mixed economy and non-alignment.

This path of development was not suited to India's requirements and led to deepening problems in the Indian society from the sixties itself. The developing crisis in the Soviet system from the mid-seventies and greater pressure from Western capitalism (as under WTO and GATT) from the early eighties led to a reduced space for manoeuvre for the Indian elite. The chosen path of development for the Indian economy floundered in the eighties and collapsed in 1990-91.

Given the inability of the ruling groups to chart an independent path and (something not attempted for 250 years) *search for a way out of the crisis ended in the adoption of the then (in the eighties) dominant model of development available in the West.* Some independent strengths developed during the independence movement and elements of autonomy achieved in the first twenty-five years of independent India's development have been completely given up with the adoption of the new model of development. The process of globalisation has become even more one-sided.

Present phase of globalisation in India since 1991 has been going on in other parts of the world for much longer. It is being overseen on behalf of international finance capital by multilateral institutions, like, IMF, WB and GATT/WTO. Because these institutions represent the interest of international finance capital, they have prescribed to all developing economies a uniform package of policies which are not based on the specificities of these economies.[11] Their view is clear, if an economy is facing problems it is because its structure is not suitable to the one required by the dominant world economic interest. Thus, the prescription is that the structure of the economy has to be adjusted to that required for its incorporation into the world markets. This is what the WTO is forcing on all economies and that is what the World Bank prescribes as Structural Adjustment Programme (SAP). The interests of the local population of the countries undertaking SAP or implementing the WTO provisions do not matter.[12] *Economic globalisation of a country represents the penetration of markets and marketisation of the structures of its economy and society.*

Markets: Undemocratic, Valueless and Amoral

What are markets? They are an institution to exchange goods and services. They are based on what Samuelson (1970)[13] called the *dollar vote.* They are governed by the purchasing power of the individuals in society. The rich have many more votes than the poor hence markets are *not democratic institutions.* In effect, left to themselves, they *lead to the marginalisation of the marginal.* This works at various levels – international, national, regional, etc. For instance, India is marginal to the world market, Assam, Uttaranchal and Pithoragarh in Uttarakhand in India. Markets do not distinguish between the old and the young or men and women – in that sense the markets are valueless. Society has to impose values from outside the market.

Markets do not decide which goods are socially good or bad. They *have no social value.* Judgement about the nature of goods is made and imposed by society from outside the markets. For instance, markets do not decide that smoking is bad or that cigarette advertising should not be allowed. Society decides that children should not be targeted with advertising or that sex and violence should not be beamed at them. There are no 'essential' or 'luxury' goods; they are just goods. So, import of luxury goods is justified and they should not be taxed higher than other goods. Whether the poor get adequate food or not, one can have one's Mercedes Benz car and one need not feel bad about it. Penetration of the markets into the social realm is undermining social values.

Unfortunately, there is as yet *no global society that sets values for the world.* This is adversely impacting nations and societies. Today the largest item of world trade is narcotic drugs. Global capital goes around destabilising national economies without any check. Soros, a staunch capitalist and a man of high finance, has decried this and argued that financial markets left to themselves can be highly destabilising.[14] Money laundering is rampant and one of the goods traded the most in international markets is narcotic drug. MNCs extract concessions from even the poor, worsening their plight. Cigarette companies target the poor, women and children in the poor nations. All this has led to growing hardships for the marginal in the world.

Markets are governed by the *principles, 'more is better' and 'Consumer Sovereignty'.*[16] Individual's welfare is supposed to increase as she/he consumes more. Markets are supposed to facilitate this increase in welfare. This underlies consumerism and results in expanding profits for producers. Consumer sovereignty means that consumer knows her/his interest best so whatever she/he wishes to consume should be made available in the market. There should be no interference with this from any quarter (government).

Efficiency is defined as the achieving of wishes of the consumers. This may be iniquitous in the extreme with one person having all and the others having nothing. But as long as this is consistent with the initial endowments, it is 'efficient'. In that sense, notion of market 'efficiency' is status quoist. Even 'waste' in society can be consistent with 'efficiency'. Baran (1973)[17] has argued that as capitalism has developed, waste in society has increased dramatically. As long as people are willing to pay for 'social bads', provision of such goods is also consistent with efficiency. Hence smuggling is consistent with 'efficiency'. That all this results in waste and lower welfare for people is of no concern to markets.

Since 'more is better', consuming less is not desirable 'as it lowers the individual's welfare.' *Restraint is then meaningless.* Sacrifice is outright stupidity. 'Consumer sovereignty' means that the focus is on self as opposed to the collective. So both these market principles weaken the idea of the community and of working towards a common good. The idea of the nation based on a shared common goal itself weakens. To build a nation a long-term goal needs to be defined and the citizens are supposed to work towards it. Short-term optimisation of one's satisfaction is then not necessarily optimal. One may have to sacrifice today for a better future. In brief, growing emphasis on markets leads to narrowing of the individuals' horizons and undermining of the idea of nation.

Blame for the misery and the poverty of the poor is put on the poor themselves. They are supposed to be uncompetitive, nonmarketable, etc. Markets are supposed to be 'objective' promoting 'efficiency' and not 'subjective' and smoothly allowing economic transitions from one state to another. They are *supposed to clear smoothly in textbook fashion* if governments do not interfere in their working.[18] But in today's world, which is the agency that can agglomerate individual's preferences into a collective or social will? Since government intervention is considered undesirable, matters have to be left to the markets.

But, *even ideal markets do not function smoothly and quickly.* There are long lags. No guarantee that they will settle down to the ideal situation in which all would be well for everyone. In the ideal situation, during the transition from one state to the other, there is misery many. Unskilled workers losing jobs in the unorganised sector have nowhere else to go since that is anyway the residual sector. Skilled clerical staff in the financial sector displaced by computerisation may be unemployable. As incomes of the poor fall, even their *children may be pulled out of school and forced to work.* Women may have to bear a *double burden of house and work outside to supplement family incomes.* Same may be the fate of coconut growers when cheap imports take place or of fishermen when deep sea trawlers dump cheap fish in the market.

Markets (which have no values of their own) are amoral and immoral. As they penetrate deeper into the individual's consciousness the society also takes on this characteristic. Consequently, notions of collectivity recede into the background. Individuals take fewer positions on social issues and indulge in individual optimisation. For instance, individual actions based on the notion of 'consumer sovereignty' are considered to be justified even if that means that some others go hungry or are malnourished or are illiterate. After all the poor are supposedly themselves to blame for their misery. The well-off need not feel guilty for their unconcern.

Income through speculation (national or international) is justified even if it causes large-scale poverty and unemployment (as in South East Asia in 1997–99). High profits need no justification as they are automatically legitimised by the functioning of the markets and the price one can get there. While earlier society used to frown on usurious interest rates of 36 per cent and 48 per cent, today a monopoly company declaring 100 per cent dividend draws little attention since it is considered justified by the normal functioning of the market.

Markets are not only undemocratic institutions, they are also *undermining democracy.* In developing countries, there is now little debate over the direction their economies should take. Even national legislatures are now being by-passed when new rules are introduced. This is done in the name of international obligations. In India some states have objected for not being consulted by the Centre when new legislation was introduced in Parliament but this has not had any effect.

Dominant western values are being imposed on the developing nations through the media, with the help of power of money, politics and dominance over ideas. Desire of the elite of the developing world to integrate with the global one has made this process voluntary. This class hardly empathises with their people. Progress means copying the dominant Western model, after all, success is also defined in these terms. This is clearly visible at the level of thinking and in the institutions of higher learning.

Any economic system sets the rules of economic gains, defining who gains and who loses. The present one-way globalisation also works with its set of rules of economic gains and defines how the product would be shared. These are based on the position of the nations and the individuals in the markets. Even those apparently not linked to the markets are affected. For instance, the tribals of Bastar may seem to be weakly affected by markets but even they are linked to international finance capital. Gains are cornered by those powerful in the market. Voluntary acceptance of the *Western domination in different aspects of our lives gives the process a legitimacy even in the eyes of those who understand what is happening and are losing out.*

Strategic Retreat of the State and the Rise to Dominance of the Markets

Since the mid-seventies there have been two important

developments in the World. Decline of the Soviet system and ascendancy of capital at the expense of labour. Rise of Thacherism and Reganism in the West accompanied by the rise of the services sector and the emergence of new labour displacing technologies weakened labour considerably. Since the mid-seventies, trade union membership has been on the decline in most countries around the globe.

These two developments have also weakened the developing world. The space that existed for them to manoeuvre in the international sphere and ward off economic and political pressures from the Western powers narrowed. This has been co-terminous with the IMF and the World Bank applying greater economic pressures on the developing world. During this period, pressures for opening up their economies mounted on the developing world under GATT also. New issues were formally introduced precisely in this period with the Uruguay Round of Negotiations starting in 1986. On 1, January 1995, with the coming into being of the WTO, many of these features,[19] strongly resisted by the developing nations, have now become a reality. Further new issues have been introduced in the Singapore and Doha rounds.[20] The developing world is simply trying to prevent its situation from deteriorating with little hope of improvement.

Advanced nations in the interest of international finance capital have found an opportunity to get the *markets of the developing world opened and integrated into the world markets that are dominated by the interests of their corporations.*[21] Hence the pressure to open up trade in agriculture and services and get a tighter control over capital and technology and obtain freedom for mobility of capital. All this has enabled capital to aggregate itself in larger and larger size and obtain more and more concessions for itself from the developing countries by making them compete with each other. This has further weakened labour in the developing world. National governments in the developing world are cooperating towards this by passing legislation. In India, the courts have given rulings making strikes illegal to varying degrees.

It is often argued that in this era of globalisation, there

are no boundaries and the nation state does not mean much. It is suggested that MNCs have no national affiliation and they work in their own interest treating all nations alike. This is the basis for the argument that the developing nations need not fear the MNCs and in fact should offer them all the concessions to attract them to their countries. This is just a *facade to confuse the developing nations and weaken their resolve for an independent path.* After all, now it is clear that in India, Enron's interest was protected all along by the might of the US Government. The US Government protects the interests of its MNCs all over the world. In WTO, only governments can file for disputes settlement so the MNCs depend on the nation states of their origin for redressal of their grievances. It is in the interest of the MNCs and the advanced nations that others open their economies for them to capture their markets; so the idea has been propagated in various ways that the nation states do not matter and should indeed retreat under globalisation.

Markets are the new buzz-word. They are to be left free to operate. This means *freedom to capital.* Labour laws that have evolved over long periods of time to check the extreme forms of exploitation by capital are now being diluted. This has happened in China, Malayasia, Indonesia, etc., and global capital has been asking India also to follow suit. To attract global capital India has been willing to dilute its various laws, like, environmental laws. For instance, lead acid waste is coming to India to be recycled. Ship breaking is a large industry. China has received imports of dangerous hospital waste. The developing world desperately seeking capital at any cost is made to compete against each other to give up command over resources and to accept damage to its environment.[22]

Market Failure and State Intervention

There are three main economic reasons given for government intervention in an economy. First, market failure, second, equity and third, development. While the former is studied in neoclassical terms, the themes of the other two are macro economic. It has been accepted that government has an important role to play in economic development of a country. This is specially so in an underdeveloped economy. Chakravarty (1987)[23] while recognising the failure of the state has nonetheless suggested in conclusion that the state has an important role to play in India. It is required to set national priorities and mobilise resources to maximise growth with equity. This role has increasingly retreated into the background with the rise to prominence of markets since the late seventies. Futility of government intervention in a capitalist economy has been repeatedly suggested by Milton Friedman.[24] This is the new orthodoxy of markets.

Failure of the markets is being ignored in the rush to embrace free markets. Such failure is known to take place in a large number of areas of economic activity. It is this which has been responsible for the rising level of government intervention in economies all over the world, right through the twentieth century.[25] Even neoclassic economics tells us that there is nothing like a free market. A state is needed to enforce rules and regulations by which society will function, otherwise there would be jungle rule with 'might is right'. Existence of society means rules by which individuals agree to work and live together. The government is required to enforce the rules.

When markets fail, government is supposed to intervene to take the economy to what is called the 'efficiency' frontier because the markets cannot do so on their own. In a hypothetical situation, the world is assumed to be 'First Best' and the government is supposed to take the economy to this frontier. However, the world is not an ideal one and the government's actions are limited by the social rules and by feasibility so that even the government cannot always take the economy to this 'efficiency' frontier. With its best efforts often it can only take the economy to a 'Second Best' frontier.[26] However this situation is still better than the one in which government does not intervene in the economy. Under Second Best conditions, neoclassical economics tells us that if one market fails, typically it leads to the failure of all the markets. Then all markets have to be taken over by the government to achieve the Second Best frontier.[27]

In brief, under realistic conditions, there are no free markets and whatever kind of markets exist they fail and require government intervention for social welfare improvement. In the hypothetical situation of 'First Best', free markets may be optimal but the realistic situation is the 'Second Best' and under this condition all markets should be taken over by the government to achieve optimality. *Thus, under realistic conditions there is no case for free markets.* So how does one argue that markets be left 'free' for efficiency and optimality? It is an ideological statement, based on the interest of capital.

Given the growing strength of capital and its dominance at the ideological plane, *it has forced society globally to accept the need for a strategic retreat of the State* to What the World Bank has called 'market-friendly state intervention'. According to this view, all those forms of state intervention which help capital are acceptable (and good) and all those which help other sections of society are bad (because they come in the way of capital) and must be withdrawn. In fact, the call is not for free markets but for selective retreat in favour of capital.[28]

What all does this imply? The government must not subsidise since that affects price formation in the markets. It must not invest in the economy and create public sector units since they limit the size of the markets for the private sector. It must not help labour since then capital's grip over labour weakens and that is supposed to make it indisciplined. It must not put restrictions on prices since then high profits cannot be generated.[29] It should only help with the setting up of cheap physical (roads, railways, ports, etc.) and social (health and education) infrastructure so as to enhance the profitability of capital. Like in Japan where MITI functions as Business Incorporated, the role of government is seen to be exclusively as a hand maiden for capital. Other interests are taken to be subordinate to the interest of capital. So MRTPC, FERA and small-scale reservation have to be diluted and/or removed. Kumar (1994)[30] gives a list of changes introduced.

Curtailing government expenditures is the best way of

checking government intervention in the economy so its budget must be truncated. Anyway, to open up the economy, customs duties have to be cut (under WTO and otherwise) and to give concessions to capital, direct taxes have to be cut. So, the Indian Government's tax/GDP ratio has fallen after 1991. Further, it is suggested that the government's deficit (fiscal) must be curtailed. Two, reduction in tax/GDP and the deficit, together imply that government expenditures have to be cut.[31] So subsidies and public investments have to be curtailed. Privatisation and disinvestment of the PSU are required to raise budgetary resources.

Worse, even essential expenditures like expenditure on employment generation, food security, health and education have to be held back in comparison to the requirements. Legitimate transfers to states have had to be restricted. They are the ones that are responsible for executing most of these programmes and a crisis in their budgets means an immediate decrease in the support they can provided to the poor.[32]

Consequences

The government has had to intervene in the economy because outcome without its intervention is considered to be inconsistent with national goals, like, equity, poverty removal, literacy, etc. Markets have been found to be unable to help society achieve these goals. If the state retreats precisely from the areas that society feels are critical then the above-mentioned desirable goals would either not be achieved or would take long to achieve. There would be a mismatch between what society considers desirable and what the economy based on freer markets would achieve. The result can only be greater social and political tensions.

The *Planning process* which was to help the economy optimally achieve the socially desirable goals has had to be curtailed to promote markets. So investment has to be guided by the dictates of the markets (as determined by the wishes of the few with command over purchasing power) rather than the goals society as a whole may wish to achieve. *Guidance of the economy by the will of the majority is not favoured under the new dispensation* – clearly reflecting the undemocratic nature of the market-based functioning. Will of the owners of global capital becomes paramount and needs of the majority becomes marginal. All in the name of economic rationality. *Clearly, democracy is undermined.*

As the government's ability to *generate employment and keep price rise in check is limited* by the new policies, there is an impact on the purchasing power of the poor households. The organised sector has gone in for more capital intensive technology under pressure from global markets (based on more advanced technology) and has been cutting back on employment.[33-34] The Central Government has cut employment from 4 million in 1991 to the present level of 3.4 million. Drop in employment would have been even faster if labour laws allowing 'hire and fire' had been introduced earlier. Voluntary Retirement Scheme (VRS), has been used to retrench workers. All this effects real incomes and *makes poverty more entrenched.*

Even in a dynamic economy like that of China, reputed to be growing at 9 per cent per annum for the last 25 years, the problem of unemployment has become acute. According to Forney (2002),[35] urban joblessness is now around 9 per cent, 100 million people move from rural to urban areas in search of jobs, number of women working for the government has dropped by 24 per cent since 1994 and the government believes that just to keep unemployment from rising, 17 million jobs per annum are required. Thus, employment has to be specifically targeted and cannot be left to the market forces. China is facing a huge social problem.

What is clear is that under the new regime, the government's actions get restricted and its ability to intervene on behalf of the poor declines. It *has fewer policy instruments to work with. The state then sheds its obligations to the individual and especially to the non-well off.* Politically it is reflected in the talk of duties of citizens to the country.

The twin process of growing disparities with the rich getting richer and rising expectations of the others which cannot be fulfilled under the new dispensations results in growing political and social tensions. With reduced government control over the economy, *business has gone in for sharp practices* to make a quick buck – the number of scams has been on the rise.[36] Even when legitimate means are used, like mergers and acquisitions, they have been to the detriment of the ordinary shareholders. This is creating an environment of a free for all, resulting in growing illegality and an increase in the size of the black economy. This is *undermining the capacity of the state to deliver even what it can still legitimately do.*

Is all this not undermining the capacity of the ruling groups in India to govern and to improve their own conditions? Indeed it is and that is visible politically and socially. It is also visible in the way India is perceived by other nations as a nation that is not able to project its policies. In WTO, India is unable to project its interests as forcefully as it should be able to.[37] In the other multilateral agencies also it is unable to defend its interest. Why this weakness?

Black Economy and Weakness of National Capital

The ruling class in India is dominated by the interest of national capital. Hence *the weakness of the ruling class is the weakness of national capital.* This weakness has not developed overnight and it is not that suddenly national capital capitulated to the interest of international finance capital in 1991 and started implementing its programme under the garb of globalisation.

National capital has been weakening itself by *resorting to the black economy, to make a quick buck.*[38] As a part of this, it has been draining the economy of capital by resorting to flight of capital. Secondly, because black economy has resulted in wasteful and unproductive use of capital, *has accumulated slower* than it could have. Thirdly, with an easy route to profits, *capital did not absorb and develop technology* and as a result lost its dynamism over the last 40 years.

The perspective guiding national capital has narrowed over time. This has resulted in missed opportunities and non-realisation of the full potential of the nation. As the economic crisis deepened in the late eighties, it increasingly allied itself with international finance capital. In 1991, it supported the

NEP and argued that these policies would enable it to become more dynamic. The threat of MNCs capturing their markets was ignored/not seen. It unrealistically believed that the MNCs needed it and wanted a partnership with it. Therefore, it was happy to be junior partners to these companies.

Now Indian companies are discovering that they are not indispensable to the MNCs who are jettisoning them from joint ventures.[39] In brief, they are neither able to compete with MNCs who have much deeper pockets, have much more advanced technology and are more dynamic in the market nor be their partner.

National capital representing the elite amongst the elite of India and having a dominant, say, in the ruling groups has also capitulated to the idea that there is only one path to development – the Western path – no indigenous path is feasible as far as they are concerned. For them, like for the other elite groups in India, progress has meant going West. Using the black economy route, they had been spurting their capital to the West. They had opened up the economy using flight of capital long before 1991. That this would weaken them further in their competition with MNCs neither occurred to them nor was it a matter of concern to them given their increasingly Western orientation. Indian businesses have been setting up their non-resident wings to manage the capital they were taking out of India. Over time, these units of capital have become important and have further changed the orientation of Indian businesses.

For the Indian elite, the emotional attachment with the idea of India has progressively weakened. They have desired to link up with the global elite. That is what they understand by progress. Vacations abroad, availability of the same goods in the Indian economy as in the Western markets, etc. For this they require high incomes. So they do not want to sacrifice and do not mind income and wealth disparities growing. They do not see its link with growing social and political tensions in the country. *They are ready to vote with their feet if the country is in trouble.*

This attitude underlies Indian capital's support to NEP

and WTO. It explains why while critics of NEP were arguing that Indian industry would be hurt, Indian industry welcomed these policies. Those who were going to be hurt the most by NEP were the ones welcoming them. Slowly, they realised that things were turning out to be difficult for them and they tried to form the Bombay Club in 1993 and the India Club in 1996 but these were non-starters given the lack of perspective. More recently, they have tried to argue for a level playing field (through FICCI) but this has not had much of an effect given the clout that international finance capital has by now acquired in the Indian economy.

With the opening up of the economy, first trade account convertibility and then current account convertibility in 1995 and partial capital account convertibility, policies have reached an irreversible phase. Any assertion by the ruling groups of an independent economic policy stance is met with threats of flight of capital and destabilisation of the precarious foreign exchange situation. The apparently large reserves currently held are built on increases in India's liabilities to foreigners (NRIs, FIIs and FDI) but given the volume of daily movements of global capital, they would be inadequate to defend the economy over the medium run.

An independent assertion is also not feasible given that policy makers are not able to deliver on policy. The black economy makes policies fail and *undermines governance. Without the capacity to deliver, there cannot be any independent assertion against the powerful interests* (inside and outside the country) representing international finance capital.

The *only force that can counter the power of international finance capital is the state but that has been weakened voluntarily* by the ruling groups who have been demanding its retreat. In brief, the ruling groups (including national capital) have weakened themselves in the last 40 years by resorting to the black economy in a big way. This has also weakened them vis-a-vis international finance capital. They have further weakened themselves by allowing the economy to be opened up and demanding the retreat of the state. This is the Catch 22 they are caught in. *They cannot take an independent stance and the instrument they could have used to take an independent stance they have voluntarily weakened.*

Impact on Food Security

It is in the context of this larger picture of globalisation and the weaknesses of the ruling groups that one can situate the problem of food security facing the Indian economy. *The problem cannot be understood in itself, without the larger macro linkages.* If there is no design to capture Indian markets and to subjugate the Indian economy, then there is no problem of food security. Food can always be imported at a price. So *the issue is not just one of agriculture but of food and the national security aspects that relate to it.*

Food in the phrase 'food security' *should not just refer to its supply from agriculture* but also demand for it. Since food is basic, interested powers can use shortages to manipulate national policies. Further, in India roughly 60 per cent of the population depends on agriculture for its livelihood (unlike in the USA where less than 1 per cent of the population is dependent on this sector) so that any disruption in this sector has serious consequences for society and governance and hence for security.

Globalisation affects food security through two separate aspects. One, due to the adverse impact on specific sections of the population and the second, due to the general impact on national policies. The former has political and social implications which affect the latter. Some of the aspects of the general impact (on planning, employment, real incomes and disparities) were presented above.

Globalisation has also posed a problem regarding analysis and this is linked to the way markets function. *Each problem is broken up into its components and viewed in isolation,* independent of the larger context. A solution is given to each of the components irrespective of what the solution to the larger problem may be. It does not matter that in dealing with the limited problem with limited solutions, contradictions arise and a more difficult macro problem follows. *Food security is a multifaceted problem,* linked to the bigger picture and it needs to be understood in its totality.

The three key features of the current phase of globalisation, as pointed above, are: the mindset of the elite, the strategic retreat of the state and the growing marginalisation of the marginal. The elite, a critical component of the Indian ruling class, have little emotional attachment with the country or it's non-rich. The former do not identify with the problems faced by the latter because they are not their problems. For instance, to the former, the availability of goods is the problem and not their price. Hence importation of food is acceptable even if it is at a high cost, at the expense of the poor and national goals.

Traditional Issues

Strategic retreat of the state as spelt out earlier has meant growing underemployment and disguised unemployment, increasing disparities in a variety of terms, decrease in public investment (specially in agriculture), decline in investment in R&D (also in agriculture), cuts in subsidies to food and attempts to reduce procurement and scope of public distribution of foodgrain.

If the *real wages* of people fall, their capacity to buy adequate amount of food for their families declines. This is the reason why in India, food stocks have risen while even according to official figures, 26 per cent of the population is below the poverty level – having inadequate income to purchase the requisite minimum of food. According to some, the figure of 26 per cent below the poverty line does not reflect reality and it should be much larger. Whichever figure one takes, the fact of a large population having inadequate purchasing power is a reality.

Marketisation has implied a further decline in the share of investment in agriculture and rural areas and specially in the backward areas. This is causing disparities to widen between non-agriculture and agriculture, between rural and urban areas and advanced and backward states.[40]

Decrease in the rate of growth of *real public investment* (net of disinvestment) *and of capital formation in the central budget has meant a slow down in* the employment generation through the budget and of stagnation of the potential of agriculture. The latter has meant that the rate of *growth of foodgrain output* has fallen below the growth rate of population. This has serious implications for the future as per capita availability of foodgrain in the country would decline or would require imports to sustain consumption. This is not desirable for a poor country like India.

Reliance on the market mechanism for satisfying a basic requirement like food is not a good idea. This is what was the case before 1967 when dual pricing was introduced, specifically recognising the fact that in a poor country, like India, certain class of consumers and producers needed state intervention for their survival. To give up this mechanism would create problems for poor consumers and for marginal producers. While in some cases these two are separate individuals, in many cases in rural areas, the same individual would be adversely affected both as consumer and producer. Under the proposed new dispensation on agriculture in WTO, procurement and public distribution are frowned upon.

Depending on imports for fulfilling the food requirements would also make the system rely on the market mechanism. For imports to be triggered off, domestic prices would have to rise. In an open environment, domestic and international prices would be equalised at the borders. As domestic shortages occur, prices would rise to trigger off imports. Since India would always be a large player in the international markets whichever commodity is imported, international prices would rise substantially. This would hurt the poor both because they would lose incomes and prices would be higher. Thus, their real consumption would be affected.

Dependence on the market mechanism would imply that production would be governed by demand. Since demand is based on purchasing power, the rich countries and the rich in the developing world would determine what is produced. Hence horticulture, floriculture, poultry, etc., may become more important than coarse grains demanded by the poor. *The cropping pattern* has been undergoing a change and would change further as the needs of the poor become more marginal.

It is often argued that comparative advantage should be the basis of trade and production. But, in the advanced countries, the basis of survival of agriculture is the huge subsidies.[41 - 42] Since in the rich countries, agriculture is a small fraction of GDP and the population involved in agriculture is negligible, these countries can afford to give substantial subsidies. The poor countries cannot afford that. Hence while advanced countries have achieved self-sufficiency, the poor countries are told that trying to achieve self-sufficiency is not a desirable goal and they should not be averse to imports of food. It is not that there are no differences between the advanced countries on the issue of trade in agriculture. (Kumar (2000) argues that was the reason for the failure of the Seattle round of negotiations). But together they want to exploit the developing world markets.

With marketisation, there is likely to be more of *speculative activity* in commodities in short supply. This has serious consequences for real incomes of the poor and even the middle classes as was seen in 1998 in the case of onion shortages. With globalisation, there is likely to be an increase in export and import of agricultural commodities. Producers of commodities whose exports increase would benefit but in the case of commodities where the imports increase their producers would suffer. This has recently been seen in the case of many commodities like rubber, edible oil seeds, etc. The gain of the one is not the gain of the other. So even if the country's trade remains in balance, a large segment of the population would be adversely affected. Further in case of exports, given the structures of trade, dominated by big dealers and international trading companies, little benefit is likely to accrue to the small and the middle farmers who have little surplus.

With the opening up of the economy, as pointed out earlier, specific prices of certain commodities have fallen. While this is of *benefit to consumers* in general, it creates a crisis for the producers of these commodities. Their incomes fall and result in a decrease in their consumption which causes demand to fall. Producers finding their incomes declining, squeeze the wages of workers and this reduces demand further. Increase in consumption of those commodities whose prices fall leads to an increase in demand in the countries from which imports take place. Hence if does not boost production locally. Overall, ceteris paribus, when cheap imports of a certain good take place, there is a fall in production in the national economy and, therefore, a slow-down of the economy.

According to Guzman (1999)[44] cheap imports of corn into Philippines adversely affected corn producers. This was done under pressure of livestock and poultry industry which wanted cheap corn. However, these industries also suffered due to cheap imports. The import share of major varieties of meat rose between 1990 and 1997. In some cases, initially imports rose slowly or even fell but they picked up momentum later. Thus, many of these industries became traders. Imports pick up slowly because lines of distribution and trade have to be established. These take time.

If many goods are *imported cheaply,* then a large number of producers suffer. In Kumar (2001)[45] it is argued that there is a fallacy of composition in the argument that cheap imports are good for the consumers and, therefore, for the economy as a whole. The question may be asked, why nations resort to dumping in other countries in spite of the loss involved and why the nations facing dumping resist it even though the consumers are supposed to benefit? The reason lies in the *primacy of production over consumption.* One is a producer first and then a consumer. If one produces, one has an income and with that one consumes. If production suffers, consumption will also fall even if prices decline. If the economy is generally opened up to the import of cheap goods and production in general suffers, then it can only lead to an economic slow down.

Under WTO, the major agricultural exporting countries in the world, like, the USA and Canada, have managed to have their subsidies legitimised and have even increased their subsidies to their farmers. In contrast, the Indian farmers are facing cuts in subsidies (electricity, water, fertiliser, pesticide, etc.) and losing their competitive position in the national markets not to speak of the international markets. As the Indian agricultural markets open out, Indian farmers' livelihood gets jeopardised. This is once again a pointer to Indian elite's lack of concern for the common people. They were the ones bargaining at WTO and GATT and *how did they allow some countries to retain their subsidies while conceding the phasing out of the subsidies given to Indian farmers?* According to Sharma (2003),[46] in 2001, OECD countries gave their farmers $ 311 billion in subsidies, 6 times their total development aid and 3.5 times India's agricultural production.

It is incorrect to argue that some subsidies are not trade-distorting so should be allowed while others should not be allowed. Each subsidy has some effect on the markets so if markets are to be the yardstick, then no subsidies should be allowed. The advanced countries cleverly floated this idea of non-trade distorting subsidies and under WTO rules devised a system of Green, Blue and Amber boxes of allowed, to be phased out and to be disallowed subsidies (See Agreement on Agriculture Article 6).

Marketisation is also setting into motion *changes in the land markets* all over the country. Land legislation is sought to be amended to allow transfer of land freely. Prior to 1991, various legislations existed, limiting the land holding size and transfer of land. These are sought to be diluted or eliminated so as to allow large commercial farms or plantations to come up. Small and medium farmers may slowly be forced to sell out and become landless.

While this would no doubt happen at market related prices, for many families this would be disastrous given that land provides security. They understand the traditional way of working in agriculture but do not fully comprehend the functioning of markets, specially the financial markets and nature of investments to protect themselves in the old age. For these people, the issue of land is linked to their food security, livelihood and through that to their long-term security. This is the reason displacement is a major issue for local people even if market compensation is paid for land.

Cuts in subsidies have led to the *decline of the PDS* which was an aid to the middle classes and the poor. The former was benefitted directly while the latter gained only indirectly. The per capita distribution from PDS has fallen 25 per cent between 1991 and 1999. Procurement continued apace specially in the 5 years up to 2001 so that foodgrain stocks mounted to crisis proportions. Under political pressure, procurement prices have been raised but because subsidies have had to be kept in check, the issue prices of foodgrain have had to be raised so that offtake fell and stocks piled up. In brief, reduction in food subsidies have caused the stocks to rise (and rot) while the poor remain under- and malnourished. It took a major drought and a sharp fall in output of foodgrains in 2002 for stocks to decline.

It has been argued that the rise in food stocks in India is a result of the changing tastes of people who are going in for more of the high value items, like vegetables and meat. According to (FAO, 1999)[47] for the Asian nations, for 1995–97, the total daily per capita dietary supply of calories rises with per capita income levels and in this the share of basic food group (cereal or starchy roots) does not fall. In other words, more is eaten rather than less of almost every kind of food. In India as the incomes of the poor rise, they will continue to eat more of foodgrains rather then less for the foreseeable future. Hence it would be erroneous to argue that India need not worry about foodgrain production since it has reached self-sufficiency.

Dual pricing was introduced in basic commodities, like, foodgrains and sugar to control free market prices and provide a certain minimum amount to the consumers at a fixed price. Under the new dispensation, this has been largely dismantled with adverse effects on the poor. Public sector banks have been told to generate profits and priority sector lending requirements have been diluted. Thus, availability of credit to the rural poor has been curtailed. Newly opened private sector banks have anyway not gone to the rural areas.

Agricultural labour is largely unorganised and mostly at the bottom of the income ladder. Spending on food takes up the major chunk of their wages. They are largely unskilled and, therefore, have few opportunities in non-agricultural employment. Lacking in capital they are unable to go for self-employment. Thus, they are adversely affected by both a rise in prices and a decrease in employment opportunities.

In brief, real incomes of many in agriculture would be adversely affected and this would deepen poverty, create alienation, and result in social and political problems. *The will and the capacity of the nation to resolve its problems would weaken.*

Technology

Under the present process of globalisation, new technology is rapidly coming into use in agriculture (as in other sectors). Given that in India functional literacy is still low and especially in the rural areas, the capacity of most farmers to absorb the new technology is limited. Further, they own little capital in comparison to their average counterpart in the advanced countries. Hence their capacity to upgrade their farms to compete in the global markets is poor. Even if Indian farms currently have comparative advantage in some commodities, this may be lost over time, as technology changes. This will affect the Indian farmers and the country's food security adversely over time.

Under the WTO regime, with TRIPS and TRIMS progressively coming under implementation, the hold of the advanced nations over technology is likely to grow. India's technological backwardness is likely to become more entrenched because of the scale of investment required to reach the frontiers of technology. India may be able to buy intermediate and low technology but at a price. For the goods produced using these technologies, the advanced nations are interested in making the developing countries compete against each other so that the world prices of these goods remain low. The terms of trade between the high technology goods and the other goods are sought to be shifted against the latter.

The new technology has tended to be *capital intensive,* suitable to the large capitalist farmers of USA, Canada, New Zealand and Australia. It is typically high-cost. Indian farmers will not be able to afford these costs. Such technology is also labour-displacing so that it reduces employment and aggravates unemployment. Finally, high-cost farming in certain commodities when the world prices of these goods have fallen has meant that incomes of farmers have been squeezed. This is what underlies the increase in suicides amongst capitalist farmers going in for new technology insay cotton or other commercial crops, (Reports have been coming in from Punjab, Andhra Pradesh and Karnataka.[48]

Research and Development (R&D) in India has been adversely affected due to the cut in budgetary support for the public sector and the universities. Drive for privatisation and the requirement that public sector units generate profits has also resulted in reduced expenditures on R&D. The focus has invariably shifted to short-run activities, like, marketing or field trials. This is making the Indian economy more dependent on imported technology and leaving the country more vulnerable to foreign pressures.

Biotechnology is being rapidly introduced in the world. This is dangerous since it has serious social implications. It is not fully tested and its long-term implications are unclear. Introduction of these technologies apart from being high cost will adversely affect Indian farmers once full consequences become clear. Then it may be too late to reverse the trends. Advanced countries with their technological lead will be able to take care of adverse effects far more quickly than the developing countries which have little understanding of these technologies. For instance, the use of terminator seeds may tie up Indian farmers into high-cost farming for all times and make them dependent on seed companies and open to exploitation.

Under WTO, *new protectionist measures* are being introduced to cut out competition from the developing world. Phyto sanitary and other measures are being used. It is said that there is pest infestation and pesticide, etc., in the imports for India. Indian farmers wanting to export will be forced to adopt the new technology packages coming from the West and they will be permanently dependent on the western seed technology. In case they are unable to absorb new capital-intensive technology, they will be locked out of the export markets.

In brief, *technology is adversely affecting the food security in two ways.* Lack of dynamism of Indian farmers because of the small size of capital ownership and their low educational status will prevent them from quickly absorbing technology and innovating on it and will affect them adversely in the developing global markets. Secondly, they will be locked into a low technology trap and will be competing against similar goods from other developing countries and will constantly find their incomes under pressure.

Challenges for the 21st Century

Many arguments given earlier may sound hypothetical. But that is true with most arguments which link consequences to certain causes. There is a time dimension to any analysis. While certain things happen quickly others take time. One may have to wait for events to unfold or read them from the past experience. For instance, because of food shortages and the requirement of imports in the past, foreign powers extracted concessions whose implications became clear later. These things can happen again and need to be taken note of for policy purposes. One cannot wait for things to occur and then to act since that may be too late.

Challenge of Food Security

Food security, in the broader sense, is being compromised in several ways as depicted above, both for individuals in society and for the nation as a whole. For the nation, *security is not just a matter of food shortage but its implications for the nations' ability to pursue its own path of development.* A 5 per cent shortage of food can always be accommodated by indigenous measures provided the political will exists. With an alienated and dissatisfied population and weak governance, this is not possible. This is what opens the country to outside pressures. As argued above, the ruling classes dominated by the elite in society, are now less committed to the task of nation building; they view globalisation as a chance to join the global elite.

Consequently, the challenge for the nation is that the prime concern of its ruling class is not the welfare of the nation and its people.

Today, a large majority of Indians do not know what the New Economic Policies launched in 1991 are or what does WTO stand for. They do not know that it is setting the agenda for the way they will live and work for the next fifty years and more. They do not understand that any economy sets the rules of economic gains – who gains and who loses – and these rules of the game are being changed in a direction that are weighed against those who are already marginal in our society and even more marginal in the world reckoning. If prices of coconut, areca nut, rubber, tea, etc., decline suddenly because of imports and the changed world situation the producers of these commodities will find their incomes falling in spite of working just as hard or more and producing as much as they did earlier. In brief, *food security is an aspect of nation building for India and a challenge posed by one-way globalisation.*

Challenge of Globalisation and Marketisation

It is not just the common people but even the educated who find these changes hard to comprehend. Our legislators and policy makers are also confused. The legislatures (like the Parliament) have not fully discussed the issues. Even when discussions take place, these have been piecemeal. Partly, this is a result of the absence of an overall perspective in the nation. Absence of an overall vision is a result of a lack of an indigenous and autonomous worldview and the tendency of the marektisation process to split any problem into its individual components and deal with them separately without allowing a holistic view to be taken. *There is a dumping down of the population.* Taking a narrow view has become acceptable and most people now accept that no effort needs to be made to understand the bigger picture. This must change if the country is to do well.

Outcomes of markets are taken to be 'objective' and, therefore, correct. Everything else is defined as 'subjective' and less desirable.

Individuals in a market environment are taken to be 'rational', optimising their gains and welfare. Welfare improvement is based on (consuming) 'more is better'. Individuals exercising restraint and consuming less or not giving into the market generated demand pattern and desires (that the producers push for) are considered irrational and are marginalised. While those who give into the market-generated consumerism are applauded as successful, automatic acceptance of market outcomes is resulting in another form of damping down of the population. Choices are expected to be exercised within given parameters and one is not expected to go against the trend.

It is argued, markets have no value of their own; these are given by society. When society gives into the dictates of the markets or suspends its judgement or accepts the outcome of the markets as correct, values are eroded. Markets are in themselves amoral and immoral. When society accepts the market outcome as its ideal, it accepts this amorality and immorality. For instance, speculative activity is a part of market functioning. Making gains through this activity are acceptable under a market-based regime and a whole tribe of people have emerged who simply earn their livelihood through this means. Globally now there are many who begin their day by placing orders for buying and selling shares. Social energy is diverted into this wasteful activity but this is legitimate in the market and no value judgement needs to be attached to it. According to Baran (1973)[49] a huge amount of waste is taking place in such activities.

If due to speculation, millions become poor or lose their employment, government policies rather than speculation needs to be blamed. Poor people do not count. *If a profit can be made, that is all that counts.* Whereas, in a feudal or semi-feudal setting, a value judgement used to be made against usurious interest rates charged by the landlord-cum-lender. Today, if a company declares a 50 per cent dividend it is considered to be well managed. It is not argued that they could have charged lower prices in the market and made lower profits so as to give a lower dividend. Their high profits are justified by the working of the markets – no value judgement need be attached to high profits. The government should not even levy a high tax on high profits. In fact, the pressure is to eliminate tax on dividends.

Globalisation is *undermining democracy in national economies.* National governments are being forced to adopt policies that may *not* be in the best interest of their population and, as argued, only in the interest of the ruling elite (in the short run). Multilateral institutions, like IMF and World Bank are not accountable to the people yet they force their conditionalities on national governments in the name of market discipline. Often the legislatures are by-passed by governments and it is argued that these are international obligations that have to be simply implemented. This has happened in India. Responsibility of society to individuals and of the state to its citizens is being diluted. In this framework, the ruling groups are now talking of the duties of the citizens and not of their rights. So, in India, where compulsory education till the age of 14 was to be achieved by 1965, now we are talking of literacy and of education up to the 5th standard without emphasis on quality. This is only a way of giving up the idea of effective literacy for all and diluting the obligation to the citizen.

The crisis in the life of individuals, in the marginalised nations, brought about by rapid changes which they do not understand and which leaves them uncertain about their future, results in their alienation and leads them to look backward rather than forward.

As the nation weakens and is found to be unable to deliver, the citizens search for a more secure identity in their *caste, community and region.* Sectarianism gains and the idea of the nation weakens and its capacity to deliver declines, creating a vicious circle of decline.[50] In the international forums, the country weakens and is unable to either define its long-term interest or to defend its interest. This damages the security of the nation in the broadest sense.

The nation suffers not only from problems on its food front (which it may be resolved through import) but as a result of *one-way globalization;* it weakens internally and is unable to define or protect its long-term interest. This needs to be rectified. The argument here is not to hark back to some glorious past but to recognise our lack of dynamism and rectify that. There is need to reinforce indigenous strengths and evolve an alternative development paradigm. India has the depth to do so.[51]

Failure of policy and the market needs to be recognised. *Society cannot go back and forth between the market and the Sate.* There is a need to work out a new paradigm. Democracy needs to be strengthened consciously through reform.[52] The elite has to redefine its long term interest.

One-way globalisation is the principal challenge before India. A deteriorating food security situation makes the nation more vulnerable to manipulation. It reinforces the notion that the nation lacks adequate resources for its own development. It sets the stage for a further acceptance of the ongoing process (for the last 250 years) of one-way globalisation as the only available path of development (TINA).

Specialisation and increased division of labour underlie the expansion of the markets. These have been considered to be good for economic development. Is this necessarily so? If it results in destruction of jobs for some and expansion for others, is it necessarily good? Similarly, the issue of comparative advantage being welfare improving also needs another look because its functioning results in the destruction of jobs for some. Those who are displaced may not be able to find jobs and this may result in suffering for their families and social tension. In brief, *the assumed smooth transitions in the market are not so smooth since there may be considerable human suffering along the path of transition.* This is not taken into account in the economic calculus of the markets.

Responsibility of society to individual and of state to citizen needs to be reasserted. Immorality and amorality of the markets needs to be understood. Man's predominance needs to be asserted while supremacy of the markets need to be reassessed. Even when markets function smoothly, can rising material prosperity based on 'more is better' be an end in itself? Can it in itself be fulfilling or will it lead to a growing feeling of being unfulfilled? The issue then is *what should have priority – Man or Market?* The answer should be obvious. But how this is to be brought about in the contemporary situation is a major intellectual challenge.

REFERENCES

1. Kumar, A., 1997, 'Freedom from the Perspective of the Poor,' *Vidyajyoti.* Vol. 61, No. 9. pp. 617-629.
2. Kumar, A., 1999, *'The Black Economy in India,'* N. Delhi: Penguin India.
3. Kalecki, M. 1976, *'Essays on Developing Economies.'* Sussex, England: Harvester Press Ltd., pp. 77-80.
4. Dasgupta, B. 2001, 'Food Security For India: Some Issues,' Mimeo. Discussion Paper 2/2001. Economics Department, Jadhavpur University, p. 6.
5. Sharma, D. 2003, 'WTO and Agriculture: The Great Trade Robbery', Mimeo. Forum for Biotechnology & Food Security. N. Delhi.
6. Bhagwati, J. and Srinivasan, T.N. 1993, *'India's Economic Reforms.'* Ministry of Finance, Government of India.
7. Kumar, A., 1994, 'Proposals for A Citizens Union Budget for the Nation for 1994-95,' Mimeo. Preparatory Committee for Alternative Economic Policies, N. Delhi.
8. Kennedy, P. 1988, *'The Rise and Fall of the Great Powers': Economic Change and Military Conflict from 1500 to 2000.* New York: Random House, 1988, p. 149.
9. Dutt, R. 1960, *'The Economic History of India,' Vol. I. Under Early British Rule 1757-1837.* N. Delhi: Publications Division, Ministry of Information and Broadcasting, Government of India, p. 216.
10. Dutt, R.P. 1947, *'India Today.'* Bombay: People's Publishing House, pp. 503–21.
11. Kumar, A. 1991, Structural Adjustment Policies: Loss of Sovereignty and Alternatives. *Lokayan Bulletin.* November December 1991, Pp. 1, 5 – 23.
12. Kumar, A., 1994.
13. Samuelson, P. A. 1954, 'The Pure theory of Public Expenditure,' *Review of Economics and Statistics* Nov.
14. Soros, G. 1997, 'The Capitalist Threat,' *The Atlantic Monthly.* February.

15. Kumar, A., 1999.
16. Tresch, R.W. 1981, *'Public Finance: A Normative Theory,'* Plano, Texas: Business Publications.
17. Baran, P. 1973, *'The Political Economy of Growth'*, Harmondsworth, England: Pelican Book.
18. Bhagwati and Srinivasan, 1993.
19.
20. Khor, M. 2002, *'The WTO, the Post-Doha Agenda and the Future of the Trade System: A Development Perspective.'* Penang, Malaysia: Third World Network.
21. Korten, D.C. 1995, *'When Corporations Rule the World.'* Connecticut, USA: Kumarian Press.
22. Kumar, A., 1994.
23. Chakravarty, S. 1987, *Development Planning: The Indian Experience.* New Delhi: Oxford.
24. Forney, M. 2002, 'Worker's Wasteland.' *Time,* 17 June, pp. 40-47.
25. World Bank. 1997, *'World Development Report,'* Oxford: Oxford University Press.
26. Lipsey, R and Lancaster, K. 1956, 'The General Theory of Second Best, *Review of Economic Studies,'* Vol. 24(1), No. 63.
27. Treseh, A., 1994.
28. Bhagwati and Srinivasan, 1993.
29. Kumar, A., 1991.
30. Kumar, A., 1994.
31. Kumar, A., 1991.
32. Kumar, A., 1994.
33. Kumar, A., 2000, 'India at the Seattle Meeting: Playing Safe,' *Economic & Political Weekly.* January 15.
34. Kumar, A., 2002, 'Factors Underlying the Economic Slowdown: Growing Disparities, Globalization and the Black Economy.' Chapter in the *Alternative Economic Survey 2001-2002.* New Delhi: Rainbow Publishers Limited, Lokayan and Azadi Bachao Andolan. 2002.
35. Friedman, M. 1977, Nobel Lecture: 'Inflation and Employment.' *Journal of Political Economy,* June.
36. Kumar, A., 1999.
37. Kumar, A., 2000.
38. Kumar, A., 1999.
39. Kumar, A., 1994.
40. Kumar, A., 2002
41. Sharma, D., 2003.

42. Dasgupta, B., 2001
43. Kumar, A, 2000.
44. Guzman, B.R., 1999, 'The GATT Agreement on Agriculture: Its Impact on the Philippine Livestock And Poultry Industry,' *Institute of Political Economy Journals,* December.
45. Kumar, A., 2001, 'The Macro View. Chapter in the *Alternative Economic Survey 2000-2001,*' New Delhi: Rainbow Publishers Limited, Lokayan and Azadi Bachao Andolan. Pp. 20-27. 2001.
46. Sharma, D., 2003.
47. FAO, 1999. *'The State of Food Security in the World.'*
48. Parvathi, M. 2003, 'Driven to Desperation' *The Hindu,* September 14.
49. Baran, P., 1973.
50. Kumar, A., 1999.
51. Kumar, A., 1994.
52. Kumar, A., 1999.

Chapter 3

Poverty and Sustainable Development

Naushad Ali Azad

Introduction

Poverty and sustainable development (SD) are two socio-economic phenomena drawing global attention of academics, researchers, policy makers as well as human activists. Traditionally the issues of poverty and SD have been treated separately and singularly but during last one decade there have been conceptual developments and paradigm shifts in these areas. They are now viewed as concepts that are *multi-dimensional* and more comprehensive. Also, there is some degree of *convergence* within and between the two in that the issue of poverty and food security (as well as many other issues of human deprivation and social welfare) are now considered an integral part of the bigger challenge known as SD. Further, most of the remedial aspects of poverty and SD require direct action and a *pro-active involvement* on the part of the government, the private sector, the civil society and the NGOs at all levels – local, national and global.

Poverty is one of the biggest challenges of the fast modernising world. Notwithstanding the new claims of a positive trickle down effects of economic reforms and globalisation,[1] about 2.5-3 billion people of the global population (6.201 billion in 2002) are 'poor' (living below the consumption of $ 2 per day) while nearly half of them (1.2 billion in 1998) are 'very poor' (living below the consumption of $ 1 per day). Most poor of the world are concentrated in the continents of Asia and Africa (WDR, 2003 and WDR, 2004). For India, national and international estimates are indicative of a declining trend during 1990s: yet the absolute number is very large. Notwithstanding the controversy about the data and the methodology, the size of 'very poor' group of India (about 350 million in 1998) is more than one-third of its own population and about one-fourth of the global 'very poor' population. Poverty of this order (often accompanied by high incidence of unemployment) not only hampers the economic growth of the economy but may also shatter the social fabric of the nation.

The immediate (or short-run) cause of poverty, faced by India and many other developing countries, is the absence of (or the lack of access to) income and employment opportunities. In the long run, however, income and employment opportunities depend on the status of health, education, skills and other parameters of human capability (defined as ability plus opportunity). That is why there is a need of going beyond 'income-approach to poverty' and the programmes of poverty alleviation need focus on these long-term factors.

SD is another potent challenge of the fast-modernising and industrialising world. Like poverty, the concept of SD was initially confined to a narrow scope of environmental issues only. Nowadays it is also evolving to encompass many other aspects of human concern – economic, social, political, cultural and spiritual. SD now relates to overall fabric of life of present and future generations. The need of such a holistic approach to SD was demonstrated at the World Summit of Sustainable Development (WSSD) held at Johannesburg during 2002. Amongst the socio-economic issues, the focal point is the incidence and prevalence of poverty and hunger in many parts of the world and the programmes of poverty-alleviation. Other issues of social relevance like health, sanitation, drinking water, human rights, etc., are also under active consideration. In other words, it is now realised that *socioeconomic sustainability is at least* (if not more) *as important as environmental sustainability.*

A large number of studies have been carried out to discuss the nature and the extent of poverty but limited efforts have been made to analyse its relationship with SD. Similarly, most literature on SD remains confined to issues of environmental imbalance and its other dimensions have not received appropriate attention. The purpose of the first section of this paper is to explore various dimensions of poverty and SD and, at the same time, examine the linkage between them. In Sections II and III, we present a broader and holistic view of the notions of poverty and SD by explaining their various dimensions. It is argued that issues of poverty and SD need to be extended beyond the boundaries of 'income-poverty' and 'environmental sustainability' respectively. In Section IV, an attempt has been made to relate SD to poverty in the same way as it is done with lack of biodiversity or ecological imbalance. There we specifically argue that socio-economic balance (or socio-economic sustainability) is as necessary a condition for SD as the environmental balance. Section V extends the argument to the case of India wherein we maintain that the objectives of a sustainable development policy as laid down in the Tenth Five-Year Plan would envisage not only the tackling of poverty in a broader sense (focusing on human poverty rather than income poverty alone) but also the integration of the rural sector (agriculture and rural development) with the modern sector (industry and services) need to become the focal point of her developmental efforts. We conclude by pointing out that both of them may remain the necessary components of a long-term sustainable development policy for India.

I

Meanings and Dimensions of Poverty and SD

The concepts of poverty and SD are multi-dimensional and relative in nature. Poverty and SD can mean differently to different groups of people in different countries at different points of time. They have varying dimensions and some of these dimensions are still in the process of evolving. For a meaningful discussion and purposeful policy implications they both need to be contextualised in terms of space and time. In this section, we examine meanings and some dimensions of SD.

What is Sustainable Development?

It appears that the term SD was first used in the context of environmental degradation across generations (Raskin et al., 1996)). However, its scope has since widened to incorporate the new realities of changing times in almost all areas of human concern. Before elaborating on the various dimensions of SD we first explore its meanings.

The notion of SD is derived from two words – sustainable and development. SUSTAIN means 'to maintain' or 'to uphold' something (e.g. a life, a system, etc.) by providing a minimum necessary support and/or a conducive environment. SUSTAINABLE implies 'capable of maintaining' or 'capable of upholding' and has the objective and subjective dimensions of *viability* and *desirability* respectively. Finally, SUSTAINABILITY refers to the capacity or capability of systems for achieving the viable and desirable results from an activity under consideration.

The meaning of DEVELOPMENT is better understood when contrasted with the notion of GROWTH. Growth (or economic progress) means a vertical change in the economy requiring an efficient use of resources (based on the criterion of cost minimisation). It is limited to an increase in the material production of goods and services produced in a year and can be measured quantitatively in terms of per capita income of a country. On the other hand, development is much more than just economic progress. It is a 'holistic' and 'multifaceted' phenomenon of horizontal change demanding a judicious use of resources (based on the notion of welfare maximisation for the society as a whole). Of late, development levels achieved by different countries are approximated with human development index (HDI) that is currently based on three variables – literacy, life expectancy and gender disparity in addition to per capita income. Many other aspects of social concern such as poverty levels and gaps in income-distribution, etc., are also the desired variables of HDI but not included in its calculations so far. However, it is clear that the notion of development requires balance and harmony amongst various components of economy as well as society. Finally, it should be noted that growth is a necessary condition for development and not the sufficient one, i.e. growth is necessary for development but growth need not always lead to development.

The Concept of SD Requires Contextualisation

The exact meaning of SD cannot be understood without defining the proper context. As mentioned above, every developmental activity should involve costs and benefits that can be either explicit or implicit. Sustainability requires that the total benefits (explicit plus implicit) derived from the activity should exceed the total costs (explicit plus implicit) involved. The implicit costs and benefits are mostly social or collective in nature and, therefore, complex in nature. *Consideration of the implicit costs and benefits makes sustainability not only difficult but also subjective in nature and their evaluation may vary with respect to time and space.* It follows that evaluation of sustainability of any activity requires its specifications (contextualisation) in terms of space and time.

Analytical and Operational Definitions of SD

The meanings of sustainability and development given above can now be used for the purpose of defining SD in analytical terms.[2] For this purpose, let us have a closer look at the viability and desirability aspects of sustainability. The criteria of viability and desirability should require a comparison of the aggregate (explicit and implicit) costs and benefits of the activity under consideration. The explicit costs and benefits so involved are normally physical in nature and, therefore, easy to calculate. On the other hand, the implicit costs and benefits are usually non-physical and non-material in nature and unlike explicit costs and benefits, they are rather difficult to compute. Further, these costs and benefits may relate to either short- or long-term periods. If, the aggregate benefits exceed the aggregate costs then the activity under consideration should be 'sustainable' in analytical terms at least. As already mentioned, to make the definition of SD operational we need to contextualise the activity in question so that the implicit costs and benefits are properly understood. *In other words, the various dimensions and the corresponding operational definitions of SD can be derived only after proper contextualisation of the development issue under consideration.*

Dimensions of SD – A Historical View

Historically, sustainability has been a matter of concern to many writers and philosophers in different stages of global development. For example, while studying the indestructible properties of land and the land-man ratio, *Malthus and Ricardo* were concerned about the *sustainability of the mother-earth for food production.* At the dawn of the post-industrial era, *Marx* was concerned about the *sustainability of the capitalist (industrial) mode of production* without using the term 'sustainability'. The sustainability of earth for food production was put to test in 1950s and 1960s when Malthus tended to be right once again. At this juncture of history, the Green Revolution came to the rescue and the rapidly growing populations of countries like China, India and Indonesia were saved from scenario of famine and starvation. These are historical examples of *initial inter-generational human concerns about sustainability of the production systems belonging to agriculture as well as industry.* The context seems to have changed when *the Club of Rome* and many other groups in 1960s and 1970s questioned the sustainability of these production systems. It was pointed out that technological advancement, industrialization, urbanization and high pressures of population were the main features of the economic system belonging to the 20th century. The Club of Rome *focused on the high opportunity cost of the development* by saying that if not checked the Earth would rapidly run out of its *key non-renewable natural resources.* The high opportunity cost was explained in terms of the overuse of earth-resources, i.e.

at a pace that is visibly much faster than what can be sustained over time. At the same time, it caused *insurmountable damage to environment and ecology* leading to various other issues and changes in the economy and the society. It follows, therefore, that though the *notion of SD did originate from our inter-generational concerns* about the use and availability of natural resources, the focus soon shifted to broader inter-generational concerns related with ecological imbalance and environmental degradation caused by over depletion of earth's natural resources. It is no wonder, therefore, that from Stockholm (First World Environment Conference, 1972) to Rio (Save the Earth Conference, 1992), the concept of SD remained confined to 'environmental sustainability' only. After the turn of 21st century, the focus has now shifted to what may be termed as *social sustainability* – a concept that includes all *major issues of human concern other than environment.* Social sustainability is emerging as an important and relevant concept in the context of the fast modernising and globalising world. Thus the Johannesburg Summit [World Summit on Sustainable Development (WSSD), 2002] took a comprehensive view of SD by defining it in terms of three pillars – environment, economy and society. WDR (2003) argues that ensuring SD requires attention not just to economic growth and environment but also to a number of social issues including poverty, illiteracy, gender discrimination, education, health, etc. Unless the transformation of society and the management of environment are addressed integrally along with economic growth, growth itself will be jeopardised over the long run. It is also realised that international (or spatial) patterns of growth and development have been uneven. With time, the poor-rich divide has deepened and widened. The striking difference in the use or overuse of these resources by the developed and the developing countries has been a moot issue at every global meet. Of late, the process of globalisation has added some new dimensions to the problem of sustainability, e.g. financial, cultural, spiritual, human rights and so on. In addition, some recognise peace and stability as an additional desirable requirement of SD. From the chronological and historical perspective of the concept of sustainability given above it follows that for a meaningful discussion and useful policy implications the concept of SD needs to be contextualised in terms of space and time. Depending on the context, SD can have various dimensions, e.g. environmental (levels of pollution in air and water), ecological (maintenance of ecosystems and the natural resource base), social (health, education, shelter, equity, etc.), economic (economic needs such as adequate livelihood and productive assets), financial (stability in the fragile capital markets and financial systems), cultural (cultural needs including cultural institutions), political (ability to participate in the decision-making processes) and so on.

Environmental Sustainability –An Operational Definition of SD

In the context of ecological and environmental concerns, a number of operational definitions of SD or 'environmental sustainability' are available.[3] The first operational definition of SD is perhaps the one given by Brundtland Commission also known as the World Commission on Environment and Development (WCED, 1987): '(economic) progress that meets the needs of the present without compromising the ability of future generations to meet their own needs.' This approach of WCED for defining sustainability (or non-sustainability) basically reflects our temporal concern about the utilisation rates of natural resources with respect to three parameters – resource-base, technology and preference structure. Similarly, Raskin et al. (1996) have defined 'environmental sustainability' as the capacity of unimpaired persistence and maintenance of the ecosystems and the natural resource base into the future.

Social Sustainability – A New Requirement of SD

This definition incorporates the concerns of 'Save the Earth' summits of Stockholm and Rio. Definitions of sustainability given by WCED (1987), Hardoy et al. (1992) and UNCHS (1996) are based on the notion of 'social sustainability'. They incorporate not only the socio-economic issues but also lay emphasis on the cultural and political aspects as envisaged by WSSD at Johannesburg.

II

Meanings and Dimensions of Poverty

For long, poverty has been a central issue of development policy. As a matter of human concern, it is perhaps much older than SD. The perennial persistence and wide prevalence of poverty across the globe has made it an essential component of the sustainable development policy (SDP). Starting from the simple 'income-approach', poverty as a phenomenon has evolved to become more comprehensive and holistic. Initially it focused on the basic needs of human survival but now factors responsible for human empowerment are also considered necessary.

Absolute versus Relative Poverty

At the very outset, a clarification of the notions of 'absolute poverty', 'relative poverty' and 'human poverty' may be useful. Conceptually, poverty can be either absolute or relative. In absolute terms, poverty is defined as the absence, lack, or denial to the access of the basic economic needs of individuals in the society. It is related to human existence in physical sense of just being alive. *Absolute poverty* is found in different guises such as lack of food, shelter and clothing. Amongst them food poverty is most prominent while hunger and malnutrition are its worst forms. (Pedro Medrano, WFP, UN). On the other hand, *relative poverty* is related to inter-personal comparison of human well-being within and across countries[4]. The common denominator between these two concepts of poverty is that both of them are measured in terms of income levels of the individuals. Both of them are important in the context of SD.

Global Dimensions of Absolute and Relative Poverty

As already indicated, global conditions about the distribution of resources (in terms of both income as well as wealth) are quite disturbing: About 2.5-3 billion people of the global population (6.201 billion in 2002) are 'poor' (living below the consumption of $ 2 per day) while nearly half of them (1.2 billion in 1998) are 'very poor' (living below the consumption of $ 1 per day). 1.2 billion people in the world earn half-a-dollar a day; The difference between the richest 20 per cent and the poorest 20 per cent of the planet was 11 times in 1913, widening to 30 times in 1960, 60 times in 1990 and to 74 times in 1997; In 1998, 86 per cent of wealth and a similar amount of income growth were appropriated by the same 20 per cent of the population; The poorest 20 per cent receive just 1 per cent of global income. Hence, fighting poverty and reducing inequalities must be priorities of the national and international agenda of development.

Beyond Income Approach - The Concept of 'Human-Poverty'

In recent times there has been a paradigm shift by *moving away from the concept of income-poverty.* To begin with, it was realized that for poor populations consumption levels are more relevant than the income levels. Hence, monthly per capita expenditure (MPCE) has been considered a better indicator of poverty than per capita income. Further, poverty has a direct correlation with the proportion of income spent on food. As the demand for cereals drops in proportion as disposable income rises, the break-up of expenditure on food in terms of cereals, milk and milk products, vegetables, edible oils, fruits, beverages, etc., can be even more revealing. Such a break-up of the consumption-expenditure can be used to reflect on the extent of malnutrition of the poor.

A more relevant concept of poverty is what is known as *'human poverty'* – a notion that takes a comprehensive and holistic view and goes beyond the income approach. Incidentally, economists and policy makers have deliberated on this dimension of poverty much before the WSSD took a holistic view of SD in 2002. They emphasised the need to go beyond the conventional definition of poverty based on income alone. It is argued that poverty should be seen as the 'denial of opportunities and choices that are most basic to human development' (see, for example, Sudarshan and Chelliah, 2002)[5]. This form of poverty is multi-dimensional involving a number of parameters of human development and human empowerment. A major advantage of this multi-dimensional approach is that the policy framework for poverty eradication has to be necessarily multi-pronged.

Thus, the multi-dimensional concept of 'human poverty' can be defined as the lack of productive employment, income (purchasing power), food (calories and nutrition), health, education, and above all opportunity (capacity and capability) and freedom of choice.

III

Linkages between Poverty and SD

Since the concepts of poverty and SD are multi-dimensional, it is difficult to conceive of an aggregate relationship between the two. However, meaningful linkages can be established after identifying the context. In India, for example, the extent and the 'depth of poverty' (defined by a change in the distribution of income below the poverty line) may be linked to SD in general in the same way as 'environmental degradation'. More importantly, the 'extent and the depth of rural poverty' in particular may have significant repercussions for SD through their linkages with 'social sustainability'. Hence, linkages between poverty and SD essentially depend on how poverty is defined and which group among the poor is more affected.

By and large, research and policy in this area have tended to focus on the relationship between poverty and environmental degradation in terms of pointing out that *the poor are both victims and agents of environmental degradation* – victims in that they are more likely to live in ecologically vulnerable areas and agents in that they may have no option but deplete environmental resources thus contributing to environmental degradation (SIDA, 1996; UNEP, 1995). At the same time, it is also acknowledged that *the poor often have practices that conserve the environment.* Great *physical and spatial variability in natural resource endowments* also complicates the picture (Redclift and Skea, 1997). In general terms, the underlying causes of both poverty and environmental degradation are structured by uneven processes of development (imbalanced growth) operating via technologies, incentives, institutions and regulations *which favor some social groups and some geographical areas over others* (Leach and Mearns, 1991).

From these observations, it may be inferred that the exact relationship of poverty and SD can be determined only after specifying their dimensions. We now discuss some dimensions of poverty in the context of Indian experience.

IV

Poverty and SD – Case of India

Estimates of poverty can be divided into categories: Type I the food poverty and Type II the poverty of income and consumption. While the former is a cruder form of poverty (and the worst form of its manifestation is in the form of starvation or hunger-deaths[6]) and poses a question mark to food-security situation in India, the latter is related to the bigger issue of SD. After a long and controversial debate about poverty estimates in India during the decades of 1980s and 1990s, the overwhelming view is that the number game is not over. The extent of poverty (both Type I and Type II) at the turn of the century may have declined but the absolute number of poor in the country may be very large and, therefore, alarming.

Poverty and Hunger Statistics in India – A Question Mark to Food-Security and SD

When poverty takes its cruelest form of hunger and hunger-deaths, it becomes a matter of immediate social and political concern. According to 1999-2000 Survey of the NSSO, roughly a quarter of the population is below the poverty line in India. This does not mean that a quarter of the population goes hungry. In fact, *the incidence of hunger (at 3 per cent as per the same survey) is distinctly lower than poverty even in rural India.* The divergence in the two ratios was noticed in the early eighties when, according to 1983-84 survey, 81.1 per cent of rural population reported that they were never hungry. This meant that barely 19 per cent were ever hungry during the year while little less than half of them were recorded as being under the poverty line. This divergence in reported figures of poverty ratio and hunger ratio embarrassed government economists and the embarrassing question on hunger was dropped altogether for the next survey of 1987-88. When some other economists expressed outrage at this, the question was restored in the 1993-94 and 1999-2000 surveys and the divergence in the two ratios has been growing ever since.

Poverty has Fallen, But Hunger has Fallen much Faster in 1990s

Notwithstanding the controversy of methodology and the accuracy of data, the comparison of the figures of 1983-84, 1993-94, and 1999-2000 surveys (19 per cent, 5.5 per cent, and 3 per cent respectively), show that the achievement on hunger front is very encouraging. Poverty has fallen, but hunger has fallen much faster. Even the proportion of the *chronically hungry population* (who said that they got insufficient food in every month of the year) has shrunk from 2.4 in 1983-84 to 0.7 in 1999-2000 in rural areas, and from 0.8 to 0.3 in urban areas. An important question that may be asked is that if only 3 per cent of Indians suffer from hunger why the media is always full of news not only about hunger but also about starvation deaths! It may be replied by pointing out that 3 per cent of India's population is huge number of 30 million people and the media can find some of them in the distressed areas. In any case, the relationship between hunger, poverty and SD is clear. The hunger ratio may have come down from 19 per cent to 3 per cent, but absolute number of poor is very large and a sustainable development policy should require bring them down to zero levels.

Controversies about Income-Poverty Estimates

Estimates of Type II poverty (income/consumption

poverty) produced controversial numbers in the decades of 1980s and 1990s. These estimates were attempted to examine the poverty impact of economic reforms and globalisation. For example, *the World Bank* in its global update on poverty in the year 1999 maintained that the number of the poor was rising in India. The bank estimated that there were 340 million poor Indians in 1997, up from 300 million in 1990. So, the level of absolute poverty in India after seven years of reforms stood unchanged at around 36 per cent. These estimates not only showed that the number of the poor was rising in India but that the number had declined substantially for China, from 280 million to 125 million during the same 1990–97 period. Earlier, the Narasimha Rao government had declared that the percentage of Indians living below the poverty line had declined dramatically to around 19 per cent in 1992 from 29 per cent in 1987-88. Income studies by NCAER also suggested that the poor were perhaps better off. On the other hand, the United Front Government went on to suggest that poverty levels had not dropped and a study by ICRIER endorsed the point. So why should different studies arrive at different conclusions? Many explanations were given. Most of the quibbling occurred about the methodology. It was pointed out that Rao Government's conclusion was largely based on Central Statistical Organisation (CSO) consumption data instead of National Sample Survey Organisation (NSSO) data and the latter was more reliable since it was obtained by questioning consumers directly. The CSO estimates, gathered indirectly, were invariably higher. An expert group headed by D.T. Lakdawala had also recommended the use of NSSO figures and suggested that poverty figures be first computed at the state level and then aggregated nationally. This was considered an improvement in the methodology of poverty estimation since price and consumption patterns varied regionally. The new formula led to a higher (39 per cent) poverty figure and fell only marginally to around 36 per cent in 1993-94 when NSSO carried out an extensive consumption survey. The bank used NSSO's data but it pertained to three consecutive yearly surveys that used a much smaller sample.

As a result, the bank's findings were criticised because the sample size in these surveys was too small to be relied upon. Many economists also quarrelled with the way the bank defines the poverty line – what an individual can buy everyday for a US dollars (that is, anyone who can't afford this is classified as poor). In rural India, the average daily consumption is just Rs 10 which goes up marginally to Rs 14 for urban India. So this dollar-a-day business just does not make sense.[7] In response, the bank clarified that it used the same approach to calculate poverty everywhere and across all time periods and, therefore, the estimates were consistent. More explanations were given in terms of change in the distribution of income below the poverty line and fluctuations in the purchasing power of the poor. For example, suppose the *number of people near the poverty line increases* so that a lot less people now live in abject poverty than they used to. Now, suppose there are periods of *high inflation* when income levels start fluctuating far more frequently than they used to. Then, the time when you measure consumption or income (and hence poverty) becomes crucial. If it happens to be a period when price levels are stable, poverty levels tend to be lower and vice versa. During the period under consideration there have been at least three bouts of high inflation. For instance, in the July 1998–January 1999 period, the consumer price index for the agricultural landless – who accounted for nearly 60 per cent of India's poor – shot up to 15 per cent. These price hikes have had an immediate and direct impact on the income and consumption of the poor.[8] Underlining the importance of the change in income-distribution below poverty line, Sen (2001) argued that there were a lot more people closer to the poverty line in the period under consideration; the majority of the poor were becoming less poor. As a result, the poverty estimates might have improved due to a decline in the 'depth of poverty.' This thesis found support in a latter study conducted by Tendulkar (2002). He calculated the number of the so-called 'ultra-poor' by using a more lenient definition for poverty. In essence, Tendulkar defined minimum consumption as what an individual could buy for Rs 15 in rural areas and Rs 18 in urban India (at 1960-61 prices) while the official cutoff mark was at Rs 49 and Rs 56 (at 1973-74 prices). The new poverty number that he got using this definition was divided by the official poverty figure. The result was a crude measure of the proportion of the ultra poor among the poor. Tendulkar was able to show that over a period of three years this ratio had come down. The advantage of this controversial debate was that the attention of researchers and policy makers shifted towards income-distribution and, therefore, the future debates had to proceed beyond the 'head-count' approach. The focus of the studies instead shifted to measuring other yardsticks such as the change in the distribution of poverty below the poverty line – and to ensuring that the crossover is not temporary.

The key issue today is not whether poverty levels have declined but the changing nature of the distribution of poor people below the line.

Rural Poverty – An Important Parameter of SDP

Several important studies on poverty, such as Deaton and Dreze (2002), Sundaram and Tendulkar (2003), Kozel et al. (2003), etc., tend to lead to a broad consensus that poverty (both urban and rural) has declined in India during the 1990s, even though the decline might not have been as marked as the official estimates by the National Sample Survey Organisation (NSSO) seem to suggest. According to the data of 56th round (2000-01) of NSSO, the all-India average monthly per capita consumer expenditure (MPCE) in urban areas was Rs 914 of which Rs 400 went for food (44 per cent). The MPCE in rural areas was Rs 495 of which Rs 279 was spent on food (56 per cent). The corresponding figures in the 43rd round (1987-88) were 56 per cent and 64 per cent respectively. In addition, the yearly rise in MPCE in rural areas (Rs 9 or 2 per cent) has been much lower while compared with the urban areas (Rs 60 or 7 per cent). Thus using the yardstick of MPCE, the data of 56th round shows a declining trend in poverty (around 10 per cent) when compared with the figures of the 43rd round (1987-88).

What is remarkable, however, is the fact that a comparison of the urban and rural estimates of poverty confirms that *poverty in the rural areas is more severely entrenched.* This evidence provides us a simple, but powerful, explanation of why the rural poor flock to urban India even if the living conditions in the cities are very bad.

The Importance of Non-farm Activities in the Neglected Rural Sector

Recognizing the neglect of the rural and agricultural sector in development planning, Pant (2003) has emphasised its importance in the following words:

> The role of the (rural and) agriculture sector in generating demand for industrial goods, through a wider dispersal of purchasing power, has been seriously underestimated in the past. It is now clear that unless the incomes of the majority of our people who are engaged in (rural and) agriculture grow rapidly, acceleration in the growth of industry and most services will simply not be possible. Therefore, unless our agricultural sector grows sufficiently fast, we face the specter of growing unemployment and of even greater underemployment of our work force. This would place an intolerable burden on the fabric of our society and may eventually thwart all our developmental efforts.

The above statement rightly brings out the importance and the neglect of the rural and agriculture sector in Indian economy, but the issues of output growth and employment growth of this sector has been clearly mixed up. It is well known that in the case of the agriculture sector these two variables (output growth and employment growth) are negatively related. It implies that even if a second Green Revolution is in the offing, the rural folk have to be absorbed in the non-farm activities and this takes us to the importance of the non-farm employment for the purpose of tackling poverty in the rural and agriculture sector.

Lanjouw and Shariff (2002) have analysed the significance of the non-farm sector in the rural Indian economy in terms of access and its impact on income and poverty. Analysis shows that *non-farm incomes account for a significant proportion of household income* in rural India with considerable variations across quintiles defined in terms of per capita income and across major Indian states. *The access to non-farm occupations has been found to be depending on education, wealth, caste, village level agricultural conditions, population densities and other regional effects.* As the poor lack the access, direct contribution of the non-farm sector to poverty reduction was found quite muted.

The policy implication of this study is that in order to maximise the impact of an expanding non-farm sector on rural poverty we need to improve the education level in rural areas. It can be pointed out that access to non-farm occupations can be further improved through the parameters of health and drinking water.

V

Efficacy of Rural Welfare Programmes and Rural Employment Schemes

At this juncture, it is important to take note of the *efficacy of the various welfare programmes and employment schemes* for the rural areas introduced and implemented by the union and the state governments. The net result of these schemes and programs has been quite discouraging.

Doubts have been raised about the long-term efficacy of these programmes by asking three supplementary questions: Is the money being spent wisely? Is poverty coming down as a result? If not, is there a better way of doing things? The first two questions pertain to the question of finding the levels of absolute poverty and determining the temporal changes in its various components e.g. how many poor are really there in India and has their number come down? They, in turn, revolve around the validity of data and the methodology used for. We have seen that there are a large number of hot debates and pitched battles related to these two questions in the literature on poverty. The time has surely come for a moratorium on technical quibbles over data and estimates because these debates contribute virtually nothing to policy.

The truth is that whether the number of those below the poverty line is 12 per cent – as recently claimed by Surjit Bhalla, or 30 per cent as often claimed by the Left, the absolute numbers are still staggering – 120 million or 300 million. It is necessary, therefore, to give an exclusive attention to the third question: namely, is there a better way for the delivery of the 'poverty alleviation programmes' and other public services?

It is possible that these programmes and schemes are helpful in the short run to fight the case of abject poverty and malnutrition (hunger-deaths), but there is strong possibility of these programmes being introduced purely due to political motives. Once governments realise that they could lose votes it they were not seen doing 'something' for voters who were poor, they had to come with an answer to the question. In response, a large number of welfare schemes could be initiated under poverty alleviation programmes. Thereafter, the governments and the political parties can capitalise on these programmes for their political ends and, in this way, their misuse is almost destined. At the same time, the taxpayers – whose money went into the funding of these programmes, may feel less guilty of being richer than the poor.

Thus it must be remembered that such welfare programmes and employment schemes are at best the immediate and short-term solutions of the problem. In the medium and long term, emphasis has to be on education, health including drinking water, infrastructure and other instruments of human development.

We conclude by saying that enhanced public investment in physical and social infrastructure of the rural areas is the key to a successful long-term SDP in India. The focus has to be on productivity improvments in on-farm activities and, at the same time, strengthening the possibilities of income and employment generation in the non-farm and off-farm activities of the rural areas. How these resources will be mobilised and how the various programmes for the alleviation of income and human poverty will be organised and implemented remain the million dollar questions?

REFERENCES

Aiyar, Swaminathan S.A., 2003, "How Hungry Are Indians?" Sunday Times of India, 1, June 2003.

Bhalla, Surjit, 2003, 'Imagine There's No Country: Poverty Inequality and Growth in the Era of Globalisation,' Penguin, New Delhi.

Chadha, G.K., 2001, 'WTO and Employment for Rural Households: Challenges from Within and Without,' paper presented at National Seminar on ECONOMIC REFORMS AND EMPLOYMENT IN INDIAN ECONOMY organized by IAMR New Delhi during 22-23, March 2001.

Deaton, A. and J. Dreze, 2002, 'Poverty and Inequality in India: A Re-examination,' *Economic and Political Weekly*, 7, September 2002.

Dubey, A. and S. Gangopadhyay, 1998, *Counting the Poor: Where are the Poor in India,* Sarvekshana Analytical Report no. 1, Department of Statistics, Government of India.

Government of India, 'The Tenth Five-Year Plan' (2002 – 2007), Government of India.

Goldar, B. and Sakthivel S., 2003, 'Employment and Poverty in Rural India: A Study of the NSS regions in the 1990s,' paper presented at the National Seminar on 'Poverty and Food Security – Problems and Policies' held at Jamia Millia Islamia New Delhi during 18-19, February 2003.

Gumber, Anil, 2002, 'Determinants of Unemployment in Rural India", NCAER Working Paper Series No. 89.

Hardoy, J., Mitlin, D. and Sattherthwaite, D., 1992, 'Environmental Problems in Third WOrld Cities,' Earthscan, London.

Kozel, V., D. Khatkhate, B. Parker, and M. Raghunath, 2003, 'Poverty Measurement, Monitoring and Evaluation in India,' *Economic and Political Weekly*, January 25-31, 2003.

Lanjouw, Peter and Shariff, Abusaleh, 2002, 'Rural Non-Farm Employment in India: Access, Income and Poverty Impact,' NCAER Working Paper Series No. 81.

Leach, M. and Mearns, R., 1991, 'Poverty and Environment in Developing Countries: An Overview Study', IDS: Brighton.

Minhas, B.S., L.R. Jain, S.M. Kansal, and M.R. Saluja, 1988, "Measurement of General Cost of Living for Urban India, All-India and Different States", *Sarvekshna*, vol. 12, pp 1-23.

NSSO, 2003, Government of India, The NSS report No. 466.

Pant K.C., 2003, 'India's Development Scenario - Next Decade and Beyond' Vol. I and II. Academic Foundation, New Delhi.

Ramachandran, Nira, 2002, *Monitoring Sustainability – Indices and*

Techniques of Analysis, Concept Publishing Company, New Delhi.

Rao, M. Govinda, 2002, (Eds.), *'Development, Poverty and Fiscal Policy - Decentralization of Institutions,'* Oxford University Press, New Delhi.

Raskin, R., Chadwick, M., Jackson, T. and Leach, G., 1996, *The Sustainability Transition: Beyond Conventional Development,* Stockholm Environment Institute, Stockholm.

Redclift, M. and Skea, J., 1997, 'Environmental Security', *Insights* 21, IDS: Brighton.

Sudarshan, R. and Chelliah, Raja J. (Eds.), 2002, *'Income-Poverty and Beyond - Human Development in India,'* Anthem Press, London.

Sundaram, K., 2001, 'Employment-Unemployment Situation in the Nineties: Some Results from NSS 55th Round Survey,' *Economic and Political Weekly,* 17, March 2001.

Sundaram, K. and S.D. Tendulkar, 2003, 'Poverty Has Declined in the 1990s: A Resolution of Comparability Problems in NSS Consumer Expenditure Data,' *Economic and Political Weekly,* 25-31, January 2003.

Swedish International Development Cooperation Agency (SIDA), 1995, *Promoting Sustainable Livelihoods: A Report from the Task Force on Poverty,* SIDA, Stockholm.

UNEP, 1995, *Poverty and the Environment: Reconciling Short-term Needs with Long-term Sustainability Goals,* UNEP, Nairobi.

Visaria, P., 1996, 'Structure of the Indian Workforce, 1961-94,' Indian Journal of Labour Economics, 39(4):725-39.

Visaria, P., 2002, 'Workforce and Employment in India, 1961-94,' in Minhas, B.S. (Ed.), *National Income Accounts and Data Systems,* Oxford University Press, Delhi.

World Commission on Environment and Development (WCED), 1987, OUR COMMON FUTURE, Oxford University Press, Oxford.

ENDNOTE

1. See, for example, Bhalla S. (2003).
2. SD AS A MISNOMER: Distinguishing the process of development from that of growth as explained above, it follows that development, if achieved, should always be sustainable. The term SD is, therefore, a misnomer. In other words, we should have been talking about 'sustainable growth' rather than 'sustainable development'. But this is perhaps besides

the point under discussion.

3. For a detailed discussion of the various dimensions and some operational definitions of 'environmental sustainability', see Ramachandaran N. (2002)
4. Absolute poverty can be measured by computing the head-count ratios based on an agreed definition of 'poverty-line'. Similarly, a simple measure of relative poverty can be the deviations of individual incomes from the average of the group of persons under consideration. In other words, poverty in relative terms is nothing but income-inequality. As a relative phenomenon, it may have different meanings to different groups of people at different points of time specially when the context changes from global to local or regional.
5. With contributions from eminent economists such as Suresh Tendulkar, Abusaleh Shariff and others, most of the subject experts have advocated for the 'human- approach' to poverty by focusing on various human aspects of the problem. The broad conclusion of this study is that measures to reduce income-poverty, including high rates of economic growth are not sufficient and that more public action is needed to counter the high prevalence of human poverty.
6. The horror stories of the starvation deaths have been the subject of intense public debate in Indian media. For example, an NGO 'Right to Food Campaign' organized a public hearing in 2002 on 'Living with Hunger' in the presence of Nobel Laureate Amartya Sen. Several persons from hunger-affected parts of the country gathered to share their stories of battling chronic starvation. Ram Ayodhya (a fictitious name) explained how he failed in getting a loan to buy food for his starving children because he neither had an asset nor a job as the security. Prof. Sen described the pervasive presence of persistent hunger as an extremely serious problem. He added that poverty in India was characterized by chronic undernourishment and its levels were more than any other country in the world. (Times of India, Sept. 15, 2002)
7. The World Bank used one-dollar-a-day definition of poverty while the Govt. of India defined the poverty line in terms of what an individual needs to spend to consume 2,400 calories daily in rural areas and 2,100 calories in urban India.

8 See, for example, Shariff (2002) and Sen (2001).

Chapter 4

Agricultural Trade Liberalisation and Food Security – Theoretical debates and Empirical Issues

S. Krishnakumar

Introduction

The importance of agriculture in the process of economic growth is well-documented in economic literature. With the concerns on growth and development gaining currency in the fifties, the development economics literature was prolific with dual models that counted on economic development with unlimited supplies of labour (Lewis, 1954). These models unfortunately had discounted the importance of agricultural surplus (which they in fact took for granted under the presumption that the marginal product in the agricultural sector was negative to begin with) for the process to be triggered, that the development experience of the less developed countries invariably drew attention in due course to the agrarian constraint to economic development. The same has also been subjected to theoretical exploration later on (Sen, 1981). In fact, the structuralist macroeconomic tradition have given due focus to the central themes like the intersectoral terms of trade between agriculture and industry and the prime role of food price inflation in the process of economic growth. The *differentia specific* of macroeconomic literature, as it has evolved in the less developed world, particularly in Latin

America and India, comes from the primacy of space it has given to agriculture *per se* in its analytical scheme.

If concerns on agricultural surplus and the terms of trade between industry and agriculture, the influence that the state wields towards the determination of the same were of importance till the eighties, ever since the focus has shifted towards the larger question of agricultural trade liberalisation. In fact, much of the liberalisation of this sector at the global level has to be seen in the wider context of the agenda of neoliberal reform. It is a noteworthy fact that there has been worldwide protests against the opening up of the agricultural sector. In less developed countries , characterised by the large scale presence of small peasants and labour force dependent on agriculture, it has also become a question of sustainable rural livelihoods.

It would be useful to locate the current debates on agricultural trade liberalisation to the Corn Law controversy which rocked Continental Europe in the early part of the nineteenth century. It was argued that the cheapening of wage goods that would result with the repeal of the Corn Laws would be important from the point of view of industrialisation in Britain. Further studies on British industrial growth has revealed that the much needed surpluses to facilitate industrialisation in Britain was not forthcoming from within the colonies and their cheap sources of raw materials and wage-foods proved to be useful to serve this purpose. But it would indeed be fallacious to argue that the same would hold true for all the countries at the same time for this would bring in a *fallacy of composition*. This could very well be one of the most important reasons that had gone into autonomous national agricultural policies focusing on agricultural self-sufficiency not only in the less developed world, once they were out of the yoke of colonialism, but also in the developed OECD countries which could very well have relied on the international markets, had the latter been able to assure certain availability from these sources. In fact the entire literature favouring agricultural trade liberalisation has as its locus a critique of the state-led industrialisation strategies that were pursued through various modes of resource mobilisation, of which one was the relative shift in the terms of trade against the agricultural sector. The reliance on agriculture as a source of resource mobilisation has been scorned at and the efforts towards industrialisation has been criticised under the garb of the static theories of comparative advantage. The overvalued exchange rates, the high rates of tariff intended towards protecting the fledgling industries – all these have been portrayed by these static theorists as deliberate efforts to discriminate against agriculture. This is precisely why they are caught unawares of the historical context of the emergence of the *dirigiste* state to which India was no exception. The rural-urban dichotomy through which Lipton and others try to attribute the poverty in the developing world to the policies of urban-bias, themselves are caught unawares of the wider context in which the nation state in itself is located in the global economy.

This paper is divided into three sections. The first section tries to brief the arguments made in favour of agricultural trade liberalisation, which is located in the wider context of trade and macroeconomic policy reforms. It is a known fact that dominant theorists of this strand are of neoclassical persuasion, who eulogise on the virtues of the *invisible hand* that would get the prices right. A critique of this neoclassical theorisation is attempted in second section. This is done not only from the perspective of agricultural trade *per se* but also from the larger context of agriculture in development theory. The third section tries to present some empirical findings. This includes tests relating to price instability in the world grain markets, the relative terms of trade of various commodities vis-à-vis the price of wheat and rice that are the dominant cereals and an analysis of the food balance sheets of the economies of South Asia.

I

Analysis of Agricultural Trade Liberalisation

Though in the early sixties, the critics of the exchange rate and trade policy regimes from the static theorists were looking at the empirical instances of industry alone, ever since research has been focused on the impact of such policies on the agricultural sector also. It has been argued that in the developed world, the agricultural sector has been largely protected and in the developing world, the same has been subjected to large amounts of extraction and 'disprotection'. Various neoclassical studies in this regard have as their focus different aspects of the trade, fiscal and macroeconomic regime. In fact much of the rationale that tries to undermine the autonomous nature of national agricultural policies comes from this sort of neoclassical theorising that tries to blind itself of the role of agriculture in development theory. In fact, the static comparative advantage which these countries have in the production of certain agricultural commodities was not a matter of which they were unaware of, but it was only that they were making deliberate efforts to negate the classical international division of labour. Let us try to have an overview of the arguments in favour of agricultural trade liberalisation before we try to develop a critique of the same.

It is by invoking the 2×2×2 model of Stolper-Samuelson that the argument is placed. The rationale is too simplistic: countries that are labour abundant would take to the track of the labour-intensive agricultural production and the others would resort to capital-intensive production, read industry. This would result in a distribution of income in favour of labour. This distribution of income would have a favourable impact on the rural livelihoods of the labour-abundant country, thus runs the argument. It is such simplistic arguments based on theorems that have assumptions in the form of constant returns to scale and the same level of technology that is used to further the case of agricultural trade liberalisation in less developed countries like India.

Over the years in the developing world, the share of agriculture in the total output has declined. This, though could be construed as a natural process in the course of economic growth (had much to do with the import-substitution industrialisation policies that were pursued at the behest of the *dirigiste* state, through high tariffs and quantitative import restrictions). Efforts were even undertaken to make available foreign exchange at favourable rates in order to facilitate the import of capital goods. In the seventies the developing countries used to even heavily subsidise the exports of various industrial commodities. It is argued by Bautista and Valdes (1993) that the producers of agricultural exports were never recipients of export subsidies and at times there were taxes slapped on them as a source of revenue mobilisation by the government.[1] The urban bias in the development policies of the developing countries, it is argued by Lipton, were focused on keeping the food prices down, and were discriminatory against the rural areas. This, he argues, is why the wages in the developing world remains low and the industry there is able to attract labour from agriculture at reduced cost. The subsidies advanced to the agriculturists provide no relief to them, for every input of any significance to them are heavily protected by the governments, in the name of industrialisation. This is essentially his urban bias thesis on the conditions of poverty in the developing world. (Lipton, 1982).

The direct price effects with regard to agriculture have also differed within agriculture. According to the findings of a World Bank study, the most important agricultural exports have been taxed more heavily than the food products – primarily due to the desire for food self-sufficiency and the administrative ease of taxing the commercial crops rather than the subsistence food crops. (Krueger, Schiff and Valdes, 1988) Apart from the direct effects, is the whole sort of indirect effect on the agricultural sector, in the form of the tariff induced increase in the relative price of the importable vis-à-vis the home produced goods. In Argentina, Peru, Colombia, Nigeria, Philippines and Zaire, the heavy protection of industrial products has placed significant indirect tax on agricultural import-competing goods and export production (Valdes, 1986). This price bias against agriculture, which comes from the indirect price effects of trade and macroeconomic policies on agricultural production incentives in the developing world, cannot be eliminated according to Bautista and Valdes, simply by adjusting the nominal exchange rate. It can be corrected only at source through the reduction in the import barriers that are used to protect domestic industry. It is in fact, this rationale provided by such trade theorising that has been used to further trade liberalisation, all in the name of agriculture, which in the post-liberalisation scenario has had its own hiccups too.

In continental economies like India which is home to many poor, the question of trade liberalisation has been viewed with scepticism, particularly so for the price of foodgrains in the international market was higher than that in the domestic market. The domestic *kulaks* who have been successful in increasing their share of the government expenditure in the form of subsidies were then expected to consolidate their post-Green Revolution gains in the form of their demand for compensation at par with international prices. Various empirical studies have found the poverty ratio to be positively correlated with the foodgrain prices or a measure of overall price index like the CPIAL, where foodgrains receive a higher weight. (Mellor and Desai, 1985). Ravallion and Dutt (1995) have also proved that the poor would invariably be hurt with price increases through the decreases in the level of real wages. But, it is argued by Kotwal and Ramaswami (1999), that the above arguments do not realise the fact that the majority of the poor live in the rural areas, and the supply responses which would be forthcoming in the wake of price signals would substantially improve their employment opportunities and this would definitely have a positive impact on their level of welfare. But it is a fact realised long back that the landless labour and the marginal and lower middle peasants are net buyers of foodgrains. Any increase in prices would definitely have a negative impact on their. This too by undermining the skewed investment in agriculture since the eighties, which has resulted in the surpluses being concentrated in a few states. In fact, trade liberalisation in developing countries has been perceived as a method of bringing the domestic prices in parlance with international prices. This argument which further counts on the high price elasticity of supply of different agricultural crops, nonetheless, does not stand the test of empirical scrutiny in our country. Even studies that have been supportive have found extremely low value for short-run elasticities as against the long-run elasticities of supply.[2] It has been argued that increased provision of necessary inputs would result in better output elasticity than the price signals from the market. In fact, the neoclassical logic of *getting prices right* would not be able to perform the magic which it is expected through the working of the invisible hand, in case there is shortage of rural infrastructure. Kotwal and Ramaswami (1999), therefore, make an argument that trade liberalisation along with increased expenditure on rural infrastructure is likely to be welfare improving. But the logical possibility of fiscal expansion being pursed under the regime on the process of liberalisation is pretty obvious.

Though the debate regarding terms of trade had figured in a prominent way in the Indian political economy in the seventies, the effective pressure groups which the farmers were able to cobble up, the minimum support prices system that had evolved over a period of time had in fact enhanced the share of the farming community in the budgetary transfers, though this is nothing compared to their developed country counterparts. Calculations made by Pursell and Gulati (1993) give the ESC (effective subsidy coefficient) to be between 0.97 and 1.07 depending on the methodology of calculation.[3] So this so-called anti-agricultural bias was not there even before the initiation of economic reform in our country.

It is often argued by the protagonists of this position that the two most important variables that explain differences in the level of agricultural protection in the developing world are one, the share of agriculture in the total income and two, the per capita income (Anderson, 1986). As the developing country grows richer and the share of agriculture decreases, so too the level of agricultural taxation becomes less necessary. Moreover, it is argued that in the political market for protection, the urban interests articulated by the industrialists and the workers get to be more heard than that of the agriculture. This sort of neoclassical political economy argument is further even used to argue for the better protection of agriculture in the higher income developing countries, where the farmers are more organised. All these genre of theorists that articulate in the neoclassical political economy tradition has cleverly gleaned out the art of pursuing political economy without classes, which in the phrase of Byres is like an oriental cat without an oriental eye. It is in this wake that the theoretical literature to the contrary presumes significance.

II

Analysis of Agricultural Trade Liberalisation – A Critique

Fundamentally erroneous nature of the various theoretical arguments that are furthered towards making a case of agricultural trade liberalisation comes from the fact that they all belong to the neoclassical persuasion, this at best can serve the purpose of addressing issues relating to static resource allocational efficiency without any intertemporal considerations. Not only are the dichotomous categories of rural and urban problematic, but the conclusions which one jumps into from the assumptions of the static trade theories while juxtaposed to the real world of international trade would only be revealing.

In fact the stream of theorising on the basis of which the suggestions for reform are being articulated in itself is based on the neoclassical schema, which according to Bharadwaj (1987), could at best serve as a tool for resource allocation under conditions of static efficiency, presuming the full employment of the factors of production. The neoclassical economic theorising which was in the upswing following the marginalist revolution saw the issues concerning growth, production and distribution being side-lined. The classical political economy not only underlined the role of food as a wage-good, but also the pertinence of agricultural surplus in serving as the foundation of accumulation in developing economies. It should be noted that the development economics literature, which emerged in the context of the planning process in the erstwhile Soviet Union and the less developed countries in the fifties and sixties , also stood to gain from the resuscitation of the fundamentals of classical political economy towards understanding the process of development.

Agriculture-industry relationships, which figured in classical political economy, have re-emerged in the new context of the renewed interest in issues related to the pace of accumulation and industrialisation. Ever since the days of classical political economy, the terms of trade between agriculture and industry was a matter of controversy. The controversy triggered by the repeal of Corn Laws[4] in the early part of the 19th century was one of the most fruitful of its kind in the history of political economy. The analytical linkages between agriculture and industry in the dynamic setting of growth can be appreciated better using the concepts of surplus, accumulation, terms of trade and the various other categories generated by the tradition of classical political economy, than under the setting of static equilibrium analysis, which tries to hide more than it reveals {see Bharadwaj (1987),[5] Byres (1996)[6] in this regard}. Right from the times of Smith, the stage was set for a political economy, whose analytic reflect the dynamics of the process of capitalist development from a predominantly agrarian, feudal economy breaking out of its shell of capitalism.

The political economy framework adapted itself to incorporate the varying institutional conditions within which the process of the generation, appropriation, distribution and utilisation of surplus is done, as against the neoclassical paradigm focusing on the relative price guided allocation of scarce resources amidst domestic agents in competitive markets. Smith clearly perceived the central facilitating role of agricultural surplus for the process of accumulation. Agricultural surplus was, therefore, considered by Smith to be the necessary condition for industrial expansion. Ricardo favoured the attempt to repeal the Corn Laws in England, under the pretext that it would reduce the level of rents in England at that time, hurting the interests of the landlords, and moreover it would result in the cheapening of the wage goods, which alone would be able to improve the pace of accumulation in the economy. Ricardo underlined the pertinence of the price of corn in determining the pace of accumulation. The fineness of classical political economy was that it had a set of well-defined categories, which underscored the underlying classes, and their correspondent revenues, and made proper distinction between the different forms of consumption, i.e. wage goods, landlord's consumption and capitalist consumption. In contrast to the historical and accumulation centred perspective that informed the agriculture-industry relationships in political economy, the neoclassical economics analysed the economy in terms of the decisions of the individual agents, given endowments and pursuit of objectives, with symmetry being postulated across factors of production. The peculiarity of land as a non-reproducible asset, and hence scarce, (as in the classical tradition), is extended to all factors of production and the notion of the diminishing returns to scale is drawn in.

In fact, the insights provided by classical political economy presume to be important from the perspective of development in continental economies like India. If the colonies were an important source of agricultural surplus, unless the domestic agrarian question is addressed, the same would provide no scope for the generation of surpluses that would be required to trigger the pace of industrialisation. In fact the current process of export orientation of agriculture has only intensified the process of the classical international division of labour. It draws out attention to the Marxist contention that export surpluses could also very well lead to the process of de-industrialisation in the less developed world.[7] Much of the developed countries. are net agricultural importers as against the developing Asian and African countries. This reveals to us the fact that much of the inflationary pressures which would have otherwise erupted in the developed OECD countries even during the time of the Golden Age of Capitalism could not have been contained, but for the agricultural import led price stabilisation that was made possible by the reorganisation of agriculture in the global economy. It is the decrease in the price of the raw materials and wage-goods imported from the developing world that permitted the miracle of the share of wages in the economy remaining intact and that of the profit also remaining stable.[8] From the latter quarter of the nineteenth century secular deterioration in the net barter terms of trade started gaining attention. It should be noted that the period also witnessed the transition of capitalism in the metropolis from competitive nature to monopoly nature, the latter of which was bent on cornering the benefits of productivity improvements to itself, rather than transferring the same to the consumers in the form of lower prices.

Therefore, too, it was not that the less developed countries were unaware of the their inherent comparative (or rather geographic) advantage in the production of primary commodities, like how the neoclassicals would like us to believe. But they were more bothered of the secular deterioration in the net barter terms of trade of their commodities and the onset of immiserising growth in the context of increases in production, for which the developing world took a tryst with the dirigiste state to negate the classical international division of labour. The agricultural policies of countries were dovetailed with the dual objectives of shielding the population against the decline in the per capita availability of foodgrains and meeting the prerequisites of agricultural surpluses that are required to trigger the pace and momentum of industrialisation. Role of agricultural surplus in the determination of the total output of an economy has been part of the debate ever since the days of classical political economy. If the low agricultural rates of growth in the economy are going to be a fetter on the overall rate of growth, could it not be appropriate indeed to go in for higher levels of public investment in this regard. Studies undertaken specifically about the agricultural sector have proved indubitably the crowding in effect, which results from of public investment in the related sectors. Kalecki (1972) was of the view that the extant production relationships, which in the absence of land reform, would result, through the disincentives operating through the system of institutions of tenancy and usury, to set a ceiling on the rate of growth of agricultural goods. Once the economy hits this, the agricultural constraint becomes dynamically binding, unless a further reduction in the real wages in the sector is not possible. Apart from this exogenous ceiling rate imposed on the agricultural rate of growth, due to the extant production relationships, the growing capital-output ratio, thanks to the energy intensity of cultivation on the post-Green Revolution scenario, erects new hurdles in the path of the rate of growth of agriculture, even at the existing rates of investment. Not only would high rates of investment be needed to sustain this rate of growth in agriculture, but also even higher levels of investment would be required to sustain the same. But, in the context of the global reorganisation of agriculture, production in the less developed countries, as of now, is directed towards the meeting of the demands of the trans-national accumulation on a world scale. Given the declining levels of public investment, attempts from the part of the policy regime of the LDCs towards exploiting to the maximum the potential of export-oriented agriculture, could turn out to be plausible, only under conditions of further decline in the level of per capita food availability in the domestic front, which could trigger a food price inflation, (see Cardoso, (1981); Taylor, (1982). Consequences would have to be borne by those at the lower rungs of the society. In a recent empirical investigation, Patnaik (2003) has established an inverse relationship between primary exports and per capita availability of foodgrains under conditions of decreasing public investment.[9]

Most of the literature in trade liberalisation so carried away with the equalisation of domestic prices with the international prices, that it has even ignored the fact that these conclusions are drawn under the small country assumptions. Continental economies like India and China, in fact are large producers and also large consumers with regard to various agricultural commodities that the price of these commodities in itself could be affected by the decision of these countries. Nayyar and Sen (1994) argue that it would be in the interests of the domestic economy to retain a wedge between the domestic and the international prices. Invoking the optimum tariff argument, it is argued that it would be in the interests of the country to retain some restrictions on exports or imports either to improve or to prevent the deterioration of the terms of trade which would have otherwise occurred. Though cheap food is an indirect subsidy to the industrial sector, it is argued that the same is desirable from the perspective of a labour surplus economy that is foreign exchange constrained.

While the whole argument of the liberalisers have been towards the equalisation of national prices with international prices, Patnaik (1996a) contests even the ratioanale behind the same. The argument that the panacea for the ills of Indian agriculture lies in linking it with the world prices is untenable on equity, efficiency and growth terms. Though the gross compensation which accrues to the average US farmer is twice as that of the Indian farmer, the ratio of the gross surplus value to the gross value added in the case of the US farmer is only 25 per cent, whereas that of the Indian farmer comes to around two-third. This, nonetheless, would reveal that much of the benefit of the linking with the international prices would accrue to the rich farmer in the countryside, as against the net buyers of foodgrains. While the difference between the domestic wages and international wages is even worse, it is not fair on equity terms to argue for international prices. The distributive implications which an increase in the level of food prices would generate in the economy, would, on the one hand, result in a decrease in the level of effective demand, thus bringing down the level of industrial output. On the other hand, agricultural output being price inelastic in the short run, would not be generating increases in the level of agricultural output. Hence, on the grounds of efficiency also, the linking with the international prices is not in the interests of the economy. Taxing the industrial sector, which benefits from the protectionist barriers and using the same revenues for investment in public infrastructure, which would definitely be having crowding-in effects in private investment in agriculture, is recommended as far better a strategy of resource mobilisation, than linking the Indian agricultural sector to the prices prevailing in the world market.

III

Some Empirical Findings

Though the recent round of trade negotiations have witnessed significant reduction in the tariffs across countries over various commodities, the farm subsidy commitments are observed more in violation, both by the EU and the United States. But simultaneously we are witnesses to the rise to ascendancy of the non-tariff barriers which could be new obstacles in the path of trade for the developing world. Coming as it is in the form of international labour and environmental standards and sanitary and phyto-sanitary measures, the same would spell problems for developing country trade.

But certain crucial concerns relating to food security remains important. The food balance sheet of China (1992 – 94) reveals that around 10 per cent of the domestic requirement of wheat is met through imports from abroad. Such large country purchases in a liberalised trade environment would further worsen the price instability in the foodgrain markets. An investigation done into the correlation between the rice, wheat and maize cereals proved to be positive and significant. This can be explained on the basis of the rationale that food patterns are evolved habits that allows only for limited substitutability during price increases of one of them. (Table 4.1)

TABLE 4.1
Correlation* between Prices of Maize, Wheat and Rice
Correlations [(112(Rice US), 135(wheat), 103(maize)]

		VAR00112	*VAR00135*	*VAR00103*
VAR00112	Pearson Correlation	1	0.743	0.674
	Sig. (2-tailed)	–	0	0
	N	30	30	30
VAR00135	Pearson Correlation	0.743	1	0.849
	Sig. (2-tailed)	0	–	0
	N	30	30	30
VAR00103	Pearson Correlation	0.674	0.849	1
	Sig. (2-tailed)	0	0	—
	N	30	30	30

*Correlation is significant at the 0.01 level (2-tailed).

Rationale of liberalisation comes from the ability of the market to deliver to the producer of the commodity, another good in exchange according to his choice. But the volatile and unstable nature of the grain markets is a matter of due concern. Predictability of the market is virtually impossible. Foodgrain markets are more of a destabilising nature. Through the data provided in International Financial Statistics from 1961 to 2000, instability index of the main cereals, i.e, maize, wheat and rice were calculated, using an appropriate equation. The index of instability is as follows:

Maize	0.213743
Rice (NO)	0.157962
Rice (Thai)	0.254326
Wheat (US Gulf)	0.244491

The secular deterioration in the net barter terms of trade of primary commodities is a much investigated issue. In this exercise, we tried to check as to how the prices of various commodities move against the price of wheat and price of rice. Here again, but for a few commodities, most of them showed high level of instability, and erratic fluctuations vis-à-

TABLE 4.2

	Vis-à-vis price of rice	*vis-à-vis price of wheat*
Banana	Stable	stable
Cocoabeans	Erratic	erratic
Coconut oil	Constant	marginally errratic
Coffee	Erratic	erratic
Copra	Errratic	erratic
Cotton	Consistent	consistent
Groundnut	Wildly erratic	wildly erratic
Jute	Erratic	erratic
Pepper	Wildly erratic	wildly erratic
Rubber	Errtic	erratic
Sugar	Stable	stable
Tea	Erratic	erratic

vis both the price of rice and wheat. Table 4.3 and chart. The data in this regard were drawn from International Financial Statistics.

Concluding Remarks

This essay has tried to locate the analytics of agricultural trade liberalisation. It has located the critique of the same in the specific context of food security. Challenges from agricultural trade liberalisation are manifold. But given the high level of instability in the market for foodgrains and the highly volatile terms of trade of different commodities vis-à-vis the food grains like rice and wheat, the developing countries ought to be cautious. Given the continental nature of economies like India and China, it is all the more important that they strategically deploy their big producer/consumer role lest the instability in the world grain markets might even worsen further.

NOTES

1. For various country studies, see this edited work.
2. See McGirk and Mundlak's(1991) study on Punjab agriculture in the period 1960-79.
3. The effective subsidy coefficient implies value added at domestic prices plus subsidies on non-traded inputs divided by value added at world prices.
4. While the anti-Corn League had argued that the price of corn is high because the rent is high , Ricardo, who was in favour of the Repeal Of Corn Laws, had argued, on the contrary that 'not that the price of corn is high for the rent is high, but the rent is high, for the price of corn is high.' The struggle against the Corn Laws could be considered to be one of the first movements against the category of rent, which was acting as a fetter on the forces of production and accumulation.
5. In this article, the author elaborates on the usefulness of the categories of economic analysis developed during the period, prior to the marginalist revolution, towards the understanding of the concepts of growth and accumulation.
6. Appreciating the Smith-Ricardo-Marx tradition and the insights it offers, Byres considers this tool of political economy

far more advanced, than the whole host of current-day neoclassical theorising.

7. For the details of this argument, see Patnaik(1996)
8. For this argument relating to the stability of metropolitan capitalism, see Patnaik (1997).
9. In this article, she makes an argument against the version in the official documents that the decrease in the per capita cereal consumption is due to the operation of the Engel's law.

BIBLIOGRAPHY

Anderson, Kym, 1986, 'Economic growth,structural Change and Political Economy of Protection,' in Anderson and Hyami 9thed.), The political economy of agricultural protection.

Bautista and Valdes, 1993, 'The Bias against Agriculture: Trade and Macroeconomic Policies in Developing Countries.' IFPRI

Bharadwaj, K., 1987, 'Analytics of Agriculture-Industry Relation,' *Economic and Political Weekly*, Vol.22, Nos. 19-21, pp. AN/15-AN/20.

Kotwal, Ashok and Ramaswami, Bharat, 1999, Economic Reforms in Agriculture and Rural Growth, in Sachs, Varshey and Bajpai(Eds.), *India in the Era of Economic Reforms.*

Krueger, Schiff and Valdes, 1988, 'Agricultural Incentives in developing countries: Measuring the effect of sectoral and economy- wide policies.' World Bank Economic Review 2(3):255-71.

Lewis, W.A., 1954, "Economic Development with Unlimited Supplies of Labour," *Manchester School of Economics and Social Studies*, Vol.22, pp. 139-191.

Lipton, M., 1982, Why Poor People Stay Poor; Oxford University Press.

McGuirk, A and Y. Mundlak, 1991, 'Incentives and Constraints in the Transformation of Punjab Agriculture', Research Report 87, IFPRI, Washington DC.

Mellor and Desai, 1985, Agricultural Change and Rural Poverty Variations on a Theme by Dharm Narain, John Hopkins University Press.

Nayyar, Deepak and Sen, Abhijit, 1994, 'International Trade and the Agricultural Sector in India,' in Bhalla, G.S.(Eds.), Economic Liberalization and Indian Agriculture, New Delhi: Institute for Studies in Industrial Development. Also published in *Economic and Political Weekly*, Vol. 29, No. 20, pp. 1187-1203.

Patnaik, Prabhat, 1996, 'Trade as a Mechanism of Economic Retrogression,' Journal of Peasant Studies, 24 (1 and 2) October/January, pp. 211-25.

Patnaik, Prabhat, 1996a, 'Should Domestic Prices Be Equated to World Prices?,' Economic and Political Weekly, September, Special Number, 31(35, 36 and 37): pp. 2425-8.

Patnaik, Prabhat, 1997, *Accumulation and Stability Under Capitalism,* Oxford: Clarendon Press.

Patnaik, Utsa, 2003, 'On the Inverse Relation Between Primary Exports and Food Absorption in Developing Countries under Liberalised Trade Regimes,' in Ghosh and Chandrashekahr (Eds.), *Work and well-being in the Age of Finance.*

Pursell, G. and Gulati, A., 1993, 'Liberalising Indian Agriculture : An Agenda for Reform': World Bank.

Ravallion, M and G Dutt, 1995, 'Growth, Wages and Poverty: Time Series evidence for Rural India,' mimeo, World Bank.

Sen, A., 1981, The Agrarian Constraint to Economic Development: The case of India, Ph.D. Thesis, unpublished, University of Cambridge.

Yotopoulos, P., 1985, "Middle-Income Classes and Food Crises: The New Food-Feed Competition" Development & Change, Vol. 33, No.2, pp. 463-83.

Chapter 5

Employment and Poverty in Rural India
A Study of the NSS regions in the 1990s

B. Goldar and S. Sakthivel

Introduction

There is a broad consensus now that poverty declined in India during the 1990s, though the decline need not necessarily be marked as the official estimates seem to suggest (see Deaton and Dreze, 2002; Kozel et al., 2003; and Sundaram and Tendulkar, 2003). There was a decline in poverty in both urban and rural areas (see, for example, Deaton and Dreze, 2002). In rural areas, headcount poverty ratio (the proportion of poor among the population) at the all-India level declined by 7 to 11 percentage points between 1993-94 and 1999-2000, (see, for example, Deaton and Dreze, 2002; Deaton, 2003; and Sundaram and Tendulkar, 2003). What is remarkable to note is that the rural poverty ratio declined in 1990s in almost all the states[1] (see Table 5.1).

In this paper, we analyse changes in poverty incidence and growth in employment in rural India in the 1990s at the level of NSS (National Sample Survey) regions. The object is to find out whether observed decline in poverty ratio at the state-level (Table 5.1) holds true also at a greater level of disaggregation. Another object is to ascertain whether the inter-regional variations in the rate of decline of poverty incidence in the 1990s was correlated with employment growth, which would be helpful in making an assessment of the contribution of employment growth to reduction in poverty.

TABLE 5.1
State-Specific Rural Headcount Ratios (Per cent)

	Estimates based on Official Methodology			*Adjusted Estimates of Deaton and Dreze*		
States	*1987-88*	*1993-94*	*1999-2000*	*1987-88*	*1993-94*	*1999-2000*
Andhra Pradesh	21.0	15.9	10.5	35.0	29.2	26.2
Assam	39.4	45.2	40.3	36.1	35.4	35.5
Bihar	53.9	58.0	44.0	54.6	48.6	41.1
Gujarat	28.6	22.2	12.4	39.4	32.5	20.0
Haryana	15.4	28.3	7.4	13.6	17.0	5.7
Himachal Pradesh	16.7	30.4	7.5	13.3	17.1	9.8
Jammu And Kashmir	25.9	30.4	4.7	15.3	10.1	6.1
Karnataka	32.6	30.1	16.8	40.8	37.9	30.7
Kerala	29.5	25.4	9.4	23.8	19.5	10.0
Madhya Pradesh	42.0	40.7	37.2	43.7	36.6	31.3
Maharashtra	41.0	37.9	23.2	44.3	42.9	31.9
Orissa	58.7	49.8	47.8	50.4	43.5	43.0
Punjab	12.8	11.7	6.0	6.6	6.2	2.4
Rajasthan	33.3	26.4	13.5	35.3	23.0	17.3
Tamil Nadu	46.3	35.9	20.0	49.0	38.5	24.3
Uttar Pradesh	41.9	42.3	31.1	34.9	28.6	21.5
West Bengal	48.8	41.2	31.7	36.3	25.1	21.9
All India	39.4	37.1	26.8	39.0	33.0	26.3

Source: Deaton and Dreze 2002). Calculations based on NSS unit record data from 43rd, 50th and 55th Rounds

Almost all available studies on poverty incidence in India are at the all-India level or at state level. An earlier study on the poverty incidence at the NSS region level was by Dubey and Gangopadhyay (1998). They estimated and analyzed poverty incidence in 1987-88 and 1993-94. They did not cover later years of the 1990s. The present study extends the analysis of Dubey and Gangopadhyay to a more recent year, 1999-00. Needless to say that an analysis of poverty incidence at the

NSS regional level, as done here, will be more revealing than a state-level analysis.[2]

The paper also examines employment growth in rural India between 1993-94 and 1999-2000 at the NSS region level. To our knowledge, there is no study in which employment growth in India has been examined at NSS region level. This is, therefore, another aspect on which little information exists, and the present paper hopes to make a contribution.

The next section describes the method applied to obtain comparable estimates of headcount poverty ratio for the rural areas of NSS regions for 1987-88, 1993-94 and 1999-2000. An analysis of trends in rural poverty ratio at the level of NSS regions during the period 1987-88 to 1999-00 is presented in preceding section. This is followed by an analysis of rural employment growth in NSS regions during the period 1993-94 to 1999-2000. Correlation between rural employment growth and decline in rural poverty in the period 1993-94 to 1999-00 is examined in the following section. Main findings of the study are summarized in the concluding section 6.

Estimation of Headcount Poverty Ratios for NSS Regions

For 1987-88 and 1993-94, we take the headcount poverty ratios for rural areas from Dubey and Gangopadhyay (1998) and then make some adjustments as discussed here. Dubey and Gangopadhyay have made several sets of estimates of headcount ratio corresponding to different ways of arriving at the poverty line. We use for this analysis the estimates they call 'APL' which makes use of poverty line based on the alternative norm (rather than the official norm) and updated using disaggregated price adjustment suggested by Minhas et al. (1988).

For 1999 we have worked out headcount poverty ratios for 59 NSS regions from unit record data from the 55th Round.[3] We have used data on consumption expenditure contained in the employment-unemployment survey rather than the data in the NSS consumption survey. In this regard, we follow Sundaram (2001a). Poverty lines for this purpose have been taken from Deaton (2003a). The poverty line for a state obtained from Deaton's study has been applied to all the regions belonging to the state (the same method was applied by Dubey and Gangopadhyay, 1998).

Since methodology (particularly derivation of poverty line) followed by Dubey and Gangopadhyay (1998) for estimates for 1987-88 and 1993-94 and that followed by us for estimates for 1999-2000 are not same, two sets of estimates may not be exactly comparable. To overcome possible problems of comparability, the following procedure has been employed.

We take the state level estimates of Deaton and Dreze shown in Table 5.1 as the correct and inter-temporally comparable estimates of headcount poverty ratio at the state level for the three years, 1987-88, 1993-94 and 1999-2000. We compare state level estimates of Dubey and Gangopadhyay with estimates of Deaton and Dreze, and compute for each state ratio of Deaton-Dreze estimate to the Dubey-Gangopadhyay estimate. Then, for each state ratio is applied to the Dubey-Gangopadhyay headcount poverty ratio estimates at the level of NSS regions, for the regions belonging to the state. This proportionately adjusts the Dubey-Gangopadhyay estimates for NSS regions in a state to bring them in line with state level estimates of Deaton and Dreze.

Same method has been followed for the estimates for 1999-2000. State-level estimates of headcount ratio are compared with the Deaton-Dreze estimates ratios between the two sets of estimates are computed and then these are applied to the estimates at NSS region level. With this adjustment, we believe, our estimates become comparable to the Dubey-Gangopadhyay estimates.

Trends in Rural Headcount Poverty Ratio, 1987 – 2000

The estimates indicate that mean headcount poverty ratio (for rural areas) across 59 regions fell from 38.19 per cent in 1987-88 to 32.99 per cent in 1993-94 and further to 26.33 per cent in 1999-00 (Table 5.2). Median fell from 35.63 per cent in 1987-88 to 33.61 per cent in 1993-94 and further to 25.37 per cent in 1999-2000. There is clear indication of a general fall in headcount poverty ratio in rural areas. Also, it appears that the fall was faster during 1993-2000 than during 1987-88.

TABLE 5.2

Basic Statistics of Poverty Ratios, Rural Areas

(per cent)

	1987-88	*1993-94*	*1999-2000*
Mean	38.19	32.99	26.33
Standard Deviation.	16.02	15.47	13.77
Coefficient of Variation (ratio)	0.42	0.47	0.52
Median	35.63	33.61	25.37
Ist Quartile	29.12	19.10	17.41
IIIrd Quartile	50.61	44.20	35.63
Maximum	76.09	78.18	69.68
Minimum	5.53	3.74	2.16

Even though there has been an appreciable fall in the average headcount poverty ratio inter-regional disparity does not seem to have come down. Coefficient of variation shows an increase rather than a fall. There is no clearly identifiable decrease in the gap between the first and the third quartile (Table 5.2, Graph 5.1).

Frequency distribution of the headcount poverty ratio among the 59 regions (rural) presented in Table 5.3 reveals wide inter-regional dispersion in the incidence of poverty. In 1987-88, the poverty ratio was less than 10 per cent in 4 regions,

TABLE 5.3

Distribution of Regions According to Poverty Ratio

Percentage	*No. of Regions*		
Poverty Ratio	*1987-88*	*1993-94*	*1999-2000*
0 – 10	4	2	8
10 – 20	4	14	12
20 – 30	10	10	16
30 – 40	15	17	13
40 – 50	11	7	8
50 – 60	10	7	1
60 – 70	4	1	1
70 – 80	1	1	
Total	59	59	59

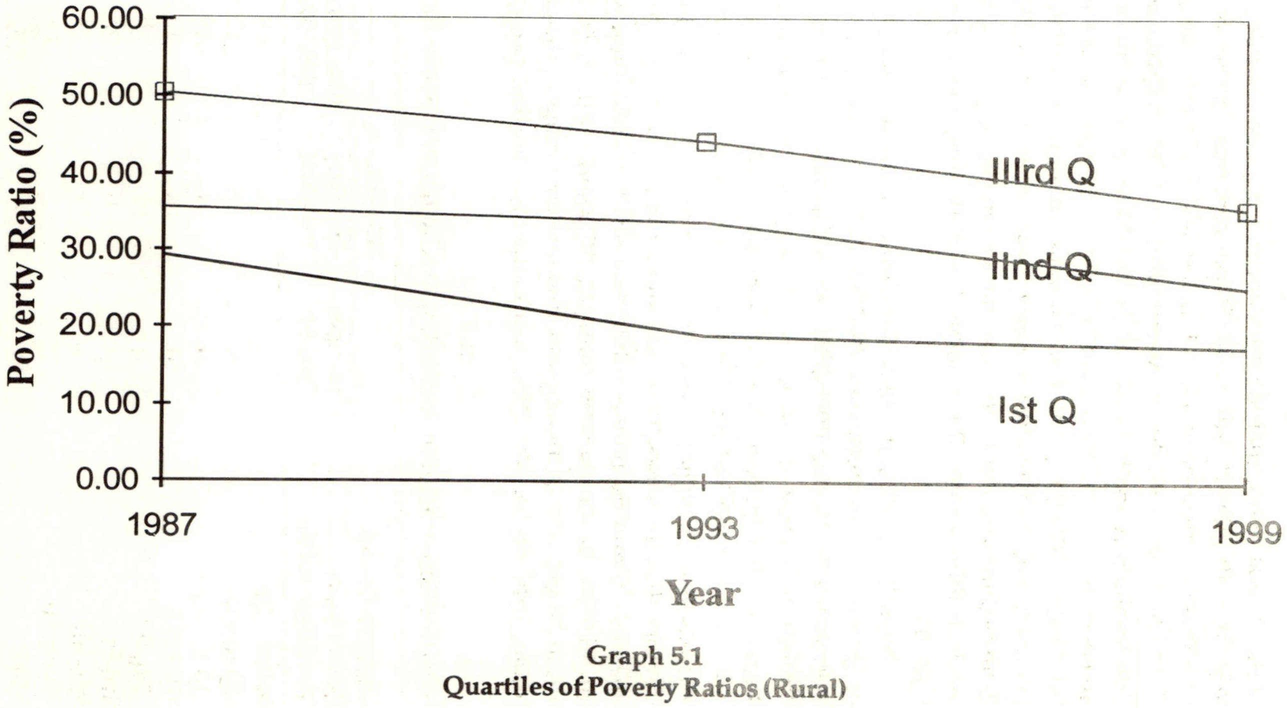

Graph 5.1
Quartiles of Poverty Ratios (Rural)

while it was more than 60 per cent in 5 regions. Number of regions with poverty ratio over 50 per cent was 15 (out of 59) in 1987-88, which declined to 9 in 1993-94 and further to 2 in 1999-2000. In 1987-88, poverty ratio in NSS regions was predominantly in the range of 20 to 60 per cent. In the vast majority of the regions (over 80 per cent of the regions), poverty ratio was in this range. In 1993-94, relevant range was 10 to 50 per cent, and in 1999-2000 it was 0 to 40 per cent. Thus, there is indication of a fall in the average incidence of poverty, but no indication of any appreciable fall in the dispersion across regions.

State-level estimates show an almost across-the-board fall in poverty ratio between 1987-88 and 1993-94, and also between 1993-94 and 1999-2000 (see for instance estimates of Deaton and Dreze in Table 5.1). But regional level estimates bring out that poverty has not declined in all regions (Table 5.4). Between 1987-88 and 1993-94, poverty ratio in rural areas increased in 21 regions out of 59, i.e. about 36 per cent of the regions. In some cases, there was more than 5 percentage point increase. Similarly, between 1993-94 and 1999-2000, there was an increase in the poverty ratios in 12 regions out of 59, i.e. about 20 per cent of the regions. Even when a longer period is taken, 1987-88 to 1999-2000, estimates indicate that poverty

TABLE 5.4

Distribution of Regions according to Change in Poverty Ratio

Change in Poverty Poverty Ratio (percentage point)	*No. of Regions*		
	1987-88 to 1993-94	*1993-94 to 1999-2000*	*1999-2000 to 1999-2000*
Below –20	3	3	6
–20 to –15	5	7	14
–15 to –10	9	9	16
–10 to –5	13	16	9
–5 to 0	8	12	7
0 to 5	14	8	5
5 to 10	5	2	1
Above 10	2	2	1
Total	59	59	59

ratio increased in 6 out of 59 regions, i.e. about 10 per cent of the regions and there was only a small decrease in 7 other regions. Evidently, decline in poverty in rural areas is not across-the- board as one may surmise by looking at state level estimates. In some regions, poverty has not declined and in some others decline has been quite low.

Employment Growth in the 1990s

Relevance and consistency of NSS data on employment-unemployment over decennial census has been well documented by now (see, for instance, Visaria, 1996). For present analysis, we harness here the unit level record data for latest two quinquennial rounds of NSS relating to the period 1993-94 and 1999-2000. Primarily, our focus is on growth of rural employment. Out of the 78 NSS regions, we carry out our investigation based on 74 NSS regions, the rest four being considered as 'disturbed areas' – two regions of Jammu and Kashmir, one each covering Nagaland and Tripura. For our analysis, we have considered both usual principal activity status and usual subsidiary status categories (UPSS) – by gender and sector (primary, secondary and tertiary) distribution of workforce.

It is interesting to note that growth of employment (rural) has been moderate across all categories and appears to have declined relative to its earlier round. Table 5.5 reveals that rural total employment has recorded a growth of 1.77 percent per annum in the 1990s (between 1993-94 and 1999-2000) as against 1.91 per cent achieved for the period 1987-88 to 1993-94[4]. Female employment, had registered a growth of 1.55 per cent while male employment grew at 1.90 per cent. Although employment growth was quite substantial measured in usual principal status alone (with over two per cent registered across the gender categories). Yet subsidiary activities in rural areas during the period from mid-1990s to end 1990s have recorded negative growth, which appears to have brought down the overall employment growth in the rural areas [measured in Usual Principal and Subsidiary Status(UPSS)].

Table 5.5
Sectoral Growth of Rural Employment in the 1990s (% p.a.)
(1993-94 and 1999-2000)

(UPSS)

Sector	Male	Female	Total
Primary	1.11	1.44	1.24
Secondary	5.11	2.55	4.39
Tertiary	3.22	1.74	2.98
Total	1.90	1.55	1.77

Performance of primary sector employment in rural areas has been lacklustre in the 1990s. While secondary and tertiary sectors witnessed the maximum growth of 4.39 per cent and 2.98 per cent respectively, primary sector on the other hand, posted only 1.24 per cent growth during this period (see Graph 5.2). Rural female employment registered a growth of 1.44 per cent, which is a little over that achieved by male employment (1.11 per cent) in the primary sector. Since female workforce constitutes a major portion of rural employment involving agricultural and allied activities, growth of female employment is likely to help achieve reduction in poverty levels. Growth of male workers has been quite significant in the secondary sector followed by tertiary sector employment.

Having looked at the overall employment growth, we now turn our attention to the regional spread of growth in employment in the 1990s. Certain interesting insights emerge from Table 5.6. It appears that overall employment growth has been fairly distributed. Secondly, the maximum number of NSS regions (19 to be specific) seem to have recorded a growth rate of 3 per cent and above while another 8 regions had posited a growth of 2 to 3 per cent during the 1990s. There are 15 regions which appeared to have experienced a fall in employment. Similar trend is discernible in case of male employment in rural areas. However, the disturbing story lies in the growth of female employment. Out of 74 regions female employment growth has been positive in 50 regions. In fact, the maximum number of 21 regions had registered a growth

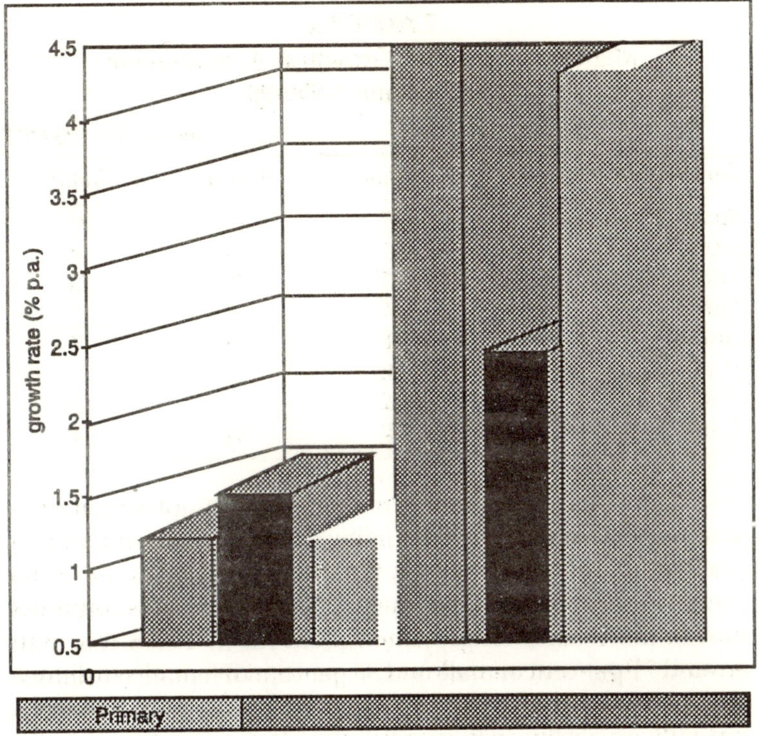

exceeding 3 per cent in the 1990s. But, 24 NSS regions had fallen into the negative territory with a maximum of 15 regions recording less than (–) 3 (negative growth of three per cent) growth of female employment. Therefore, it appears that although the spread of growth in male employment in NSS regions during 1994–2000 is widespread in positive territory, female employment, however, shows signs of distress in many regions of India. This is particularly worrisome in view of the fact that female employment in rural India is a stronger component in total employment of the country.

TABLE 5.6
Regional Spread of Growth in Employment
(1993-94 and 1999-00)

(no. of NSS regions)

Growth Rate (% p.a.)	*Male*	*Female*	*Total*
Above 3	15	21	19
2 to 3	21	4	8
1 to 2	17	12	20
0 to 1	7	13	12
–1 to 0	8	6	7
–2 to –1	4	3	3
–3 & Above	2	15	5
Total	74	74	74

We next turn to examine the changing sectoral distribution of employment in the 1990s. Table 5.7 and the accompanying chart amply demonstrate continuation of earlier trend in the composition of rural employment. Primary activities continued to dominate rural employment scenario in 1990s too with around 71 per cent of male and 86 per cent of female workforce engaged in primary sector. It must be noted that there is virtually no decline in the contribution towards primary sector between the two successive NSS rounds in the 1990s, particularly in the case of female employment. While tertiary sector appears to employ little more than the secondary sector involving male workforce, secondary sector is ahead of the latter in the case of female employment.

TABLE 5.7
Sectoral Distribution of Employment

	Male Employment		*Female Employment*		*Total Employment*	
Sector	*1993-94*	*1999-00*	*1993-94*	*1999-00*	*1993-94*	*1999-00*
Primary	74.76	71.32	86.61	86.05	79.01	76.53
Secondary	10.42	12.64	7.91	8.40	9.52	11.14
Tertiary	14.82	16.04	5.48	5.54	11.47	12.33
Total	100.00	100.00	100.00	100.00	100.00	100.00

It may be pointed out that our results are at variance with Sundaram (2001, 2001a). For instance, Sundaram's estimate shows that employment in rural area between 1993-94 and 1999-2000 has virtually stagnated particularly in the category of female employment and has in fact declined in *growth terms. But our analysis here suggests that all categories of employment in rural areas (male, female and total) witnessed moderate growth for the period under consideration. This inconsistency could arise due to the fact that while Sundaram's estimate is grounded on interpolation areas based on census population figures, ours is from unit level records of NSS rounds.*

Links between employment and poverty

Having discussed trends in employment and poverty in rural India in the 1990s, it would be useful to explore next the links between employment and poverty. In regions where employment opportunities are inadequate, a rapid growth of employment opportunities should lead to reduction in poverty.

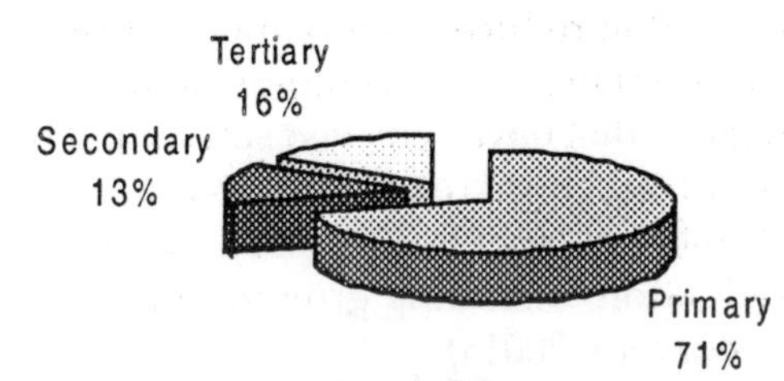

Graph 5.3
Sectoral distribution of rural male employment, 1999-2000

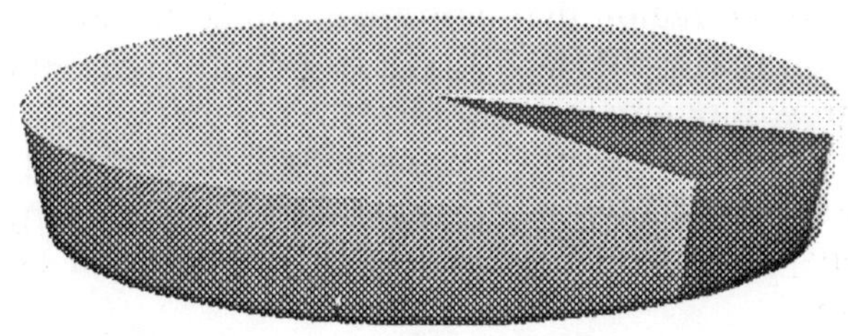

Graph 5.4
Sectoral distribution of rural female employment, 1999-2000

Changes in the industrial structure of employment are also expected to have an effect. If a rapid expansion takes place in employment opportunities in non-farm activities, this may augment the income of the rural people and help them shift from low productivity to relatively higher productivity activities. On this ground, one may hypothesize a negative relationship between changes in the share of secondary and tertiary sector employment in a rural region and changes in poverty incidence in that region.

Analysis of data, however, does not reveal any significant relationship between growth rate of employment and reduction in poverty. Rank correlation coefficient between the change in headcount poverty ratio and growth rate of employment across regions in the period 1993-94 to 1999-2000 is found to be – 0.027. The same secondary 0.01 and tertiary sectors is found to be 0.01 and 0.09 respectively. These two correlation coefficients do not have the expected sign, and are in any case statistically insignificant. A closer examination of the data reveals that some regions have failed to reduce poverty much during 1993–2000 even with significant increases in employment, while there are some other regions that have achieved substantial reduction in poverty without much increase in employment. There are obviously a number of other factors that may have contributed to poverty reduction, including growth of productivity and wages (see Sundaram, 2001a).

Table 5.8 above presents for each state a comparison of employment growth in the region that performed best in terms of poverty reduction (during 1993–2000) with employment growth in the region that performed worst. In seven states, the region that performed better in poverty reduction had faster growth of employment than the region that performed worst. In five states the opposite is true. Evidently, the comparison presented in the table does not show any clear relationship between employment growth and poverty reduction.

A more clear relationship that is visible from the data relates to non-farm employment. Correlation coefficient between poverty ratio and the share of employment in secondary sector is – 0.23 for 1993-94 and – 0.37 for 1999-2000. Correlation coefficient between poverty ratio and the share of employment in the tertiary sector is –0.38 for 1993-94 and –0.29 for 1999-00. All these are statistically significant. Evidently, a change in the structure of employment from primary to secondary and tertiary sectors is associated with a reduction in poverty.

Regressing poverty ratio on the share of secondary and tertiary sector (combined), we obtain the following equations (t-ratios in parentheses):

For 1993-94

$$P_i^{93} = \underset{(9.4)}{45.86} - \underset{(-2.87)}{0.61}\, SHARE(i)_{S+T}^{93} \quad R^2 = 0.13 \quad n=59$$

TABLE 5.8
Employment growth and Poverty Reduction:
State-wise comparison of regions

State	*Region that performed best in poverty reduction*	*Region that performed worst in poverty reduction*
	Employment growth (% p.a.)	*Employment growth (% p.a.)*
Andhra Pradesh	0.94	–1.03
Assam	1.27	0.48
Bihar	3.68	4.67
Gujarat	3.32	2.50
Haryana	1.24	-0.16
Karnataka	0.70	2.74
Kerala	1.62	4.39
Maharashtra	2.27	1.92
Madhya Pradesh	2.92	1.43
Orissa	–0.15	0.24
Punjab	5.63	–0.38
Rajasthan	0.71	0.80
Tamil Nadu	–1.00	1.96
Uttar Pradesh	--0.08	2.44
West Bengal	–0.18	5.25

For 1999-00

$$P_i^{99} = 39.43 - 0.55\ \text{SHARE (i)}_{S+T}^{99}\quad R^2 = 0.14\ n{=}59$$
$$(8.91)\ (-3.19)$$

In these equations, P_i^{93} and P_i^{99} are headcount poverty ratio in the i'th region in 1993-94 and 1999-00 respectively, and $SHARE(i)^{93}_{S+T}$ and $SHARE(i)^{99}_{S+T}$ are the share of secondary and tertiary sectors in employment in the i'th region in these two years, respectively. Results suggest that one percentage point increase in the share of the secondary and tertiary sector (combined) in employment reduces poverty ratio by about 0.55 percentage point. The estimates of employment presented in Table 5.7 above suggest that between 1993-94 and 1999-2000 there was about 2.5 percentage point increase in the shares of the secondary and tertiary sectors in rural employment. This may have contributed to about 1.5 percentage point lowering of poverty ratio. Overall decline in the poverty ratio between 1993-94 and 1999-2000 was by about 5-6 percentage points. Clearly, the increase in the share of secondary and tertiary sector in employment in rural areas can account for a part of the observed decline in poverty incidence.

Conclusion

There has been a general reduction in rural poverty in India in the 1990s. However, inter-regional dispersion in poverty has not come down, and in a significant proportion of regions there has been either an increase or only a marginal decline in poverty.

A moderate growth has taken place in rural employment in the primary sector, with somewhat better performance in secondary and tertiary sectors. Estimates on rural employment suggest that growth of male employment has been fairly distributed across all regions while growth of female employment does not follow this trend. In a majority of regions, rural employment has grown. Overall rate of growth has been 1.77 per cent per annum. But female employment, witnessed mixed results wherein 50 out of 74 regions displayed positive growth while the rest had slipped into the negative growth territory. On an average there has been a moderate growth of women employment in rural areas.

An analysis of association between employment growth and poverty reduction suggest that there is no significant relationship. It appears that even with a significant growth in employment, some regions have failed to make any dent on poverty. And, on the other hand, without any significant growth in employment in some regions, poverty reduction has been possible.

A significant negative relationship is found between poverty ratio and the share of secondary and tertiary sector in rural employment. Based on the estimates, it seems that there was about 2.5 percentage point increase in the share of secondary and tertiary sectors in rural employment and this has made a part contribution to the reduction in rural poverty in India in the 1990s.

NOTES

1. The same is true of urban poverty.
2. There have been two recent studies on the poverty incidence at District level: the study of Kozel and Parker (2003) for Uttar Pradesh and Murgal, Suryanarayana and Zaidi (2003) for Karnataka. These have looked at the poverty incidence at a level of disaggregation beyond the NSS regions.
3. We have made estimates for regions belonging to the states listed in Table 1, but have left out Jammu and Kashmir.
4. The growth rate for the period involving the earlier two NSS rounds, viz., 1983-88 and 1988-94 is compared here from Visaria (2002).

REFERENCES

Deaton, A., 2003, 'Adjusted Indian Poverty Estimates for 1999-2000,' *Economic and Political Weekly*, 25-31, January 2003.

Deaton, A., 2003a, 'Prices and Poverty in India, 1987-2000,' *Economic and Political Weekly*, 25-31, January 2003.

Deaton, A. and J. Dreze, 2002, 'Poverty and Inequality in India: A Re-examination", *Economic and Political Weekly*, 7, September 2002.

Dubey, A. and S. Gangopadhyay, 1998, *Counting the Poor: Where are the Poor in India*, Sarvekshana Analytical Report no. 1, Department of Statistics, Government of India.

Kozel, V., D. Khatkhate, B. Parker, and M. Raghunath, 2003, 'Poverty Measurement, Monitoring and Evaluation in India,' *Economic and Political Weekly*, January 25-31, 2003.

Kozel, V. and B. Parker, 2003, A Profile and Diagnostic of Poverty in Uttar Pradesh", *Economic and Political Weekly*, 25-31, January 2003.

Minhas, B.S., L.R. Jain, S.M. Kansal, and M.R. Saluja, 1988, 'Measurement of General Cost of Living for Urban India, All-India and Different States,' *Sarvekshna*, 12:1-23.

Murgal, R., M.H. Suryanarayana, and S. Zaidi, 2003, 'Measuring Poverty in Karnataka: The Regional Dimension,' *Economic and Political Weekly*, 25-31, January 2003.

Sundaram, K., 2001, 'Employment-Unemployment Situation in the Nineties: Some Results from NSS 55th Round Survey,' *Economic and Political Weekly*, 17, March 2001.

Sundaram, K., 2001a, 'Employment and Poverty in 1990s: Further Results from NSS 55th Round Employment-Unemployment Survey, 1990-2000,' *Economic and Political Weekly*, 11, August 2001.

Sundaram, K. and S.D. Tendulkar, 2003, 'Poverty *Has* Declined in the 1990s: A Resolution of Comparability Problems in NSS Consumer Expenditure Data,' *Economic and Political Weekly*, 25-31, January 2003.

Visaria, P., 1996, 'Structure of the Indian Workforce, 1961-94,' *Indian Journal of Labour Economics*, 39(4), pp. 725-39.

Visaria, P., 2002, 'Workforce and Employment in India, 1961-94,' in B.S. Minhas (edited), *National Income Accounts and Data Systems*, Delhi: Oxford University Press.

Chapter 6

Food Security through Improving Rural Female Employment – Need to Develop Gender Specific Strategies and Institutions

Shahid Ashraf & Tauqeer Alam Farooqui

Introduction

Poverty breeds powerlessness, the inability to control one's own life. The poorest of the world tend to be women. The poorer a woman the less chances she has to protect herself and survive a decent life. Issues of women employment, food security and equality point to the multiple burden that women have to bear poverty and food security are inter-linked and the road map towards decreasing poverty and improving food security, specifically of the rural women is through their access to employment. The focus of the present paper is to understand and analyse female rural employment and its importance towards a more gender equal world. The inference is that for the vast majority of rural female the most viable strategy is the sustained self-employment for their individual and household food security. The paper suggests that developing gender specific institutions for increasing rural female employment is an important and viable strategy towards food security. The emphasis of the paper is, therefore, on exploring the issues of rural female employment.

Poor women have the least access to basic needs such as food, health and education, both within the family and outside. Their work remains primarily invisible permitting little social recognition. In fact, the only sectors of the economy in which women remain a dominant section of the labour force are those which demand low skills and repetitive functions and generate low returns. As such poor women function mainly in the informal sectors (Wingnaraja, 1990). Alongside exploitation and invisibility in the economic sphere, women face social oppression which demonstrates the hazardous and insecure nature of their lives. Further in India, women workers are not a homogeneous group.

Female Employment

Ability to earn and control income is one of the most powerful determinants of women's status in the family. World Bank Discussion Papers (1990 and 1991) point that, 'female employment was more significant than present wealth or parent's educational status in explaining variations in sex-specific survival rates. Significantly, a rise in male employment exacerbated the difference between boy's and girl's survival in favour of boys.' Further, whether on- or off-farm female employment was a more important determinant of the dietary intakes of children than income or landholding size.

According to 2001 Census, 58.4 per cent of the total workers in the country are engaged either as cultivators or agricultural labourers. A sizeable number is engaged in agriculture-related industries and are thus employed indirectly by the agriculture sector itself. Dependence on agriculture is much higher for some states. For example, in Bihar 77.35 per cent of the total workers are engaged directly in agriculture (see Table 6.1).

Employment as agricultural cultivators and labourers differ from state to state. Bihar and Orissa have a higher percentage of female workers as compared to the well-off states of Punjab and Haryana.

Chatterjee (1990) quotes studies concerning overall time allocation and household work. On an average, women

Table 6.1
Workers employed in Agriculture State-wise (in %)

States	*Cultivators*			*Agricultural Labourers*		
	Total Popu-lation	*Total Males*	*Total Females*	*Total Popu-lation*	*Total Males*	*Total Females*
Andhra Pradesh	22.6	24.3	29.6	39.64	19.9	56.2
Bihar	29.1	31.6	42.7	48.1	22.4	63.2
Gujarat	27.5	27.4	17.3	24.4	27.8	39.7
Haryana	36.3	32.7	12.4	15.2	44.1	21.1
Karnataka	29.4	32.1	17.0	26.4	24.5	43.8
Madhya Pradesh	42.93	42.8	21.5	28.6	43.1	40.7
Maharashtra	28.56	25.1	18.3	26.85	34.6	42.1
Punjab	22.96	25.9	15.9	16.4	13.1	17.8
Rajasthan	55.3	48.1	7.1	10.6	67.1	16.4
Tamil Nadu	18.3	18.2	23.6	31.1	18.7	45.4
Uttar Pradesh	40.9	42.9	20.1	25.1	34.3	41.2
West Bengal	19.1	20.7	22.5	24.9	13.4	32.4
Orissa	29.6	34.3	26.2	35.1	19.4	54.3
Kerala	7.1	16.1	8.1	14.1	4.7	21.9

Source: Population Census 2001, Government of India (GOI).

contributed 70 per cent of total household labour time, though only 31 per cent of total income (both cash and kind) were earned by them. Thus incapacitation of women due to illness, particularly recurring and debilitating illness, may well be far more significant in terms of household functioning than illness of men, particularly among the poor. Obviously, with the death of woman the situation becomes acute, leading to the potential dissolution, or total dysfunction of the household as a unit.

According to Visaria (1996), from 1950 onwards to the late nineties, data indicate that in the rural sector women constituted about 34–36 per cent of the workforce. Labour market favours men over women and the division of labour within the occupations is highly sex-biased. Work done by women within a given occupation is considered inferior and subordinate, and accordingly woman's overall earning from the job done is less than man. Not only that for the same job within the occupation, women are paid less than men.

Gender-based wage discrimination continues even for identical tasks performed by men and women such as weeding or even a typical female labour-intensive tasks such as transplantation. Though both male and female agricultural wages are often inadequate from the point of view of minimum needs, a lower average rate of remuneration, combined with a shorter period of employment over the year is likely to push a typical woman agricultural labourer way below the poverty line. Choudhry (1993) points that, animal husbandry has gained a new importance in view of the intense commercialisation of milk. In dairy keeping women perform intensive labour and supervisory work. Men whose work are marginal compared to that of women, are the key controlling authorities in the crucial sphere of marketing and collection of income as well as sale and purchase of livestock.

Kothari (1997) points that financial security does not necessarily mean women have greater control over their lives though it potentially allows greater participation in decision-making within the household. Furthermore women's powerlessness in gaining access to employment independently is highlighted when a daily agricultural labourer loses his job or no longer wants to work, usually, his wife must also leave her employment with the same household.

According to Choudhry (1993), women are spending more time today in doing both agricultural and domestic work specially with the coming of the green (agriculture) and white (dairy) revolutions. Their economic participation is undisputed yet what seems to be crucial is not the work done by women but its evaluation and adequate remuneration. An increase in their work load makes no difference to the way their economic contributions and work is valued. Paradoxically the family females also perceive only male work as income generating.

Rural Female Work Participation Rate

According to Jain (1996) difficulty in appropriately netting female labour is because of the nature/style of women's work. Women whether in Rajasthan, a high Female Work Participation

Rate (FWPR), state or West Bengal, a low FWPR state report at least three if not six hours per day in domestic work. In Rajasthan women engage more in outside home activities (even though there is strict, age-sex segmentation of tasks) whereas in West Bengal they engage in much more home-based work. Though these women were actively engaged in what are identified as productive activities, the system is not able to capture this because the activity is lost in the female domain of kitchen. In Rajasthan, however, rural women since they are on farms like men, appear in the labour force. Thus the more male-like the activities of females the more likely they will be measured and noticed.

According to Chadda and Saha (2002), rural labor force participation rate has declined from 44.9 per cent in 1993-94 to 42.3 per cent in 1999-2000. Both in rural and urban areas, workforce participation rate (workers in relation to labour force) is much lower for females compared with males in respect of all 15+ age groups.

TABLE 6.2
Work Participation Rate (WPR)
(principal + subsidiary status)

Year	*Rural Male(RM)*	*Rural Female(RF)*	*Rural Person (RP)*
1987-88	53.9	32.3	43.4
1993-94	55.3	32.8	44.4
1999-2000	53.1	29.9	41.7

Source: NSS, 1983/2000, GOI.

Table 6.3
Work Participation Rate

	WPR current weekly status			*WPR current daily status*		
	RM	*RF*	*RP*	*RM*	*RF*	*RP*
1983	51.1	22.7	37.2	48.2	19.8	34.2
87-88	50.3	22.0	36.4	50.1	20.7	35.8
93-94	53.1	26.7	40.3	50.4	21.9	36.6
99-2000	51.0	25.3	38.4	47.8	20.4	34.4

Source: NSS, 1983/2000,GOI

Economic reforms of the 1990 seems to have ushered in relatively harder times for female workers. Female WPR under the usual (principal + subsidiary) status of 29.9 per cent goes down to 25.3 per cent for weekly status and 20.4 per cent under the daily status in 1999-2000. This signals the greater degree of casualness in employment of rural female workers.

TABLE 6.4

Rural Female (Principal+subsidiary) Mode of Employment

	Self-employed	*Regular employees*	*Casual labour*
1983	61.90	2.80	35.30
1987-88	60.80	3.70	35.50
1993-94	58.60	2.70	38.70
1999-2000	57.30	3.10	39.60

Source: NSS Data 1983/1999-00, GOI.

Employment on a casual basis has increased at the cost of self-employed. The declining incidence of self employment may be throwing some people out of self-cultivation only to swell the ranks of the landless agricultural labourers.

TABLE 6.5

Annual compound growth rate of employment for Rural Female usual status (Principal + subsidiary)

	1983 to 1993-94	*1993-94 to 1999-2002*
Agriculture	1.24	–0.02
Field crop production	1.71	–0.08
Plantation	1.57	–0.15
Livestock	–2.00	–0.68
Total Manufacturing	2.21	1.75
Agro-based manufacturing	2.19	1.81
Non-Agriculture	2.58	1.21
All Sections	1.41	0.15

Source: Chadda and Sahu (2002).

TABLE 6.6
Employment Elasticity and Output Growth

	Output Growth (Percentage)			*Employment Elasticity (relative to GDP)*	
	1993-2000	*10th Plan**	*1983 to 93*	*1993to 2000*	*10th Plan**
Agriculture	3.1	4.2	0.70	0.01	0.23
Manufacturing	7.8	10.0	3.8	0.33	0.50
All sectors	6.7	8.0	0.52	0.16	0.34

* Projected
Source: Economic Times, 20 January, 2003.

For the agriculture sector the employment elasticity has declined sharply from 0.7 during 1983 – 1993 to a low of 0.01 during 1993 – 2000. The Tenth Plan document expects the employment elasticity to increase to 0.23. Employment elasticity of output growth is declining. It has fallen from 0.52 during 1983–94 to 0.16 during 1993–2000 for all sectors. Higher output growth has not been accompanied by higher employment growth. Growth rate of employment declined from 2.7 per cent per annum during 1983-94 to 1.07 per cent during 1993–2000, when during the same periods GDP went up from 5.2 per cent to 6.7 per cent (Tables 6.2–4 for more details).

In case of employment for rural females growth rate of employment is more precarious. Growth rate of employment for rural females has declined from 1.41 per cent during 1983–93 to only 0.15 per cent during 1994–2002. Agriculture and field crop production employment shows a negative growth rate during 1994–2002. Census data show that growth of main worker declined from 2.34 per cent during 1981–91 to just 0.81 per cent in 1991–2000. A fall in employment elasticity of output growth generally indicates a rise in labor productivity and or a shift in favour of capital intensive technology. According to the Planning Commission (Mahant, 2003), labour productivity increased by 5.6 per cent annually during 1993–2000 against 2.3 per cent during 1983–94. Also there has been a higher incremental capital-output ratio. But the Planning Commission is silent as to how will the country achieve its 10 million a year employment growth target during the 10th Plan if employment elasticity of output growth declines.

Female Access to Economic Resources

Customarily access to land has been largely confined to male household members. Based on ethnographic information among 145 communities where the households had some access as owners or tenants, the overwhelming normative pattern in 131 of these communities is clearly patrilineal. According to Rao and Rana (1997) it is only in small pockets of the Northeast and Kerala that matrilineal and bilateral inheritance patterns prevail among certain communities. Islamic law did recognise women's rights to inherit ancestral property, including immovables but not equal to men's. Official policies and programmes reflect and reinforce traditional attitudes. Prevailing biases tend to affect both court judgements and the formulation and implementation of government policies, including land reform programmes. Rao and Rana (1997) provide two illustrative examples. In Bodhgaya (Bihar) landless women, after an extended struggle for land, were granted rights by the government in two villages. But when they sought to formally register the land in their names, the district officer initially refused, on the grounds that titles could only be given to men since they were the heads of households. Again, when landless women in Udaipur district (Rajasthan) claimed a part of the village wasteland to grow herbs, fodder, etc., the bias of the local official was clear. 'But we do not allot to women.' When asked why not, he said with unbeatable logic, 'Because we never have, so that is why we won't.'

Rao and Rana (1997) say that, land rights for women is a necessary precondition for their empowerment. To rural women, land rights do not just imply control over land, but its meaning is found in social, cultural and economic terms, whether it be higher status, security against absolute poverty, the capacity to challenge male oppression and domestic violence, the ability to improve intra-household distribution of resources, the access to credit.

According to Mehta (1996) while it is true that women's access to independent sources of income is positively related to their participation in household decision-making and the treatment they receive from family members. For the large mass of women who work, the use of the incomes they earn is determined by the male head of the family. Income alone inadequately reflects access to resources, for even if earnings were to be gender equitably distributed, it does not follow that use of it will be too.

Access to credit is a critical index of empowerment. Winnaraja (1985) highlits the inappropriate nature of existing institutions, namely, banks, vis-à-vis the needs of the rural poor, especially women. Lack of flexibility and requirement of collateral and certified identification effectively puts state-sponsored credit out of their reach.

Sangwan (1997) describes the efforts of a bank to reach out to the women. It is being realised in India that Self Help Groups (SHG) can establish relationship between the formal financial institutions and the poor for providing credit and other banking facilities. Oriental Bank of Commerce (OBC) is implementing the SHG approach in the two districts Dehradun (UP now in Uttaranchal), and Hanumangarh (Rajasthan) since May-June 1995. Development manager says initially the villagers avoided him for fear of recovery of earlier loans. After a few interactions the women were prepared to save in the hope of getting some work. Groups consisting of five persons were formed, pickle making, knitting, livestock, poultry and other activities were taken up. From 5 groups it has increased to 150 groups, 143 consists of women members as on March 1996.

Women are much more disadvantaged in their access to employment and earnings than men. For a number of reasons as pointed out by Aggrawal (1989):

> They have lesser job mobility due to their primary and often sole responsibility for child care, the ideology of female seclusion, and the vulnerability to caste/class related sexual abuse;
>
> There is more limited access to information on job opportunities due to lower literacy levels, lesser access to mass media, and less interaction with the market place;

> Women are confined to casual work in agriculture. Only men being hired as permanent labourers – feature that appears to be related, among other things, to the need for permanent workers to substitute for family men in ploughing, in market transactions and in night operations that is, in work from which women tend to get socially excluded.

Female – Self Employment and Organisational Structure

Targeted credit programmes for poor men and women, such as the conventional government or credit institutions and delivery of inputs approaches have failed to achieve the desired results. Two major failings are, wrong identification of beneficiaries and selection of activities undertaken without consideration of the beneficiaries.

There are several constraints in the existing formal credit systems which poor women find difficult to overcome despite the rhetoric of policy pronouncements. Formal system requires certifications of identity, ownership of assets and other legal restrictions. Its system management and processing costs are high because of the small amounts involved.

Poverty alleviation programmes should focus on: (i) savings, credit and assets creation for poor women; (ii) strengthening their capacity to save; (iii) meeting their social needs; (iv) entering into income generating activities; (v) increasing their saving; (vi) utilising these savings along with available credit both for further improving their socio-economic condition and part of their families and sustaining the process. Two urban-based organisations, the Self-Employed Women's Association (SEWA) and Working Women's Forum (WWF) have done commendable job in organizing women in the area of self-employment.

The WWF has involved the poorest of women by mobilising and organising them through a participatory process into cooperatives that are totally managed by poor women workers themselves. There are no elite intermediates, it combines human resource development and credit with conscience raising so as to bring out the untapped potential of poor women leading to sustainable social and economic development.

SEWA means service and the term self-employed give a sense of dignity to the participant in the organisation. Thus SEWA provided poor women a support system not only in the work place but also in their homes and in relation to the totality of their lives. It attempted to address not only the gender issue but also the poverty and equity issue. All poor women are part of the informal system of the economy which implies that their dealings are of small size based, on trust or dependence on known people and on verbal transaction rather than written communication. They have little control, real or documented over their assets and means of production.

These two effective projects have emerged from and as a result of the organisation of women for collective action. Problem is essentially not one of credit for poor women but that of addressing the problem of their powerlessness, which cannot be accomplished by isolated individuals but through collective action. The forms of organisation may vary from project to project and are to be determined by the circumstances, and needs of effective organisation. Group action is dependent on mutual acceptance and trust among all concerned – the rural women, the rural panchayat and donor agencies acting only as catalysts. Activities are implemented by the catalytic intermediary itself functioning as an NGO and at the village level by organisations of poor women in which they are part of the participatory process.These participatory processes of work would be the backbone of food security for the large number of rural female workers.

REFERENCES

Agarwal, Bina, 1985, 'Women and Technological Change in Agriculture: The Asian and African Experience,' in Ahmed, I. (ed.), *Technology and Rural Women: Conceptual and Empirical Issues,* George Allen & Unwin, London.

Agarwal, Bina, 1989, 'Rural Women, Poverty and Natural Resources: Sustenance, Sustainability and Struggle for Change,' *Economic and Political Weekly,* October, 28.

Chadda, G.K. and P.P. Saha, 2002, 'Post Reform backs in Rural Employment, Issues that Need Further Scruting,' *Economic and Political weekly,* May 25.

Chhabra, Rami and Nuna, Sheel C., 1995, 'Abortion in India, An Overview,' Report, Sponsored by Ford Foundation, New Delhi.

Chatterjee, Meera, 1990, 'Indian Women: Their Health and Productivity, World Bank Discussion' Paper No. 109.

Choudhry, Prem, 1993, 'High Participation, Low Evaluation: Women and Work in Rural Haryana, *Economic and Political Weekly*, December 25.

Duvury, Nata, 1989, 'Women in Agriculture: A review of the Indian Literature,' *Economic and Political Weekly*. October, 28.

Franke, Richard W. and Chasin. Barbara H., 1996 'Female Supported Households; A Continuing Agenda for Kerala Model,' Economic and Political Weekly, March 9.

Jain, Devaki, 1996, 'Valuing Work: Times as a Measure': *Economic and Political Weekly*, October 26.

Jha, Manish K., 2002, 'Hunger and Starvation Deaths, Call for Public Action,' *Economic and Political weekly*, December 28.

Kothari, Uma, 1997, 'Women's Paid Domestic Work and Rural Transformation a Study in South Gujarat,' *Economic and Political Weekly*, April 26.

Mahant, Tushar K., 2003, 'GDP Growth doesn't mean Jobs,' *Economic Times*, January 20.

Mehta, Aasha Kapur, 1996, 'Recasting Indices for Developing Countries: A Gender Empowerment Measure,' *Economic and Political Weekly*, October 26.

Mukherjee, Mukul, 1996, 'Towards Gender-Aware Data Systems Indian Experience, *Economic and Political Weekly*, October 26.

Rao, Nitya and Kumar Rana, 1997, 'Land Rights and Women Care of Santhals, Pursuing Third World Women's Interests Compatibility of Feminism with Grass Roots Development,' *Economic and Political Weekly*, June 7.

Sangwan, S.S., April-June 1997, 'Financing through Self-Help Groups: An Experience of a Commercial Bank in Dehradun.' *The Journal of the Indian Institute of Bankers.*

Shiva Kumar A.K., 1996, 'UNDPs Gender Related Development Index: A computation for Indian States,' *Economic and Political Weekly*, April 6.

World Bank, 1990, 'Indian Women: Their Health and Productivity,' World Bank Discussion Paper No. 109.

World Bank, 1991, 'Gender and Poverty in India,' A World Bank Country Study.

Wignaraja, Ponna, 1990, 'Women, Poverty and Resources,' Sage Publications, New Delhi.

Chapter 7

Human Rights, Agricultural Deregulation and Food Security

Shahid Ahmed & Ghulam Yazdani

Food Security and Food Sovereignty is an essential condition for life with dignity. Liberalisation of agriculture under Agreement on Agriculture (AoA) is threatening the livelihoods of millions, especially the most vulnerable rural population in the world's poorest countries. Globalisation of food trade is leaving behind those who are unable to participate for lack of land or other assets, skills, technology, market weight or ethnic and gender-based discrimination. In the liberal economic regime, governed by the instinct of self-interest, decisions are taken on the basis of market forces leaving behind the interests of the poor. The reality is that the economic policies of most governments, (which are often influenced or imposed by the World Bank, the IMF and the WTO, and are promoted by trans-national corporations), have widened the gap between wealthy and poor countries and have accentuated the unequal distribution of earnings within countries. Poor cannot be left at the mercy of free market mechanism where purchasing power of an individual decides his living conditions. This process of development has no meaning without guaranteeing right to life with dignity. Right to life is basic human right. Human rights include all those rights essential for human survival, physical security, liberty and development with dignity. They stem from the recognition of the inherent equality and dignity of all human beings. Every man, woman and child is entitled to enjoy their human rights, merely on the basis of their humanity and regardless of any distinguishing characteristics such as race, gender, creed, opinion and class. The first and most important right of all human beings is the right to food. In view of this, the objective of the paper is to analyse the prevailing and changing food scenario, particularly in the context of AoA and to discuss constitutional rights of the people, commitment made to the United Nations and its various bodies, international conventions and declarations to meet the needs of the hungry and vulnerable. The paper also identifies some necessary conditions essential to establish food and nutritional objectives and policies.

The 1996 Plan of Action and the Declaration of the World Food Summit, defines Food Security as 'the access of all people to sufficient, safe and nutritious food to meet their dietary needs and food preferences for an active and healthy life.' In other words, food security symbolises a situation where everyone has access, at all times, to the food needed for an active and healthy life. Thus, the essential elements of food security are: (a) adequate availability of food, (b) availability of adequate purchasing power in the hands of the people, and (c) efficient distribution through trade and/or public distribution system. Food sovereignty is defined as the right to determine policies and strategies for the sustainable production, distribution and consumption of food. Food sovereignty is considered to be a prerequisite for food security. It is, therefore, essential that the global and national rules must encompass food sovereignty a commitment to justice in order to ensure that people have what they need to survive and develop, including food security.

Eight years after the World Food Summit and ten years after the Agricultural Agreements of the Uruguay Round, the promises and commitments made to satisfy the food and nutritional needs of all are far from being fulfilled. They have worsened the conditions of food production and access to healthy and sufficient nutrition for the majority of the world's people, even in the developed countries. As a consequence, right to food and nutritional well-being is not guaranteed to the majority of the world's people.

The philosophy of economic development in developing countries has changed considerably during the eighties. Self-reliance as a strategy for growth was devalued in favour of an increased orientation towards the world market. Accelerating industrialisation of food systems and globalization of food trade is leaving behind those who are unable to participate for lack of land or other assets, skills, technology, and gender-based discrimination. Private sector is taking over the public sector. This sector is governed by the instinct of self-interest and decisions are taken on the basis of market forces leaving behind the interests of the poor. However, the poor cannot be left at the mercy of the free market mechanism. This process of development has no meaning without guaranteeing the right to life with human dignity.

India is a poignant example of how food sufficiency at the macro level does not translate necessarily or evenly into food security at the family or individual level. Despite strong economic growth approximating six per cent annually in the 1990s, and well past the landmark attainment of self-sufficiency in cereals at the national level, India has staggeringly large number of undernourished – about 208 million. In addition, about 40 million are exposed to one or more natural disasters every year. One in every four chronically food insecure persons in the world lives in India. In every five Indians one suffers from overt or covert hunger. Among women and children, hunger prevalence is higher. About 50 per cent of India's children in India (more tribal and rural than urban) are undernourished and stunted, 33 per cent have a low birth weight (below 2500 gm), and 69 out of 1,000 die before the age of one year. Almost 36 per cent women are malnourished and 52 per cent suffer from anaemia and other micronutrient deficiencies, resulting in the shocking high maternal mortality rate of 540 per 100,000 live births.[1] Add to it the figures of the poor and ailing who die for want of adequate food, medical and healthcare facilities to complete the sordid picture of the indifference of the leadership to protect the Constitution they are oath-bound. The state is responsible for the violation of the rights of the individuals guaranteed by the Constitution. Right to life (including food) is denied to countless citizens everyday. We do not know of a single agent of the state having ever been punished for failing to protect the Constitution. Do we take it that the Constitution has never been violated?

Agricultural Deregulation Under Agreement on Agriculture

The most important change regarding food security is expected to be brought about by the implementation of Agreement on Agriculture in WTO. AoA has three pillars: market access, domestic support and export subsidies. In general terms, it amounts to: increase in market access, and reduction in domestic support and export subsidies. All parties to the agreement had to take steps in this direction, although the least developed countries (LDCs) were exempted from some obligations and developing countries overall had smaller reduction commitments. AoA also opens and closes with explicit reference to non-trade concerns some countries view as a fourth pillar.

There are a number of provisions in AoA, which directly and indirectly affects the food security. There are measures outlawed by the agreement known as *Red Box*. For example, non-tariff measures such as variable levies had to be replaced by tariffs. Under *Amber Box* category, some payments and subsidies paid to producers that were to be reduced, but have not yet been eliminated. These measures are based on the Aggregate Measure of Support (AMS), which is a cash equivalent of total government support for agricultural producers, including both direct and indirect spending (for example input subsidies and price supports). The AMS excludes certain kinds of spending that is exempted under various articles of the agreement.

Article 6.5 of the AoA allows countries an unlimited spending for direct payments to farmers as long as these are linked to production-limiting programmes (*Blue Box category*) based on fixed areas and yields, or per head of livestock.

Ironically, government support to limit production is allowed, while many forms of government support to increase production are not, even though that is precisely what is needed to tackle food insecurity in many developing countries. The *Green Box* list includes payments linked to environmental programmes, pest and disease control, infrastructure development, and domestic food aid (paid for at current market prices). AoA also includes payments to producers that are not linked to changing levels of production (so-called decoupled payments) and government payments to income insurance programmes. Also exempted from AMS commitments are levels of spending on the agricultural sector and on particular commodities that fall below a specified ceiling – the so-called *de minimis* levels, which are 5 per cent of the total value of production of that crop for developed and 10 per cent for developing countries. Article 5 of the agreement specifies that countries that are at the outset converted non-tariff measures into tariffs ('terrified') for each crop could reserve the right to apply safeguard tariffs to protect against sudden import surges or falls in world prices for a limited time, to protect their domestic industry. It was mainly developed countries that torrified in this way. Only 21 developing countries have access to this provision, the rest having opted to declare general ceilings for tariffs across all their imports, a choice that precluded them from using special safeguards measures.

The AoA contains clear discrepancies and imbalances. In the case of agricultural trade, many developing countries are seeking greater special and differential provisions to guarantee food security and support for local farmers. However, while developed countries make a show of listening to developing countries' needs, the nature of negotiations ensures that the strongest players extract the greatest concessions and shape the outcome to suit their immediate interests. The most flexible part of the AoA is in spending levels, exactly where developing countries have the least flexibility, because their governments are so strapped for cash and are often tied into onerous debt repayments. Developing countries, which are generally forced to rely on border taxes to protect their farmers, found the constraints on these measures a good deal tighter than those on northern-style farmer support.

AoA does not currently include the World Food Summit commitment to halve world hunger by 2015. In promoting the industrial model of agriculture worldwide, it has jeopardised food security in developing countries. AoA rules (together with structural adjustment programmes) have pressurised developing countries to intensify their agriculture, producing a bias against small farmers in favour of larger producers, agri-business and export crop production. Most of the gains from trade liberalisation have gone to the trans-national agri-business corporations (TNCs). The sector has seen an increasing trend of mergers and takeovers concentrating even more power and influence with TNCs. Trade reform has thus been accompanied by growing land alienation, declining food entitlements, a growing number of hungry people, greater intensive farming and erosion of agricultural biodiversity.

Some of the major implications of Agricultural Deregulation under AoA for developing countries are as under:

(*a*) The agreement has legitimised the use of subsidies in developed countries, while narrowing the options available to developing countries, which must compete in an increasingly global market. Food security, and the potential of agriculture as an engine of growth for the South, has been undermined;

(*b*) Products for which little or no imports took place in the past because of the highly restrictive nature of the then-existing regime, countries were required to give minimum market access opportunity commitments. These provide for the establishment of tariff quotas equal to 3 per cent of domestic consumption in the base period 1986–88 which rise to 5 per cent by the end of 2000 for developed countries and 2004 for developing countries. Lower rates (specified in the national schedules but generally not greater than 32 per cent of the bound terrified rates) are applicable to imports up to the quota limits, while the higher rate resulting from tariffication applies to imports over quota limits. As a result of these minimum access commitments, countries will have to import modest amounts of their most restricted products. Products covered by minimum access commitments include meat, dairy products, and specified fresh vegetables and fruits;

(*c*) Developed nations while maintaining high protection and subsidies for their own agricultural and food sectors, deny developing countries the use of the very support measures (import controls and producer subsidies) which enabled the EU and US to develop their farming sectors;

(*d*) Developed countries have exploited the ambiguous nature of commitments such as the changes in tariff levels on sensitive commodities;

(*e*) Most of the allowable agricultural support measures are beyond the financial or technical resources of many developing countries;

(*f*) Special and differential treatment provisions for developing countries, meant to recognise their particular problems, are currently mostly non-binding and amount to little more than longer transition periods;

(*g*) The Trade-Related Intellectual Property Rights (TRIPs) agreement does not specifically recognise the rights of local communities to their traditional and indigenous knowledge and this could lead to the unjustified patenting of their agro-biodiversity by foreign corporations.

Globally, the liberalisation of agriculture is threatening the livelihoods of millions, especially the most vulnerable rural papulation in the world's poorest countries. The frequent cases of starvation deaths reflect not only the ineffective implementation of development policies but also inappropriateness of development strategies. The global food chain is increasingly distorted by the disparities in power between global agri-businesses, on the one hand, and farmers and consumers on the other. This is driving the liberalisation of agriculture and the food trade in directions inimical to the public interest. In this environment, there has been growing recognition that all developments, and in particular so called long term sustainable development, had to be founded on a society's human resources, and these will have to be developed first through proper food supplies, healthcare and education.

International Concern

Right to adequate food starts from the recognition that hunger and malnutrition are almost always the result of poverty.[2] Article 1 of the Universal Declaration of Human Rights[3] asserts, with spiritual sensitivity and moral maturity, that all human beings are born free and equal in dignity and rights. They are endowed with reason and conscience and should treat one another in spirit of brotherhood. This profound position is central to the charter of the United Nations, which affirms its faith in fundamental human rights, and in the dignity and worth of the human person. Any person anywhere and every person everywhere is heir to the progressive promise for the human dignity and the basic right.

Right to adequate food includes the right to a standard of living adequate for the health and well-being of human beings. It was originally included in Article 25 of the Universal Declaration of Human Rights promulgated in 1948 and was more explicitly formulated in the International Covenant on Economic, Social and Cultural Rights (ICESCR), approved in 1966 and enforced since 1976. Article 25 of the Declaration lays down that everyone has the right to a standard of living adequate for the health and well-being of himself and of his family, including food, clothing, housing and medical care and necessary social service, and the right to security in the event of unemployment, sickness, disability, old age or other lack of livelihood in circumstances beyond his control. Similarly, Article 11 of ICESCR states the right of everyone to an adequate standard of living including food. A number of other International Agreements, Conventions and laws also deal with the right to food for special groups, for instance, the Convention on the Right of the Child. They may also protect the right to food indirectly, as in the case of Convention on the Protection of Migrant Workers, the Convention on the Elimination of all Forms of Discrimination against Women (CEDAW) and other ILO conventions for the purpose. The ICESCR has so far been ratified by 142 countries, but the acceptance of the right to food as legally binding, rather than broadly guiding, principle is not universal. Some key countries have still to ratify the ICESCR and few have amended national legislation to suit the Convention. Food and Agriculture Organisation (FAO) has an obligation enshrined in its Constitution to assist member states in raising the levels of nutrition and standards of living and thus ensuring humanity's freedom from hunger.

Article 11, para 2, recognises the right of everyone to be free from hunger as a fundamental right. Pursuant to Article 11.1 of the Covenant, States recognise the right of every one to an adequate standard of living for himself and his family, including adequate food, clothing and housing, and to the continuous improvement of living conditions. While pursuant to Article 11.2 recognises that more immediate and urgent steps may be needed to ensure the fundamental right to freedom from hunger and malnutrition. On the request of the Member States during the 1996 World Food Summit, the general comment of the Committee aims to identify some of the principles important issues in relation to the right to adequate food for a better definition of the rights relating to food in Article 11 of the Covenant and to give particular attention to the Summit Plan of Action in monitoring the implementation of the specific measures provided for in Article 11 of the Covenant.

The General Assembly of the UN convened the World Food Conference at Rome on 5-6 November 1974. The Conference adopted 22 resolutions and the Universal Declaration on the Eradication of Hunger and Malnutrition.[4] It was affirmed that the participating states would make full use of the United Nations system in the implementation of the declaration and other decisions taken at the conference especially the conference called upon the people of the world to work together to bring about the end of the age-old scourge of hunger. The resolution and the Universal Declaration on the Eradication of Hunger and Malnutrition so adopted at the Conference as endorsed by the General Assembly on 17th Dec. 1974. In the preamble to the Declaration it has been noted that there exists a grave food crisis, which afflict the people of the developing countries.

There is an obligation cast by a Universal Declaration on the Eradication of Hunger and Malnutrition in the many countries where half of humanity starve without shelter and clothing The Universal declaration must, therefore, be immediately implemented and the dichotomy between the haves and the have-nots must be eliminated to achieve peace and order in the human world. The Declaration, which fundamentally opposes starvation and houselessness, has been one of the international instruments slumbering for decades. At the international level, there have been world summits reiterating the commitment to eliminate hunger and achieve universal food security. The United Nations Millennium Development Goals and the World Food Summit also emphasised the commitment to halve the number of undernourished in the world by 2015.

Developing Human Rights Approaches to AoA

At the heart of adopting a human rights approach to the liberalisation of agricultural trade is the issue of whether a 'one-system-fits-all approach' is appropriate. Agricultural sector plays starkly different roles in the development of every country. In the case of low-income countries, it plays an essential role in ensuring food security and alleviating poverty. In these countries, it is still the major employer, it is a significant contributor to GDP as well as an important source of foreign exchange and revenue. Further, food consumption accounts for a significant share of expenditure of households in many developing countries.

Food-insecure developing countries in particular need to deal with inadequate production and lack of resources to raise agricultural productivity and food production in line with their needs and potential. Opening of markets in a manner that is conducive to the protection of human rights in fact requires a different form and pace, depending on the country in question. This requires an approach to trade rules that guarantees affirmative action for vulnerable individuals and groups. A human rights approach would consider the impact of trade liberalisation on different groups and set rules accordingly. Despite including several special and differential measures for developing countries, the AoA does not sufficiently take into account the highly varying levels of development of the agricultural sectors among countries and of the people.

Applying the human rights principle of non-discrimination to trade law encourages affirmative action for the poor. While non-discrimination is also a principle of international trade law there is a distinction in the application of the principle. 'National treatment' envisages equal treatment for nationals and non-nationals – whether they are poor farmers or large agri-business or industrial firms. Treating unequals as equals is problematic for the promotion and protection of human rights and could result in the institutionalisation of discrimination against the poor and marginalised. Under human rights law, the principle of non-discrimination does not envisage according equal treatment to everyone in all cases. Affirmative action is necessary in some cases to protect vulnerable people and groups. Doha Ministerial Declaration has emphasised on making special and differential treatment an integral part of the rules and disciplines of the AoA so as to enable developing countries the flexibility to take into account food security and rural development objectives.

India's Concern and Constitutional Recognition

The preamble of the Constitution guarantees to all citizens of India social, economic and political justice... and equality of status and opportunity and seeks to promote fraternity among the Indians in order to assure the dignity of the individual and the unity and integrity of the nation. By 42nd amendment of the Constitution made in 1976, the country was as a to set sovereign, socialist, secular and democratic republic. The expression 'socialist' was intentionally introduced into preamble for removing the difficulties, which have arisen in achieving the objective of socio-economic revolution directed to: end poverty, ignorance, disease and inequality of opportunity. Chapter III of Constitution deals with the right to live with human dignity as given in Article 21, Article 38 provides that the State shall strive to promote the welfare of the people by securing and protecting as effectively as it may, social order with justice. The State shall, in particular, strive to minimise inequalities in income, and endeavor to eliminate inequalities in status, facilities and opportunities, not only amongst the individuals but also amongst groups of people residing in different areas or engaged in different vocations. Article 39, as amended by 42nd Amendment in 1976, provides that the State shall, in particular direct its policy towards securing: the right to an adequate means of livelihood; ownership and control over the material resources; equal pay for equal work, etc.

Food as Basic Human Right and the Poor: Judicial Recognition

The right to life necessarily includes the right to food. Even so, it must be possible to vest power in the people through enacted legislation so that they may secure their basic human right. The right to life and food is wide and not pedantically narrow. The Supreme Court of India, speaking through Chief Justice Chandrachud, observed:

> The question which we have to consider is whether the right to life includes the right to livelihood. We see only one answer to that question, namely, that it does. The sweep of the right to life conferred by Art 21 is wide and far-reaching. It does not mean merely that life cannot be extinguished or taken away as, for example, by the imposition and execution of the death sentence, except according to procedure established by law. That is but one aspect of the right to life. An equally important facet of that right is the right to livelihood because; no person can live without the means of living, that is, the means of livelihood. If the right to livelihood is not treated as a part of the constitutional right to life, the easiest way of depriving a person of his right to life would be to deprive him of his means of livelihood to the point of abrogation. Such deprivation would not only denude the life of its effective content and meaningfulness but it would make life impossible to live. And yet, such deprivation would not have to be in accordance with the procedure established by law, if the right to livelihood is

> not regarded as a part of the right to life. That, which alone makes it possible to live, leave aside what makes life livable, must be deemed to be an integral component of the right to life. Deprive a person of his right to livelihood and you shall have deprived him of his life. Indeed, that explains the massive migration of the rural population to big cities. They migrate because they have no means of livelihood in the villages. The motive force which propels their desertion of their hearths and homes in the village is the struggle for survival, that is, the struggle for life. So unimpeachable is the evidence of the nexus between life and the means of livelihood. They have to eat to live: Only a handful can afford the luxury of living to eat. That they can do, namely, eat, only if they have the means of livelihood. That is the context in which it was said by Douglas J. in Baksey, (1954) 347 M.D. 442 that the right to work is the most precious liberty that man possesses. It is the most precious liberty because, it sustains and enables a man to live and the right to life is a precious freedom. 'Life,' as observed by Field, J. in Munn v. Illinois, (1877) 94 US 113, means something more than a mere animal existence and the inhibition against the deprivation of life extends to all those limits and faculties by which life is enjoyed.[5]

In another case, Justice Kuldip Singh of the Supreme Court observed that: 'The State is under a constitutional mandate to create conditions in which the fundamental rights guaranteed to the individuals under Part III could be enjoyed by all.'[6] The Hon'ble Supreme Court held[7] that in any oraganised society, the right to live as human being is not ensured by only meeting the animal needs of a man. It is secured only when a man is assured of all facilities to develop himself and is freed from all restrictions which inhibit his growth. All human beings are designed to achieve this object. The Right to Live that is guaranteed in any civilised society implies the right to food, water, shelter, education, medical care, and a decent environment. These are basic rights known to any civilised society. The similar view was also expressed by the Hon'ble Court in Francis Coralie Mullin's case.[8] The right to life enshrined in Article 21 cannot be restricted to mere animal existence. It means something much more than just physical survival. The right to life includes the right to live with human dignity and all that goes along with it, namely, the bare necessities of life such as adequate nutrition, clothing and shelter over the head and other facilities.[9]

Former judge, Supreme Court of India, Hon'ble Justice Bhagwati opined in the Asiad Workers, 'The poor too have civil and political rights and the rule of law is meant for than also, though today it exists only on paper and not in realty.'[10] The Supreme Court, in the Pavement Dweller case approved of Francis Coralie Mullin decision and derived a guarantee for the minimum needs of existence directly from the right to life. This is, however, a defensive right against encroachment on the basic prerequisite of life or to put it differently, on the basic necessities of life. The road from such a negative right to a claim on the State for actively securing and providing basic necessities is yet uncertain but some day, it will have to be explored by the Supreme Court.

One of the Public Interest Litigation initiated by the People's Union of Civil Liberties (PUCL) before the Supreme Court represents a new front in the battle for right to food, which has been waged with varying degrees of the intensity in the States worst affected by adverse weather conditions over the last few years. After hearing the petition, the Supreme Court bench comprising Justice B.N. Kirpal and Justice K.G. Balakrishnan on 28 November, 2001 issued directions and ordered to the Union of India and other concerned States to implement immediately the existing schemes[11] such as TDPS, AAY, MDMS, NOAPS, AS, ICDS, NMBS and NFBS regarding food Supply to the poor. The Court directed the governments to give grain free to people who are too poor to buy it, provide cooked mid-day meals in all government and government-aided schools, and empower Gram Panchayat to frame food for work schemes with focus on poor, Dalits and women.

Hearing another petition relating to right to food the Supreme Court lends its weight to the cause of the deprived. This second petition was also filed by the People's Union of Civil Liberties on 20 August, 2002. The three-judge Bench comprising justice B.N. Kirpal, Santosh Hegde and Brajesh

Kumar affirmed that the Central and state governments had the principal responsibility to see that food reached the poor and the indigent. The Bench was requested to deal with a series of questions, which could have far-reaching consequences for the directions of economic and social welfare policy. First, did the right to life, as guaranteed by Article 21 of the Constitution, imply that people who were too poor to buy their own food should be guaranteed the minimum means of subsistence by the state. In other words, did the right to life include the right to food? And did this not in turn imply that the state was obliged to provide sufficient and adequate redress to vulnerable sections in circumstances that threatened to impair seriously the right to food

Implementation of Right to Food

Rights-based approach obliges states that have not yet done so, to establish food and nutrition objectives and introduce policies to meet them. This approach to food security imposes obligations on the State towards its citizens, the rule of law and the involvement of the poor and hungry themselves in articulating, planning and implementation of anti-hunger programmes. Following the prevailing concept on food security, the key issue is entitlement to food. A policy for the creation of food entitlements must therefore do one of the two things: help the food-insecure with their own production, if they are farmers, and, if they are not, with acquiring purchasing power to buy food from the market. This approach is, however, only part of the solution. A large number of food insecure and hungry persons cannot, in the short or medium term, be helped in this fashion. This is because there are market failures of various kinds, inequitable access to land, vulnerability to external shocks, illness, financial, social, educational, ethnic and gender-related exclusion, conflicts, natural disasters and failures in the intra-household food distribution. To make the right to food feasible, there is immediate need of following steps:

In the changing economic environment, it is important to develop market access mechanism that targets the poor, small farmers and producers and to promote sustainable agriculture. Policy makers should strive for:

1. Collaboration with developing countries to counter and bargain from the powerful developed countries. In this context, movement of non-alligned countries and the group of G-15 countries can play an important role. Revitalisation of these organisations is the need of the hour. More collaboration with CIS and east European countries will make our position stronger;
2. Implementation of Marrakesh Decision in 1994;
3. Amendment to the TRIPs agreement [Article 27.3(b)] that would enable WTO members to exclude all genetic resources for food and agriculture from the TRIPs agreement;
4. Recognition of traditional knowledge, bio-innovations and practices of indigenous people and farming communities; precedence of Convention on Biological Diversity takes over the WTO TRIPs agreement in provisions relating to the requirement for prior informed consent of peoples and communities before use of their knowledge or plants and that benefits from any commercial exploitation are equitably shared with these communities (Article 15);
5. Identification of the vulnerable people at village level by the Gram Panchayat;
6. Establishment of Community Food Banks at local level control which should be managed by the Gram Panchayat. There may be an Insurance Schemes to the rural people which can be managed and operated on a collective basis through the Panchayats;
7. Avoidance fluctuations in prices and prevention of distress sales by small farmers;
8. Creation of an efficient delivery systems;
9. Coordination of food supply and distribution, (There is an urgent need to establish Commission for Poor at State and National level at par with other commissions. Right to Food is one of the human rights which itself gives 'life' to the Right to Life to every human being to enjoy his right and along with other freedoms. In case the violation of this very essential rights which requires attention at all levels to realise the importance of it and thereafter fix the responsibility for the criminal neglect and consider it as a crime against humanity and punish the guilty whosoever).

Accountability is the medium through which we can strike and maintain a balance between the governors and the governed.[12] In recent years, starvation deaths have been receiving attention both by the government and non-governmental organisations. The judiciary in this matter has played a very humanistic role in declaring the right to food to poorest of the poor within the ambit of the fundamental rights to life under the constitution. But it may be stated that the problem of food to the poor is of such enormous magnitude that all that has been done till now is not sufficient. All that the administration needs to do is to uphold constitutional rights of the people and operationalise the commitment made to the United Nations and its various bodies, their international convention and declarations to meet the needs of the hungry and vulnerable.

NOTES

1. World Food Programme(2002)
2. Frank Walter, 'The WTO and The Right to Food,' Istituto Internazionale Jacques Maritain, Rome (2000)
3. Universal Declaration of Human Rights (1948)
4. Report of the World Food Conference
5. AIR 1986 SC 180 at Pages 193-194
6. AIR 1992 SC 1858
7. Chameli Singh v. State of U.P., 1996(2) SCC, 549.
8. Francis Coralie Mullin v. Administrator, Union Territory of Delhi, 1981(1) SCC, 608; AIR, 1981 SC 746.
9. Francis Coralie Mullin v. Administrator, Union Territory of Delhi, 1981(1) SCC, 608; AIR, 1981 SC 746 as cited by V. D. Mahajan, 'Constituional Law of India' 7th Edition, 1991, p. 230.
10. People's Union for Democratic Rights v Union of India (Asiad Case). AIR 1982 SC 1473: 3SCC 235.
11. Targeted Public Distribution Scheme (TDPS), Antyodaya Anna Yojna(AAY), Mid Day Meal Scheme (MDMS), National Old Age Pension Scheme(NOAPS), Annapurna Scheme (AS), Integrated Child Development Scheme(ICDS), National Maternity Benefit Scheme(NMBS), National Family Benefit Scheme (NFBS).
12. Upendra Baxi(1994)

REFERENCES

Baxi, Upendra, 1994, 'Inhuman Wrongs And Human Rights-Unconventional Essays' Har-Anand Publications, New Delhi. p. 2.

FAO, 1998, 'Assessment of the Impact of the Uruguay Round on Agricultural Markets,' CCP 99/12.

FAO, Technical Background Document,' 1996

Food and Agriculture Organisation, 2003, 'The State of Food Insecurity in the World 2003, Monitoring Progress Towards The World Food Summit And Millennium Development Goals.

Gulati, Ashok and C.H. Hanumantha Rao, 'Indian Agriculture: Emerging Perspectives and Policy Issues,' India's Economic Reforms, edited by Uma Kapila, 2nd Edn, Academic Foundation, Delhi.

Krishna Iyer, V.R., 1995 'Human Rights – A Judge's Miscellany,' B R Publishing Corpn., pp. 24-26

Report of the World food Conference, 1974, 'United Nations Publication,' Sales No. E-75, II.A.3

Rodrik, D., 1998, 'Globalization, Social Conflict and Economic Growth,' *The World Economy,* vol. 21, No. 2, March.

Sen, A., 1996 'Economic Reforms, Employment and Poverty: Trends and Options,' *Economic and Political Weekly,* Special No.

Staatz, J., V. D'Agostino and S. Sundberg, 1990, 'Measuring Food Security in Africa: Conceptual, Empirical and Policy Issues.' *Amer. J. Agr. Econ.* 72, December, pp. 1311-17.

Universal Declaration of Human Rights (1948) was adopted and proclaimed by General Assembly Resolution 217 A (III) of 10th December.

V. D. Mahajan(1991), 'Constitutional Law of India' 7th Edn, p. 370.

Weber, M.T. et al., 1988, 'Informing Food Security Decisions in Africa: Empirical Analysis and Policy Dialogue.' *Amer. Journal of Agriculture Economics.* 70, December, 1044–1052.

World Bank (1995), 'Agricultural Trade Liberalization in the Uruguay Round, Policy' Research Working Paper.

World Bank, 1986, 'Poverty and Hunger: Issues and Options for Food Security in Developing Countries,' Washington DC: World Bank, 1986.

World Bank. World Development Report 2000/1: Attacking Poverty (Internet, WWW). 2000 (cited May, 2000).

World Food Programme, 2002, New Delhi: Tackling Hunger-United Nations World Food Programme's Effort to Help Eliminate Food Insecurity in India, pp. 2-3.

Chapter 8

Nutritional Food Insecurity in India*

Abusaleh Shariff

Introduction

Apart from the requirements of energy, human body at different age groups also requires certain essential nutrients. Deficiency or inadequate intake of these might lead to diseases and disabilities carried over through generations. This is more relevant for women and children suffering from dietary diseases that have a noticeable effect on their ability to meet nutritional needs. Within the households the nutritional needs are different according to age and sex. Several factors like diet preferences, nutrition knowledge and caring practices and intra-household distribution influence these needs.

There are some groups of people who are more at risk than the chronically food insecure. The most vulnerable under this category are the pregnant and nursing mothers, unborn babies, children under the age of five years as they have special nutritional needs. The main objective of this paper is to elaborate some critical aspects of this nutritional food insecurity in India.

Food Absorption

Food absorption is a major problem in developing countries. In the words of Amartya Sen and Jean Drenze, 'the capability to be nourished depends crucially on other characteristics of a person that are influenced by such non-food factors as medical attention, health services, basic education, provision of clean water, eradication of infectious epidemics, and so on.' This can be termed absorption food insecurity when the body is not in a position to absorb the nutrients from the food taken due to factors mentioned above. The problem of hunger, nutrition and food security is thus related to the whole developmental process. In remote rural areas, communities have little access to safe drinking water, sanitation, and health care facilities. Worm infestation and malaria are common in India. In case of sickness, nutrient reserves in the body and the capacity to absorb new nutrients decrease rapidly. Severe and frequently recurring shocks can turn transitory food insecurity into chronic situations of poverty and under nutrition.

Assetless, those living in drought prone areas and people belonging to tribal and forest areas and on high altitudes have higher degree of food insecurity. Female-headed households are highly vulnerable and food-insecure. Infants, children, the old and women have higher levels as well as higher degree of undernourishment. Besides intra-household food distribution seems to disfavour particularly the women and children. The infirm, chronically sick and disabled are others who have high degree of food insecurity and risk of under nutrition. Malnutrition is persistent amongst the above groups across India and it varies only marginally between states.

Low birth weight is the most important indicator of under-nutrition both at household and national level. More than 60 per cent of births taking place all over India are underweight. This points to extremely precarious health and nutrition conditions of pregnant women. Under nutrition among the infants and children besides being a manifestation of low birth weights is also associated with poor post-natal maternal and child care practices relating to food intake and health. Often the modern public health programmes have not addressed these special nutritional and health care needs in India. Access to food is also affected by food prices.

A trend analysis using monthly data of food price since

1981 suggest that the price of rice and wheat increased substantially during the 1990. The rate of price rise was the highest in the case of pulses followed by rice. It is also noticed that the relative differences between the food and all commodity prices during 1981–92 has been narrow compared with the 1991–98 period suggesting a favorable terms of trade for agricultural products.

There are a number of situations when the food insecurity may become more apparent; such as those during a bad agricultural season, droughts, floods, extreme cold conditions and so on.

Outstanding vulnerability of agricultural laborers, artisans marginal and small farmers, and slum dwellers has been widely noted. Besides, a large number of manufacturing workers such as in *bidi* and *agarbatti* (incense sticks) industry, construction works, the rickshaw pullers, head loaders, petty traders, garment factory workers and so on (just to name a few) become food insecure due to fluctuations in demand for their labor and irregularity of work. There is also an increase in rural to urban migration from exclusive areas in the states of Bihar, eastern parts of Uttar Pradesh, Orissa and Gujarat. Often these migrants are in family units. Among all such identifiable groups the women and children are often the worst affected due to irregular food intake, lack of adequate food during pregnancy and lactation. In terms of caste and religious identities, the most food insecure are those belonging to the SCs and STs all over India, and the minorities in selected states.

Nearly 35 per cent or about 45 million rural households undertake wagework both in agricultural and non-agricultural activities to eke out a living on a daily basis. This number is growing each year as a number of landed households become landless. They do not own any cultivable land nor do they posses other assets, but entirely depend upon others to provide them daily work and wage. This group of people is nutrition insecure from more than one dimension. First, they do not have capacity to store food grains say during the harvest seasons when the prices are low. The only mechanism to undertake this is by selling their labour at relatively cheaper or discounted rate in advance and secure a loan so as to buy stocks of grains. But often the trade-off is such that the laborers may find it more practical to fend wage work on a daily basis and also buy food products on a daily basis. It has been found that the market price of cereals is 2 to 3 times more than the harvest prices during the lean agricultural seasons. It is during this period that children and women are susceptible to very low levels of food intakes while men are allocated normal quantities of food so as to maintain calorie levels as they are conceived as the real bread earners and that they have to undertake manual work. But women also undertake a number of labour-intensive but low productivity tasks during this period while consuming less food.

The third substantial group that has been facing food insecurity since long is the artisans. The artisans in the Indian villages were closely associated with the landed households through the *jajmani* relationships. This enabled them to provide regular services to a specific number of landed households around the year. Due to the onslaught of modern centralised manufacturing of agricultural implements and instruments the artisans got affected and the *janmani* system of relationships collapsed. The artisans are often landless and not reputed to undertake agricultural occupations.

Gender Dimension

Gender differentials at household level are paramount in the South Asian societies with the exception of Sri Lanka and Maldives. Often these differentials emerge from cultural stereotypes prevalent over centuries. These have barely changed with the advent of modern education, information and media technologies. Women (cutting across the economic class, caste and religion and regions) in India have relatively lower access to food within the household. Even if they happen to be producers and managers of food at home, women restrain from consuming adequate food so as to enable higher allocations to men and male children who are considered the breadwinners.They usually eat last after having served adult men and children first, often left with no adequate food to eat. Men, on the other hand, are advantaged. They at times consume food and beverages outside home also. Women and children do not have access to such source of nutrition at all.

In addition to above types of nutritional disadvantages, women are also hard-pressed by nutritional denials during pregnancy, childbirth and lactation (Shariff, 1993). A number of cultural practices restrain women in maternity from eating adequate and often locally available cheap food. These practices impair nutrition supply not only to women but also to the foetus and newly born child. This is one single reason as to why birth weights are low. Similarly, nutritious food is restrained due to the belief that this causes the foetus to get stuck to mother's womb. On the other hand, women are encouraged to consume relatively larger amounts of edible oil which is believed to lubricate the internal parts of mothers' womb. Similarly, a large number of food items is avoided by lactating mothers in anticipation of protecting the infant from the harmful effects of such food items.

Although there are a number of biological and physiological mechanisms to withstand dietary energy stress yet, women and children in India are at risk. In this connection it is appropriate to recall '...that inadequate iodine intake during pregnancy, iron deficiency anemia in infancy, and early protein-energy malnutrition in infancy and early childhood only contribute to increased morbidity and mortality in childhood, but also resulting stunting means lower physical work capacity of adults' (Scrimshaw, 1997).

Effects of food insecurity and the incidence of stress caused by food shortages can be gauged by the prevalence of anemia among women and low birth weights. Prevalence of anemia measured as below 11 gram per decilitre is extremely high in states for which data are available. Incidence of anemia varies across the Indian states. It was about 50 per cent in Andhra Pradesh and Tamil Nadu, but was as high as 95 and 98 per cent in Haryana and Rajasthan, closer to 90 per cent in Maharashtra and Gujarat and over 80 per cent in Bihar and Uttar Pradesh. A level of anemia below 8 gram per decilitre was as high as 41 per cent in Maharashtra, 21 per cent in Gujarat and 14 per cent in Andhra Pradesh (Measham and Chatterjee,1999).Women, who regularly consume green, leafy vegetables, but not fruits, have the highest prevalence of anemia (NFHS-II).

Anemia is a serious concern for young children because it can result in impaired: cognitive performance, behavioural and motor development, coordination, language development, and scholastic achievement, as well as increased morbidity from infectious diseases (Seshadri, 1997).

Malnutrition is directly or indirectly responsible for more than half of the deaths of children under four years of age worldwide. While India has successfully brought down infant mortality (IMR) from 146 per 1,000 live births in 1951 to 72 in 1996, most of the children who survived are malnourished (GOI, 1998). Infant mortality declined from 110 per thousand live births in 1981 to 72 in 1996 in the overall . In Rural India, it declined from 119 to 78 and Urban India from 62 to 46 in the respective years. In 1996, the IMR in India was 73 as compared to 65 in all developing countries, 13 in industrialised countries and 60 the world average (Human Development Report 1998: 157).

Child Anthropometric Measures

Anthropometric measurements are dependable indicators of child nutrition and cumulative health both in long (height-for-age) and short (weight-for-height) term perspective (Waterlow et al., 1977). These measures also highlight children's susceptibility to disease and their chances of survival. Child anthropometric levels are primarily determined right from the time the child grows in mother's womb. Thus it is mother's nutritional intake during pregnancy, which determine birth weights and lengths. Subsequently, breast feeding practices and timing of supplementation determine the growth in athropometric measures. Often fully breastfed children up to the age of 4 months and then long duration partially breast fed children with adequate supplementation grow normally. Another reason that causes serious damage to anthropometric growth of young is very high levels of diarrhoea.

For India as a whole, the occurrence of both severe and mild under-nutrition among the under 3 years old children is strikingly high, at 23.0 and 45.5 per cent respectively. The incidence of severe undernutrition is particularly acute in the states of Uttar Pradesh, Bihar, Madhya Pradesh, Assam Haryana and Gjuarat. Bihar is singled out as a state with the dubious distinction of having the highest levels of both severe and mild undernutrition. Stunting (both mild and severe) is more pronounced in Uttar Pradesh and Bihar. Kerala has registered the lowest occurrence of stunting for children under-four years of age. Wasting in its mild form is more prevalent in of Punjab, Rajasthan, Bihar, Orissa, Gujarat and Maharashtra. In its severe form, it is most pronounced in Rajasthan, Bihar and Maharashtra. Incidence of undernutrition in rural area has been found to be 60 per cent compared to 45 in urban parts. Similarly, stunting and wasting proportions in rural India are found to be 54 per cent and 18 per cent respectively.

Dietary Practices: Nutrition Pattern

Food and eating habits are regulated by a number of cultural practices. These practices not only have broader pattern in terms of vegetarianism and non-vegetarianism but are closely related to caste and religious identities. The type of food eaten has a strong association with the class identities as well. However, most often locally available food stuffs such as coarse cereals, vegetables and fruits are the least preferred although often they have relatively higher nutritive value. Food avoidance through fasting and ban of eating specific types of food during certain days and months of the year is also practised. During pregnancy and lactation, women may drain their own energy to provide nourishment to the child. During the time of acute food shortages, it is also expected that women draw upon their body fat to sustain themselves a bit more than the men.

Dietary Energy Supply (DES): DES per capita measured

calories in India has improved over years although during the mid-1970s it was less than 2000 kcal which improved to about 2300 kcal by 1990 and to 2500 kcal by 1997. In spite of recent lower growth rates in agricultural production, DES has been increasing largely because of a fall in rate of population growth. Share of cereals in household food consumption is declining across all expenditure class. For example, the top 20 per cent of population spends about 50 per cent of their income on cereals while this percentage still is about 70 to 80 amongst the bottom 20 per cent. Share of expenditure on items such as milk and milk products and meat, fish and poultry has been increasing considerably. It is expected that while there will be some rise in consumption of cereals as income increases during the next 20 years, the per capita increase in milk and milk products will increase considerably followed by meat and eggs. Projections are that cereal consumption per capita is likely to increase from 458 gram in 1993 to 509 gram in 2020. Milk and milk products will increase from 162 gram to 597 gram in 2020. Consumption of meat and eggs may increase from 16 grams per day to 41 gram per day per capita (Bhalla, 1999).

Calorie Intakes: Nutritional pattern based on NSS consumer expenditure survey data for 1987-88 and 1993-94 suggests that energy intake is low compared to the recommended levels in both rural and urban parts of India. In rural India, the calorie deficits compared with the recommended level of 2400 kcal increased from 10.6 per cent in 1987-88 to 12.5 per cent in 1993-94. In urban India the deficits narrowed down from 10 to 8.4 per cent during the same period. Calorie deficients are found to be far higher amongst the bottom 20 per cent and subsequent 20 per cent of the population both in rural and urban areas. By 1993-94, calorie deficits amongst the bottom 20 per cent increased from 34 to 44 per cent and for the next 20 per cent from 20 to 31 per cent in rural India. In urban areas respective deficients increased only marginally.

Protein: In case of protein, deficits amongst the bottom 20 per cent increased from 25 to 37 per cent during this period, but protein supply increased from 42 to 62 per cent amongst the top 20 per cent in rural areas. Over all deficits remain low only at about 2 per cent level. But protein deficits are in Urban India (at 10 per cent less than the recommended level). The protein deficits were found to have increased to 30 per cent for the bottom 20 per cent in urban areas.

Fat : Overall deficits in fat consumption continue to be very high at 16 per cent in rural areas. In urban parts the deficit is marginal at 3 per cent of the recommended level. In both rural and urban fat consumption remained low among all population groups excepting the top 20 per cent. The bottom 20 percent had a deficit of 26 per cent in rural and 22 per cent in urban areas. The top 20 per cent however, enjoyed an excess of 20 per cent in rural and 22 per cent in urban India.

Iron: Iron deficiencies were 3.6 per cent in rural and 14.3 per cent in urban India. The bottom 20 per cent of the population has recorded a very high level of iron deficiency at levels 27.9 per cent in rural and 34 per cent in urban areas. Only the top 20 per cent enjoyed an excess of 27 per cent and 5 per cent respectively in rural and urban parts.

Coping Strategies

Coping strategies to mitigate food risks are large and complex. These differ substantially between rural and urban areas and within rural areas among ago-climatic regions and between different population groups. Strategies may be as simple as borrowing grains from kins and neighbours, or withdrawing children from schools and make them work long hours. Others in the household may work long hours in the hope of increasing income, but this possibility is low as the demand for labour in the local areas would have disappeared. Since food shortages mean low or no cash reserves, there certainly will be denial of health and medical care which will affect women and children more than the others. Families who own properties may resort to liquidating assets. Often it is seen that households sell their highly valued livestock to ward off temporary shocks. Large-scale indebtedness and sale or mortgaging of agricultural lands, property, permanent migration in search of employment are extreme responses to such crises.

Food and Nutrition Programmes

In 1970, a number of targeted programmes aiming to improve food output were initiated. These were, the small farmers development agency, the marginal farmers and agricultural laborers agency and the drought prone area programme (DPAP). An evaluation, a decade later suggested that these programmes did not succeed because of leakages, implementation and management problems (Paul, 1983). Subsequently during the early 1980s, programs such as Integrated Rural Development Project, the Employment Guarantee Scheme and Old Age Pension were launched so as to improve the purchasing power of the poor. These programmes did have some impact it was not sufficient to reduce the number and extent of malnutrition among the poor. A number of employment-oriented programmes have been recently restructured.

To reduce malnutrition among the rural poor the Government of India launched *Antyodaya Anna Yojana* Scheme in December 2000. It contemplated identification of 10 million poor families and providing them with 25 kg of foodgrains per family per month at a lower price of Rs 2 per kg for wheat and Rs 3 per kg for rice. Another scheme, *Annapoorna Anna Yojana* was also launched in 2000-01. In this scheme, 10 kg of foodgrains are given free per month to those who though eligible for old age pensions remained uncovered under National Old Age Pension Schemes (NAOPS). In the Union Budget 2001-02, the scheme has been modified to extend the coverage to those persons who are covered under NAPOS (approximately 69 lakh), besides those initially targeted to be covered under 'Annapurna' (14 lakh).

Public Distribution System (PDS), was initiated after independence largely to distribute the PL 480 aid. It is considered relatively more effective. Cereals are distributed at subsidized prices under PDS. This is considered an income transfer strategy for the poor. Under the first five-year plan, the PDS was extended to those rural areas where food grains deficit was most prominent. These were defined as 'statutory rationing areas'. Supply from the ration shop or Fair Price

Shop (FPS) was obligatory. Other areas were to be covered by non-statutory rationing. Its scope was widened to include both urban and rural areas. As early as in 1957, a Food Grains Enquiry Committee recommended the creation of 'buffer stock' and control over cereal trade and 'progressive socialization of trade in food grains'. In view of the statutory prices, national trading in food grains was attempted by fixing prices in 1959. At this stage other essential commodities such as sugar was also included in the PDS.

In 1965, two important organisations, viz; Agricultural Prices Commission now called Commission for Agricultural Costs and Prices (CACP) and the Food Corporation of India (FCI) were set up. Procurement prices offered by the FCI are fixed by CACP are generally lower compared to open market, FCI was made to implement Government's policy on procurement, storage, transportation, distribution of food-grains and other commodities through Fair Price Shops (FPS). CACP is an institution that is to give advice on support and procurement prices.

Integrated Child Development Services (ICDS)

National Policy for children 1974, acknowledged that majority of India's children live in impending conditions like poverty, poor environmental sanitation, disease/infections, inadequate access to primary health care, inappropriate child caring and feeding. Special interventions were therefore required to provide equality of opportunity to these children. Founded on this conviction, the ICDS program was launched on 2nd October 1975, in 33 blocks. Today, ICDS represents one of the world's largest and most unique programs for early childhood development.

Currently, ICDS has many a meaning for the community-homely child care center, a play/learning center, a peripheral health center, a meeting place for women/mothers, a source of support during calamity, a means to fulfil aspirations for millions of young children. All the ICDS services are provided through an *anganwadi* (child care centre) that is used to house all the children collected on a daily basis so as to provide all the listed inputs that includes daily nutrition supplement, some teaching and schedule of immunization services. Each 'anganwadi' is run by an anganwadi worker (AWW) who is always a woman and supported by an 'anganwadi' helper in service delivery, and improved linkages with the health system on the one hand and community especially women (mother-for childcare). A number of services provisioning activities through the ICDS seem to be better than those that are provided through public health infrastructure.

Though ICDS facilities have been extend to all the districts in the country, yet there are large areas left uncovered. A basic lacuna in the scheme is poor coverage of children under three years. Since these children are too young to be taken care of at the anganwadi, they must be either brought to the center especially for feedings, or their rations must be taken home. This scheme has also sidestepped the issue of inequality within the families.

There has not yet been a comprehensive national level evaluation of the ICDS. However, a few studies seem to highlight the fact that the nutritional levels of children in the ICDS areas have been marginally better than the non-ICDS areas. Strategies to augment just the levels of income levels are not adequate to eliminate undernutrition. Employment generation, as an empowering strategy, needs to be strengthened. Any amount of safety net will be inadequate due to resource constraint. State policies and programs relating to nutrition and health are too weak to make the desired impact.

Sustainability of our agriculture is as crucial issue today. Increase in production in the future will come not from area expansion, but from enhanced productivity through improved and sustainable agricultural practices. Innovative packages are needed which harness our traditional skills and strengthens to novel cropping systems, precision farming methods and advances in frontier of sciences and technologies. In view of the fact that large areas of the country are becoming prone to soil degradation, community-based programmes for conservation and enhancement of land-water resources combined with sustainable system of use, need to be developed through micro-planning.

The realities of the agriculture scenario today underscore the importance of diversification. Horticulture has proved to be an ideal alternative to agriculture. Not only does it improve the productivity of land in terms of biomass production and returns per unit area, but it also provides increased employment opportunities. Apart from these, new avenues for gainful employment are the production of eco-foods, bio-fertilisers, bio-pesticides, bio-processing, health foods, herbal medicines etc.

Livestock and fisheries sectors provide yet another set of avenues for supplementing farmer's incomes and generating gainful employment in the rural sector. India has already become the world's largest milk-producing country – now the sixth largest producer of fish in the world and second largest producer of freshwater fish after China. The availability of animal protein in Indian diet needs to be increased at least two-fold from the present level of ten gram with special emphasis on maintaining the nutritional levels of growing children and nursing mothers.

It is disturbing that about 10 per cent of foodgrains, 30-40 per cent of the horticultural produce, and around 10–12 per cent of livestock and fisheries produce of the country get spoiled or damaged for want of adequate post-harvest and processing facilities. We can ill afford such huge losses. The processing levels of agricultural produce in the country are extremely low, even in comparison with other developing countries.

High cost of managing our food stocks is a major problem in the way of reaching cheaper good to a greater number of needy families. There is an urgent need to ensure that the subsidy is better targeted. One way to reduce costs is to decentralise the buying and distribution of food.

Implementation of the PDS is not living up to the expectations. Limited off-take in the States where the majority of our poor live, points to serious deficiencies in the administrative capability of the system. Even though the penetration of PDS (access to PDS) is very high in rural India (92 per cent), the actual use of PDS seems to be as low as 35 per cent (NCAER/HDI survey 1994).

Even the implementation of free food provided to schoolchildren under the mid-day meal scheme leaves much to be desired. Our Panchayati Raj institutions and other citizen's organisations have to play an active role in making these laudable schemes successful.

NOTE

* Transcribed version of a recorded lecture

REFERENCES

Andersen, Per Pinsturp, and Pandya-Lorch Rajul, (eds.), 1999, *World Food Prospects: Critical Issues For The Early Twenty-First Century.* International Food Policy Research Institute, Washington, DC.

Bhalla, G.S, Peter Hazell and John Kerr, 1999, *Prospects for India's Cereal Supply and Demand to 2020*, Food, Agriculture, and the Environment Discussion Paper 29, International Food Policy Research Institute, Washington DC.

Dreze, Jean and Amartiya Sen, 1995, *The Political Economy of Hunger*, Selected Essays, Clarendon Press, Oxford.

Government of India, 1988, *Sample Registration Bulletin*, New Delhi.

Khullar, Vandana, 1998, 'Integrated Child Development Services- A Critiques of Evaluation Techniques,' *Economic and Political Weekly*, Vol. 33, 7 March.

Measham, Anthony R and Meera Chattejee, 1999, *Wasting Away: The crisis of Malnutrition in India*, The World Bank, Washington DC.

Mooij, Jos, 1999, 'Dilemmas in Food Policy: About Institutional Contradiction and Vested Interests,' *Economic and Political Weekly*, 34(52) pp. A-114 – A-120.

Payne, Philip and Michael Lipton, 1994, *How Third World Rural Households Adapt to Dietary Energy Stress: The evidence and the issues*, International Food Policy Research Institute, Washington DC.

Planning Commission (GOI), 2001, 'Towards Hunger Free India,' M. S. Swaminathan Research Foundation & UN World Food Programme, 2001.

Sen, Amartya, 1997, 'The Lasting Damage of Early Malnutrition,' in *Ending the Inheritance of Hunger,* Lectures given by Robert William Fogel, Navin S. Scrimshaw and Amartya Sen, WFP/ UNU Seminar, Rome, 31 May.

Scrimshaw, Navin S., 1997 'The Lasting Damage of Early Malnutrition,' in *Ending the Inheritance of Hunger,* Lectures given by Robert William Fogel, Navin S. Scrimshaw and Amartya Sen, WFP/UNU Seminar, Rome, 31 May.

Seshadri, Subadra, 1998, A Data Base on Iron Deficiency Anemia (IDA) in India; Prevalence, Causes, Consequences and Strategies for Prevention. Vadodara: The Maharaja Sayajirao University of Baroda.

Shariff, Abusaleh, 1993, 'Factors Affecting Child Health: Search for Maternal Education Effects in Rural Gujarat,' Working Paper No. 47, Gujarat Institute of Development Research, Gota, Ahmedabad.

Shariff, Abusaleh and Ananatha C. Mallick, 1999, 'Dynamics of Food Intake and Nutrition by Expenditure Class in India,' *Economic and Political Weekly,* 34.

Vyas, V.S and Pradeep Bhargava, 1999, *Poverty reduction in Developing Countries – Experience from Asia and Africa,* Rawat Publications, Jaipur.

World Food Programme, 2001, 'Enabling Development - Food Assistance in South Asia,' Oxford University Press.

Chapter 9

Poverty Alleviation Programmes in India

Some Issues and Concerns[1]

Ananya Ghosh Dastidar

Since Independence government has undertaken numerous policies to eradicate poverty, yet poverty persists. Latest estimates indicate as much as 26.1 per cent of the total population still below the officially defined poverty line (Planning Commission). As such, there is a need to review the role of the government in addressing the issue of poverty alleviation and ask what went wrong. In this paper we focus on a particular aspect of the government's poverty alleviation strategy – we analyse the working of the specially designed Poverty Alleviation Programmes (PAPs), which were meant to launch a 'direct attack' on poverty. We review the performance of these programmes over the eighties and the nineties and in the light of this discussion evaluate the main changes in the design of these programmes undertaken under the Ninth and Tenth Plans. First, we outline the important features of some of the main components of the PAPs (in the form they existed before 1999) (Section I). Next, we review the existing body of literature that focuses on the functioning of the PAPs in order to identify what are perceived as their main strengths and weaknesses (Section II). We take up the Wage Employment Programmes first, followed by the Self-Employment Programmes. Next we discuss certain problems, endemic to the overall economic and social environment, that affect the implementation of the PAPs (both self-employment and wage-employment programmes) at the village level. Thereafter we review the main changes in the programmes put in place since 1999, with a view to identifying whether such changes are geared to address some of the main weaknesses inherent in programme design and implementation (Section III). In this section we also evaluate the changes envisaged under the Tenth Plan. Finally, we outline the main recommendations that emerge from the literature for improving the effectiveness of the PAPs, and point out a few lacunae in the existing body of writing that evaluates the government's role in alleviating poverty in the Indian context (Section IV).

I

A Brief Overview of the Poverty Alleviation Programmes

Poverty eradication policies of the government have two broad aspects. On the one hand, there is an emphasis on fostering economic growth; on the other, there are the PAPs which are meant to launch a 'direct attack' on poverty. Dynamic process of economic growth creates new employment opportunities and enables people to enhance their incomes and overall standards of living. As more and more people are integrated within the overall growth process, benefits of a fast growing economy spread and with time, 'trickle down' to even the lowest economic strata. However, the *eradication* of poverty via trickle down is a slow process. Hence specific PAPs supplement policies that promote growth. In particular PAPs are designed to achieve broadly two sets of targets. First, they attempt to guarantee the poorest classes a certain minimum standard of living when they lack other viable means of sustenance. Second, these are geared to relax certain basic constraints (such as poor infrastructure, limited or no access to credit) facing the poor in the rural areas. This helps to create certain basic capabilities among the poorest classes and enables them to better their economic prospects in the long run.

In this paper we mainly focus on three Programmes which address specifically the problem of rural poverty, viz., Jawahar Rozgar Yojana (JRY), Employment Assurance Scheme (EAS)[2] and Integrated Rural Development Programme (IRDP) and its Allied Programmes[3]. Target population for all three consists of the rural poor whose incomes lie below officially defined Poverty Line. JRY and the EAS are *wage-employment* programmes. Primary objective of these programmes is to create employment opportunities for the rural poor, particularly during lean season. IRDP (and allied programmes) are essentially *self-employment* programmes. Their main objective is to facilitate asset creation (either physical assets, or intrinsic assets such as skill, via training programmes) which would yield a stream of returns and enable the rural poor to improve their economic condition. We discuss the main features of each of these programmes in greater detail below, starting with the wage-employment programmes.

Wage-employment Programmes: JRY was introduced in 1989 by merging two existing wage-employment programmes, National Rural Employment Programme (NREP) and Rural Landless Employment Guarantee Programme (RLEGP). EAS was introduced later in 1993. It is designed after Employment Guarantee Scheme (EGS), a successful wage-employment programme in Maharashtra. Aim of this programme is to guarantee about 100 days of employment during the lean agricultural season to all those (between 18 and 60 years of age) looking for work. Both JRY and EAS are sponsored by the Central Government.

JRY funds were allocated to the States proportionally, on the basis of the share of the rural population below the poverty line in each State. Within each State funds were allocated to various districts based on a backwardness index which takes into account the shares of population below the poverty line, of people belonging to the Scheduled Castes and/or Tribe (SC/ST) and agricultural performance of the area.[4] In this respect the main difference between JRY and EAS is that fund allocation for the latter was demand driven. No fixed allocations were made at the district level in case of EAS. Rather only notional allocations worked out at the beginning of the year and EAS funds were released only after a specific request was made, accompanied by a list of the unemployed and details of the project to be undertaken. Additional funds were made available based on the demand for supplementary employment and the actual utilisation of allocated funds. Regarding the administration of allocated funds, this decision rested almost entirely with the Gram Panchayats in case of JRY (70 per cent of JRY funds were disbursed via the village Panchayats). For EAS, funds were administered at the district level while muster rolls (containing details of the unemployed) were prepared by the Panchayats.

Primary objective of the wage-employment programmes was to create employment opportunities for the poor in rural areas, especially during the agricultural lean season.[5] This was expected to provide the landless poor an alternate employment opportunity and thereby prevents overcrowding in rural labour markets (this in turn was envisaged to arrest the downward pressure on the wage rate and to some extent checks migration to the urban areas). A *secondary* objective was to create rural infrastructure in the process of employment generation (this was supposed to alleviate binding constraints on productivity growth in medium and long run and thereby to facilitate agricultural growth and rural development).

An important feature of wage-employment programmes like JRY and EAS was their 'self-targeting' nature. The work requirement associated with these was supposed to function as a screening device. It was expected that only the poorest, who do not have any other opportunities open to them, would participate in these programmes, as payment of wages is contingent on fulfilling the work requirement. A demand for unskilled labour could be created via these programmes as skill accumulation tended to be low among the poorest classes. It was stipulated that all projects undertaken under these schemes would use labour and capital in the ratio 60 : 40 (i.e. the ratio between wage and non-wage cost of projects).[6] This was to ensure that these projects had a high labour content and hence high employment potential.

Benefits accruing to the poor from these programs were classified into Transfer (direct and indirect) and Stabilisation benefits (Gaiha, 1997a). *Direct transfer benefits* relate to the short run income gains to the poor from being employed, whereas *indirect benefits* relate to the benefits accruing to the village community in terms of the infrastructure and/or other community development projects undertaken as part of the programmes. As for *stabilisation benefits*, the wage incomes earned through JRY or EAS provided a stream of income during the lean season and thereby prevented the distress selling of assets by the rural poor. In this sense these schemes had a stabilising effect on the income streams of the poorest classes. Several attempts have been made in the literature to quantify these benefits and evaluate the performance of the employment programmes in the light of the findings of this exercise (Gaiha, 1997c, 1998b). World Bank (1998) summarises the findings of *benefit incidence analysis* of the PAPs carried out by several researchers in the Indian context. Such analysis measures how government subsidies on the PAPs are distributed across the poor and the non-poor groups in society. Two broad factors that determine the distribution have been studied, the size and allocation of government spending and the behaviour of beneficiary households. Benefit incidence analysis therefore brings together two sources of information: data on government subsidy (estimated as the unit cost of running the program less cost recovery, if any) and information, usually obtained from household surveys on the usefulness of the programs to the beneficiary-households or individuals. The evidence from these studies shows that wage employment programmes were by far the most effective in reaching the poor, while the self-employment programmes ranked second with a relatively higher proportion of non-poor beneficiaries (World Bank, ibid). Public distribution system fared the worst according to this analysis in terms of both the money spent on the programme and the its targeting of the poorest classes.

Self-Employment Programs: IRDP has been in place since 1980. This is the most important self-employment programme run by the Government of India (GOI). The main objective of the

IRDP was to provide access to subsidised credit for the rural poor. Typically the poor in rural areas are excluded from the credit market as they lack assets which could be used as collateral against the borrowed funds. This exclusion perpetuates a vicious circle [see, for instance, Banerjee and Newman (1993) for a theoretical exposition of this issue]. Lacking collateral, the poor do not have access to credit. Thus they cannot invest in human or physical capital which would enable them to break out of poverty. As a result, they remain poor and are unable to acquire assets that might act as collateral and are thus shut out of the formal credit market. IRDP tried to make a difference precisely in such situations by providing subsidised credit to those below the poverty line, so as to enable them to acquire some form of income-earning asset. It was expected that this investment would enable poor to both repay the loan and improve their economic status in the long run. Activities eligible for financing under IRDP ranged from traditional land-based enterprises to non-traditional projects such as pisciculture, sericulture, floriculture, etc.

Recently there has been a change of focus within the IRDP. From lending to poor individuals the emphasis has shifted to *groups* of poor individuals. Collective borrowing could lead to economies of scale as far as loan utilisation is concerned. Further, within-group pressures may reduce the likelihood of default on loan repayment. Another new feature involves the backending of subsidy. This measure was aimed at reducing corruption and improving the targeting of the loans. Further, fund allocation for the development of programme infrastructure has been increased with a view to improving its effectiveness. A number of Allied Programmes with similar objectives were 'implemented' as sub-plans of the IRDP, [7] viz., Training of Rural Youth for Self-Employment (TRYSEM), Supply of Improved Toolkits to Rural Artisans (SITRA) and the Development of Women and Children in Rural Areas (DWCRA). TRYSEM and SITRA attempted to create certain basic capabilities among the poor. First, by providing training opportunities, and facilitates for human capital formation;

second, by providing improved tools to small artisans, facilitates access to physical capital. DWCRA is specially targeted to meet the needs of women in poor rural households. By providing training, credit and other support services to *groups* of women, this programme triend to enable them to take up income generating activities jointly. It was envisaged that economic empowerment of women through this scheme would serve to improve their social standing to a large extent. Support programs aimed at improving childcare, health care and family welfare supplemented this scheme.

II

An Evaluation of the Performance of Poverty Alleviation Programmes

A great deal has been written on the performance of the PAPs in India. Critical analyses focus on the design of the PAPs and on problems that arise at the implementation stage. Broadly speaking, two types of approaches can be identified. First, Benefit Incidence Analysis. Using data on government expenditures and on large-scale household surveys, these studies attempt to gauge the effectiveness of the PAPs in targeting the intended beneficiaries, viz., poor households. Second, detailed 'village studies' which focus closely on a sample of households from a particular village or a small group of villages. These studies provide information, which cannot always be easily distilled from larger-scale household surveys. Using benefit incidence methodology a World Bank study (World Bank, 1998) shows that the poorest quintile (in terms of the distribution of per capita consumption expenditure) is best served by wage employment programmes like the JRY and EAS. Credit programme (IRDP) comes in second place, while subsidised food-supply program (PDS) does least well in reaching the poor. Another important finding of this study is that non-negligible shares of program beneficiaries are 'non-poor', both in case of IRDP and wage employment programs.

In what follows we focus on the literature that evaluates the performance of PAPs in India (either on the basis of village studies or using large-scale household survey data). Basically we attempt to identify some of the main issues raised by various studies regarding the functioning of programmes like JRY, EAS, IRDP, DWCRA, TRYSEM, etc. In particular, we discuss three sets of issues-*design* of anti-poverty programmes, *implementation* and *systemic failures* that come in the way of effective implementation of PAPs.

Wage-Employment Programs

Design Issues: Most analysts view JRY and EAS as effective ways of dealing with the problem of poverty alleviation. In particular, the self-targeting nature of these programmes is considered one of their major plus points. Further wage offered under these programs help to make the employer-labourer relation more market-based. In this context Gaiha (1997a) outlines some specific mechanisms through which wage employment schemes like the EGS may influence agricultural wages. Employment projects undertaken through these programs directly affect the demand for labour. Another mechanism operates through effects the projects have on agricultural productivity and via that on the agricultural demand for labour. In addition, the infrastructure created through these programmes can potentially raise agricultural productivity, enhance farm output and incomes and indirectly contribute to enhanced demand for rural labour. Second, to the extent that the employment programmes contribute to a greater awareness of the potential for collective action among rural workers, the oligopsonistic power of large landholders in wage bargaining is likely to be weakened. This puts further upward pressure on agricultural wages. Additional employment opportunities created during the agricultural lean season via these programmes, prevent the market wage rate from falling below a certain minimum level and help to reduce migration to the urban areas.

Parthasarathy (1995) points out that employment programmes led to upward pressures on minimum wages in rural Andhra Pradesh; while Sharma (1995) cites evidence from Bihar to show that the JRY influenced the rural labour market and led to upward pressures on the agricultural wage rate. In effect, by providing alternative employment opportunities, these programs led to a uniform wage rate rather than a segmented labour market in a single locality, as suggested by the experience of West Bengal (Dasgupta, 1995). An evaluation of the Employment Guarantee Scheme (EGS) in Maharashtra by Gaiha (1997a) reveals that both EGS and non-farm wages together influence agricultural wages. In particular the short-term effect of EGS on agricultural wages is small, while the long-term effect is relatively large.[8] In this context it has been argued that the EGS has played a signal role in preventing effective demand failures during drought in Maharashtra. Further, a study on four drought-affected districts in Rajasthan actually finds that due to employment created through the wage employment programs, consumption of foodgrains by households was actually *higher* in drought years compared to a normal year (GOI, 2003).

Regarding the choice of projects taken up under the wage-employment programmes, it is argued that these should be chosen not only for their employment potential but also with a view to improving agricultural productivity, or more generally the overall quality of life at the village level. That is, the strategies for poverty alleviation should be closely inter-linked with the strategies for agrarian development or more broadly rural development[9] (Rao, 1992). A number of analysts cite the example of Punjab in this context to underscore the importance of economic growth, in particular agricultural growth, for poverty alleviation (Desai, 1995; Shergill et al., 1995). An empirical study by Shergill et al. (1995) traces a declining trend in rural poverty in Punjab over the entire period 1960-61 to 1990-91. The authors find that the proportion and absolute number of poor fell at a steady rate both during the initial and mature phase of the green revolution technology. As such they assign an important role to agricultural growth in alleviating rural poverty.

Importance of agricultural development in poverty alleviation is further stressed in Bhalla (1995). A case study of Haryana reveals that the role of PAPs is at best 'marginal' in this state which has witnessed impressive agricultural growth and implemented a deliberate policy of income and occupational diversification. PAPs in Haryana were carried out, it seemed only because funds were allocated for these schemes. These programmes mainly generated demand for unskilled workers for which there did not seem to be too many takers in the prosperous state, particularly since the market wage is higher in many cases than the programme wages offered. Rather than the Central Government run PAPs, it is better if State government run programmes for building rural infrastructure, old-age pension schemes, educational subsidies for SC/ST students have proved more popular in Haryana (Bhalla, ibid).

In actual practice, however, poverty alleviation and agricultural development are viewed as very different issues. A case study of the performance of the PAPs in Karnataka reveals, for instance, that there was no coordination between irrigation and other rural development activities, which led to the misuse and even wastage of valuable resources (Vyasulu, 1995). Vohra (1996) also stresses this point. According to Vohra, the most important reason for rural poverty is the sub-optimal use of our natural resources of land and water. As such he advocates that programmes like the JRY and EAS be merged into one scheme for 'soil and water conservation' and be run by a single department. This will also save wasteful expenditure currently incurred in the absence of inter-departmental coordination. In general, adopting policies that acknowledge the close inter-linkages between overall agrarian development and poverty alleviation enables more efficient resource use.

Implementation Issues: One of the most serious problems of implementation of the PAPs involves effective targeting, i.e. making sure the benefits from these programmes reach only the target population (the population below the poverty line). At the very outset there is the problem of correctly identifying who are the poor. In practice, those qualify whose incomes are less than the officially defined poverty line. However, verifying information about levels of income can be quite difficult. Non-poor may misreport income in order to qualify for the benefits, especially for the credit scheme. In view of this many suggest the use of a composite index that incorporates easily verifiable family characteristics (such as e.g. ownership of consumer durables, highest literacy standard of the head of the family and so on) for identification (Dev et al. 1998; Suryanarayana, 1996).

A number of studies report widespread mis-targeting (see for instance, Gaiha et al., 1999; Dev, 1995) where the benefits meant for the poor fail to reach them altogether. This is a serious problem even in Kerala which is a highly developed state, as studies report widespread inclusion of ineligible beneficiaries in the anti-poverty programmes in the state (Kannan, 1995). In particular, two aspects of mis-targeting have been estimated empirically. One refers to E-errors, which measure the proportion of non-poor among the total number participating in the program. Second, F-errors, measure the proportion of poor population in the program area excluded benefits. Sum of the E- and F- errors give an aggregate measure of accuracy of targeting of the programmes. Greater the value of (E+F) the lower is the overall accuracy. Studies by Gaiha et al. (1999) and Gaiha (2000) reveal substantial E- and F-errors in case of both the wage employment programs and the IRDP. In particular, the magnitude of F-errors tends to be substantially greater (than E-errors) in both cases, which suggests that the PAPs are not being able to address the problems of the poor effectively; as such this is a matter of great concern. In case of the wage employment programmes, one channel via mistargeting tends to occur as the level of wages offered under the JRY or EAS. If these wages are higher than the prevailing market wage rate in the village, there is an incentive for the non-poor to participate in the programme.

Other problems encountered at the implementation stage relate to corruption and excessive administrative controls (Rao, 1993; Dev, 1995). Bureaucratic procedures delay the disbursement of funds and at a lower level this translates into delays in the payment of wages to those employed. In particular, when part of the wages are payable in kind (in terms of food), delay in wage payment creates immense difficulties for the programme beneficiaries (Iyer, 1994). It also acts as a disincentive for the poor to participate in these programs. In fact in a concurrent evaluation of the JRY, *less than half the workers* surveyed wanted part of their wages in terms of foodgrains (Neelakantan, 1994).[10] Corruption among officials and others responsible for the disbursement of the loans leads to misdirection of funds and results in reduced cost-effectiveness of the PAPs. It also leads to poor quality of asset creation via the programmes. It was also found that line departments played a very limited role in asset maintenance. Thus corruption together with the lack of maintenance often lead to the creation of assets that are of little long-lasting value. On a more positive note results from a concurrent evaluation of the JRY reveal that in the poverty-stricken states (Bihar, Orissa, MP, Rajasthan and West Bengal), in 98 per cent to 100 per cent of the cases JRY assets were considered very useful (Neelakantan, 1994). In this context there is a case for focusing on more effective implementation of the existing PAPs, rather than increasing allocations each year. For instance, leakages occurring through the panchayats can be checked by regular audit of accounts (Dev, ibid).

Finally, it is often pointed out that the PAPs are far too target, oriented and mechanically implemented, in the sense that officials responsible are mainly concerned with meeting statistical targets rather than with the *quality* of program administration (Mathur, 1995). Lack of motivation at the implementation stage, no doubt, goes a long way in explaining the poor performance of the wage employment programs.

Self-Employment Programs

Design Issues: Regarding the design of the IRDP, the main concern mirrored in the literature is that it does not pay sufficient attention to the existence of linkage effects. Existence of backward and forward linkages is extremely important for efficient loan utilisation and ultimately for loan recovery. For self-employment to be economically viable it is important to ensure that the credit can be effectively utilised. For this there must be marketing channels open to entrepreneurs, cold-storage facilities in case of perishable products, easily accessible sources of raw materials and so on. In most cases loans are forwarded without sufficient attention to these aspects; as a result, the poor are unable to use the loans productively. In effect there is little post-disbursement support (or after-care) provided via IRDP and there is virtually no post-disbursement monitoring of activities of the loan-recipient. Almost all the studies stress this point (see, for example, Sharma, 1995; Parthasarathy, 1995; Mathur, 1995).

On a positive note, village studies found that IRDP loans were virtually the only form of formal credit locally available to poor (World Bank, 1998). This shows that programme can potentially play an important role by filling in a lacuna in the market for rural credit. It can reduce the dependence of rural poor on village moneylenders. However village studies also reveal that few loan recipients actually acquired and retained any productive assets. A high percentage of the loans underwrote consumption in the case of marriages, sickness and other unproductive expenditure. Overall, access to IRDP loans has actually led to greater indebtedness in many cases rather than sustained income generation (World Bank, ibid).

It has been argued that in general the poorest groups lack exposure to the market and as such it is wrong to thrust an 'entrepreneurial market model' upon them (Sagar, 1995). In fact World Bank (1998) study bears out that without forging backward (e.g. input supply) and forward (e.g. marketing) linkages and without post-disbursement support programs such a move may well prove counterproductive. It might be better to raise exposure to market gradually and provide some training before thrusting self-employment programs involving an element of risk-taking, on the target population. Experience with the DWCRA in Gujarat brings out this point clearly (Hirway, 1995). Case studies from Gujarat revealed that poor women were incapable of bearing entrepreneurial risks, rather fixed wage porgrams were more suited to their conditions. Hirway puts this down partly to weak project design – programmes are not tailored to meet specific micro-level needs of the women. In this context voluntary agencies (such as SEWA in UP) have an important role in making the programmes more effective by providing necessary support services to the women's groups and acting as a feedback channel for the program administrators. However evidence from Andhra Pradesh where the DWCRA is relatively successful, suggests that with continuous training and the right kind of support programs poor women's groups can make successful entrepreneurs. Government of Andhra Pradesh (1998) cites a number of instances of successful women entrepreneurs who have benefited tremendously from the DWCRA and also the SITRA schemes.

Implementation Issues: In case of the IRDP, reports of corruption and pay-offs to middlemen are pervasive (World Bank, 1998). Very often middlemen 'captured' the subsidy component of the loans, thus increasing the cost of such operations both for the borrower and for the government. Another common finding regarding the performance of the IRDP is that a significantly large number of the program beneficiaries tend to be non-poor (see, for example, Vyasulu, 1995; Kannan, 1995; Hirway, 1995). In terms of the E- and F-errors (defined above), Gaiha (1999) finds that the E-errors are greater for IRDP than the wage employment programs, implying that the inclusion of the non-poor is greater in case of the IRDP. Also the combined index (E + F) is greater for IRDP, implying less accurate targeting of the self-employment component than the wage employment component of the PAPs. Some authors argue that in fact, the poorest are deliberately kept out of the programme as they lack motivation and capacity to make use of self-employment opportunities (Rao, 1998).

In general, reports from case studies reveal that in most cases *almost no* IRDP beneficiary satisfied the eligibility criteria. Their participation in the programme came about primarily through political interference and connivance with corrupt bank officials. However, some studies reveal that greater decentralisation can help in bringing about some improvement in the situation. In case of West Bengal, it seems that initially distrust and ignorance of the panchayats regarding the role of banks kept the IRDP from being much of a success in the State (Dasgupta, 1995). But greater involvement of Panchayats made a difference in terms of the greater number of program beneficiaries able to cross the poverty line.[11] Further, involvement of the Panchayats also made for more efficient identification of schemes under the JRY in West Bengal. This points to a greater need for local level planning and inputs for more effective functioning of the IRDP.

In view of the above discussion, the need for local level planning, in designing the projects undertaken via the IRDP, must be emphasised.[12] Lack of such planning can give rise to problems of mismatch between (a) assets created under the programs and the demand for them; (b) demand for assets generated by the programs (i.e. input-demand, in some sense) and their supply; and (c) type of assets created and the pre-existing resources of the beneficiary household. Even where beneficiary-targeting is relatively better, as for instance in West Bengal in case of the IRDP, the mismatch problem means that poverty persists (Mathur, 1995). One way to take care of this problem is to go in for greater decentralisation. This has been done in case of the JRY but the IRDP continues to be a 'top down' programme. What is needed is a greater local level input in the choice of self-employment schemes in case of the IRDP.

From 1999 onwards, the government redesigned several aspects of its PAPs. In particular there are welcome changes in the IRDP. For one, there is a shift in emphasis from lending to individuals to collective lending. This will lead to economies of scale in loan utilisation. Till recently, the amount of loan at the level of the individual was often sub-critical, in the sense, the level of investment is too low for any self-employment project to be economically viable. Also greater attention is now being paid to selection of self-employment schemes. Ideally these schemes should be chosen with greater consideration for the endowments and capabilities of the target population. Lakshmi et al. (1998) clearly brings out this point. The study examines the characteristics of loan-defaulters in the related context of users of agricultural credit and underscores the need to increasingly link the flow of credit to individual-specific requirements in order to reduce chances of default.

Summing Up: An important point to bear in mind is that ultimately PAPs are *short-term*, temporary measures for dealing with the *long-term* problem of poverty. Thus they should be designed to create conditions so they can ultimately be phased out. Choice of projects undertaken under the PAPs should therefore be influenced by this consideration. In reality the poor, typically, are unwilling (and often unable) to bear the risks associated with self-employment and tend to be economically dependent on the wage-employment programmes. As such political pressures build up to keep these programmes going. It is also important to realise that the PAPs are still not an integral part of our overall rural and agricultural development strategy (say, as the Green Revolution was).[13] As such the momentum for formulating an effective implementation strategy is absent. In this context there is a strong case for decentralisation to allow for better planning and programme administration. Village politics can create pressures for Panchayats to function to some extent, in contrast to the bureaucracy who are not answerable to the people (Sharma, 1995). For instance, the experience of West Bengal shows that greater involvement of the Panchayats in implementing the PAPs can have very positive effects (Dasgupta, 1995). In a welcome move, the government pays greater attention to more effective empowerment of the Panchayati Raj Institutions in the Ninth and Tenth Plans. These are discussed in greater detail here.

Systemic Failures affecting Poverty Alleviation Programmes

There are certain institutional factors that come in the way of effective implementation of the PAPs. We focus on these in the following discussion.

The most important issue relates to the functioning of Gram Panchayats, the elected institution at the village level responsible for the administration of JRY-funds. Seventy-third

Constitutional Amendment Act devolves greater powers to the Gram Panchayats. Further, under the Ninth Plan greater responsibilities were passed on to the Panchayats regarding the administration of funds under the PAPs. In view of this, steps should be taken to make Panchayats truly accountable to the people. One way of doing this is by vesting greater powers to the Gram Sabha, a body consisting of village residents. On paper the Gram Sabha is supposed to hold regular meetings and discuss the working of the Panchayat. But in practice such meetings are held only at irregular intervals and even where they are held, proceedings are dominated by those in power while the voices of the poor are rarely heard (Gaiha et al., 1998b; Srivastava, 1998).

Case studies (for example, Gaiha et al., 1998b) reveal that these institutions are typically dominated by a coalition of the village-elite. This may be a caste coalition or a coalition of the economically better off or otherwise powerful people in the village; typically the poor are not a part of the coalition. In case of the JRY funds, it is seen that in the study villages, there is a tendency for funds to be siphoned off and used for the economic betterment of the powerful groups instead of the poor. Further, beneficiaries of programmes like the IRDP are not chosen by using an objective, poverty criterion, rather they are chosen, very often, on the basis of their personal relations with programme officials. For instance, reports from a case study of Bihar reveal that the social structure in the State is one of the biggest handicaps in the way of effective targeting of the PAPs (Sharma, 1995). However the PAPs can contribute by promoting social cohesion among the poor and building pressure among them for the implementation of the PAPs and enforcement of other rights.

A valid point made by several authors (see, for example, Gaiha et al., 1998c; Sharma, 1995) is that ultimately the pressures for effective implementation of the PAPs must come from the poorest classes themselves. In practice, however, a coalition of the poor, which can voice their joint demand, is non-existent. There are several reasons for this (Gaiha, 1998b). For one there are caste hierarchies, which create divisions even among the poor. Also lack of education among the poor causes lack of awareness about the details regarding government programs and about the effectiveness of joint action. Without structural change in rural society the poor cannot share equitably in the gains from development (Roy, 1997). The experience of certain NGOs, such as the Self-Employed Women's Association (SEWA) shows how economic empowerment and greater awareness can overcome other barriers and create greater cohesiveness among the poor groups (Gaiha et al., 1998c). Insofar as economic empowerment serves as a precondition for collective action by the poor, the role of the PAPs assumes yet another dimension.

III

Evaluating Changes in the Design of the PAPs under the Ninth and Tenth Plans

In 1997 the Planning Commission set up a Committee to review the existing PAPs. Following the Committee's recommendations several changes were made in the design of both wage-employment and self-employment programmes. Rural poverty alleviation programmes were revamped and re-focused during the Ninth Plan to increase their effectiveness. In what follows we discuss the changes introduced under the Ninth and Tenth Plans, as we attempt to evaluate whether they address some of the main problem areas related to programme design and implementation identified above.

The Wage-Employment Programs: The JRY was revamped in April 1999 with a major change in program emphasis. Renamed the Jawahar Gram Samridhi Yojana (JGSY), this was now *primarily* a programme for creating rural infrastructure with the objective of employment generation relegated to second place. The specification that the wage labour to material cost be kept at a ratio of 60 : 40 was now relaxed. Payment of wages under the scheme was to be partly in cash and partly in kind: 5 kg. of foodgrains were provided as wages with the balance paid in cash.

Thereafter in September 2001, a single wage-employment program Sampoorna Gramin Rozgar Yojana (SGRY) was launched integrating the three existing programmes: JRY, EAS and FWP (Food For Work Program). This is an attempt to internalise the complementarities inherent in these wage employment programs and to pool the resources available for rural infrastructure creation and employment generation. Under the Tenth Plan the programme emphasis is to be on three main streams. General stream', uniform cross States, is to emphasise the creation of minimum rural infrastructure (e.g. water tanks, anganwadies, primary school buildings, sanitation facilities, primary health centres etc.). Second stream seeks to cater specifically to areas facing chronic unemployment and poverty by providing an employment guarantee of at least 100 days in the year.[14] Third stream of the SGRY is designed to provide temporary employment opportunities in calamity stricken areas.

Certain welcome changes have been introduced in the design of the WEPs. Literature on the subject points out that given the importance of agricultural growth for poverty alleviation (borne out by the experience of Punjab and Haryana for example), the choice of projects under the programmes should be closely linked with strategies for agrarian growth. Changes in the design of the WEPs can be viewed as an effort in this direction. For, rural infrastructure creation rather than employment generation has been made the main thrust of the JGSY and the SGRY. Insofar as the infrastructure created through the programmes cater to the specific needs of the agro-climatic region, there is scope for linking poverty alleviation with agricultural development.

However, problem areas remain. For instance, we have discussed above the problems associated with part payment of wages in kind. Yet there is renewed emphasis on this under the new scheme. Problems related to payment of wages in kind are mainly corruption-related and arise primarily in the implementation stage. In fact, the literature reviewed above clearly indicates that corruption is the single most important problem affecting the implementation of the PAPs. Given this it is somewhat disturbing that there is no attempt on the part of the government to address the issue either directly or indirectly.

Further, a review of the WEPs under the Ninth Plan reveals a worrying trend: there has been *substantial reduction in fund allocation and in employment generation* under the WEPs in the Ninth Plan. Allocation by the Centre and the States under the JRY went down from Rs 18691 crores in the Eighth Plan, to Rs 11,688 crores in the Ninth Plan. In any case coverage of every village panchayat in a country as vast as India means that often funds available for a single panchayat may be as low as less that ten thousand rupees per annum.[15] Reduction in total allocation would further squeeze the amount available at the village level. According to the Tenth Plan document, on an average only about fifteen per cent of the population at the village panchayat level could be employed through JRY schemes, where close to forty per cent of the total population in a panchayat sought work. This points to the need for stepping up employment generation through such wage employment programmes.

A decline in allocation coupled with increasing cost of providing employment meant that as against 513 crore mandays of employment generated under the JRY and EAS in the Eighth Plan, only 286 crore mandays of employment were generated under the JRY/JGSY and EAS in the Ninth Plan.[16] This trend is particularly disturbing given the evidence that wage employment programs are the best targeted among the existing PAPs. Also much has been achieved through these programs in terms of asset creation and employment generation in the rural areas.[17] Further, there is evidence to suggest that JRY wages have often been instrumental in affecting rural wages. According to the Tenth Plan document, reduction in allocation on the JRY/JGSY has been compensated by increased expenditure on other programmes such as Indira Awas Yojana (IAY), rural connectivity, watershed development and so on. However, as yet there has been no study on whether employment generation via these alternate schemes has offset the reduction in employment through the WEPs.

Self-Employment Programmes: Planning Commission Committee constituted in 1997, recommended merger of all self-employment programmes and suggested that there should be a move away from individual beneficiary to group lending. It also emphasised identification of activity clusters in specific areas and setting up of strong training and marketing linkages. As such in April 1999, IRDP and its allied programmes including the Million Wells Scheme (MWS) were merged to create an independent scheme called the Swaranjayanti Gram Swarozgar Yojana (SGSY). For greater effectiveness in programme implementation now the stress was on promoting a network of agencies such as line departments of state governments, banks, NGOs and Panchayati Raj Institutions (PRIs). Further, it was decided that fifty per cent of groups formed would be exclusively by women and that fifty per cent of programme benefits would accrue to members of scheduled castes and tribes, for improved targeting of the weakest sections in society. These are welcome changes in programme design, which are to be carried further under the Tenth Plan. In particular the emphasis on group lending, enhanced role of support groups (such as NGOs, PRIs, etc.), stress on linkage effects (such as training programmes, access to markets for finished products etc.) and on building up programme infrastructure all serve to address what the existing literature has identified as some of the most important problem areas.

However, areas for concern remain. In recent years there has been a sharp drop in the numbers of programme beneficiaries. Under the Eighth Plan programme coverage was 22 lakh beneficiaries per year; this figure dropped to 9.34 lakh in 1999-2000, and was 10.3 lakhs in 2000-01. Moreover, in the Tenth Plan Document the government acknowledges a number of shortcomings relating to programme implementation. For instance, DRDAs responsible for programme administration lacked requisite skills in social mobilisation. Linkages with NGOs, were not in place. Clearly this calls for further improvements in the quality of program administration at the village level.

IV

Conclusion

From the above review what emerges is the need to focus on better targeting of the existing PAPs rather than increasing their outlays or introducing new schemes. Also, in designing the PAPs greater attention should be paid to closer integration of these with overall programmes for agrarian and rural development.

Redesigning of the PAPs, with a view to improving the targeting aspect should be a top priority of the government, where in particular the attempt must be to enhance coverage of the poor population. Also, administrative procedures related to funds disbursal should be simplified and made more transparent. This would reduce delays in disbursals and help create greater awareness among village residents about the working of the programmes. Alongside these measures, the institution of the Gram Sabha should be made functional and the Panchayats made more accountable to them. This will serve to reduce corruption and ensure that funds earmarked for village infrastructure projects are used properly and not siphoned off to serve the interests of those in power. Government also recognises the need to strengthen the PRIs especially the Gram Sabha (GOI, 2003). If the intentions articulated in paper are translated into actual policy measures, this would go a long way in making the PAPs much more effective.

There is need to draw attention, at the same time, to some serious lacunae in the literature that focuses on the design and implementation of PAPs in the Indian context. In particular we focus on two sets of issues. First of these relate to government's stance regarding the role of NGOs in alleviating poverty. It is recognised, time and again, by various authors, that NGOs such as SEWA play an important role in effective implementation of the PAPs (for example, Gaiha et al., 1998c). Yet, there is no attempt in the literature to explore policy implications of this important finding. There is no indication in the existing literature as to how the government should go about framing a 'NGOs-policy' that incorporates what role these agencies could play in making PAPs a success. Indeed there is no sign that the authors even feel that there is need for the government to formulate such a policy. This is rather surprising given the immense importance of this issue. However, changes envisaged in the PAPs, under the Tenth Plan, clearly indicate greater involvement of NGOs. This is an indication that government recognises the importance of the potential role these agencies could play especially at the program implementation stage.

Second issue concerns a serious problem related to the design of the PAPs in general. It is widely recognised by almost every author that one of the most serious problems faced at the implementation stage is that of widespread mis-targeting (both in case of wage- and self-employment programmes), which in turn stems largely from rampant corruption encountered at each level. Yet the following questions are not clearly raised in the existing literature: 'What incentive do program officials have, to implement the programs effectively?' Is there a proper system of accountability built into the program-administration system itself, which attempts to take care of the problem of corruption?' These are very important questions which must be answered before any kind of rethinking can be done regarding the design of PAPs. As such it is surprising that these are not clearly raised in the vast literature that attempts to analyse the government's role in alleviating poverty via the PAPs. There is urgent need to analyse these questions and come up with serious *suggestions* as to how the government can internalise the problems of incentives (for programme administrators) and accountability, within the overall design of the PAPs.

At the end of the day it should be noted that these special programmes were designed with a view to *alleviate* poverty in a short to medium-term perspective. Reviewing the overall performance of the PAPs in this context, it appears that while the functioning of these programmes do indeed suffer from a number of shortcomings, nevertheless much has been achieved via this route in terms of making a dent on poverty at the micro level.

NOTES

1. I would like to thank Dr Rohini Nayyar for an extremely helpful set of comments and for guidance in writing this paper. I would also like to thank Dr J.V.Meenakshi for her comments and suggestions. Thanks are also due to Prof. A.N. Sharma, Prof. Amitabha Kundu and other participants at the 'National Seminar on Poverty and Food Security in India', Department of Economics, Jamia Millia Islamia University, for their comments. I gratefully acknowledge financial support from the Rural Development Division, Planning Commission. The usual disclaimer applies.
2. These wage employment programmes (along with the Food For Work program) were merged into a single programme, 'Sampoorna Gramin Rozgar Yojana' (SGRY) in Septermber 2001.
3. The IRDP and its allied programmes, along with the Million Wells Scheme (which was originally a part of the JRY) were merged into a single program called the 'Swaranjayanti Gram Swarozgar Yojana' (SGSY).
4. Inverse of agricultural productivity is taken as a measure of agricultural performance.
5. However, since 1999 there has been a shift in programme emphasis with infrastructure creation being the primary, and employment generation the secondary objective of the wage employment programmes.
6. In 1999 this norm was relaxed under the JGSY.
7. Since 1999 the IRDP and all its sub-plans were merged to create a single programme: the Swarnajayanti Gram Swarozgar Yojna.
8. According to Gaiha's estimates, if EGS wages rise by a rupee, agricultural wages would rise by 10 paise in the short run and by about 18 paise in the long run.
9. For instance, Rao (1992) suggests that wage-employment programmes can be easily integrated with programs for area development such as the National Watershed Development Project for Rainfed Areas (NWDPRA). This point is also stressed in Chopra (1993) who points out that in addition to employment and asset creation, watershed development also creates the potential for the regeneration of natural capital.
10. However, under the new scheme SGRY, part of wages is now payable in kind, i.e. wages constitute 5 kg. of foodgrains and the rest in cash payable at the minimum wage rate.

11. However, only 11 per cent of the programme beneficiaries could cross the Rs 6400 poverty line, while 75 per cent could cross the lower Rs. 3500 poverty line.
12. In fact the recent changes in programme design reveal an understanding of these issues. For instance, it is recognised that 'Micro enterprises succeed only if they cater to specific needs of the area' (GOI, 2003).
13. A number of studies (for instance, Samal, 1998) point out that programs such as the JRY play only a marginal role in employment creation. Survey of a tribal area in Orissa reveals that the JRY provided only 6.51 per cent of total employment (from all sources) per family. As such these programmes have very little impact on unemployment.
14. In essence this corresponds to the EAS which was started with the objective of providing employment for 100 days in drought-prone, desert, hilly and flood-prone areas in the country.
15. On an average panchayats get less than fifty thousand rupees per annum except in States like Kerala, West Bengal and Orissa where village panchayats cover a larger area.
16. Insofar as increasing costs of employment are due (at least in part) to the problem of corruption, these statistics simply underscore the urgency of addressing this problem which time and again has come up as a prime factor affecting the efficacy of the PAPs.
17. In the poverty stricken states (Bihar, Orissa, Madhya Pradesh, Rajasthan and West Bengal) in 98 per cent to 100 per cent cases JRY assets were considered useful (Neelakantan, 1994).

REFERENCES

Banerjee, A.V., and A.Newman, 1993, 'Occupational Choice and the Process of Development,' *Journal of Political Economy* 101 , 274-298.

Bhalla, S., 1995, 'Development, Poverty and Policy : The Haryana Experience,' *Economic and Political Weekly* XXX (41- 42), 2619 – 2634.

Bhuvaneswari, S. and Varadarajan, S., 1998, "Role of Credit in Capital Formation on Farms,' *Financing Agriculture* 30 (3).

Chopra, K., 1993, 'Watershed Development : A Contrast with NREP/ JRY,' *Economic and Political Weekly* XXVIII (26), A-61–A-67.

Dasgupta, B., 1995, 'Institutional Reforms and Poverty Alleviation in West Bengal' *Economic and Political Weekly* XXX (41- 42), 2691-2702.

Desai, B.M., 1995, 'Growth with Social Justice : Sweet Slumber or Big Leap,' *Economic and Political Weekly* XXX (47), 3019 – 3020.

Dev, M., 1995, 'Economic Reforms and the Rural Poor,' *Economic and Political Weekly* XXX (33), 2085 – 2088.

Dev, M., 1995, 'Alleviating Poverty : Maharashtra Employment Guarantee Scheme,' *Economic and Political Weekly* XXX (41- 42), 2663-2676.

Dev, S.M. and A. Ranade, 1997, 'Poverty and Public Policy,' in *India Development Report*, Oxford University Press, 61-76.

Dev, S.M. and A.Ranade, 1998, 'Persisting Poverty and Social Insecurity : A Selective Assessment,' *mimeo.*

Gaiha, R., 1997a, 'Do Rural Public Works Influence Agricultural Wages? The Case of the Employment Guarantee Scheme in India,' *Oxford Development Studies* 25, 301-314.

Gaiha, R., 1997b, 'Rural Public Works and the Poor : The Case of the Employment Guarantee Scheme in India,' *Research in Labor Economics* 16, 235-269.

Gaiha, R., 1997c, 'Do Rural Public Works Stabilize Incomes? The Case of the Employment Guarantee Scheme in India,' *mimeo.*

Gaiha, R., 1998a, 'On the Persistence of Poverty in Rural India,' *Canadian Journal of Development Studies* XIX, 281-314.

Gaiha, R., P.D. Kaushik and V. Kulkarni, 1998b, 'Jawahar Rozgar Yojana, Panchayats and the Rural Poor in India,' *Asian Survey* XXXVIII, 928-949.

R. Gaiha and V. Kulkarni, 1998c, 'Policy Reforms, Institutions and the Poor in Rural India,' *Contemporary South Asia* 8, 7-28.

Gaiha, R., K. Imai, and P.D. Kaushik, 1999, 'On the Targeting and Cost-Effectiveness of Anti-Poverty Programmes in Rural India,' *mimeo.*

Gaiha, R., 2000, 'Do Anti-Poverty Programs Reach the Rural Poor in India?,' *Oxford Development Studies* 28, 71-95.

Government of Andhra Pradesh, 1998, 'DWCRA and Women's Empowerment,' Commissionerate of Rural Development, Government of Andhra Pradesh.

GOI, 2003, 'Tenth Plan Document, Planning Commission : Government of India.

Hirway, I., 1995, 'Selective Development and Widening Disparities in Gujarat,' *Economic and Political Weekly* XXX (41- 42), 2603-2618.

Iyer, P., 1994, 'Creating Rural Employment : JRY's New Thrust Areas,' *Economic and Political Weekly* , XXIX (32) , 2065-2066.

Kannan, K.P., 1995, 'Declining Incidence of Rural Poverty in Kerala,' *Economic and Political Weekly* XXX (41- 42), 2651-2662.

Lakshmi, S. et al., 1998, 'Characteristics of Defaulters in Agricultural Credit Use: A Micro Level Analysis with Reference to Kerala,' *Indian Journal of Economics* 53(4), 640-647.

Mathur, K., 1995, 'Politics and Implementation of Integrated Rural Development Programme,' *Economic and Political Weekly* XXX (41- 42), 2703-2708.

National Bank for Agriculture and Rural Development (NABARD), 1997, 'Dairy Development in Mandi District in Himachal Pradesh : Ex-Post Evaluation Study.'

Neelakantan, M., 1994, 'Jawahar Rozgar Yojana : An Assessment through Concurrent Evaluation,' *Economic and Political Weekly,* XXIX (49), 3091 – 3097.

Parthasarathy, G., 1995, 'Public Intervention and Rural Poverty: Case of Non-Sustainable Reduction in Andhra Pradesh,' *Economic and Political Weekly* XXX (41- 42), 2573- 2586.

Rao, C.H.H., 1993, 'Integrating Poverty Alleviation Programs with Development Strategies,' *Economic and Political Weekly* Nov. 28, 2603-2607.

Rao, C.H.H., 1998, 'Agricultural Growth, Sustainability and Poverty Alleviation: Recent Trends and Major Issues of Reform,' *Economic and Political Weekly,* XXXIII (29 & 30), 1943 – 1948.

Rao, V.M., 1998, 'Economic Reforms and the Poor : Emerging Scenario,' *Economic and Political Weekly,* XXXIII (29 & 30), 1949 – 1954.

Roy, S., 1997, 'Globalisation, Structural Change and Poverty : Some Conceptual and Policy Issues,' *Economic and Political Weekly,* XXXII (33 & 34), 2117 - 2135.

Sagar, V., 1995, 'Public Intervention for Poverty Alleviation in Harsh Agro-Climatic Environment : Case of Rajasthan,' *Economic and Political Weekly* XXX (41- 42), 2677-2690.

Sharma, A.N., 1995, 'Political Economy of Poverty in Bihar,' *Economic and Political Weekly* XXX (41- 42), 2587- 2602.

Shergill, H.S. and G. Singh, 1995, 'Poverty in Rural Punjab : Trend over Green Revolution Decades,' *Economic and Political Weekly* XXX (25), A-80 – A-83.

Srivastava, R., 1998, 'Anti-Poverty Programs in Uttar Pradesh, India, in the Context of Decentralization,' *mimeo.*

Samal , K.C., 1998, 'Poverty Alleviation after Post-Liberalisation:

Study of a Tribal Block in Orissa,' *Economic and Political Weekly,* XXXIII (28), 1846 – 1851.

Suryanarayana, M.H., 1995, 'Growth Poverty and Levels of Living: Hypotheses, Methods and Policies,' *Discussion Paper* 175-1995, Indira Gandhi Institute of Development Research.

Suryanarayana, M.H., 1996, 'Poverty Estimates and Indicators: Importance of Data Base,' *Economic and Political Weekly,* XXXI (Special Number), 2487 – 2497.

Tewari, D.D. and A.G. Isemonger, 1998, 'Joint Forest Management, South Gujarat, India : A case of Successful Community Development,' Community Development Journal 33 (1), 32-48.

Vohra,B.B., 1996, 'Better Resource Management for Poverty Alleviation,' *Economic and Political Weekly,* XXXI (23), 1397 – 1404.

Vyas, V.S. and P. Bhargava, 1995, 'Public Intervention for Poverty Alleviation : An Overview,' *Economic and Political Weekly* XXX (41- 42), 2559-2572.

Vyasulu,V., 1995, 'Management of Poverty Alleviation Programmes in Karnataka : An Overview,' *Economic and Political Weekly* XXX (41- 42), 2635-2650.

World Bank, 1997, 'India : Achievements and Challenges in Reducing Poverty,' *World Bank Country Study.*

World Bank, 1998, 'Reducing Poverty in Indian : Options for More Effective Public Services,' *World Bank Country Study.*

Chapter 10

Social Orientation and Women Empowerment

An Analysis and Future Strategy

Rashmi Agrawal & B.V.L.N.Rao

Women constitute half of the world's population but their share in fruits of development is not commensurate with that ratio. Male-female disparities may be observed in every sphere of life, i.e. education, employment, remuneration, access to social assets etc. In 43 countries of the world, male literacy rates are higher than the female rates by at least 15 percentage points. Such disparities lead to situations where 544 million of the world's estimated 854 million illiterate adults are women and 60 per cent of the estimated 113 million children out of school are girls. Human Development Report (2002) indicates that women earned around three-fourths as much as men; about half a million women die every year as a result of pregnancy and child birth. Patel (1993) points out that 'Women account for more than one half of humanity and they work for nearly two-thirds of the work hours, but they receive only some one-tenth of the world income, and own less than a bare one per cent of the world's productive assets.' Women make up 70 per cent of the world's one billion absolute poor and one half of the women in Asia and Africa are malnourished.

Discrimination against women cuts across geographical boundaries or levels of development. It varies, however, in degree and areas of operation. While gender bias in South Asian countries, for example, is often deliberately practised and offends all canons of human rights and dignity, even in highly developed countries gender-based discrimination, exists. To take an extreme example the United States of America has never had a woman President and only one-eighth of its parliamentarians are women.

Indian Scene

Situation in India, in spite of various efforts at national and regional levels to achieve gender parity, is not very encouraging. Social attitudes hardened over ages do not change easily. Even if change per se is accepted, the deep-rooted prejudices do die hard. A majority of people, men and women alike, still have a preference for a son, and pay relatively less attention to girl child in matters of education, health, etc. Education even when provided to girls does not, generally, aim at their main-streaming in the society but only to find a suitable match at a lower dowry. Lopsided sex ratio of 933 females per 1000 men has been result of such favours for the male child. More worrisome is the fact that sex ratio has been declining steadily during the last century instead of showing improvement. There is even a hypothesis, which can not be dismissed off hand, that affluence heightens the desire for a male child. [Even though in the decade 1991–2001, the overall sex ratio improved slightly (from 927 in 1991 to 933 in 2001), the under-6 sex ratio declined from 945 to 927. Declining trend is perceptible in almost all states including economically prosperous States like Punjab and Haryana, Maharashtra, Gujarat etc. These States have a sex ratio of less than the national average of 933 in 2001 and in all of these, ratio declined sharply during 1991–2001 (Table 10.1). This shows with economic prosperity deep-rooted societal prejudices do not change automatically.

TABLE 10.1
All Age and Under -6 Sex-Ratios in Different States and Union Territories, 2001

State/Union Territory	*Sex Ratio*					
	All Ages		*Age 0–6*		*Age 7 +*	
	1991	*2001*	*1991*	*2001*	*1991*	*2001*
Andhra Pradesh	972	978	975	964	972	980
Assam	923	932	975	964	910	926
Bihar	907	921	953	938	895	916
Chattisgarh	985	990	984	975	986	992
Goa	967	960	964	933	967	964
Gujarat	934	921	928	878	936	927
Haryana	865	861	879	820	862	869
Himachal Pradesh	976	970	951	897	980	981
Jammu & Kashmir	—	900	—	937	—	894
Jharkand	922	941	979	866	908	935
Karnataka	960	964	960	949	960	966
Kerala	1,036	1,058	958	963	1,049	1,071
Madhya Pradesh	912	920	941	929	905	918
Maharashtra	934	922	946	917	931	923
Manipur	958	978	974	961	955	981
Meghalaya	955	975	986	975	947	974
Mizoram	921	938	969	971	911	932
Nagaland	886	909	993	975	864	899
Orissa	971	972	967	950	972	976
Punjab	882	874	875	793	883	886
Rajasthan	910	922	916	909	908	925
Sikkim	878	875	965	986	860	858
Tamila Nadu	974	986	948	939	978	992
Tripura	945	950	967	975	940	947
Uttaranchal	936	964	948	906	933	976
Uttar Pradesh	876	898	927	916	863	895
West Bengal	917	934	967	963	907	929
Andaman & Nicobar	818	846	973	965	790	830
Arunachal Pradesh	859	901	982	961	829	888

Table 10.1 contd.

State/Union Territory	*Sex Ratio*					
	All Ages		*Age 0–6*		*Age 7 +*	
	1991	*2001*	*1991*	*2001*	*1991*	*2001*
Chandigarh	790	773	899	845	772	763
Dadra & Nagar Haveli	952	811	1,013	973	937	779
Daman & Diu	969	709	958	925	971	682
Delhi	827	821	915	865	810	813
Lakshadweep	943	947	941	974	943	943
Pondicherry	979	1,001	963	958	982	1,007
All India	927	933	945	927	9236	935

Source: Registrar General of India, Paper 1, Census 2001, Final Population Count.

Gender differentials in mortality rates may also be observed (Table 10.2). Some reasons associated with higher IMR in case of females are neglect of girl child, high maternal mortality, sex determination before birth and elimination of female births. Human Development Report (2002) referred to a 'recent survey in India (which) found 10,000 cases of female infanticide a year.' Further ratio of IMR for females to that of males does not exhibit any falling trend, which belies hopes of narrowing gender gap.

TABLE 10.2
Infant Mortality Rates by Sex

Year	*Infant Mortality*			*Ratio of Female to Male Rate*
	Female	*Male*	*All*	
1985	98	96	97	1.02
1990	81	78	80	1.04
1997*	73	70	71	1.04

Source: Registrar General of India. Sample Registration System;
* excludes Jammu & Kashmir

Neglect of the girl child in terms of providing nutrition is the main cause of higher mortality among girls. Gender biases are widely prevalent in allocation of food and health care. Mishra (1996) refers to a study in Tamil Nadu which found that male children were breast-fed for 5 months longer than female children in landed families and for about 10 months more in agricultural labour household. Another study of children under five by Institute of Health Management, Pachod, showed that disparity in nutritional status is the highest in age group of 1–3 years. Same study also showed that percentage of severely malnourished female children was consistently 2-3 times higher than that of boys.

While neglect of girl child in matters of nutrition and health are responsible for higher female mortality below age of 15, it is early marriages which result in higher female mortality rates till the age of 30 years. Although mean age at marriage has increased about 15 years to about 20 years during the last 50 years and law prohibits marriage of girls before the age of 18, data from Sample Registration Scheme for 1996 indicate that 20 per cent of females in the age group of 15 to 19 were married. It shows inadequate enforcement of prevention of Child Marriages Act. A UNICEF study conducted in 12 North Indian villages with a sample of 400 girls in age group of 10 to 16 shows that about 45 per cent were either married or were in process of getting married. Pathetic status of Primary Health Services available to pregnant women, particularly in rural areas seems to be responsible for high mortality rate in this age group. There are about 450 maternal deaths per 1,00,000 live births in India compared to 10 to 20 in developed countries and less than 100 in countries like Thailand. The highest number of maternal deaths in 1998 was due to haemorrhage (29.7 per cent) followed by anaemia (19 per cent) Sepsis (16.1 per cent) which could have been prevented easily by better health care and nutrition (Tenth Plan).

Education is of basic importance in women's development and empowerment but it has not received deserved attention. India has the largest number of illiterates in the world. Literacy rates no doubt have improved over the years, but India still lags behind the developed countries as well as some of the developing countries like Vietnam, Philippines and Thailand. Situation is worse in case of female literacy. Although gender gaps have narrowed down substantially, about half of the female population is still illiterate (Table 10.3).

TABLE 10.3
Literacy Rates by Sex

(In per cent)

Census	*Females*	*Males*	*Persons*	*Male-Female Gap in Literacy Rate*
1981	29.76	56.38	43.57	26.62
1991	39.29	64.13	52.21	24.84
2001	54.16	75.85	65.38	21.69

Note: (*i*) The literacy rates relate to the population aged seven years and above; (*ii*) The 1981 Census Literacy rates exclude Assam. The 1991 Census Literacy Rates exclude Jammu & Kashmir.

Source: Census of India, 2001 : Provisional Population Totals, Registrar-General & Census Commissioner, GOI, New Delhi.

The gross enrolment ratio at different stages of education for girls has increased substantially over the years. However, efforts in this direction get neutralised due to high dropout rates. Gender disparities in the enrolment ratios at different stages and dropout rates in school education may also be observed (Table 10.4).

Gender disparity in work participation rate is also a matter of concern. Female work participation rate increased from 19.7 per cent in 1981 to 25.7 per cent in 2001, it is still much lower than the male work participation rate (Table 10.5).

It is also pertinent to mention that even working women are not at par with working males. More than 90 per cent women work in unorganised informal sector with low incomes, poor working conditions and without any social security. Drudgery is passed on to women, they are assigned work

TABLE 10.4
Gross Enrolment Ratio of different
Stage of School Education

Year	*Primary Classes (I–V) Age group 6–11 years*		*Middle Classes (VI–VIII) Age group 11–14 years*		*High/Higher Secondary Classes (IX–XI/XII) Age group 14–17*	
	Boys	*Girls*	*Boys*	*Girls*	*Boys*	*Girls*
1971	92.6	59.1	46.5	20.8	27.1	10.2
1981	95.8	64.1	54.3	28.8	23.1	11.1
1991	115.3	86.0	73.4	46.1	31.2@	16.3@
1999*	100.6	82.9	65.3	49.1		

* Provisional @ Relate of 1990. Data for subsequent years not available

Source: Ministry of Human Resource Development reproduced in Institute of Applied Manpower Research, Manpower Profile India, Year Book 2000.

TABLE 10.5
Work Participation Rate by Sex (1981 to 2001)

Census	*T/R/U*	*Female*	*Male*	*Persons*
1981	Total	19.7	52.6	36.7
	Rural	23.1	53.8	38.8
	Urban	8.3	49.1	30.0
1991	Total	22.3	51.6	37.5
	Rural	26.8	52.6	40.1
	Urban	9.2	48.9	30.2
2001	Total	25.7	51.9	39.3
	Rural	31.0	52.4	42.0
	Urban	11.6	50.9	32.2

Source: Census of India, 1991, Series 1 and Census of India 2001, Provisional Population Totals, Registar General & Census Commission, GOI, New Delhi.

which requires low skills and they are placed at the lowest point of occupational spectrum in terms of prestige. Disparities in incomes of men and women for the similar kind of work may be seen from Tables 10.6 and 10.7.

Representation of women in decision-making bodies is almost negligible except in local bodies where there is statutory system of reservation. In political matters while their representation in the lower house of national parliament has shown some improvement (percentage of women members has increased from 4 to 7 in the 30 years), their share in the upper house has fluctuated around 10 per cent (Table 10.8). These shares are nowhere near the one-third level aimed at in international commitments. Representation of women in some All India Services is extremely low (Table 10.9).

Table 10.10 shows Gender Empowerment Rank of some of developed as well as developing countries published by the UNDP in its Human Development Report. India ranks 95 behind even Bangladesh, as per 1998 ranking.

Low social status of women is also evident from crimes against them. A number of legislations are there to prevent various types crimes against women, these continue unabated. In comparison to 1999, year 2000 saw an increase in crimes against women like dowry deaths, rapes, sexual harassment and cruelty by family members. Report of the National Crimes Record Bureau, 2000 provides some quick analysis crimes against women as follows:

- There was 4.1 per cent increase in crimes against women in 2000 over 1999;
- 960 per cent increase in cases of buying of girls for prostitution, 42.9 per cent increase in foeticide cases over 1999;
- 6.6 per cent increase in rape cases. Every 54 minutes a woman is raped.

What is of greater concern is that 77.8 per cent IPC (Indian Penal Code) cases that were investigated, 78 per cent were charge-sheeted, 15.8 cases tried and of those only 39.6 per cent resulted in convictions. These percentages compound to an overall conviction rate of hardly 4 per cent of the registered cases. A large number is unreported and unrecorded.

TABLE 10.6
Average Daily Wage Earnings of Casual Wage Labour in Various Industries

(in Rupees at 1982-83 Prices)

Activity Status/Sector	*Male*		*Female*	
	1987–88	*1993–94*	*1987–88*	*1993–94*
Rural Casual Labour in Public Works	8.36	9.46	6.16	7.01
Other types of work in Agricultural Sector	8.19	8.91	5.41	6.25
Non-agricultural Sector Urban Casual Labour in Works (other than public works)	10.25	11.36	5.87	6.54
Agricultural Sector Mining and quarrying				
Manufacturing (of which)	9.49	10.54	5.60	6.81
Consumer goods	11.56	12.68	5.20	6.00
Capital Goods	11.11	12.12	5.74	5.80
Electricity, Gas and Water	11.19	15.39	6.98	8.87
Construction	**12.83**	**14.41**	**7.86**	**9.56**
Trade	9.93	10.62	5.58	7.71
Transport, Storage and Communication	11.67	13.18	9.92	7.57
Financial and Business Service	11.16	10.90	1.15	9.88
Community, Social and Personal Service	10.96	10.30	5.87	7.15
Non-agricultural Sector	11.61	12.72	6.1	7.27

Source: NSSO 43rd Round (July 1987 to June 1988) and 50th Round (July 1993 to June 1994); taken from Singh (2000).

TABLE 10.7
Average Wage Rate in the Handicrafts Sector (current prices)

Year	*Daily Wage Rate (Rs)*	
	Male	*Female*
1980–81	17.62	9.26
1981–82	18.78	9.90
1982–83	20.02	10.58
1983–84	21.34	11.31
1984–85	22.75	12.09
1985–86	24.23	12.94
1986–87	25.85	13.83
1987–88	27.59	14.78
1988–89	29.43	15.81
1989–90	31.41	16.90
1990–91	33.43	18.08

Source: Vijayagopalan, 1993

Empowerment Efforts

Efforts have been made at several levels for main-streaming of women in the society. Our Constitution has made specific provisions to enforce equality between men and women. Special attention had been given in the Third, Fourth and Fifth Five-Year Plan(1961–80) to girls education and immunization programme for children and supplementary nutrition programmes for children and expectant and nursing mothers. Sixth Five Year Plan (1980–85) incorporated for the first time a separate chapter on 'Women and child Development' which expressed concern about the declining sex ratio, lower life expectancy among women and lower status of women in the society. Seventh five Year Plan (1985–90) focused on need for an integrated approach for development of women in education, health and family welfare, nutrition and employment. National Perspective Plan for Women released in 1988 considered women as equal partners with men. In the background of National Perspective Plan, Eighth Plan expected that 'Women must be enabled to function as

TABLE 10.8
Women in Parliament

Year	*Lok Sabha*			*Rajya Sabha*		
	Total seats	*Women members*	*Percentage of women*	*Total seats*	*Women members*	*Percentage of women*
(1)	*(2)*	*(3)*	*(4)*	*(5)*	*(6)*	*(7)*
1971	521	22	4.2	243	17	7.0
1977	544	19	3.4	244	25	10.2
1980	544	28	5.1	244	24	9.8
1984	544	44	8.1	244	28	11.4
1989	517	27	5.2	245	24	9.7
1991	544	39	7.2	245	38	15.5
1996	543	36	7.2	223	20	9.0
1998	545	41	7.0	236	18	8.0

Source: Parliament

TABLE 10.9

Representation of Women in some all-India Services

Service	*1077*			*1997*		
	Total members	*Women*	*Percentage of women*	*Total members*	*Women*	*Percentage of women*
(1)	*(2)*	*(3)*	*(4)*	*(5)*	*(6)*	*(7)*
1. Indian Administrative Service	4,204	339	7.5	4,991	512	10.2
2. Indian Foreign Service	480	53	11.4	575	71	12.3
3. Indian Police Service	2,418	21	0.9	3,045	67	2.2
Total	7,102	413	5.8	8,611	650	7.5

Source: Ministry of Home affairs. Ministry of External Affairs and Ministry of Personnel. Government of India quoted in the Ninth Five Year Plan. Planning commission. (Government of India)

TABLE 10.10

Gender Empowerment Rank

Countries	*Ranks*
Sweden	1
USA	11
China	35
Pakistan	100
Bangladesh	80
India	95

Source: Human Development Report (1998)

equal partners and participants in development and not merely as beneficiaries of various schemes.' Basic thrust in this Plan was on organisation and strengthening of women so that they could play a decisive role in planning and implementation of various programmes. Hence, Eighth Plan initiated a change in the approach from welfare to empowerment. Ninth Five-Year Plan committed itself to empower women as agents of social change and development. Tenth Plan lays emphasis on empowerment of women with a more integrated approach and considers 'empowering women as a process which demands a life cycle approach. Therefore, every stage of their life counts as a priority in the planning process.'

Ninth Plan approach was to enable women to exercise their rights by creating a conducive environment. It also attempted convergence of existing services available in both women-specific and women-related sectors. A Women Component Plan was visualised through which about 30 per çent of all benefits had to flow to women from development sectors. National Health Policy 2001 (Draft) emphasises need for increased access to women to basic health care. National Nutrition Policy of 1993 explores strategies for tackling problems of malnutrition. Various other programmes have been initiated like Integrated Child Development Services (ICDS), Universal Immunisation Programme, etc. which aim at better health care for women. Education recently has been declared as fundamental right. Mahila Samakhya Scheme launched in 1989 aims at education and empowerment of women in rural areas. Anti-poverty training programmes have been implemented to impart various skills to increase employability of women in rural areas. Swaranjayanti Gram Swarozgar Yojana relates to rural development programme for families below poverty line. Launching of 'Sw-Skakti', 'Stree Shakti Puraskar', adoption of 'National Policy for Empowerment of Women', introduction of gender budgeting to attain more effective targeting of public expenditure, launching of 'Stree Swadhar', induction of Bill on Domestic Violence Against Women (prevention) are some of milestones in the process of empowerment of women. National Commission for Women, a statutory body was set up in 1992 to safeguard rights and interests of women. A strong legislative support is available for women in the country which is reviewed from time to time to make them more effective. No doubt condition of women has improved with these efforts but they still lag behind in almost all spheres. Tenth Plan approach is based on the recently adopted National Policy for Empowerment of Women (2001) which will be put into action through

- Creating an environment, through positive economic and social policies, for the development of women to enable them to realize their full potential;
- Allowing *de-jure* and *de-facto* enjoyment of all human rights and fundamental freedoms by women at par with men in all spheres-political, economic, social, cultural and civil;
- Providing equal access to participation and decision-making for women in social, political and economic life of the nation;
- Ensuring equal access to women to health care, quality education at all levels, career and vocational guidance, employment, equal remuneration, occupational health and safety, social security and public office, etc.;
- Strengthening legal systems aimed at elimination of all forms of discrimination against women;
- Changing societal attitudes and community practices by active participation and involvement of both men and women;
- Main streaming a gender perspective into development process;
- Eliminating discrimination and all forms of violence against women and girl child; and
- Building and strengthening partnerships with civil society, particularly women's organisations, corporate and private sector agencies.

Strategy adopted to empower women in the Tenth Plan are Sector-specific three-fold strategy which include:

- Social Empowerment – to create an enabling environment through various affirmative developmental policies and programmes for development of women besides providing them easy and equal access to all the basic minimum services so as to enable them to realize their full potential;
- Economic Empowerment – to ensure provision of training, employment and income generating activities with both 'forward' and 'backward' linkages with ultimate objective of making all potential women economically independent and self-reliant; and
- Gender Justice – to eliminate all forms of gender

> discrimination and thus, allow women to enjoy not only *de-jure* but also *de-facto* rights and fundamental freedom on par with men in all spheres, viz., political, economic, social, civil, cultural etc.

As outlined above, for the last two decades, multi-directional, multi-dimensional and multifaceted programmes for empowerment of women have been in vogue. Things have not, however, improved up to the desired extent. There are lacunae in visualisation, conceptualisation and implementation of programmes. It has been well documented that efforts are not synergised and approach is piecemeal. But in our opinion there are certain more fundamental issues that require immediate attention. The relevant question is whether economic, social and political empowerment imposed from outside by external agencies, by themselves, are enough to make the women come out of the traditional stereotypes and become empowered.

The Indian social-cultural structure has dichotomous power structures, i.e. 'Strongly powerful' and 'extremely weak' which is reflected in so many facets of socio-political structure such as caste system, religions, geographical variations, political structures, family structures, etc. These have created class society of 'haves' and 'have nots' – there are 'dominating men' the most powerful and 'dominated women' the least powerful. Concept of empowerment emerged perhaps due to this dichotomy which aimed at balancing powers especially between the two halves of humanity 'men' and 'women'. In social terms, empowerment attacks the existing power structures. Empowerment programmes have been visualised in our country perhaps on the basis of this conceptual framework. But things are not happening the way they were planned or visualised. For example, educational development visualised as instrument of empowerment does not always lead to the goal. Many women who have access to excellent education ultimately end up as house wives. In the political sphere, even though seats have been reserved for women in local bodies, this is not in practice translated into actual decision-making powers, Our experience in some villages of

Uttar Pradesh, Madhya Pradesh and Orissa shows, for example, that women *Sarpanches* mostly depend on their menfolk in discharging their responsibility. Often decision about the engagement of women in work is the prerogative of men. One evaluation study conducted by IAMR in KBK region of Orissa (2002) shows that houses given under Indira Awaas Yojana are many times in the names of males while as per guidelines they should be in the names of females or in the joint empowerment process is perhaps due to the fact that they have not led or contributed to women's realisation of their innate potential to utilise the opportunities that have been thrown up. They lack self-confidence and often times do things at the bidding of their menfolk. Unless such self-confidence is instilled in women and the feeling of 'I cannot do it is replaced by the feeling 'I can', efforts towards empowerment will not have the desired effects.

Empowerment of Women through Personality Development – A model for future

Empowerment through personality development is actually giving power to 'self' which is a process involving realisation of self, acceptance of self (its potential and short coming) and its development through training. No doubt self-empowerment cannot come in isolation, it has to be integrated with other programmes like imparting knowledge, social participation, development of capability to cope with barriers etc.

Self-empowerment comes automatically with adequate social orientation and cognitive development and at the same time can be induced through proper training and motivational inputs. In Indian case, the second approach is necessary because social orientation of women in our country varies from that of men, as females have been placed subordinate to males in the family hierarchy. Women have been conditioned in such a way that they submit to such notions and accept themselves inferior to males. According to sex role theory, women acquire sex role learning during social orientation in their early childhood which lead to attitudinal mind sets. Claes (1999) defines it as a form of 'culture trap.' Social roles have been bifurcated as 'domestic' for women and 'public and social' for men.

Of late, women have started crossing such gender barriers and have started entering labour markets. But job markets have also been segregated on the basis of sex. Women have been found suitable for occupations, which match the roles they perform at home like caring for sick people. Bem's Gender Schema Theory (1980) and sex typing of occupation suggests that not only men but also many women think that jobs in which women pre dominate and are doing for long time are more appropriate for them. Oppenheimer (1968) found some of the socio-economic factors responsible for such phenomena like 'cheapness plus availability' and 'cheapness plus skill.' In other words, jobs with less pay, lower skills and ready supply of workers are for females. Recently, women have been found entering into hitherto male dominated occupations but these are exceptions. In a quick survey of hundred women with a list of thirty three jobs we tried to study, the respondents were asked to rank the jobs whether the women who have crossed over from their stereo-typed roles have been able to change their attitudes in general as traditional jobs and non-traditional jobs for women. These hundred women were selected from various categories like advocates, doctors, administrators, nurses, business women, teachers, etc., working in Delhi. The results show that women still segregate labour markets and consider certain occupations as suitable and appropriate for men only. Informal interaction with these groups of professional women as well as other educated and also the illiterates reveals that highly professionally qualified and working women want their girl children to be educated and opt for a career as per their aptitudes and interests. Educated women, who were either housewives or working in traditional jobs generally, opined that 'although education is necessary for girls, it is mainly for getting a suitable match for them. Match is a priority and choice of a career depends on the thinking of husband or in-laws.' This group of women also thought that their girl children should take up jobs compatible with the responsibilities of their married life. Many women preferred a teaching job for their female child. While a few illiterate wanted their daughters to be educated and self-earning, others felt that girls should learn to do the household work instead of studying. Our results show that women are going through a slow but sure change and it may be observed that highly educated professional women have been able to come out from the ambit of their early childhood social orientation.

Another major factor that restricts women development of a positive self is the learning of socially assigned role behaviours that are feminine in nature. Aggressiveness is valued when shown by men and denigrated if demonstrated by women. This makes them feel negatively when a question of showing self-confidence, making an independent decision or risk taking, etc., comes up. For these matters they depend on men. Researches suggest that while dependency in boys is discouraged by parents and teachers, it is acceptable in respect of girls (Kagam and Moss, 1962; Sears, Rau and Alport, 1965). Women are discouraged to develop an independent self. The view that certain personalities are suited only to certain jobs leads to conservative decisions. Perhaps a positive self-image among women contrary to the traditional stereo-typical social orientation of subordinate status may make for a sure and certain change in the direction of empowerment of women which is possible through intervention in early stages of development. Authors conducted an investigative study to measure levels of self-esteem among women working in traditional and non-traditional jobs with a total sample of 200 women in the metropolitan city of Delhi, in which hundred women were selected from a traditional job, i.e. senior secondary school principal and 100 from non-traditional jobs, i.e. research scientists in natural science. Women in the selected sample, in general, were found having high self esteem. No significant differences were found in levels of self-esteem of women working in traditional and non-traditional jobs. It appears that women who have non-stereotypic social orientation developed high self-esteem and chose higher level jobs. Role of higher professional education in development of positive self cannot also be ignored.

As has been stated earlier, women are allowed to develop feminine behaviours in their personality. Researches show that due to this reason they are not found suitable for higher level jobs that require leadership qualities and managerial skills (Gilmer, 1961; Bowman, Worthy and Greyser, 1965). Even when they take up such roles they are not effective in these roles. However, Situational Model of Leadership suggests that in modern times' a manager has to change his leadership behaviour according to the situation and an 'Autocratic' leader is not as effective as compared to the 'democratic' leader.

Authors also studied whether women selected to measure their self-esteem were effective in their managerial roles. It was seen that women managers, in general, were effective in their leadership behaviour. Leadership effectiveness was studied on four major leadership styles i.e. High Task – Low Relationship (S1); High Task – High Relationship (S2); High Relationship – Low Task (S3); and Low Relationship – Low Task (S4). It was found that women managers who followed pattern 1 as their basic leadership of self-esteem and effectiveness was also observed. It was seen that women managers with high self-esteem were effective in their leadership behaviour as compared to women managers with low self esteem. The study also shows that women were able to vary their leadership styles as per the situation.

The above discussion suggests that women can excel in fields which have been the preserve of men so far, provided they are allowed to develop their personalities along with access to other requirements like education, training and employment. This calls for change in mind sets and alterations in the social orientation for which interventions are required at various levels – the individual, the family and the society. What is required is a mutually supportive and complimentary effort on the part of all the social partners – government, non-government organisations, social activists and community at large. No programme of empowerment will succeed unless development of personality is strongly embedded into it.

Road Map

Empowerment of 'self' is an essential pre-requisite to socio-economic and political empowerment of women. This, of necessity, has to be taken up in a phased manner. A practical programme to operationalise this process would involve the following steps:

1. Identification of specific target groups of women such as highly educated/educated/literates/illiterates; working/ non-working, etc.;
2. Assessment of personality characteristics – strengths and weaknesses specific to each identified target group through psychological tests and observations;
3. Designing and organisation of personality development programmes for each target group;
4. Provide individual or group counselling wherever required;
5. Exploration of potential for income generating activities with area specific approach;
6. Matching of these potential activities with the potentials of target groups and establish linkages for credit, marketing facilities, etc.;
7. Creation of general awareness about the world of work, emerging field of occupations, requirements, etc.;
8. Motivate women to take up income generation activities on individual and or collective basis;

Modalities

There should be a national plan of personality development of women. Implementation of the program may be in a phased manner to cover all women gradually with special focus on most needy women or where some kinds of empowerment strategies have been adopted. For example, to start with, these programs may be organised for all women *Sarpanches* in the country. Mapping of grassroot level organisations may be done for their involvement in the project. Existing institutions providing training may train these organisations to further implement the programme at local level.

REFERENCES

Agrawal, R. and Rao, B.V.L.N., Women Empowerment. (under print)

Bem, S.L., 1980, *'Gender Schema Theory: A Cognitive Account of Sex Typing,'* Psychological Review,

Bowmen, G.W. Worthy, N.B. and Greyser, S.A., 1965, *'Are Women Executives People?'* Harward Business Review, 43, p. 14–17.

Claes, M.T., 1999, *'Women, men and Management Styles,'* in International Labour Review, Vol. 138, 4.

Gilmer, B, 1961, 'Industrial Psychology' Mc Graw Hill, New York.

GOI, Census of India, 1991, Series 1, Registrar General and Census Commission, GOI, New Delhi,

GOI, Census of India, 2001, Provisional Population Tables, Registrar General and Census Commision, GOI, New Delhi,

GOI, Five year Plans (First to Ninth), Planning Commission, New Delhi.

GOI, 1998, National Perspective Plan, Planning Commission, New Delhi,

GOI, 2001, National Policy for Empowerment of Women, New Delhi,

GOI, NSSO Rounds.

GOI, Tenth Plan,Planning Commssion, Yojana Bhawan, New Delhi.

Institute of Applied Manpower 2000, Research, Manpower Profile India-Year Book, New Delhi,

Kagan, J. and Moss, 1962, H.A. Birth to Maturity, Wiley, New York,

Kagan, J., 1964, *'Acquisition and Significance of Sex-typing and sex-role identity'* in M.L. Hoffman and L.W. Hoffman (eds)—Review of Child Development Research, Vol. 1, Russel Sage, New York,

Mishra, L.N., 1996, Introduction to Women Labour in India. V.V. Giri National Labour Institute, New Delhi.

NCRB, 2000, Report of the National Crime Record Bureau, New Delhi,

Oppenheimer, V., 1968, *'The Sex-Labeling of Jobs,'* Industrial Relations, 7, 219-234.

Patel, K.A., 1993, *'Gender distance among countries,'* Economic and Political Weekly, Bomby, 13, Febrauary.

UNDP, 1998, Human Development Report.

UNDP, 2000, Human Development Report.

Vijaygopalan, S., 1993, Economic Status of Handicraft Artisans, National Councial of Applied Economic Research, New Delhi, WWW. Parliamantofindia. nic. in.

Chapter 11

Spatial and Sectoral Patterns of Growth in India
A Comparison between the 1980s and 1990s

Subir Gokarn & D. Joshi

Introduction

India's growth rates during eighties and nineties were higher not only in comparison to previous decades but also most other countries. Figure 11.1 shows that while on an average, decades of 1980s and 1990s clocked similar growth rates, there was a clear compositional shift in favour of services during the 1990s. Growth rates of both agriculture and industry fell from 4.6 and 6.8 per cent in the 1980s to 3.1 and 5.8 per cent in 1990s respectively. Services sector, however, raised its growth rate from 6.5 to 7.5 per cent per year in the corresponding period.

Pattern of growth was not consistent all through 1990s. Period from 1993-94 to 1996-97, when the rate of growth was over 7 per cent, can be classified as the boom period. After that the growth slowed down. Boom was characterised by buoyancy in all sectors. Slowdown, however, saw a dramatic decline in growth rates in agricultural and industrial sectors. Only services sector was able to hold on to its annual growth rate of 8.1 per cent.

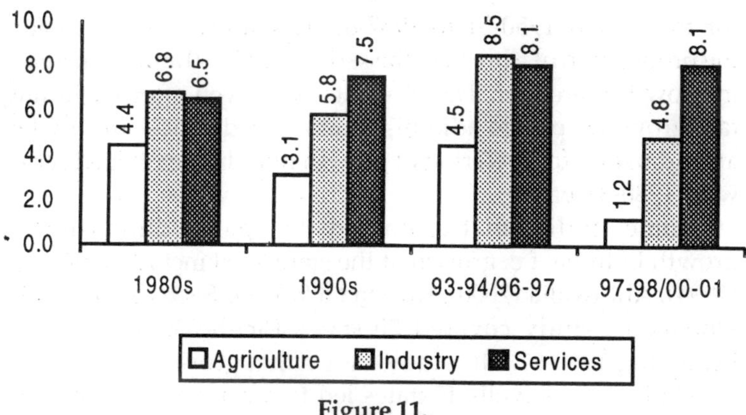

Figure 11.
Sectoral Growth Rates

Source: National Accounts Statistics, CSO (GOI)

This impressive aggregate growth performance, however, disguises spatial dimension which has important implications. Did all the states gain from the reforms? What was the sectoral composition of growth across states? What are the implications of observed patterns? We examine state-wise growth performance to identify gainers and losers of the reform process.

Past Studies

A number of studies have looked at the dynamics of growth process in India. These studies were triggered both by the need to explain the shift to a higher growth trajectory since 1980s, as well as by the periodic revision of the base of the National Accounts data.

Focus of some of these studies has been on analysis of growth rates at the aggregate sectoral level and structural breaks in it. Notable among these are Raj (1984), Rudra (1985) and Nagaraj (1990). K.N. Raj was probably the first one to point out improvements in growth rates (significantly above the Hindu rate of growth[1]) since middle/late seventies. Nagaraj statistically scrutinised Indian growth performance for the period 1950-51 to 1987-88. His study does not reject the proposition of a break in the series at 1979-80 and an increase in growth thereafter. These results hold even after excluding fast growing 'public administration and defence' from GDP and adjusting for lowering of growth rates in the revised series with 1980-81 base.

Some studies that examined the spatial dimension of growth in India. i.e. growth at the state level include Dholakia (1994), Ahluwalia (2000), Kurien (2000) and Sachs et al. (2001). Dholakia's study covered 20 states for the 30-year period beginning 1960-61. His study shows that growth acceleration in relatively less well-off states led to a convergence of long-term growth among Indian states. He also corroborates his earlier finding of there being a sharp north-south divide in the manufacturing sector – manufacturing growth accelerated in the Northern states and stagnated or decelerated in the Southern states.

Ahluwalia's study covering 14 major states and focusing on the decades of 1980s and 1990s, finds an increased growth variation in 1990s leading to increased inter-state inequality. Kurien's study focuses on the two decades beginning 1980 and concludes that economic and social disparities increased in 1990s. Sachs et al focus on the last two decades. They point out that India's growth favoured urbanised states either due to coastal access or high agricultural productivity. Their study concludes that there was little to ensure that growth would equalise across states in future. Thus, Dholakia's conclusions of convergence of growth rates among states for the three decades beginning 1960-61, is not borne out by later studies covering eighties and nineties.

State Level Analysis

Before analysing presenting the analysis across the states a brief on the data used and its limitations is in order.

States that improved their growth performance in 1990s include Karnataka, Gujarat, Maharashtra, Tamil Nadu, Kerala, Madhya Pradesh and West Bengal. Although growth in Rajasthan did not accelerate in 1990s, 7 per cent per year SDP

Box 11.1
Data and Limitations

Analysis is restricted to 15 major states also referred to as 'non-special category states'. North-Eastern states, Jammu and Kashmir, Delhi, Goa and union territories are excluded from the analysis. Fifteen major states account for the bulk of Indian population and GDP (over 90 per cent).

State level GDP data are compiled by State Statistical Departments. Although states broadly follow the methodology followed by the Central Statistical Organisation, no attempt is made to ensure consistency between state GDP estimates and National GDP estimates. CSO merely compiles the state estimates and disseminates them.

Data from 1993-94 are as per the revised series (at 1993-94 base). Prior to that, state level sectoral data are available only at 1980-81 base. The present analysis is, therefore, lacking on account of methodological differences in the two series.

Period growth rates used in the analysis are simple averages of annual growth rates and not the compound annual growth rates that are commonly used. For such short period, average measure is useful because it takes into account performance in all the years of the period.

growth clocked by it was second only to Karnataka.

Karnataka stands out as the best performing state in the 1990s. It clocked the highest average annual growth of 5.5 per cent in agriculture. Industrial and services sectors too boomed during the nineties. What is remarkable about Karnataka's growth performance is its ability to avoid the recession, which hit the economy after 1996-97. When the GDP growth in the Indian economy slid from 7.1 per cent during the boom period to 5.3 per cent during the slowdown, Karnataka notched up its growth SDP rate from 7.1 to 9.2 per cent in the corresponding period. Karnataka also improved its per capita SDP rank from 10th in 1990-91 to 6th in 1999-2000. Despite a growth slippage in 1999-00, industrial sector registered a healthy average annual growth rate of over 9 per cent even in the slowdown.

TABLE 11.1

Relative growth performance of states: 1990s vs 1980s

Growth acceleration in 1990s		*Growth deceleration in 1990s*		*Growth stagnation in 1990s*	
Total GDP					
Gujarat	7.2 → 6.5	Assam	4.3 → 2.9	Andhra Pradesh	4.9 → 4.8
Karnataka	5.1 → 7.1	Bihar	4.3 → 2.8	Rajasthan	6.9 → 6.9
Kerala	2.0 → 5.7	Haryana	5.8 → 5.2	Uttar Pradesh	4.3 → 4.5
Maharashtra	6.1 → 6.6	Punjab	5.4 → 4.5		
Tamil Nadu	5.2 → 6.4	Orissa	5.1 → 2.3		
West Bengal	14.3 → 6.5				
Madhya Pradesh	3.2 → 5.1				
Agricultural GDP					
Karnataka	3.0 → 5.5	AndhraPradesh	4.2 → 2.3		
Kerala	–1.1 → 3.4	Assam	4.6 → 1.2		
Madhya Pradesh	0.3 → 3.7	Bihar	2.1 → 1.3		
Uttar Pradesh	1.6 → 3.0	Gujarat	10.4 → 2.9		
		Haryana	4.7 → 3.0		
		Maharashtra	5.5 → 3.1		
		Orissa	4.0 → -1.0		
		Punjab	5.7 → 2.8		
		Rajasthan	8.2 → 4.0		
		Tamil Nadu	5.2 → 3.7		
		West Bengal	4.9 → 4.4		

Table 11.1 Contd.

		Industrial GDP			
Andhra Pradesh	5.5 → 6.1	Assam	7.7 → 3.3	Punjab	7.0 → 6.8
Gujarat	7.2 → 9.3	Bihar	7.6 → 4.4	Uttar Pradesh	7.2 → 6.5
Karnataka	5.9 → 7.2	Orissa	7.5 → 3.7	Haryana	6.4 → 5.8
Kerala	3.3 → 6.9				
Madhya Pradesh	5.2 → 6.0				
Maharashtra	6.1 → 6.7				
Rajasthan	6.9 → 11.1				
Tamil Nadu	4.3 → 6.6				
West Bengal	13.2 → 12.7				
		Services GDP			
Andhra Pradesh	5.5 → 6.0	Assam	5.0 → 4.5	Gujarat	7.0 → 7.0
Karnataka	7.1 → 8.6	Bihar	6.1 → 4.7		
Kerala	4.1 → 6.6	Haryana	7.9 → 7.3		
Madhya Pradesh	5.5 → 6.0	Orissa	6.4 → 5.6		
Maharashtra	6.8 → 8.4	Uttar Pradesh	6.1 → 4.8		
Punjab	4.3 → 5.3				
Tamil Nadu	6.7 → 7.9				
West Bengal	4.6 → 8.5				

Source: CSO

Note: Growth rates are average annual growth rates.
A → B; where 'A' is average growth in 1980s and 'B' is average growth in 1990s.

Rajasthan registered high growth rates in all the sectors in 1990s. Agriculture (4.0 per cent), industry (11.1 per cent) and services (7.0 per cent). Overall growth of almost 7 per cent in the last 2 decades pushed up its ranking from 14th in 1980-81 (in terms of SDP per capita at 1993-94 prices) to 12th in 1999-2000. Had it not been for high rate population growth in Rajasthan, the gains could have been even more. High agricultural growth also brought a sharp decline in percentage of population below poverty line from 27 per cent in 1993-94 to 15 per cent in 1999-2000. Logging double-digit growth rates, industry outpaced the national industrial growth rate. This raised share of Rajasthan in India's industrial GDP from 4 per cent in 1990-91 to 6 per cent in 1999-2000.

In Andhra Pradesh (AP), overall SDP growth at 4.8 per cent per year was marginally below 4.9 per cent in the previous decade. Since growth in industry and services picked up in 1990s, stagnation in overall SDP growth is attributable solely to the poor performance of agriculture. Unlike in Karnataka, agricultural SDP growth in AP slid from 4.2 per cent in the 1980s to 2.3 in 1990s. Second half of nineties saw a pick up in SDP growth to 5.5 per cent. During the slowdown, industrial SDP growth in AP fell, a pattern seen in almost all the states, Karnataka being the exception. While growth in industrial and agricultural SDP decelerated during the slowdown, services sector improved its growth performance to 7.6 per cent.

Gujarat and Maharashtra are the two most industrialised states. Their industrial sectors contribute 40 per cent and 33 per cent respectively to the SDP. Together they contribute over 28 per cent to India's industrial SDP. Both the states witnessed high industrial growth in the boom phase. However, industrial growth decelerated after 1997-98. Industrial slowdown in Gujarat (4.9 per cent growth) was more pronounced than in Maharashtra (6.4 per cent growth) during this period. Deceleration in industrial growth was accompanied by a severe slide in the agricultural growth during the slowdown. Average SDP growth in agriculture in Gujarat and Maharastra during in this period was (–) 12.1 and (–) 3.0 per cent respectively. Services, however, continued to boom even in the slowdown.

Not all the states benefited from the liberalised environment in 1990s. Three eastern states (Assam, Bihar and Orissa) emerge as the losers in the reform process of 1990s. Growth rates in all the sectors (agriculture, industry and services) decelerated during 1990s in comparison to 1980s. These three states had the lowest per capita SDP and the highest poverty levels to begin with. A slowdown in SDP growth in the 1990s reduced the per capita SDP growth to anaemic levels of below 1 per cent per year. Also, these states were particularly hit by a slowdown in agricultural growth due to their high dependence on agriculture. Not only are the poverty levels in these states above the national average, poverty reduction too has been pathetically slow (Figure 11.2).

Poor performance of the industry in these states does not come as surprise. These states lack in infrastructure and skilled manpower. They could not take advantage of the dismantling of Licence Raj, which reduced the role of government in directing private investment and increased the role of enabling environment that a state could provide. During 1993-94 to 1996-97, when the Indian industry was growing at an average

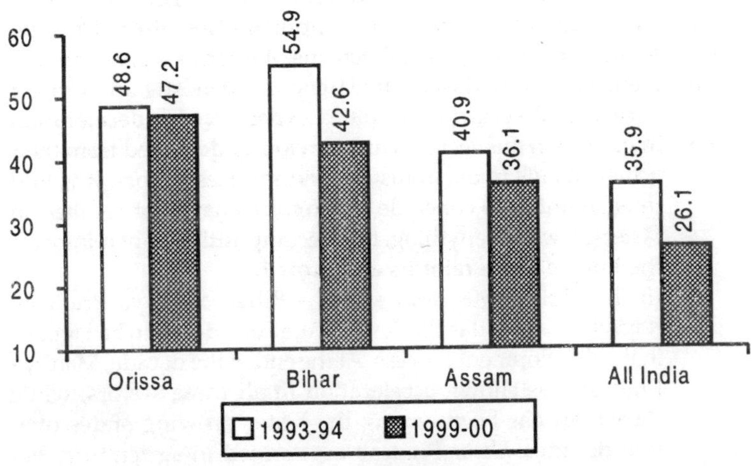

Figure 11.2
Percentage of Population below Poverty Line

Source: Human Development Report, Planning Commission, 2002.

rate of 8.5 per cent; Bihar, Assam and Orissa clocked growth rates of 1.2, 3.6 and 3.3 per cent; respectively. These developments underscore the need for these states to grow at higher rates to catch-up with others and a specific policy focus on these states.

It is not only the poorer states that lost out in the 1990s. Punjab and Haryana, which are among the richest states, too witnessed a significant growth deceleration. A deceleration in agricultural growth, together with the fact that agriculture has a high share in state GDP of Punjab (40 per cent) and Haryana (35 per cent), pulled the overall GDP growth down. Growth in industry and services in these states during the 1990s was also relatively weak.

Conclusion

Following generalisations can be made on the basis of sectoral growth comparisons across states.

- Most states have witnessed acceleration in both industry and services. Since the reforms of the 1990s were oriented primarily towards these two sectors, it may be reasonable to conclude that these states were, by and large, able to take advantage of the increased opportunities offered by the reforms. However, the full benefits of reforms were denied to them, because of the negative trend in the mostly unreformed agricultural sector. Most states experienced a deceleration in growth in this sector, which obviously detracted from their achievements in the industrial and services sectors. It would thus be unfair to conclude that reforms have not resulted in faster growth. If anything, this decomposition only reinforces the link between reforms and growth;
- In the early 1990s, four states – Bihar, Madhya Pradesh, Rajasthan and Uttar Pradesh – were considered to be laggard in the development process. At the end of the decade, Madhya Pradesh has shown acceleration in all three sectors, while Rajasthan has been among the faster growing states over two decades. Uttar Pradesh accelerated in agriculture, but stagnated elsewhere. Three states – Assam, Bihar and Orissa decelerated in all three sectors over the 1990s. Clearly, not all states were equally equipped to take advantage of reforms. Also, being laggard in the early 1990s did not necessarily

mean that such advantage could not be taken. There may be grounds here to consider putting an additional thrust on the laggard states to enable them to catch up.

NOTES

1. The term 'Hindu rate of growth', coined by Raj Krishna, refers to the 3.5 per cent growth rate to which the Indian economy was locked into until mid-seventies.

REFERENCES

Ahluwalia, M. S (2000): 'State Level Performance under Economic Reforms under Economic Reforms in India, Paper presented at the Conference on Indian Economic Prospects: Advancing Policy Reform, Stanford University, May.

Dholakia, R.H., 1994, 'Growth in India', *Economic and Political Weekly*, pp 2303-2309, August 27.

Kurien N.J., 2000 'Widening Regional Disparities in India: Indicators', *Economic and Political Weekly*, 538-550, February 12.

Nagraj, R., 1990, 'Growth Rate in India's GDP, 1950-51 to 1987-88: Examination of Alternative Hypothesis', *Economic and Political Weekly*, 1396-1403, June 30.

Raj K.N., 1984, 'Some Observations on Economic Growth in India over the period 1952-53 to 1982-83' Economic and Political Weekly, Vol. 19, No 41, October 13.

Rudra, Ashok, 1985, 'Economic Growth in India,' Economic and Political Weekly, Vol 20, No 15, April 13.

Sachs, Jeffrey D.N., Bajpai A, Ramiah, 2001, 'Understanding Regional Economic Growth in India', Paper prepared for Asian Economic Panel Meeting held at Seoul, October 26.

Chapter 12

Trade Liberalisation and the Poor
A Framework for Poverty Reduction Policies with Special Reference to Some Asian Countries, including India[1]

Somesh K. Mathur

Introduction

One of the most prominent features of the world economy over the last twenty years, has been the liberalisation of international trade and payments under the auspices of the GATT (and now the WTO), the IMF and the World Bank. This is one of the reasons that world trade has grown nearly five times faster than world output. However developing economies like India have insignificant share in the world trade less than 1 per cent. The purpose of this paper is to explore some aspects and consequences of the liberalisation process that affect the overall economic performance of countries and welfare of peoples within countries.

Trade liberalisation involves reducing tariffs and non-tariff barriers. This is achieved not simply by eliminating quotas and reducing average tariffs and dispersion across tariff, but also by strengthening trade related institutions, in particular customs and standards bodies. In general, liberalisation refers to all measures taken to reduce anti-export bias and import controls, including non-tariff barriers and exchange rate distortions.

Proponents of globalisation argue that greater integration with the world economy may reduce poverty. Two mechanisms usually identified in this context are firstly, reduced industrial protection should turn terms of trade in favour of agriculture and thereby raise agricultural (and rural) incomes; and, second, that this should increase industrial employment, since comparative advantage would favour labour intensive manufacturing in regions with abundant labour.

There is ample empirical evidence that trade liberalisation increases growth rate of income and output (Sachs & Warner, 1995; Dollar, 1992; Edwards, 1993 and 1998; Ben David, 1993; Frankel and Romer 1999, among others). Also, the link of overall growth to poverty alleviation has been demonstrated both in cross country analyses (Dollar and Kray, 2000) and for individual countries.[2] Trade liberalisation can therefore be expected to help the poor given the positive association between openness and growth. The paper tests the hypothesis that whether trade openness promotes growth for fourteen Asian countries included in our sample. The study also examines the impact of growth rates, trade openness and inequality of incomes on poverty. Significance of growth rates and trade openness on inequality of incomes is also measured. Cross-country regression is used for analysis. This paper provides the basic elements of a good trade policy regime and how it can work for the benefit of the poor. These can provide a benchmark against which to judge the prevailing trade and provide guidance for the direction of reforms for the poor in future. It is organised as follows. Section I examines the benefit of the globalisation process for some South Asian countries included in our study. Section II discusses the linkages between trade, trade policy and poverty. A framework is given to examine the impact of trade liberalisation on poverty through its impact on prices (and hence consumption) and income (Production). Section III reviews some literature which links trade liberalisation with growth rates, poverty and inequality. Section IV gives empirical evidence between poverty and growth rates, trade openness and inequality of incomes for cross section of fourteen Asian countries included in our study. Section V discusses the various trade policy instruments which can work for the benefit of the poor. Section VI gives some general guidelines for poverty reduction. The last section gives conclusion.

Gains of Globalization

Greater integration with the international economy may reduce poverty through two routes: terms of trade and employment effect. Two mechanisms usually identified are first, that reduced industrial protection should turn terms of trade in favour of agriculture and thereby agricultural(and rural) incomes; and, second, increase industrial employment, since comparative advantage would favour labour intensive manufacturing in regions with abundant labour. Sen(2003) however notes that reduced protection to industry in South Asian countries have not been able to raise agricultural terms of trade. He notes that agricultural terms of trade have actually worsened in Bangladesh, Pakistan and Nepal. The domestic policies regarding food subsidies and price support in India and Sri Lanka, however, has raised cereal prices and thus improved terms of trade (Table 12.1). In the South Asian Region it is services that gained from the shift in the terms of trade against manufacturing, suggesting not only that skill differentials increased but also considerable part of the dividend from reduced tariffs was retained by trade

TABLE 12.1

Sectoral Price Relatives to Overall GDP Deflator

	1979 (Ag)	*1989 (Ag)*	*1998 (Ag)*	*1979 (Man.)*	*1989 (Man.)*	*1998 (Man)*
Bangladesh	100	83.5	85.8	100	101.4	95.4
India	100	107.0	119.1	100	101.4	90.5
Nepal	100	82.2	86.6	100	92.7	94.5
Pakistan	100	116.0	104.0	100	95.7	91
Sri Lanka	100	109.9	121.0	100	95	81.7

Source: World Bank Country Tables, 2000.

and finance. Despite overall GDP growth being maintained or slightly improved the growth of agricultural GDP decelerated throughout the region (Table 12.2). This combination of slower output growth in agriculture with deteriorating terms of trade is the major reason why rural incomes in South Asia have tended to lag behind urban incomes. Globalisation would have had greater effect if agricultural growth would not have lagged due to falling terms of trade, low technology diffusion and cuts in public investment including investment in rural infrastructure, public irrigation, roads and power.

As far as employment is concerned there is complicated picture among the South Asian countries (Table 12.3). It is true, for example, that garment exports and employment has expanded rapidly, particularly in Bangladesh and Sri-Lanka. However in both countries this occurred alongside significant decline in employment in other import substituting industries. In Pakistan, manufacturing as a whole experienced a severe slowdown. In India, the 1990s patterns is more complicated with manufacturing employment stagnant in unorganized sector (covers approximately 93 per cent of the employment), but a marginal increase in employment in organized firms after reforms (Tendulkar, 2000). However, data from labour surveys by ILO show that industrial employment in India had declined in the late 1990s (Table 12.3).

TABLE 12.2
Growth Rates of Sectoral GDP

	1980s (Agri)	*1990s (Agri)*	*1980s (Ind)*	*1990s (Ind)*	*1980s (Serv)*	*1990s (Serv)*
Bangladesh	2.7	1.6	4.1	7.3	5.4	5
India	3.4	3.1	6.6	6.5	6.7	7.5
Nepal	3.8	2.4	8.5	7.4	3.5	6.3
Pakistan	4.6	4.4	7.3	4.3	7.2	4.5
Sri Lanka	3.5	2.1	5	7.1	6.5	5.6

Source: World Bank Country Tables, 2000.

TABLE 12.3
Sectoral Distribution of Employment

	Bangladesh	*India*	*Pakistan*	*Sri-Lanka*
Agr. Early 80s	57.1	68.7	52.7	45.9
1990	66.4	62.1	47.5	41.4
Late 90s	63.2	63.9	50.0	35.1
Inds Early 80s	12.1	13.8	18.9	18.6
1990	13.0	15.5	19.1	25.7
Late 90s	9.6	14.3	16.7	22.4
Serv Early 80s	26.4	17.5	28.4	29.3
1990	16.2	22.3	33.4	29.6
Late 90s	25.0	21.8	33.3	38.8

Source: ILO, KLIM data set from Labour Force Surveys.

Trade, Trade Policy and Poverty

It is useful to consider the linkages that exist among trade, trade policy, and poverty. In a comprehensive paper on this topic, Winters (2000a, b) identifies several key linkages, which are reiterated in large part by Bannister and Thugge (2001). Potential links include changes in:

(a) price and availability of goods;
(b) factor prices, income and employment;
(c) government transfers influenced by changes in revenue from trade taxes;
(d) incentive for investment and innovation, which affect long-run economic growth;
(e) external shocks, in particular, changes in terms of trade;
(f) short-run risk and adjustment costs.

Our paper develops a framework linking trade with poverty using link (a) and (b).

Linkages (b) through (f) tend to be less frequently considered. A study by Levin (2000) focuses on transfers, link (c). A number of economy-wide analyses account for terms of trade effects, link (e) Factor price, income, and employment link (b) may have the greatest relative importance of all the links between trade and poverty. Household survey data as well as casual observation suggest that people tend to be much more heterogeneous with respect to income than with respect to consumption. In other words, two households may have identical commodity budget shares, and same level of income, but entirely different sources of income. This point is underscored by the fact that opposition to free trade initiatives often arises from groups with highly specialised income, such as steel workers and sugar farmers in the US, to name just two examples.

Income effects are the key to the famous Stolper- Samuelson theorem, which relates international trade to the domestic distribution of income (Dixit and Norman). By the Heckscher-Ohlin theorem, a country has a comparative advantage in a good that intensively uses the country's relatively abundant factor. Free trade will increase the relative price of that good increase real return of the relatively abundant factor by an even larger percentage. At the same time, trade will reduce the return to the relatively scarce factor, though to a smaller degree. As a result, it can be said that changes in commodity prices due to trade liberalisation magnify the resulting changes in factor prices.

Presence of this Magnification Effect (Jones, 1965) in theoretical trade models is one reason why trade economists tend to focus on factor market effects when analyzing trade liberalisation and poverty. Some (for example, Winters, 2000a, b) have argued that the practical relevance of the Stolper-Samuleson/Magnification result is negligible, since it rests on so many restrictive assumptions. Nevertheless, this theoretical insight underscores the importance of considering factor earnings effects when examining the relationship between trade liberalisation and poverty.

Three empirical studies reinforce this view. A general equilibrium analysis of technical change in the Philippines by Coxhead and Warr (1995) found earnings effects to be substantially more important than consumption effects. In particular, income effects accounted for two-thirds of poverty alleviation when there was a rise in agricultural productivity. Nature of the shock is not dissimilar since the adjustments are transmitted through commodity and factor markets. Harrison,

Rutherford, and Tarr(World Bank studies, 1996) find that factor price changes drive the incidence of trade liberalisation in Turkey. They demonstrate this by employing three counterfactuals in which the 40 representative households in the analysis (differentiated by rural/urban orientation and by income level) have (i) identical consumption shares, (ii) identical factor income shares, and then (iii) identical consumption and factor income shares. Since counter-factual (i) provided nearly identical results to those generated when the heterogeneity of the 40 households is left intact, The authors conclude that 'clearly, for the poor it is the source of income, not the pattern of expenditure that is driving the adverse impact relative to the average household.'

A general equilibrium analysis by Warr (2001) of Thailand's proposed rice export tax also suggests that factor earnings effects are the driving force behind welfare and distributional effects. Although an export tax generates government revenue and lowers the price of rice for consumers, it also lowers the return to unskilled labour, which is used intensively in the Thai rice industry. Because both rural and urban poor derive more than 40 percent of their income from unskilled labour (according to the Thai survey upon which the stylised households are based), negative income effect ends up outweighing consumption benefit, such that both rural and urban poor are harmed by the export tax.

Despite the apparent importance of factor earnings effects, they are often not accounted for in studies that quantify the effects of external shocks on the poor in developing countries, This is particularly the case for analyses based on detailed household surveys, because abstracting from this particular linkage may be quite misleading, this paper will pay particular attention to how each analysis deals with the income side of the story. At the same time, the issue of whether a focus on 'factor markets' is the same as a focus on 'income' is not explored in depth here. It can be argued that many of the poor are subsistence farmers and largely disconnected from markets, is largely determined by their net trade position in a food commodity such as rice. Studies that explore this in detail include Ravallion (1990) and Ravallion and van de Walle (1991). As to the importance of thinking about a household's income in terms of commodities versus factors, Cranfieid, Hertel, Preckel, and Ivanic (2001) provide interesting survey evidence on this issue for seven developing countries.

Trade Reform and the Poor: A Simple Framework

In order to provide an overview of the various possible effects of a trade policy reform we follow Hoekman et.al. (2001a). The model assumes three types of sectors [those producing import-substitute goods(M), exportable goods(X) and non-tradable or home goods(H)] and two factors of production, labour and capital. The only asset of the poor consists of labour,while the asset owned by non-poor is capital.

The effects of trade policy reform on the poor depend on the consumption and production of the poor in these three sectors. Effects also differ in the short and long run. In the short run,factors of production are immobile, while they are mobile in the long run.

The model assumes that countries have no power to affect world prices of trade goods and that labour markets functions efficiently. Nominal and real wages are flexible. Domestic prices of M(Pm) and X(Px) depend on their world price and on policy variables such as exchange rate and import tariffs. On the other hand the price of H (Ph) is determined fundamentally by domestic supply and demand. In the long-run resource allocation depends on relative prices only, such as Px/Pm and Px/Ph.With three nominal prices, there are only two independent relative prices.For instance choosing Px/Pm and Px/Ph, the third relative price(Pm/Ph) is obtained by dividing Px/Ph by Px/Pm.[3]

Trade liberalization(a reduction in tariffs) raises Px/Pm,and labour and capital have an incentive to move from M to X.Whether Pm falls or Px rises makes an enormous difference in the short run and is likely to determine the success of the reform. This is where complementary policies play crucial role, including exchange rate policy.

Suppose the nominal exchange rate (ER) remains

unchanged following a tariff reduction. Then Pm falls while Px remains unchanged, and labour and capital in sector M are hurt in the short run. Groups that are hurt are likely to lobby for a policy reversal. Also, though in the long run both imports and exports increase with a tariff reduction, imports tend to increase faster than exports, with a likely deficit in the balance of trade that may be unsustainable. Pressure from short-term losers and the balance of trade problem may result in a failure of the reform. This outcome can be avoided or its effects mitigated by depreciation of the domestic currency. This raises the price of importables relative to non-tradables, and helps dampen both the increase in import demand and the decline of labour and capital's nominal income in sector M. On the other hand, labour and capital in sector X benefit from the devaluation since Px increases.[4]

Thus, a policy package of tariff reduction and currency depreciation should make it easier for the factors of production in sector M in the short run and during the transition period, and should dampen the resistance to the reform. In countries with a flexible or floating exchange rate policy, lower tariff will raise the demand for imports and foreign exchange. This will raise the price of foreign exchange or lower the value of domestic currency. In other words, exchange rate will depreciate.This is similar to a devaluation except that it is determined by market and not by monetary authorities.

Effect of trade reform on the poor also depends on Px/Ph. It depends not only on policy but also on consumer reaction to the policy since it is determined by supply and demand. Px/Ph rises following a tariff reduction, though less than Px/Pm.

When the value of the nominal exchange rate cannot be changed, a tariff reduction has no impact on Px but lowers Pm. This leads to a shift in consumption from H and X to M, and thus to a reduction in Ph (though less than the reduction in Pm). This implies an increase in Px/Ph. With a full devaluation equivalent to the tariff reduction, Pm remains unchanged and Px rises by the magnitude of the depreciation, shifting consumption from X to M and H, raising Ph. Px/Ph rises by the exact same amount as in the absence of devaluation. Finally, with flexible exchange rates, the depreciation is less than the reduction in the tariff, so Pm fails, while Px rises. Consumption shifts from X to H and M, and from H to M, so the net effect on the demand for H is ambiguous, as is the effect on Ph. Note, however, that Px/Ph rises exactly as in the other two cases.

Effects on Real Income in the Short Run

Impact of trade reform on the poor in the short run will critically depend on their location in terms of consumption and production (income), in particular whether they are employed in tradable or nontradable activities. Three cases to consider that indicate types of effects that may arise:

(i) Poor employed in the exportable sector. Relative price of sector X increases. Thus, in the short run, as factors are not mobile across sectors, wage rate of labour employed in X increases. On the consumption side, labour (and the poor, by assumption) would gain as long as they consume either some M or some H or both (since their prices fall). Thus, labour's real income must improve; and the higher the proportion the poor spend on H and M, the larger the gains. Thus, the real income of labour in X must rise, or remain unchanged in the unlikely circumstance that the poor spend their entire income on the exportable X.

(ii) Poor employed in the importable sector. If, poor produce in the importable sector, a tariff reduction would lead to a decline in the wage of the poor (labour) employed in the importable sector. How much they would lose depends on the consumption effect: if they spend all their income on importables, the income and consumption effects would cancel out and the net effect of trade liberalisation on their real income would be zero. However, if they also consume X and H, they will lose. The expected result is that the poor lose in the short run, but their loss is smaller than the decline in their wages, because of the gains from the effect of trade liberalization on the prices of things they consume.

(iii) Poor produce only in the non-tradable sector. With the decline

in the price of H, the wage rate in that sector also declines by about the same percentage. On the other hand, labour in H also benefits from the lower cost of consuming M and H. It is possible that the impact on real income of the poor rises because the cost of the consumption bundle falls more than their wages. In general, impact on the real income of labour in H is ambiguous and depends on the shares of M, X and H in the consumption basket, and on the response of the price of H to trade liberalisation. Larger the share of M in the consumption basket of the poor, greater the likelihood that they will gain. They must gain if they only consume M, they must lose if they only consume X, and they are unaffected if they only consume H.

These results are summarized in the matrix in (Table 12.4). Each cell in the matrix represents the 'location' of the poor in terms of production and consumption. First sign represents effect of trade liberalisation on income of the poor, i.e. the return to their assets (labour). Second sign represents effect on their real income due to changes in the cost of their consumption basket. Thus a '+' after the 'I' sign means that cost of their consumption basket has fallen following trade liberalisation. Sign in parenthesis gives the net effect of changes

TABLE 12.4

Location of the poor and effects of trade liberalization in the short-run

	M	*X*	*H*	*TOTAL©*
M	-/+(0)	-/-(-)	-/+(-)	-/(+)(-)
X	+/+(+)	+/-(0)	+/+(+)	+/+(+)
H	-/+(+)	-/-(-)	(-)/+(0)	-/+(?)
TOTAL®	?/+(+)	?/-(-)	?/+(?)	

Note: The Total© gives the effect for the poor that receive their income from production in only one sector but their consumption basket includes products from the three sectors.

Total® gives the effect for the poor that consumes products from only one sector but receive their income from the three sectors.

in their nominal income and cost of their consumption baskets on their real income in different 'locations.' To summarise, the best outcome is when the poor are employed primarily in the exportable sector X and consume importable goods M. And the worst outcome occurs if the poor are primarily employed in sector M and consume primarily exportable goods X.

Although the discussion has focused on trade reform involving tariffs, in practice, reforms often involve the abolition of quantitative restrictions (QRs) such as import licenses. As discussed above, due to rent-seeking, shifting from QRs to tariffs could significantly help the poor.

Effects in the Long Run

In the long run, labour and capital are mobile across sectors. Then, trade liberalisation results in a contraction of sector M and an expansion of sector X. If, as is likely for most low income developing countries, M is on average capital intensive while X is relatively labour intensive, then, in the new output configuration results in an increased demand for labour and a higher nominal wage rate. As the prices of M and H fall, labour's real income rises as well. Consequently, while in the short run some labour employed in M loses from trade liberalisation and the impact on labour in H is ambiguous, when factors are mobile, labour in both sectors gain. Of course, for this to apply to all the poor, labour markets need to be integrated. If they are segmented, then some poor could lose, especially if they are employed in the import competing sector and are unable to move. In order to ensure that poor are better off following trade liberalisation, conditions affecting functioning of the labour market are therefore critical.

In the analysis presented above, it is assumed that all factors are fully employed and changes in trade policy are reflected in changes in relative factor prices. In practice, there may be a large supply of unskilled labour in the subsistence sector that can be employed at a fixed real wage in the modern sector. Trade reform may have a positive impact in this case, not through increase in the wages of the unskilled workers but rather by reducing the amount of unemployed or underemployed in the subsistence sector and inducing an expansion of output of modern sector. Indeed, following Indian trade reform in 1991, manufacturing employment increased faster while wages increased slower than before the reform (Winters, 2000 a, b). In most cases, one can expect a lasting trade policy reform to have a mixture of quantity and price effects on the labour markets. But no matter what the situation, labour mobility is essential in order to ensure movement of workers from the contracting to expanding sectors.

Sector-Specific Issues

Above framework is highly stylised and abstracts from many factors that are important in determining the impact of reform on the poor. Such factors include the existence of imperfect competition and inter-sectoral dependencies. For example, although the agricultural sector is generally made up of small farms, this is typically not the case for marketing and distribution services. In a number of LDCS, marketing is organised by public agencies, who usually fix producer prices at levels below world prices and do not always change them in response to changes in world prices or in exchange rates. An issue to take into account is the degree to which farmers consume their own output. The greater the share of own consumption, the smaller the impact of the reforms on real income of the farmers. If farmers consume exactly what they produce, then the real income effect of trade reform on them is nil. If farmers are net buyers, it is often argued that in that case farmers lose from an increase in price of the product they produce. This may well be the case. But one must also consider that in order to be net buyers, they need to obtain additional income. If this additional income is obtained by working on other farms, real income need not decline given that nominal rural wages will tend to increase with the price of farm products (or increase with trade reform in the long run).

Trade Liberalisation, Growth, Inequality and Poor

Trade is likely to make impact on the poor through higher growth. However, impact on the poor over a period of years would depend on how steady growth is and, also whether growth is poor-friendly. There are numerous individual country studies which suggest that 'trade does seem to create, even sustain higher growth (Bhagwati and Srinivasan, 1999). A country's trade policy is the key link in the transmission of price signals from world markets. In combination with exchange rate, it allows resource allocation consistent with comparative advantage,thereby increasing productivity. An open trade regime and investment regime encourages integration into global trading environment and import of diverse and modern technologies that are important for productivity improvements (Coe, Helpman and Hoomaister, 1997) for evidence and Romer (1994) for a further discussion. However, it has been argued that from 1960 to mid-1990s in some of the East Asian Economies (like Hong Kong, Korea, Singapore, Taipei, Indonesia, Malaysia and Thailand) it was domestic investment boom which sustained growth process rather than outward oriented policies (Rodrik, 1995). According to him, exports were initially too small in relation to GDP to have a significant effect on aggregate growth. Boom was the outcome of number of strategic government interventions and favourable initial conditions,such as presence of an educated labour force and equality of income and wealth. Many have contested their argument. Bhagwati (1996) opined that even if it originated from sources other than trade policy reform, investment boom could not have nurtured in a closed economy.

However, for most of developing economies agricultural growth is important. Strategy of inward-oriented development, in which exports are not encouraged because imports are kept to a minimum, proved to be ineffective everywhere, even in most populous countries such as Brazil,China,India and the former Soviet Union(Bajpai and Sachs, 1998).

Trade can affect the poor adversely if economic growth worsens the income distribution. Table 12.5 documents the data for India. This table reports worsening of distribution in 1997.

TABLE 12.5
Distribution of Per-Capita Expenditure in India

Year	*Lowest* 20%	*Second* 20%	*Third* 20%	*Fourth* 20%	*Highest* 20%
1972	8.5	12.6	16.5	21.8	40.6
1973	9	13.1	17.2	22.6	38.1
1977	8.5	12.5	16.4	21.7	40.9
1983	8.6	12.7	16.5	21.7	40.5
1987	8.9	12.5	16.3	21.3	41
1992	8.8	12.5	16.2	21.4	41.1
1994	9.2	13	16.8	21.7	39.3
1997	8.1	11.6	15	19.3	46

Source: The figures for 1994 are from World Bank Development indicators on CD-ROM. All other figures are from NSS,reported in Datt(1999).

However, Deininger-Squire(1996) and the WIDER(2000) data suggests that there is virtually no change in income distribution (defined as share of bottom 40 percent) over twenty-five year period (1972 to 1997). The constancy of the share of the bottom 40 per cent has implication for studies on poverty. It means that the poor have shared equally in whatever economic growth has occurred.

Xavier Sala-I-Martin(2002) using data for 125 countries concludes that poverty rates as well as absolute headcounts declined significantly from 1970 to 1998. Moreover, income inequality also declined, particularly in the last two decades. The author uses nine inequality indices to offer the same result: though inequality remained more or less constant in 1970s, it declined substantially in the 1980s and 1990s. As a result, the shape of the income distribution has changed, from a bimodal distribution with peak of poor people and peak of rich in 1970 to a smoother distribution in 1998, suggesting emergence of world middle class.

Dollar and Kray (2001) defined the poor as the lowest 20 percent of the population, and assumed that poverty falls if the mean income of the bottom 20 percent goes up relative to the mean income of the population. Dollar and Kray's regression analysis, which used data from 80 countries for four decades, indicated that trade openness enhances growth, which affects all income groups proportionately. This result was robust with respect to variation over time, between rich and poor countries, and between crisis and non-crisis periods. However, openness does not have any direct impact on income distribution – either positive or negative – other than through growth.

There are three reasons why growth is crucial to poverty reduction (Panagariya,2002). First, when the growth is nearly 3 per cent or more in per capita terms, it overwhelms any negative effects resulting from increased inequality. It gives rise to what Jagdish Bhagwati call the powerful pull-up effect rather than what skeptics call the trickle down effect. This effect rapidly brings the poor into gainful employment. Second, faster growth generates much more resources to finance anti-poverty programmes. Finally, growth also improves the ability of the poor to access public services. At low levels of income, most poor people send their children to work. It is only increased incomes that result in the children being able to switch from work to school.

Trade Openness, Growth, Inequality and Poverty: Empirical Evidence from Some Asian Economies

We have run OLS regression on cross country data for fourteen Asian countries. Statistical software Statmost is used for the analysis. The countries included are India, Pakistan, Bangladesh, Nepal, Sri Lanka from South Asia and Indonesia, Malaysia, Philippines, Hong Kong, China, Japan, Singapore, Thailand and South Korea from East Asia. Dependent variable is poverty as measured by population below the international poverty line of $ 1 per day; the independent factors are average annual trade openness and average annual per capita GNP and GNP growth rates(1960–97) and measure of inequality - 'Gini average' (the average Gini across all observations for the given sample period for each country included in the sample). Gini coefficient[6] in 1990s is also regressed on economic growth rates and trade openness to examine the impact of such factors on income distribution.

Regression analysis results shows that trade openness is one of the significant factors in explaining variation in growth of PCGDP for fourteen Asian countries (note in Table 12.6 for the regression result). In turn economic growth process(1960–1997) has significant impact on reducing poverty for these economies in the 1990s (note of Table 12.7 for the regression results). Trade openness has significant effect in reducing poverty for all countries in the sample. However, it becomes an insignificant factor in explaining poverty when per capita growth rates are included as an additional explanatory factor. Effect of trade openness is captured by per capita growth rates. This suggests that trade openness has impact on poverty via raising economic growth rates (note in Table 12.7).

Inequality of income(Average Gini) during the last three decades has no significant impact on poverty for the Asian economies in the 1990s t-values are insignificant but surprisingly they come out with negative signs for the sample included in our study suggesting that higher inequality tend to reduce poverty (note in Table 12.7).

Also, neither economic growth nor average trade openness from 1960–1997 are significant factors in explaining inequality of incomes in 1990s as measured by Gini coefficient for the fourteen Asian economies. Signs of the independent factors suggest that higher economic growth rates tends to reduce inequality while higher trade openness tends to increase inequality (see note in Table 12.7).

Above analysis for fourteen Asian countries confirms the results of other studies (Dollar and Kray, 2001) that raising economic growth rates is the factor which reduces poverty across economies.Trade openness tends to increase economic growth rates. No significant relationship could be however found in our study between changes in inequality and poverty, and economic growth rates, trade openness and inequality of incomes (see notes in Table 12.8).

TABLE 12.6
Average Trade Openness, Growth of GNP, Per-Capita GNP and Volume of Trade for Some Asian Countries

	Average Annual Growth Rate of Volume of Trade (1960–97)	*Average Annual Growth Rate of GNP (1960–97)*	*Average Annual Growth Rate of Per-Capita GNP: 1960–97*	*Average Trade Openness (Trade (Exports +Imports) / GNP) in % 1960-97*
Bangladesh	5.6	3.879	1.58	26.33
China	11	7.725	6.215	27.92
Hong Kong	8.7	7.977	5.61	280.31
India	7.9	4.712	2.55	15.43
Indonesia	8	6.26700	4.24	50.94
Japan	5.100	5.5100	4.45	18.21
South Korea	12	7.94100	6.16	74.84
Malaysia	8.8	7.073	4.37	144.66
Nepal	6.9	3.465	1.12	34.83
Pakistan	6.7	5.743	2.78	34.82
Philippines	8.3	4.179	1.45	55.41
Singapore	9.4	8.6	6.43	354.18
Sri-Lanka	4.1	4.572	2.88	70.40
Thailand	10	7.516	5.13	70.12

Source: GNP and Per Capita GNP data is in constant 1995 US $.GNP, PCGNP and Trade data from World Bank World Development Indicators in CD-ROM for various years.

Note: Regressing Average Annual Growth Rate of GNP(Y-Column 2) on Average Trade Openness(X-Column 4) yields

$Y = 3.0545 + 0.5915X$

t- (5.1640) (2.192)

$R^2 = 0.28$

$F = 4.809$

TABLE 12.7
Economic Growth, Poverty and Inequality Index for Some Asian Countries

	Average Annual Growth Rate of GNP (1960-1997)	*Average Annual Growth Rate of Per-Capita GNP: 1960-97*	*Average Population Below $ 1 a day in 1990s*	*Gini Average*	*Gini Coefficient in % in 1990s*
	Col. (1)	*Col. (2)*	*Col. (3)*	*Col. (4)*	*Col. (5)*
Bangladesh	3.879	1.58	29.1	36 (1963-86)	33.6
China	7.725	6.215	18.5	32.68 (1980-92)	40.3
Hong Kong	7.977	5.61	0.1	41.58 (1971-91)	42
India	4.712	2.55	44.2	32.55 (1951-92)	37.8
Indonesia	6.26700	4.24	7.7	33.67 (1964-90)	31.7
Japan	5.5100	4.45	0.1	34.82 (1962-90)	24.9
South Korea	7.94100	6.16	1	34.52 (1965-88)	31.6
Malaysia	7.073	4.37	0.1	50.76 (1970-84)	49.2
Nepal	3.465	1.12	37.7	36 (1960-90)	36.7
Pakistan	5.743	2.78	31	31.55 (1969-88)	31.2
Philippines	4.179	1.45	49	48.53 (1957-85)	46.2
Singapore	8.6	6.43	0.1	40.12 (1973-89)	38
Sri Lanka	4.572	2.88	6.6	42.50 (1953-87)	34.4
Thailand	7.516	5.13	2		41.4

Source: GNP and Per Capita GNP data is in constant 1995 US $. GNP and PCGNP data is from World Bank World Development Indicators in Cdrom. for various years. Poverty data (international poverty line) and Gini index (area between lorenz curve and line of equality) are from the World Bank World Development Indicators 2001. Note Higher values of Gini index indicate higher levels of inequality. Gini Average data in Column 4 for years indicated in the bracket (Sarel, 1997)

Note: Regressing Poverty (Column 3 of Table 12.7) on Trade Openness (Column 4 in Table 12.6)

Poverty = 24.21 -.088 Trade Openness

t-values (4.06) (2.00)

$R^2 = 0.25$

F = 3.1

Regressing Poverty (Column 3 of Table 12.7) on Per Capita Growth Rates (Column2 of Table 12.7) and Trade Openness (Column 4 in Table 12.6)

Poverty = 46.037 -7.1471PCGNPGR-.019452 Trade Openness

t-values (5.862) (-3.347) (-.503) R^2 = 0.1179
F = 9.28
Regressing Poverty (Column 3 of Table 12.7) on Growth rates(Column I in Table 12.7) and Trade Openness(Column 4 in Table 12.6)
Poverty = 61.285- 7.2272 GNPGR-.012184 Trade Openess
t-values (4.048) (-2.588) (-.259)
R^2 = 0.533
F = 6.285
Regressing Poverty (Column 3 of Table 12.7) on Per-Capita Growth Rates (Column 2 in Table 12.7) and Gini Average (Column 4 in Table 12.7)
Poverty = 70.1027 -7.755PCGNPGR -0.61 GINI Average
t-values (3.30) (-4.51) (-1.18)
R^2 = 0.662
F = 10.8
Regressing Inequality of Income (Gini)-(Column 5 of Table 12.7) on Growth rate(Column I in Table 12.7) and Trade Openness (Column 4 in Table 12.6)
GINI = 36.04 - 1.78GNPGR +.023 Trade Openess
t-values (4.88) (-.1315) (1.0265)
R^2=0.06279 ,F=.7447
Regressing Inequality of Income (Gini)-(Column 5 of Table 12.7) on Per-Capita Growth Rate (Column2 in Table 12.7) and Trade Openness (Column 4 in Table 12.6)
GINI = 37.533 -.78803PCGNPGR +.0228 Trade Openess
t-values (-.691) (1.416)
R^2 = 0.154
F = 1.005

Identifying Good Trade Policies to benefit the Poor

In practice, the most practical way of stimulating trade and opening up to international economy is through liberal trade regimes rather than through a complex structure of protection and export incentives. Basic elements of a good trade policy regime involve predictability, transparency and uniformity. A liberal trade regime provides guidance for the direction of reforms.

As a practical matter, duty drawback mechanisms are ineffective in most of the developing economies, Thus, a regime with high protection will diminish exports and growth. Moreover, differentiated structures of protection and subsidisation creates opportunities for the elite and powerful producers groups to capture trade policy for their special interests. This lobbying for protection and subsidies engenders corruption and inefficiencies which, in the end hurt the poor.

These problems can be avoided by simple and transparent protection regimes of low uniform tariffs. Most low income countries have differentiated tariff structures with significant tariff escalation. Main reason include fiscal objectives, import substitution motivations combined with the political weight of vested interests. Tariff escalation is a problem since it affords high effective protection to final goods producers,thereby discouraging the development of intermediate industries. Exporting of intermediate products is an important way for developing countries to participate in modern global economy; but these activities are discouraged by the escalation of tariifs.

A uniform tariff conveys a number of advantages (Tarr, 2001), the most important of which is that if tariff is uniform, gains to industry lobbying are much smaller (and may be negative), creating a kind of free rider problem for the lobbying industry and dramatically reduces the incentive to lobby for protection[7]

A uniform tariff greatly simplifies custom operations, eliminates a number of ways used to avoid paying tariff and should help reduce corruption and save on scarce administrative resources. There will also be a direct saving of resources from reduced lobbying for higher protection and an associated gain from encouraging scarce entrepreneurial talent to be employed more productively in the creation of better and cheaper products. Overall, level of protection is likely to be lower as incentive to lobby for higher tariffs is attentuated. Many of these factors are pro-poor as they greatly reduce scope for the exercise of power and rent seeking.

Uniformity does not imply that there can be no exemptions for products that are deemed to be of great social importance such as essential medicines. However, care should be taken that such exceptions target only products that are critical to attain social and public health objectives.

If tariffs are important for revenue generation, uniformity

implies that overall level of the tariff should be such as to generate the revenue required. However, some products such as alcohol and tobacco products may be subjected to high duties to raise revenue as long as equivalent excise taxes are imposed on domestic production. Dispersion often generated by exemptions and tariff escalation will lead to high effective rates of protection and is likely to entail significant inefficiencies.

Many countries tend to use anti-dumping as a safeguard instrument. India, for example is largest perpetrator of anti-dumping duties (Mathur, 2001a). This is not advised. Anti-dumping is a trade policy instrument that allows duties to be imposed on imports that are sold for less than what is charged in the exporters home market. That is, it can be invoked to offset price discrimination across markets. Such differential pricing usually reflects economic conditions and is not detrimental to welfare. As anti-dumping is an instrument that is easily captured by industries to raise price of imports, and requires use of scarce administrative resources. It is counterproductive to economic development and poverty reduction. If there is need to raise protection because imports injure domestic industry it is preferable to use WTO consistent safeguard actions as they allow the country to consider impact of taking action on the economy as a whole, including the poor as opposed to simply the industry that confronts import competition.[8]

The best policy option from a development perspective in this area is to have no anti-dumping instrument. If anti-dumping procedures are adopted efforts should be made to establish procedures that allow for national interest and impact on the poor to be taken into account prior to the imposition of an anti-dumping duty.

In addition to the commercial policy instruments there are number of trade related institutions that can have important implications for the impact of trade reforms. Custom clearance efficiency and transparency is an important determinant of costs associated with trade. Burdensome and redundant procedures can give rise to substantial uncertainty and are often associated with rent seeking and corruption. Minimising discretion by simplifying as much as possible clearance process, elimination of exemptions and providing officials with training and appropriate information technology are important dimensions of trade reform. An efficient customs clearance process is required.

Non-tariff barriers are in place for reasons other than for health or safety these are the most pernicious of trade barriers in terms of their harm to growth and poverty alleviation. Partly this is because non-tariff barriers encourage competing interest to lobby to obtain the valuable licenses to import. This competing lobbying wastes valuable resources. Non-tariff barriers also lack tranparency,and and thereby may allow protection to go relatively unnoticed. As discussed above, the political economy of protection suggests that import controls (and then sometimes export controls) are usually put in place to benefit powerful interest groups.

Overall analysis of the trade regime should yield a preliminary judgement on the desirability of trade reform. Analysis of both the impact of the status quo policy and the alternative reforms on the poor is important. Tools to undertake such an analysis can be constructed for most economies; basic requirements include detailed data on imports and exports, trade barriers that apply to those goods, household survey information on the consumption pattern of the poor and sources of their income and data on basic structure of the economy.

This judgement should be reviewed in the light of the potential short-term effects of trade reform on the poor. If there are possible negative affects, it is important to identify the relevant products and sectors early on, in order to help design remedial arrangements.

It might appear tempting to design a pro-poor trade reform by identifying sectors that are important to poor and signaling out these sectors for differentiated cuts in protection. There are atleast two problems with this approach. One is fundamental and the other relates to political economy. Fundamental problem is that trade policy is a single instrument and cannot be expected to address multiple targets. Political economy problem is that once a highly differentiated trade regime is adopted, it is essentially impossible to stop special interests building a case that their sector deserves special treatment for one reason or the other.

A better approach is to focus on developing two different sets of instruments – one trade policy, focussed on providing the incentives appropriate for efficient production and use of goods and services and another distributional policy, focussed on alleviating poverty. A set of distributional instruments will necessarily have a much wider range of dimensions, including investments in expanding access to education, the provision of safety nets, and a range of infrastructure investments needed to allow people in poorer regions access to the markets and other amenities enjoyed by relatively disadvantaged people.

Conclusion

There is unambiguous empirical evidence from economies around the globe and for some of the Asian economies included in our sample that trade openness promotes economic growth. Raising economic growth in a sustained manner reduces poverty. However, most of the poor in the developing economies are in the agricultural sector, therefore raising growth in the agricultural sector is essential ingredient for making the reform process successful. Further, for a cross-section of fourteen Asian economies included in our study, no significant relationship could be found between changes in inequality and poverty, and inequality of incomes with economic growth rates and trade openness .As there is no convincing evidence that economic growth per se could lower income and wealth inequalities. Policies like fully government funded public and social services with land reforms may be the key for promoting distribution of incomes in the countries.

A policy package of tariff reduction and currency depreciation should make it easier for the factors of production in importable sector in the short run and during the transition period, and should dampen the resistance to the reform.

Impact of trade reform on the poor in the short run will critically depend on their location in terms of consumption and production (income). The best outcome is when the poor are employed primarily in the exportable sector and consume importable goods. And the worst outcome occurs if the poor are primarily employed in importable sector and consume primarily exportable goods. Long-run effects of trade reform are beneficial to the poor if labour market functions efficiently. Labour market segmentation dampens the positive effect. Overall analysis of the trade regime should yield a preliminary judgement on the desirability of trade reform. Tools to undertake such an analysis can be constructed for most economies. Basic requirements include detailed data on imports and exports, trade barriers that apply to those goods, household survey information on the consumption pattern of the poor and sources of their income and data on basic structure of the economy.

In the South Asian Region it is services that gained from the shift in the terms of trade against manufacturing, suggesting not only that skill differentials increased but also considerable part of the dividend from reduced tariffs was retained by trade and finance.

Simultaneously, despite overall GDP growth being maintained or slightly improved growth of agricultural GDP decelerated throughout the region. This combination of slower output growth in agriculture with deteriorating terms of trade is the major reason why rural incomes in South Asia have tended to lag behind urban incomes. Globalisation and trade reform would have had greater positive effect if agricultural growth would not have lagged due to falling terms of trade, low technology diffusion and cuts in public investment including investment in rural infrastructure, public irrigation, roads and power. As far as the effect of trade reform on employment in South Asian countries are concerned there is complicated picture as employment in the unorganized sector is stagnant.

Basic elements of a good trade policy regime involve predictability, transparency and uniformity. A liberal trade regime provides guidance for future reforms.

Appropriate mix of trade policies with complementary macro and microeconomic policies is needed to benefit from interaction with the global economy. Macroeconomic and micro-economic stability and a competitive exchange rate should be in place.

Safety nets are absolutely essential to alleviate and minimize pains of adjustment atleast in the short run. But if these pains are necessary to put the economy on a higher economic growth path, the society and polity will have to evolve credible mechanisms of cost sharing and conflict resolution.

NOTES

1. Thanks are due to Professor M.S. Bhat, and Professor Naushad Ali Azad for discussion on the theme of the paper. Abridged version of the article published in Indian Development Review, vol. I, No. 2 (2003) pp. 179-230.
2. For example, Srinivasan (2000) found that of the 17 percentage point reduction in the population below the poverty line over some 40 years(between 1951–55 and 1993-94), a 15 percentage point reduction is to be attributed to growth and 2 to redistribute policies. Agricultural and rural growth in a sustained manner is though important.
3. With three nominal prices, there are only two independent relative prices. For instance, choosing Px/Prn and Px/Ph, the third relative price (Pm/Ph) is obtained by dividing Px/Ph by Px/Pm.
4. A devaluation has no impact on the relative price Px/Pm because both prices increase in the same proportion.
5. The cross-country regression approach has a number advantages for understanding the links between trade and poverty. First of all, it enables the use of traditional statistical tools for testing results and hypotheses, as opposed to only making predictions. Secondly, cross-country regression results are typically much more general than the country-specific results of many applied simulation models. Thirdly, cross-country regression may be able to account for some of the dynamic aspects of trade reform that are missed by static simulation models. Given the differing advantages and disadvantages associated with the cross-country regression

and simulation approaches, they should probably be viewed as complementary forms of analysis as opposed to substitutes.

6. The Gini coefficient, although not a perfect tool, is relatively good summary indicator of income inequality. For discussion on the merits and drawbacks of using the Gini indicator see Deninger and Scquire(1996, pg. 567).
7. Chile which has had a uniform tariff since 1979,is a dramatic case in point. In Chile in 1998, the legislature considered a progressive reduction of the uniform tariff from 11 to 6 per cent, to be accompanied by one percent per year reductions through 2003. Chilean industry groups supported a reduction of the tariff, which passed the Chilean legislaturer. Evidently, uniform tariffs led industrialists to conclude that a reduction was in their collective interest.
8. Under the WTO, safeguards also require compensation to be offered to exporting countries if the action lasts more than 3 years.This is useful mechanism to ensure that protection is temporary. See Hoekman and Kostecki(2001) for more detailed discussion.
9. Poverty is not only due to lack of income but also due to lack of capabilities (skill, education), livelihood, security and assets, troubled and unequal gender relations, exhausted and weak body, disregard and abuse by the more powerful, dis-empowering institutions, lack of radical and comprehensive land reforms, degraded environment, inadequate rural infrastructure, among others. Effective domestic policies for poverty reduction should cover all the above stated issues.Pre-occupation for long–with minimal concept of poverty has impaired the capacity of anti-poverty strategies in eradicating poverty. The scope of this paper is however limited.
10. Microeconomic stability refers to economies having competent governance, technological and managerial innovations, impartial judiciary, efficient legal system and improvement in the quality of human resources.

REFERENCES

Bannister, G and K. Thugge, 2001, 'International Trade and Poverty Alleviation,' *Finance and Development*, Vol. 38 (December) No. 4.

Bagpai, Nirupam and Jeffrey Sachs, 1998, 'Strengthening India's Strategy for Economic Growth,' *Economic and Political Weekly*, July.

Ben, David D., 1993, 'Equalizing Exchange: Trade Liberalization and Income Convergence,' *Quarterly Journal of Economics*,108(3).

Bhagwati, J., 1996, 'The Miracle that Did Happen;Understanding East Asian in Comparative Perspective.' Keynote Speech delivered at the conference on Government and Market: The Relevance of the Taiwanese Performance to Development Theory and Policy in honour of Professors Liu and Tsiang, May 3, Cornell University, Ithaca, New York.

Bhagwati, J. and T.N. Srinivasan, 1999, 'Outward Orientation and Development: Are Revisionists Right,' Yale University *Economic Growth Centre,* Discussion Paper No 806.

Coe, D and E. Helpman, 1995, 'International R&D Spillovers,' European Economic Review, 39, 859-887.

Coxhead, I and Peter Warr, 1995, 'Does Technical Progress in Agriculture Alleviate Poverty? A

Philippine Case Study.' *Australian Journal of Agricultural Economics,* 39(1), April, pp. 25-54.

Cranfield, John A.L., Thomas W. Hertel and Paul V. Preckel, 2000, 'Multilateral Trade Liberalization and Poverty.' Paper prepared for the Conference on Poverty and the International Economy,organized by the World Bank and Swedish Parliamentary Commission on Global Development, Stockholm, October 20-21

Deinninger, Klaus and Lyn Squire, 1996, 'A New Data Set Measuring Income Inequality,' *World Bank Economic Review* 10(3):565-91.

Dollar, D and Kraay, Aaart, 2000, 'Growth is Good for Poor,' World Bank Policy Research Working Paper No. 2587

———, 2001, 'Trade, Growth and Poverty', World Bank Policy Research Working Paper No 2615.

Datt, G, 1999, 'Has Poverty Declined Since Economic Reforms? Statistical Data Analysis', Special Article, *Economic and Political weekly,* 11 December.

Edwards, S, 1993, 'Openness,Trade Liberalization and Growth in Developing Countries', *Journal of Economic Literature,* 31(3), September, 1358-1393.

————, 1998, 'Openness,Productivity and Growth : What Do We Really Know?,' *Economic Journal,* 108 (March), 383-398.

Frankel, J. and D. Romer, 1999, 'Does Trade Cause Growth?' *American Economic Review,* 89(3), 379-399

Hoekman, B. Michalopoulus, C, Schiff, M and Tarr, D, 2001a, 'Trade Policy Reform and Poverty Alleviation,' Policy Research Working Paper No. 2733, The World Bank, December.

Hoekman, B and M. Kostecki, 2001, 'The Political Economy of the World Trading System.' Oxford University Press, Oxford.

Jones, R.W., 1965, 'The Structure of Simple General Equilibrium Models,' *Journal of Political Economy* 73, (December), 557-572

Levin, J., 2000, 'Kenya-Poverty Eradication Through Transfers', Paper Prepared for the Conference on Poverty and the International Economy organized by the World Bank and Swedish Parliamentary Commission on Global Development, Stockholm, October 20-21.

Mathur, Somesh. K., 2001a, 'Multilateral Trading System and Developing Countries:Prospects and Perspectives with Special Reference to India' Asian-African Journal of Economics and Econometrics, Volume 1, No 2, December, New Delhi, India.

Panagariya, A., 2002, 'Poverty, Inequality and Trade Openness,' Comments on the papers by Juan Louis Londono and Martin Ravallion presented at the Annual Bank Conference on Development Economics -Europe Conference, 24th June, Oslo.

Ravallion, M., 1990, 'Rural Welfare Effects of Food Price Changes Under Induced Wage Responses: Theory and Evidence for Bangladesh'. Oxford Economic Papers 42:574-585.

Ravallion, M and D. Van de Walle, 1991, 'The Impact on Poverty of Food Pricing Reforms : Welfare Analysis for Indonesia,' *Journal of Policy Modeling,* 13:281-99.

Rodriguez, F and Rodrik, D., 1999, 'Trade Policy and Economic Growth : A Skeptic's Guide to Cross-National Evidence,' Centre for Economic Policy Research Working Paper No. 2143, London.

Rodrik, 1995, 'Getting Interventions Right : How South Korea and Taiwan Grew Rich.' *Economic Policy* 10(20) : 55-107.

Rodrik, 1998, 'Why is Trade Reform so Difficult in Africa,' *Journal of African Economies,* 7, 10-36.

Romer, P., 1994, 'New Goods,Old Theory and Welfare Costs of Trade Restrictions,' Journal of Development Economics,' 43(1):5-38 (February).

Sachs, J and A. Warner, 1995, 'Economic Reforms and the Process of Global Integration,' Brooking Paperson Economic Activity, 1-118.

Sarel, M., 1997, 'How Macroeconomic Factors Affect Income Distribution : The Cross Country Evidence,' IMF Working paper/97/152.

Sen, Abhijit, 2003, 'Globalization,Growth and Inequality in South Asia : The Evidence from Rural India' in J. Ghosh and C.P.

Chandrashekar (ed.) 'Work and Well Being in the Age of Finance,' Tulika Publishers, New Delhi.

Srinivasan, T.N. (2000), 'Eight Lectures on India's Economic Reforms,' Oxford University Press.

Tendulkar, S.D., 2000, 'Planning and Markets in Indian Development Process,' Artha Vynana, Vol. XLII, No 3, September, pp. 191-215.

Tarr, D., 2001, 'On the Design of Tariff Policy : Arguments for and Against Uniform Tariffs' in B. Hoekman, P. English and A. Mattoo (eds.), Trade Policy Reform and Multilateral Negotiations : A Sourcebook,Washington : World Bank.

Warr, Peter G., 2001, 'Welfare and Distributional Effects of an Export Tax : Thailands Rice Premium,' *American Journal of Agricultural Economics.* 83 (4) (November) : 903-920.

WIDER-UN, 2000, 'World Income Inequality' Database, available at www.wider.unu.edu

Winters, L.A., 2000a, 'Trade and Poverty : Is there a connection?' in WTO : Special Studies#5 : Trade, Income Disparity and Poverty, Geneva.

Winters, L.A., 2000b, 'Trade,Trade Policy and Poverty,' Background paper for the World Bank World Development Report 2001. Washington DC.

World Bank, 1999, 'Panama Poverty Assessment: Priorities and Strategies for Poverty Reduction, Human Development Department,' Latin American and the Carribean Region, Washington, DC.

World Bank, 2002, 'Global Economic Prospects and the Developing Countries : Making Trade Work for the Worlds Poor.' The World Bank, Washington, DC.

Xavier, Sala-I-Martin, 2002, 'The World Distribution of Income,' Columbia University, January.

Chapter 13

Sabotaging Public Distribution System (PDS) the High Level Committee goes Dangerously Astray

Colin Gonsalves

Built up painstakingly over the last 3 decades is an incredible structure for the maintenance of national food security. It rests on three pillars: (a) a reasonable price paid to farmers so that production levels of cereals are kept up; (b) The FCI system for large scale and efficient procurement, storage and transportation of grain; and (c) a public distribution system (PDS) for the transfer of subsidised grain to the poor.

The IMF now says stop this subsidy. The High Level Committee falls in line. The committee recommends:

- Cut the price paid to the farmers thus discouraging procurement and the cultivation of cereals;
- Cut the food subsidy almost entirely by raising the PDS grain prices to almost market prices; thus effectively dismantling the PDS; and
- Import cereals.

Of course, lip service is paid to Food for Work (one page of the 200 page report) and Antyayodhya Anna Yojana (1/2 page). And yes, self-sufficiency!

Operating on two presumptions, both wrong, the High Level Committee on Long-Term Grain Policy has made recommendations which appear in favour of the poor in the short term but which are against them in the long run. The first presumption is that the surplus stocks in the FCI godowns are an indicator of excess procurement. The second is that the food subsidy standing at 1 per cent of GDP must be reduced to 0.2%. Accordingly, it recommends that procurement be discouraged by cutting minimum support price to farmers thereby reducing procurement by 12 million tonnes. Then it suggests that there be a uniform PDS price virtually at acquisition cost, thus allowing the BPL prices to shoot upwards. The poor indeed have reason to be very alarmed.

Ironically these suggestions have been made at a time when reports of deaths by starvation have come in from Orissa, Jharkhand and Uttar Pradesh and elsewhere. Today there are 60 MT of grain in the godowns well above the 15 MT buffer.

Food for Work

Procurement every year is 40 MT. Offtake (*excluding food for work*) is 30 MT. Assuming that the food for work programme will remain at their present low levels, the Committee concludes that procurement must be reduced. This is a fatal error.

Food for work programmes during British rule were governed by the Famine Codes. These provided an extensive code of conduct for officials for the recognition of the onset of famines, the immediate starting of FFW programmes available to all irrespective of income, and the payment of subsistence amounts to those who cannot work. Studies show that the British were able to control deaths by starvation by the effective implementation of these Codes. Over time these Codes came to be disregarded. Governments today, in contrast, appear to be worse than the British. Food for work programmes began only after crops were decimated, cattle migrated and starvation deaths had occurred. Moreover, the FFW programmes had ceilings leaving out large sections of the population.

As is usual in every Red Fort address to the nation, Prime Ministers began to announce schemes. Employment Assurance Scheme (EAY) promised 100 day of FFW to all. Prime Minister

Vajpayee then announced a new Sampoorna Gramin Rozgar Yojana (SGRY). Everyone assumed it was an improvement on EAY. With the facts came the shock. It would provide on average of 10 days employment! Rs 5000 crores and 5 MT grain was all government could spare.

Chandrababu Naidu demonstrated that 5MT was a pitiable amount for the country when he managed to grab 3MT for Andhra alone. A genuine FFW implemented nation wide can easily absorb 30 MT. Thus, procurement is not 10 MT in excess but about 20 MT less than required. *The piling up of stocks is therefore not because procurement is too high but because there is a deliberate decision not to feed the poor. This brings* us to the subsidy issue.

Subsidy

To argue that the subsidy should be reduced is to say that food security for the poor through the PDS should be done away with. Subsidies were reduced in two ways; first by targetting and second by the introduction of food stamps.

The High Level Committee concludes, what everyone has known for a decade that the shift from universal to targeted PDS was a mistake. Targetting restricts the PDS benefits to persons below a particular income level. Targeted Public Distribution System (TPDS), has 'excluded a considerable part of the poor and undernourished population.' The classification into BPL and APL was 'seriously flawed.'

If the international standard for the definition of the poor i.e. a household that spends more than one third of its income on food, is followed in India, 95 per cent of all households would be considered poor. If the Chinese standard of a food share of 60 per cent is followed, then 70 per cent of all households would be considered poor. However, only 27 per cent are considered falling within BPL. This is why angry complaints are coming in from all over the country about the wrongful exclusion of the poor from the BPL list. Tribals who say they eat meat or drink liquor are out. Tiles on the roof or a fan in the room knock the family out of the list. The Planning Commission's definition of BPL as a family income less than of Rs. 20,000 p.a. is rarely followed.

But was targetting a mere mistake or was it a deliberate attempt to sabotage the PDS? And is the Committee using the failure of TPDS to dismantle the PDS system altogether in the guise of reforming it?

PDS was sabotaged in five ways. First by targetting, then by increasing the APL and BPL prices to such an extent that APL offtake collapsed and BPL offtake declined, thirdly by relaxing Fair Average Quality Norms so that people were disgusted with the grain they received, then by rendering uneconomical the running of ration shops save by the black marketeering in grain, and finally, when the APL prices were marginally reduced, by not communicating this to the public.

When targetting was introduced in India in 1997 the experiences of Mexico, Zambia, Jamaica, Tunisia and Sri Lanka were well-known. The targeted food stamps in Mexico were aimed at cutting the food subsidy and led to an 80 per cent decline of those receiving subsidized food. Sri Lanka's effective universal PDS was converted to one based on income in order to pander to the IMF direction to cut food subsidies. As a result, there was a 50 per cent fall in participating households and a significant number of low income groups were excluded from the food stamps program. Food stamps replaced general price subsidies in Jamaica to reduce the subsidy from 1 per cent GNP to 0.23 per cent. The real value of the food stamps fell until the cost of the minimum food basket was 3 times the minimum wage. The poor were excluded. Similarly in Tunisia there was a dramatic fall in the calorie and protein intake after subsidies came under attack. And in Columbia targetting was the method by which food subsidies were done away with.

The heart of the matter is money. India's food subsidy at 1 per cent GDP is not high by international standards. Moreover 66 per cent of this is worthless as it is storage cost. The hidden agenda of the committee is to reduce this food subsidy to 0.2 per cent i.e. to virtually do away with the subsidy for the poor. To disguise this with an offer of price indexed linked coupons for the poor and cash transfers to the state in lieu of price subsidies is laughable. State governments that cannot pay the salary of their employees will put this cash into the general account. Coupons have failed worldwide. In India counterfeiting will be an additional problem.

With the largest population of malnourished people in the world and with half the nation's women and children malnourished, 'business as usual' will not do. Drastic steps are called for. India must consciously dedicate a part of its GDP towards subsidising food for the poor. The subsidy must go up, not down. In the present extreme situation, 2 per cent GDP is not excessive. Jamaica in the 1970s and Tunisia in the 80s had these subsidy levels.

Once the decision is taken for a massive FFW programme, the gap between procurement and disbursement will disappear, the minimum support prices must be maintained to keep up the level of procurement and benefit farmers, and the movement of grains from the godowns will reduce that part of the food subsidy relating to storage (which is 66 per cent of the total food subsidy). A massive FFW programme will reduce hunger, provide employment and improve rural infrastructure.

As the grain component of SGRY rises from 5 MT to 30 MT, so too will the cash component. But this can be kept in check by enforcing the labour/capital ratio on public works to 70/30 and by paying almost the entire wage in grain. Additional funds could be raised by the states by imposing a levy as Maharashtra has done in the case of the Employment Guarantee Act. All it needs is the will to act.

PDS Prices

In recommending that BPL and APL prices be increased close to acquisition cost, (which is today higher than the APL level) the Committee goes over the top. Surely it must understand that the current BPL/APL rates are too high for the poor to purchase grain.

Distribution is very low not because PDS is inherently unworkable, but because the poor are too poor to buy the grain at the prices fixed. The BPL rate has to be fixed at the

Antyayodya rate level, and the APL rate brought down to the BPL level for there to be any significant increase in offtake. Starvation does not just happen. It is caused by high PDS prices.

Contractors

Seeking to capitalise on the huge surpluses lying in FCI godowns, Reliance and others have moved in. Privatising storage is the catch phrase. Once it is understood that the grain should be distributed and not stored for years, then the FCI capacity ought to be sufficient. There is no need for contractors. Initial calculations show that it should be cheaper to give the grain away free rather than pay contractors!

Food rots in the FCI godowns not because the FCI is inefficient. FCI operations have in fact been efficient given the sheer scale of the operations but its hands are tied and it has no say in the release of grain for the poor. FCI has been critical in sustaining production incentives over thirty years and in maintaining overall national food security.

Self-sufficiency

A salient feature of India's cereal situation is that most states are deficit. Growth rates of cereals have decelerated. Non-foodgrain yields have also declined. Inter-state imbalances are expected to widen. Critical in sustaining the production of cereals is the system of procurement now in vogue and the fair prices fixed for procurement. This has maintained overall national food security for 30 years. It is essential to maintain cereal self-sufficiency because the devious policies of rich countries and the highly volatile nature of international cereal prices make the import of cereals a very dangerous policy. Surplus production of a few advanced countries accounts for 4/5 of the global trade in cereals. US farm subsidy is expected to be about a 50 billion dollars a year. Once the US grain exporters get a monopoly on the basis of highly subsidized grain exports, prices will be pushed up leading to a grave crisis.

India has the world's largest malnourished population. Malnutrition among children is higher than sub-Saharan

Africa. Since cereals account for 60 per cent of nutrient intake, decline in production is a serious concern.

I have heard Amartya Sen saying on TV that 'procurement should be curtailed, market forces be allowed to prevail and then prices will fall and the poor will get food cheap.' Quite the contrary. Prices may fall initially. Farmers will then move away from cereal production. Shortages will occur. Imports of highly subsidised wheat from the US and elsewhere will cause a further collapse of cereal production. Prices will then be pushed up by grain-exporting cartels leading to chaos and deprivation.

Chapter 14

Poor under Reform Era
Some Reflections

S.A.R. Bilgrami

Since the initiation of economic reforms in 1991, one widely discussed issue has been its impact on the poor. Popular notion that has emerged is that the on-going reform measures are 'anti-poor'. It is argued that these do not envisage welfare-based support to economically weaker sections of the society. Five decades of our 'planned' development present extreme divergences. On the one hand, at the bottom, are the ever-expanding vulnerable sections of our society largely deprived of most of the benefits, opportunities and facilities. On the other hand, is the small affluent class, at the top, enjoying every bit of comfort and squeezing major benefits of the plans. Fifty years of 'equity-with-social justice' based approach of our plans remained unsuccessful in reducing the struggles of the poor. But succeeded, from all angles, in multiplying the comforts of the rich. The gist of our achievements is that we have given too little to poor and too much to rich.

Though a number of poverty alleviation programmes have been put in place, the magnitude of poverty and its intensity have not been appreciably reduced through 'growth-with-social justice', 'direct-attack' and 'trickle-down' routes. Various studies and reports reveal that the beneficial effects of various employment and income generating programmes, subsidised distribution of essential commodities and provision of essential services (such as health and education) on the poverty ridden segments of the society have been marginal even and selective. Official statistics, may demonstrate a declining trend in poverty. But the fact is that the bare necessities of life are yet scarce for a common man. Ad-hocism, improper and ineffective implementation, leakages, loose monitoring and widespread corruption are often cited as the major factors responsible for the failure of poverty alleviation programmes. These factors, are no doubt, important. Yet I feel one important element always remained missing in over-all approach towards the poor and the poverty. And that element is dignity of the poor. Unfortunately, a poor is always viewed as a person who deserves only sympathy, help and mercy. As a result, the framework of all poverty alleviation programmes is based on help, consolation, sympathy and charity. Human dignity is absent in overall approach to poverty alleviation. As a result, we fail to treat them as equal partners of the society with dignity and honour.

As mentioned earlier, the current phase of economic development started since the initiation of economic reform measures in 1991. Overall thrust is to place the market forces at the centre of all development activities. These market-based economic reform measures have transformed the role of the government. Processes of decontrol, cutting and reducing subsidies, curtailment of public expenditure and closing of 'unprofitable' public sector units has shrinked the role of the government. This has a direct bearing on the poor. Curtailment of public expenditure and reducing, or withdrawing of subsidies have important repercussions on income, employment and the welfare levels of the poor. Curtailment of public expenditure on welfare-based programmes (such as education, health and sanitation and nutrition has a direct bearing on the poor. These programmes are closely associated with the weaker sections of the society. If expenditure is reduced further, the welfare level of the poor will certainly come down. Similarly closing of uneconomical public sector undertakings also goes against the poor. This will lead to retrenchment of the poor workers, particularly those who are easily dispensable. Market is our best friend and partner till we demonstrate our efficiency and competitiveness. The weaker sections are handicapped in responding to market signals as they find their entry into markets difficult due to lack of required qualifications.

During the decade (1991–2000), the reform measures have been quite visible in the areas of trade, communication and industries. But this success has been selective. These have entered into those areas which have a strong economic base and avoided those which are traditionally backward and weak. Social services, small industries, small trade and farming and the whole unorganised sector come under this category. Advocates of economic reform measures have chosen a track for a faster and safer run and believe that the demonstration of miracles in these areas will force the weaker to follow. Hence there is no need for an exclusive attention towards the vulnerable and under preveleged sections. Developed areas with assured growth has been accrorded prominence. Backward and underdeveloped have remained unattended.

Instead of giving more attention on reforming our own policies to make them more effective and useful for the poor, we have introduced unbalanced reform policy, which is bound to aggravate poverty. When the role of government is gradually reducing and the markets are dominating, the emergence of frustration amongst the poor is quite natural. The 'human face' of economic reforms or its 'Swadeshi-texture' proposes to take care of this critical dimension.

REFERENCES

Bilgrami S.A.R., 1997, "Economic Reform and the poor" in Kausar J.Azam, "Economic Liberalisation in India, Implications for In Indo- U.S. Relations (ed.) Delta Publishing House, Delhi, 1997.

Dev S. Mahendra 1998, Public Distribution System, Impact on poor And options for Reform, E.P.W. August 29,1998.

Nayar Deepak 1993, 'Indian Economy at the Crossroads Illusions and Realities', E.P.W., April,1993.

Padgaonker Dileep, 2002, 'Hard Times Ahead', Times of India Dec. 1,2002.

VyasV.S. 1993, 'New Economic Policy and Vulnerable Sections Rationale for Public Intervention', E.P.W., March 6,1993.

Regional Perspective

Chapter 15

Rural Poverty and Agrarian Power[1]
Village[2]-level Evidence from Bihar[3]

M.S. Bhatt & Brajesh Kumar

Introduction

Poverty debate in India has centered round such issues as: definition of poverty line, nutrition and undernutrition, deflators to be used to update/down-date the normatively defined national poverty line, identification, aggregation of characteristics of poverty, determinants of poverty, quality of the data utilized (in particularly, National Sample Survey Consumption Expenditure Data, henceforth NSS data) official strategies for poverty alleviation, and evaluation. An number of studies been conducted on these aspects of the debate. Most of these studies deal with the issues in a highly aggregated framework. This context is important but not sufficient. These studies indeed added new insights to the poverty debate. However, local, social, and institutional aspects of rural poverty have received inadequate attention.

Absence of systematic attempts to identify the poor households at the local levels have resulted in a lot of wrong identification and left gates open for the powerful sections of the society to harvest the benefits of government sponsored anti-poverty programmes. It is in this context that present study assumes significance. Our main argument is that there is need for a paradigm shift in the approach to poverty analysis. Studying the causality between rural poverty and agrarian power and rural poverty and land concentration provides one such new paradigm. It can provide fresh insights into the incidence, intensity, and determinants of rural poverty. It is with this purpose in mind that the present study explores and explains the causality between rural poverty[4] and agrarian power and land concentration. The study has been organised in seven sections. Section I deals with the concept of agrarian power. Section II presents definition of poverty line and methodological developments. A macro view of approach to poverty alleviation has been outlined in Section III. Section IV presents an overview of the related literature on poverty. Hypothesis, proposed model and the sampling design employed in the present study form the subject matter of Section V. Results and discussion are presented in Section VI. Summary and conclusions are covered in Section VII.

I

Agrarian Power

In the received literature, the concept of agrarian power has defied consensus. This can be traced to a variety of reasons. The definition of power varies along a continuum that concentrates exclusively on a particular academic discipline/ research paradigm, at the one end, and hybrid definition of agrarian power/power on the other end (Desai, et. al., 1984). Historians, sociologists, and economists have attempted to define power with respect to their discipline-specific requirements. In sociological studies of: welfare, deviance and social control concept is used more prominently embracing many disciplines simultaneously. Even in this domain the concept has been subjected to a variety of criticisms. Nevertheless, it continues to display remarkable resilience.

The concept power/social control was first popularized by Ross (1901) and the early American sociologists (Mead, 1925). There are a variety of ways through which it can be utilized (Janowitz, 1975; Meier, 1982; Edwards, 1988). A more critical understanding of social control, however, received a strong impetus in the 1960s and 1970s, when Marxism and Feminism made their presence felt and many sociologists became critical of the central features of functionalist social sciences. Much of the social theory written since that time was oriented towards the development of a *sociology from below.* In the process there developed a highly critical attitude towards the regulatory and interventionist activities of the state, which was reflected both in the sociological and economic examinations of poverty, welfare and social policy (Piven and Cloward, 1972; Platt, 1977; Cohen, 1979; Donzelot, 1979; Bailey and Brake, 1975; Corrigan and Leonard, 1978).

A definition of power, which seems more appropriate to overpopulated underdeveloped agrarian society of Lewisian[5] types relates power to command over food. The acquisition of food is not to be by means of its distribution by government institutions. Rather, it is through an intensive mixing of the hitherto under-utilised labourwith legally secured access to productive farmland (El Ghonemy, 1990).

In agrarian economics the concept of power is often premised as: *reflexive of the economic framework in which it is conceived or proposed to be utilised* (Desai et. al., 1984). For example, it can assume different meanings depending upon the following frameworks one has in mind:

(*a*) Pre-classical world;
(*b*) Powerless universe of classical economists;
(*c*) A Neoclassical frame in which concept of power is absent;
(*d*) A Marxian or Neo-Marxian world of structurally generated economic power where power is mainly determined by and reflexive of economic conditions; and
(*e*) Webarian world of politically generated power emerging from a frame, which is partially or wholly autonomous of economic relations.

Most of the definitions of agrarian power do not readily fit into the above paradigms. Economists who have contributed to agrarian debates in South Asia, are contrastingly divided on this issue. According to Srinivasan (1981):

> In the competitive world no agent has economic power in spite of asymmetric information (in view of actual or potential com-

petition with numerous others similarly placed employers) in the sense of his being able to strike a deal more favorable than the market would allow.

For Rudra (1984) power means:

> A social phenomenon given rise by such institutional factors as caste hierarchy, distribution of wealth and income, occupational pattern, etc. and such ideological forces as customs, traditions, taboos, affecting the process of decision making by the economic agents. It includes political power so far as it is bound out by local social structures. And applied by the local power agents and excludes the state power as applied by the representative of the state or local community on the question of economic power.

Desai (1984) is more explicit when he opines:

> In its economic and political meaning power involves access to resources and control over certain instruments and social relationships. It involves access in the sense of outright ownership of resources with freedom to dispose them of as the other wishes, or in so many cases access to institutions and agencies, which may provide and withhold such resources. . . . in the final analysis power is a social relationship mediated by unequal access to resources and consequently unequal control over instruments.

Herring (1984) uses the economic power in two senses:

(*a*) Power to make decisions about the employment of resources in production and their redeployment over time can be termed economic power. Such power has both structural component (property, institutions and class configuration, or more broadly the mode of production) and a conjunctural component (state policies, shift in macro economic policies, collective action by opposite classes);

(*b*) *The power to extract economic surplus from production.*

Herring (1984), Harris (1980), and Rudra (1984) also argue that the economic power of a local-dominant class is not absolute . . . But is fundamentally and differentially affected by:

(*a*) State policies (minimum wage laws, tenancy legislation, land-use restriction, etc.);

(*b*) The economic and political power of the subordinate classes which in turn is heavily influenced by the demographic, organizational and resource endowment variations regionally;

(*c*) Various economic forces in environment (prices of inputs and outputs, interest rates, access to credit) which are in turn profoundly affected by the politics of national, state and the local political/administrative apparatus; and

(*d*) Local norms of custom and legitimacy and their relative resistance to change.

Unlike Europe, (where urbanization and commercialization were powerful facilitators of agrarian change) slow and highly skewed commercialisation of agriculture in overpopulated agrarian societies like on under reference, makes the relevance of the European experience and debates originating suspect. Concept of agrarian power in the context of these societies has been land-centric wherein control over land has traditionally coincided with control over political and economic power, which in turn has pervasively affected the poverty alleviation strategies. The importance of land is undoubtedly central to agrarian societies. However, as Herring rightly argues *land-centered model requires significant qualifications.*

Centrality of land is a necessary but not a sufficient condition to understand and analyse the causality between rural poverty and agrarian power as poor have to struggle against *five interlocking disadvantages, viz., poverty itself, physical weakness, isolation, vulnerability and powerlessness which trap them in deprivation* (Chambers, 1983). Similarly, control over or access to: environment resource-base, *common access* and *common property resources* are equally critical. An exalted view of this approach even suggests, *ecological variations shape agrarian class systems, which in turn shape opportunities for economic change* (Atwood, 1984). The empirical base of this argument needs to be enlarged and recast. In case of common property resources Jodha (1986) has demonstrated their positive contribution in the alleviation of rural poverty.

Given these variations, a possible solution could be a hybrid concept of power. Though theoretically very appealing, it is riddled with practical difficulties.

In the light of above overview, we recast and employ Desai's (1984) definition of agrarian power as: *adequate/effective control and access to critical inputs and commodity markets.*

This power should be legitimate and enforceable since it is necessary to increase productivity and capability and convert these into well-being. Economic power and control over social relationship subsume each other. The nature, composition and magnitude of control and access will understandably vary across the locations. But these have to be effective and of required magnitude to enable the poor persons or households to overcome interlocking disadvantages which trap them in vicious deprivation circles. The significance of this definition can be further gauged if seen in the context of disadvantages for a poor person/a poor household is in and what bearing powerlessness has on such a household (Chambers, 1992).

The causality between rural poverty and agrarian power is obvious in the context of an agrarian economy (like Bihar) but the direction of this causality needs to be empirically tested. For example, whether the differences in the agrarian power structure have played an important role in the location-specific success of the green revolution has been a subject matter of seminal studies from contrasting perspectives. Harris (1980), Bhaduri (1973), Prasad (1975) and several Planning Commission (Government of India) documents (1976 in particular) Bardhan and Rudra (1978, 1980, 1981) have approached the problem from this perspective.

Irrespective of these contrasting views, it is clear that the character of the local power structure is indeed a crucial determinant of productivity, which in turn affects poverty. In the opinion of the Planning Commission's (Government of India) Task Force on Agrarian Relations (1976), local power structures are *insurmountable hurdles in the path of spread of modern technology and improved agricultural practices.*

However, relationship between agrarian power and productivity (in turn between rural poverty and agrarian power) is variable and it becomes more difficult to prescribe which power structure (and under which circumstances) favors productivity. Moreover, variations in trans-local factors cannot be sidetracked. The nature of distribution of resources also matters, both on efficiency and equity grounds. A significant implication of such a power-productivity relationship is that poverty removal requires restructuring of the agrarian power structures (Chakaravarty, 1984).

After defining agrarian power and its causal relationship with rural poverty, it is imperative to identify the link between the two. Our study lays special attention on: Landless agricultural laborers, marginal and small farmers. The relative share of these categories, both in the incidence of poverty and rural workforce, is quite high. Most of these belong to the Scheduled castes. The crucial factors of production are: land; labor; irrigation; fertilisers; pesticides; credit; and extension services. And the important commodity markets are: market for selling excess produce like rice; vegetables; straw; manure; milk; etc.

We assume agrarian power first reduces labour-productivity, which in turn increases the severity of poverty. Since poor have no control/access to commodity markets, therefore, they are not being in a position to sell marketable surplus. There are possibilities of distress sale. These obviously will work backwards and compound the intensity of poverty. Thus, agrarian power works both ways against the poor and the net result is what Chambers called *vicious circles of deprivation*. The peculiar caste configuration in Bihar villages further aggravates the problem. Significance of these linkages can be better appreciated if seen in the context of the villages studied and the prevailing production conditions therein (for more elaboration see Section V).

II

Definition of Poverty

The concepts, measurement and methodological issues relating to poverty in the Indian context have been examined by a number of distinguished groups on the subject {viz., Working Group (GOI, 1962), Task Force (GOI, 1979), Study

Group (GOI, 1984), Expert Group (GOI, 1993)} set up by the Planning Commission (GOI) and also individual researchers.

Officially, the estimates of poverty have been worked out by Planning Commission (GOI). The first attempt to define a minimum standard of living was made in 1962 through a seminar on 'Some Aspects of Planning' and by a Study Group. The group recommended: (i) The national minimum for each household of five persons (4 adult consumption units) should be not less than Rs. 100 per month in terms of 1960-61 prices or Rs. 20 per capita per month. For urban areas, this figure will have to be raised to Rs. 125 per month per household or Rs. 25 per capita to cover the higher prices of the physical volume of commodities on which the national minimum is calculated; (ii) This national minimum excludes expenditure on health and education both of which are expected to be provided by the state according to the Constitution of India; and (iii) An element of subsidy in urban housing will have to be included after taking Rs. 10 per month or 10 per cent as the rent payable from the proposed national minimum of Rs. 100 per month.

The criteria for computing the monetary norms and the definition of minimum level of living are not available in published form. However, a note from Planning Commission (GOI, 1978) and Pant (1997) point out that the Working Group considered the recommendations of a balanced diet made by the Nutritional Advisory Committee (NAC) of the Indian Council of Medical Research (ICMR) in 1958. Later, the concept of poverty line was modified and recast on the recommendations of Task Force on 'Minimum Needs and Effective Consumption Demands' (GOI, 1979). The Task Force was to work out daily per capita calorie requirements for rural and urban areas on the basis of age, sex and activity specific calorie allowance recommended by the Nutrition Expert Group (GOI, 1979). Norms of nutritional requirement for the rural and urban sectors were obtained as 2435 kcal and 2095 kcal respectively.

The official approach thus started by fixing a standard of calorie intake and observing the level of per capita consumption expenditure with this calorie intake level is associated. An allowance for non-food consumption is also made in the construction of poverty line on a behavioral basis. The poverty lines at 1973-74 (base year) prices for the rural and urban sectors were worked out as Rs 49.09 and Rs 56.64 respectively using NSS data on consumer expenditure. The poverty line so defined was updated using various inflators. Initially, the Wholesale Price Index was used. Later, Implicit Private Consumption Deflator from National Accounts Statistics (NAS) for the year 1977-78 was used for this purpose. Study Group on: 'Concept and Measurement of Poverty' set up by the Planning Commission (1984) recommended the use of a price index approximately weighted by the consumption basket of the poor as an index for reflecting price changes relevant to the poor.

For calculating the incidence of poverty using Head Count Ratio the use of NSS data on size distribution of consumer expenditure (with adjustment for differences in the two sets of estimate as available from NAS and NSS) was adopted to maintain comparability between the two sets of data. The population below poverty line was thus worked out using the updated poverty line to the corresponding adjusted NSS distribution of population by levels of consumption expenditure. To estimate the incidence of poverty at the state level, all India poverty line and the adjustment factor were used on the state specific NSS distribution of population by level of consumption expenditure uniformly across the state.

Planning Commission (GOI, 1981) has also used the NSS 32nd round (July 1972–June 1978) data on consumer expenditure and applied a similar procedure resulting in rural poverty line of Rs 76 per capita per month and urban poverty line of Rs 88 per capita per month.

The official methodology has been criticized by several scholars including Sengupta and Joshi (1979), Minhas et. al., (1988, 1989, 1990, 1991), Expert Group (GOI, 1993) and Dandekar and Rath (1971). The bases of this criticism are: (*a*) Derivation of calorific norms; (*b*) The procedure of adjustment of consumption expenditure generated by the NSS with the aggregate private consumption expenditure; (*c*) The choice of price deflators to represent changes in the poverty line; (*d*) The ignorance of differences among state price; (*e*) The uniformity of consumption basket over time; (*f*) The uniformity of consumption basket among the states; and (*g*) Estimates based on the all India poverty line and the all India size distribution of per capita total expenditure (PCTE) vis-a-vis the population weighted average of state specific head count ratio using state specific poverty lines and state specific size distribution of PCTE.

The Planning Commission constituted an Expert Group in 1989 for looking into the methodology of poverty estimation at national and state level and also to go into the question of redefining the poverty line. The group in its report submitted in 1993 recommended: (i) Abandonment of NSS-NAS adjustment procedure; (ii) Derivation and application of state-specific poverty lines as against all India poverty line for rural and urban areas for working out state-specific poverty estimates and its aggregation to derive national level poverty estimates; (iii) Use of state-specific cost of living indices for updating the poverty line separately for rural and urban areas; and (iv) Use of Consumer Price Index Number for Agricultural Labour(CPIAL) for updating the rural poverty line and a simple average of Weighted Commodity Indices of Consumer Price Index for Industrial Workers (CPIIW) and Urban Non-Manual Employees (CPIUNME) for updating the urban poverty line. Most of these suggestions were earlier proposed by Minhas et. al. (1989, 1990, 1991). Recently, the Planning Commission (1997) has accepted these recommendations and the methodology adopted by the Expert Group with a slight modification in adopting the price deflator for updating the poverty line in the urban sector. Accordingly, the most recent official methodology (Modified Expert Group) uses CPIIW (instead of weighted average of CPIIW and CPIUNM) along with the other recommendations made by the Expert Group in working out the poverty estimates for the rural and urban areas at the state level and its aggregation at national level. According to official estimates, in the 1999 incidence of poverty works out to be 37.3, 32.4, and 36.0 for rural, urban and total respectively (see Appendix 14.1). However, unofficial studies suggest that incidence of poverty has not declined sharply as revealed by official estimates. Most of the writers relate these declines to shift of recall period of household consumption expenditure surveys by NSS from 30 days to 7 days in case of food items (for more details see Sen, 2000).

III

Approaches to Poverty Alleviations in India

India's poverty during the colonial rule assumed scandalous proportions. Hunger, malnutrition, disease, illiteracy and deprivation stalked the country. A series of dietary surveys conducted by the Indian Council of Medical Research during the period 1935–48 revealed that about one-quarter of the households were undernourished (Sukhatme, 1991). This estimate squares up with 30 per cent put forward by the Famine Inquiry Commission, which argued that this proportion of the poor were hungry even in normal times (Famine Inquiry Commission, 1945). Conditions in the rural areas were appalling (Ansty, 1952)

After the achievement of independence, the poor in the country have occupied a prominent place in all the Five Year Plan strategies. The change in attitude has been captured by A.K. Sen. He says:

> The Indian Poor may not be accustomed to receiving much help, but he is beginning to get used to being counted. The Poor in this country have lately been lined up in all kinds of different ways and have been subjected to several sophisticated head counts (Sen, 1974).

Poverty removal has been a major objective of development planning in India since 1951. The strategies to achieve the objective have, however, differed widely, reflecting divergences in the appreciation of the development process. Policy shifts have also taken place in response to experiences accumulated over a period of time. The change in approach has been particularly sharp since the *mid-seventies.*

In the initial phase (1951–65), it was believed that structural and institutional modifications in the economy through direct state intervention would generate an inbuilt mechanism to ensure sustained and self-reliant economic growth on the one hand and the gradual removal of poverty on the other. Poverty was perceived to be a consequence of lack of economic growth and the nonegalitarian agrarian structure. Industrialization, therefore, was viewed as an indispensable means to accelerate the tempo of economic growth and poverty removal. Agrarian restructuring was considered as necessary precondition to unleash the productive forces from the shackles of predatory landlordism. It was stipulated that this would help mobilisation of agricultural surplus for enhanced growth and welfare. The theoretical premise that underlay this perception was that economic growth sets in motion dynamic changes in a stagnant economy.

Direct state intervention was sought to be regulated through centralized planning. However, economic planning was tailored to the compulsions of a mixed economy. Roles of sectors – public and private – were defined and delineated. Public sector was assigned the key role of developing heavy industries and building up of infrastructure, while private sector was provided various incentives to raise output levels in agricultural and consumer goods. It was sought to be regulated through various measures so that the broader social purpose could be sub-served and the growth of monopolies be checked.

Industrialisation, it was envisaged, would absorb rural surplus labourin non-agricultural occupations and raise the incomes and standards of living of wage workers. Land reforms were expected to raise the income and consumption level of the deprived sections of the rural population. The poor would thus be benefited through an axiomatic *trickle-down* mechanism. Fiscal policies, the provision of public/social facilities like health and education and a certain measures of technological diffusion would reinforce the mechanism. It was further assumed that the imperatives of economic growth and technological impulses would induce changes in the traditional mode of production and social institutions like the repugnant caste system.

However, experience in the first decade of development planning (1951 – 60) demonstrated that the planner's optimism about the country's ability to achieve higher rates of growth and to reduce poverty was not justified. It was found that a bare 3.5 per cent average annual growth of the material product (as against 5 per cent targeted for), in the face of a 2.5 per cent population growth annually, yielded a per capita income growth rate of a mere 1 per cent per annum. The meagre increases in per capita incomes could hardly benefit the poorer segments of the society. Inflationary pressure, in fact, worsened the lot of the poor. It was found that prices of coarser varieties of food had risen more sharply to the detriment of the poor. [The Committee on: Distribution of Income and Levels of Living (called *Mahalonobis Committee*) Report, Vol. I, 1960.] Concentration of income, wealth and economic power had increased during the period.

In case of land reforms, it has been found that the first round was, by and large, successful. Intermediaries in land were abolished within a few years after independence and the actual tillers became owners. However, the reforms did not have uniform success in all parts of the country (Thorner, 1976). Land reforms, in the successful areas, provided major incentives for investment and growth. However, in case of imposing ceilings on land-holdings and distributing the surplus land among the landless, the land reform measures have not been successful. Inequality in the distribution of holdings has, therefore, persisted (Rao, 1991). Due to these factors development planning could not make a significant dent on poverty in the country (Nehru, 1963).

Perspective Planning Division of the Planning Commission (GOI, 1974) produced a document, which for the first time, highlighted and quantified the magnitude of absolute poverty. The document emphasised that economic growth alone could not solve the problem of poverty.

Third Five-Year Plan, however, did not make any specific

departure from the earlier two plans in tackling the problem of mass poverty. The Plan did mention that '*the essential problem is to reduce the spread between the higher and the lower incomes and to raise the level of the minimum.*'

Fourth Five-Year Plan constituted a watershed in India's development process. Earlier emphasis on industrialization was tempered by assigning agricultural growth a bigger role in the development process. Experience of the droughts of 1965-66 and 1966-67 went into the formulation of the technology-based agricultural development. It was only in the Fifth Five-Year Plan, a direct interventionist strategy at the macro level was evolved to combat the problem of absolute poverty. The contents of the anti-poverty programme consisted of: (i) provision of employment opportunities so that the poor have income; (ii) gearing the pattern of investment and composition of output to the consumption pattern of the poor; (iii) ensuring the availability of basic elements of consumption at stable prices; and (iv) the provision of social consumption, i.e. education, health, nutrition, etc. The Plan postulated that modifications in the production structure coupled with price stability and public social facilities would enable the bottom 40-50 per cent of the poor sections of the population to improve their levels of living. Minimum Needs programme (MNP) was initiated during this period. The programme had two components, viz.,

(*a*) Provision of basic infrastructure and social amenities such as rural roads and drinking water supply which were considered essential for improving the living conditions of the poor; and
(*b*) Provision of the basic needs of the people like elementary education and rural health.

The Plan formulated two variants of GDP growth – a 6.5 per cent and a 5.5 per cent. The former would eliminate the decline in the average level of consumption of the first three deciles altogether. Fifth Plan strategy had to be recast due to the structural problems of adjustment caused by the oil crisis of 1973 and the weather-induced harvest failures in 1972 and 1973. However, the Plan did sharply highlight the stark truth that poverty removal was predicated on: (a) a high rate of economic growth, particularly in the agricultural component; and (b) modifications in the production structure. In the absence of either or both, a direct attack on poverty was inevitable.

It was in the background of this experience that the target group-oriented approach for the removal of poverty was launched during the Sixth Five-year Plan (1980 – 85). A number of programmes were launched to alleviate poverty. Notable among these was: (a) IRDP, (b) NREP, and (c) TRYSEM. The stipulated targets of poverty reduction were 30 per cent by 1984-85 to less than 10 per cent by the end of 1986. These anti-poverty programmes became an integral part of the Seventh Five-Year Plan. Approach to poverty alleviation in Eighth, Ninth and Tenth Five-Year Plans remained same despite new economic policies initiated in the early nineties.

In sum, India's development efforts since 1951 represent a period of attempted transition from agrarianism towards economic growth. In the first phase, reliance was placed on industrialisation-led strategy to put the economy on the trajectory of growth and modernisation. Institutional restructuring was to supplement the design. In the Second Phase, technology-based agricultural growth was formulated to meet the twin objectives of growth and social equity. In the third phase, modifications in the production and consumption structure were attempted through priority to *food* and *fuel* sectors to achieve growth and a certain measure of reduction in absolute poverty. In the current phase, the twin objectives of economic growth and poverty alleviation have been sought to be juxtaposed and policy instruments redesigned and adjusted accordingly. Direct state interventionist strategy to alleviate poverty is the chief feature of the new strategy.

In spite of constraints, the country is witness to the *solid gains registered by our economy during the fifty seven years since independence.* The national income registered an increase of 4.2 per cent compounded annually in the period 1950-51 to 1964-65, fell to 2.7 per cent annual during 1966-67 to 1974-75. It, however, rose to 5.0 per cent during the decade 1975-76 to

1988-89 and has been around 5.6 per cent in the eighties and 5.8 per cent in nineties. Per capita growth of national income at 1.9 per cent in the period 1950-54 fell to 0.2 per cent in the period 1965-74, rose to 2.6 per cent annual since 1975-76 and has been around 3.4 per cent in the eighties. The corresponding percentage for nineties works out to be 5.6 per cent. Over the period, a broad and diversified industrial structure has grown in the economy. The country has achieved self-sufficiency in food-grains. This has saved foreign exchange reserves from being used for importing food-grains. Structural changes, as reflected in the sectoral contribution to aggregate growth, have taken place. The country has succeeded in averting large-scale famines, in spite of natural calamities like droughts and floods. The skilled manpower available in the country now is an achievement of far-reaching significance. All these achievements have imparted strength and resilience to the economy. However, poverty persists across the regions and among social classes. There is a consensus among policy-planners and economists that the problem of poverty has not been solved satisfactorily. It has also been acknowledged that the persistence of poverty and the marginalization of the poor have the potential of undermining the very process of economic development and social stability.

IV

Review of Related Studies

As mentioned earlier, some of the abiding concerns of the debate on rural poverty in India have been:

(*a*) Definition and construction of poverty norms/lines;
(*b*) Time trends in the poverty ratio across the states/regions/ country; and
(*c*) Determinants of poverty and their interpretations.

Much empirical work has been carried out on these issues. This work can broadly be grouped into:

(*i*) Studies, which focus on inter-regional variations in the incidence of poverty (Bardhan, 1984; Gaiha, 1988; Sawant, 1990; Sundaram and Tendulkar, 1983); and

(*ii*) Studies, which examine inter-temporal variations in rural poverty in India as a whole or among different states separately (Ahluwalia, 1978, Bardhan, 1986; Bhattacharya et. al., 1991; Dandekar and Rath, 1971; Narain, 1979; Griffin and Ghose, 1979; Joshi, 1974; Nayyar, 1991; Panikar, 1980; Rajaraman, 1975; Rao et. al., 1986; Rao and Kakwani, 1990; Saith, 1981; Walle, 1981; Vaidyanathan, 1974).

Without undermining the significance of studies, which could not be accommodated in the present review, we outline below some of the studies in order to highlight the central themes, concerns and significant conclusions of the study. Though no single study is available on the theme of the present paper, yet we think that this review will be instructive.

Ahluwalia (1978) observed an inverse relationship between rural poverty and net domestic product from agriculture at constant prices for India as a whole and for a few states. His study confirmed the *trickle-down* effects of agricultural growth on rural poverty. Ahluwalia was supported by Mundle (1984) but hotly contested by Griffin et. al. (1979) and Saith (1981).

Saith (1990) introduced consumer price index and time trend as explanatory variables and inferred that poverty ratio is directly related to these two variables and inversely to agricultural production.

Dharam Narain (1979) also found a very strong positive association between rural poverty and the consumer price index of agricultural labor. These conclusions were questioned by Mathur (1985). He contends that though inflationary pressure tends to raise the extent of rural poverty and agricultural growth tends to reduce it. But if one takes into account the effects of these two variables in conventional linear specification, there is no evidence of a positive time trend in the rural poverty.

Walle (1981) introduced population as a separate explanatory variable and observed significant adverse effects of population on growth in addition to favourable effects of agricultural growth and real agricultural wages on poverty.

Rao et. al. (1986) examined the relationships between institutional, infrastructural-technological factors, agricultural growth, productivity, and consumer price index of agricultural labourers and incidence of poverty. Their main conclusions are: (i) poverty and inequality in consumption expenditure are positively related to prices; (ii) rise in the proportion of agricultural labourand scheduled castes/tribes are negatively related to agricultural growth; and (iii) the relationship between various infrastructural levels is complex. Some reduce poverty while the effects of some are not conclusive.

Bardhan (1986) states that agricultural growth and productivity improvements in general tend to raise incomes all around, but certain types of growth processes generate negative forces for the poor, particularly an institutional-setting of highly unequal distribution of assets and access to resources.

Some studies identified landlessness as an important cause of poverty, for example, Dandekar and Rath (1971) found rural poverty and proportion of agricultural labourers in the rural workforce positively associated. Minhas (1974), Vaidyanathan (1974), and Kerala Study (1976) too supported this view.

Nayyar (1991) estimated a function in which per capita production of foodgrains, per capita availability of foodgrains, the prices of cereals, the per capita state domestic product in agricultural sector at constant prices, per capita income, coefficient of variation in the distribution of ownership holdings and proportion of agricultural laborers in the working population were used as the explanatory variables with three alternative estimates of poverty as dependent variables. In each case price factor emerges as the most important variable explaining the differences in the rural poverty among the states. Next to prices landlessness emerges as the most significant determinant of poverty.

Bhattacharya et. al. (1991) builds a theoretical model to identify the factors, which are closely linked to rural poverty. Postulating a close inverse relationship between incidence of poverty and average real per capita expenditure on all items in the rural sector they examine the factors which influence the most important component of real per capita expenditure i.e., per capita quantity of cereals consumed.

Empirical testing of this model reveals: (1) per capita current output of cereals, government policy of procurement and distribution of food and per capita cereal output in the previous year are inversely related to poverty; (2) relative prices of cereals in previous year and per capita non-agriculture real income are positively related to poverty.

Kakwani and Subba Rao (1992) utilize NSS Rural State level data of 1973-74, 1977-78, 1983-84, and 1986-87 rounds to identify linkages among: growth, inequality, and poverty over time and across the states. A major conclusion of this study is:

> Trickle-down can happen but is seldom automatic. The beneficial effects of growth on incidence of poverty can, but need not, substantially offset, even nullified increases in the inequality of consumption.

Sen (2000) examined NSS data, and focuses on the recent methodological changes employed by NSS. He questions the wisdom and utility of using 7 days recall period in the 55th round NSS consumption surveys for food items. Sen opines that this is bound to underestimate the incidence of poverty and make the task of targeting (through poverty alleviation programmes) difficult and untenable. The study concludes that in order to maintain the integrity of the India's statistical system, it would be necessary to conduct another large Consumer Expenditure Survey using the 30-day reference period as soon as possible.

Palmer et. al. (2001) surveys the debate on poverty and the key issues rose therein. The authors presented new evidence on the divergence between caloric-based poverty measure and the official poverty line, and explore the alternative explanations for this divergence.

Thakur et. al. (2000) analysed the rural poverty and income distribution. This study is based on an intensive survey (1996-97) in eight villages representing all agro-ecological regions of Bihar. The study's results indicated that income distribution was less unequal in technologically *developed villages* than in *less developed villages*. Agriculture and/or rice income was more equally distributed than non-agriculture income. Thus, the diffusion of modern agricultural technology reduced inequality of overall income distribution. Further, rural poverty was lower in technologically *developed villages* than in *less developed villages*.

Ravallion (2000) tries to assess the case for re-estimating poverty using NAS instead of NSS data. He opines, *if one replaces average consumption from India's National Sample Surveys with private consumption per capita from the National Accounts, while retaining the survey-based distributions, then one finds a faster rate of poverty reduction in the 1990s. However, to assess the case for anchoring India's poverty measures to the National Accounts one cannot ignore the fact that this topic has become intermeshed with the larger debate about India's economic reforms*. Ravallion argues that there are legitimate concerns about the various aspects of NSS survey data and these must be addressed to. Possibilities of combining the two data sets should be carefully assessed.

Sundaram and Tendulkar (2001) also addressed the question of using the NAS estimate of private final consumption expenditure (PFCE) in place of NSS-based estimate for calculating proportion of the population below the poverty line. The study arrived at two major conclusions: (i) the issue of accepting NAS estimate of PFCE as more correct and reliable than NSS estimate is far from settled; and (ii) the item-groups that accounted for a very large proportion of the aggregate discrepancy between NAS and NSS estimates had a much smaller budget share in the consumption basket of the bottom 30 per cent fractile group in the rural and urban areas. Whereas in respect of item-groups which together accounted for over 75 per cent of the consumption of the bottom 30 per cent, the divergence between the two estimates was much smaller than on the average for all item groups and negative in some cases.

Deaton and Dreze (2002) presented a new set of integrated poverty and inequality estimates for India and Indian states for 1987-88, 1993-94 and 1999-2000. They believe that the poverty estimates are broadly consistent with independent evidence on per capita expenditure, state domestic product and real agricultural wages. Which shows that poverty decline in the 1990s proceeded more or less in line with earlier trends. Regional disparities increased in the 1990s, with the Southern and Western regions doing much better than the Northern and Eastern regions. Economic inequality also increased within states, especially within urban areas, and between urban and rural areas.

V

Methodology and Data Sources

Hypothesis

In consonance with the main objective of the present study, the following hypothesis is proposed for testing:

> *There is significant causal relationship between rural poverty as dependent variable and land concentration and agrarian power as predictors.*

Symbolically,

$$Y = f(X_1, AP) \quad ....[1]$$

Where Y = Incidence of Rural Poverty;

X_1 = Concentration of Land Holdings[6]; and

AP = Agrarian Power.

The linear probability model of equation [1] is as follows:

$$Y = \alpha + \beta_1 X_1 + \beta_2 AP + \mu_i \quad ....[2]$$

Where α is constant;

β_1 & β_2 are the coefficients of the predictors;

μ_i is the standard error term.

Precisely,

$H_0: \beta_1 = 0$ and $H_0: \beta_2 = 0$

$H_1: \beta_1 \neq 0$ and $H_1: \beta_2 \neq 0$

Econometric Model

To test the aforesaid hypothesis, two logistic regression models/logit models have been employed. General form of a logistic regression is as follows:

$$\ln\left(\frac{\hat{\pi}}{1-\hat{\pi}}\right) = \alpha + \beta_1 X_1 + \beta_2 X_2 + \beta_3 X_3 + \beta_4 X_4 + ... + \beta_n X_n + \mu_{ij} \quad ...[3]$$

where
ln is the natural logarithm, $\log_{exp}$, where exp = 2.71828;
$\hat{\pi}$ is the probability that the event 'Y' occurs, $\pi(Y = 1)$;
$\hat{\pi}/(1 - \hat{\pi})$ is the 'odds ratio;'

$\ln\left(\frac{\hat{\pi}}{1-\hat{\pi}}\right)$ is the log odd ratio, 'logit;' and

all other components of the equation [3] are same as in equation [2].

Dependent Variable

Y = Incidence of Poverty is defined in terms of ***Below Poverty Line (henceforth, BPL)*** and/or **Above Poverty Line (henceforth, APL).** 'Y' is a dummy variable (in 0 & 1 form), computed from the sample survey on the basis of *Expert Group Recommended Poverty Line.*[7] *Zero (0)* is assigned to those who are *Above the Poverty Line* and *One (1)* to those who are *Below the Poverty Line.*

Independent Variables/Predictors

X_1 = Gini Co-efficient of Ownership land holdings (village-wise); X_2 = Land Owned; X_3 = LabourHired; X_4 = Assured Irrigation; X_5 = Use of Fertilizers; X_6 = Credit Borrowed; X_7= Assured Supply of Extension Services; X_8= Marketed Food Surplus; X_9 = Appropriate Price for Marketed Surplus; X_{10}= Marketed Vegetables; X_{11}= Marketed Straw; X_{12}= Marketed Manure; and X_{13}= Marketed Milk.

Model 1

The general form of logit model used here is as follows:

$$\ln\left(\frac{\hat{\pi}}{1-\hat{\pi}}\right) \quad ...[4]$$

Model 2

From X_2 to X_7 and X_8 to X_{13} we have used Binary Indexing Method to generate one single variable as a representative of control over and access to factor markets (Z_1) and commodity markets (Z_2), where

$$Z_1 = \frac{\sum_{i=2}^{7} X_i}{N} \quad ...[5]$$

$$Z_2 = \frac{\sum_{i=8}^{13} X_i}{N} \quad ...[6]$$

Using equations [5] and [6], one single variable has been computed, which is the true representative of 'agrarian power,' where

$$AP = \frac{\sum_{i=1}^{2} Z_i}{N} \quad ....[8]$$

The general log-linear function of the Model 3 is as follows:

$$\ln\left(\frac{\hat{\pi}}{1-\hat{\pi}}\right) = \alpha + \beta_1 X_1 + \beta_2 AP + \mu_{ij} \quad ...[9]$$

Sampling Design Information

On the basis of agro-climatic conditions in Bihar, the state is divided into two zones, i.e. North Bihar Plains and South Bihar Plains. The former is very fertile and constitutes about 54.75 per cent of the total area of the state. It has a number of big rivers and afflicted occasionally by heavy floods, causing huge damages to crops and property. The area is heavily populated – the density of population in this region is one of the highest in the country. The area is predominantly rural. The economy of the region lacks diversification. Infrastructural facilities are extremely meagre. There is a large disparity in irrigation facilities, electricity consumption, rail and road communications, etc. It is no wonder, therefore, that North Bihar is an area of endemic poverty, backwardness and unemployment.

South Bihar plains, constituting 45.25 per cent of the total geographical area is not subject to frequent floods, except for lands on the banks of rivers. This region is more diverse than the North Bihar plans. It has the lowest rainfall and is considerably more urbanized. Position in regard to infrastructure is also better. A large part of the rural area of this region is currently witnessing the radical peasant and labourmovement leading to considerable violence and turmoil (For details see Sharma, 1995).

Keeping these features into consideration, the study area has been sampled first on the basis of geographic features, i.e. Upper Ganga Region and Lower Ganga Region. Second stage sampling has been done using purposive random sampling techniques keeping in view the socioeconomic characteristics of Bihar. The state is far from homogeneous with regard to the distribution of its socioeconomics characteristics. Four villages viz., Bhavdevpur Got (Sitamarhi District) and Barasra (Siwan District) from Upper Ganga Region and Sonahri (Gaya District) and Kanaudi (Gaya District) from South. The sample size (50 samples from each village) has been taken on the basis of calculations done by *'The Sample Size Calculator'* provided by the *'The Survey Systems' (http://www.azplansite.com* developed by *Michael T. Martin).* The survey was conducted after testing the questionnaire in Pilot Survey over the 5 respondents from each village for smooth surveying.

Table 15.1 presents the sampling design information used in the present study. The details of the description of vectors used in table specify Sampling Design given in Table 15.1a.

VI

Results and Discussions

The variables used in the empirical analysis are described in Table 15.2. Descriptive statistics are presented in Table 15.3. Logistic regression results are presented in Table 15.4. Two models are presented where the dependent variable in each is 'Whether the respondent will be in BPL or APL category' (Yes = 1 if they are in BPL, 0 Otherwise). Each model includes different blocks of independent variables.

The results from Model 1 support our hypothesis. The Wald statistics of *Gini Co-efficient of Ownership Land Holding*

(X_1); LabourHired by the Respondent (X_3); Assured Supply of Extension Services (X_7); Marketed Vegetables (X_{10}); Straw Sold by the Respondent (X_{11}); and Manure Sold in the market by the respondent (X_{12}) are significant. From this evidence the model establishes a robust link between rural poverty and agrarian power. There is significant positive correlation between rural poverty and land concentration also.

The β coefficients on *Gini Co-efficient of Ownership Land Holding (X_1); LabourHired by the Respondent (X_3); Assured Supply of Extension Services (X_7); Marketed Vegetables (X_{10}); Straw Sold by the Respondent (X_{11}); and Manure Sold in the market by the respondent (X_{12})* has a Wald statistics significant at the 0.05 level (95 per cent confidence level). The overall Model 1 is significant at the 0.01 levels according to the Model Chi-square statistics. The Model 1 predicts 78.77 per cent of the responses correctly. The McFadden's R^2 is 0.379 (Amemiya, 1981).

The Model 2 also establishes a significant causal relationship between rural poverty and agrarian power. The overall Model 3 is significant at the 0.01 levels according to the model Chi-square statistics. The model predicts 73 per cent of the responses correctly. The McFadden R^2 is 0.31 (Amemiya, 1981).

The pseudo-R^2 and model chi-square statistics both decrease with the log functional form indicating that the Model 1 is superior in terms of model fit. The Model 2 includes an arithmetic average of indicators of control over and access to factor and commodity markets as an independent variables. The Wald statistics of land concentration become significant in both the models that this is superior specification whereas the computed 'AP' in Model 2 has also turned out significant, which proves our hypothesis that the land concentration and agrarian power acts as a causal factor for determination of rural poverty in Bihar.

The above results establish that:

(*a*) A robust causal association between rural poverty and land concentration and agrarian power; and

(*b*) The direction and linkages along which these association work.

Lot of literature has come in recent years suggesting that rural markets are interlinked [see Basu (1990) and Debraj Ray, 2000]. Imperfections in one market are bound to affect the functioning of other markets. Studies have also shown that ownership acts as an incentive for higher production. Control and access to these markets are necessary for increasing the overall agricultural growth.

The basic premise of the present study is that the present land tenure system in Bihar generates: landlessness, chronic indebtedness and eviction of tenants. Besides economic consequences like high incidence of rural poverty it has resulted in social polarisation and unrest. Big landowners (called *bhumihars*) have organised their own private armies parallel to the state structures of law and order. On the one hand, land, water, credit, and other inputs, markets have completely become monopolised and use of labor, on the other hand, has become monopsonistic. Landless agricultural labourers, marginal and small farmers are forced to live in the conditions of poverty and deprivation. In collaboration with state revenue-development machinery *bhumihars* are in complete control over production and exchange relations. The incidence of poverty, size distribution of assets (in particular land), land-related violence and leakages in the poverty alleviation strategies have consistently remained one of the highest in the country.

A typical Bihar village can be personified as what Basu (1986 and 1990) calls a three persons' world – landlord (we replace this term by big landowners called *Bhumihars* with his private land army), a labourer (we redefine him as landless agricultural labourer and marginal/small farmer, who invariably belongs to the lower castes) and the merchant (who for our analysis serves as a strong link between the village and non-governmental urbanised part of the state). All the three depend upon one another in a triadic interaction. The *Bhumihar* has inherited the wealth with which he buys labour from the labourer and goods from the merchant. He does not undertake production on a full time basis and cannot be described as capitalistic farmer in the Lewisian sense but a member of Veblen's Leisure class. Merchant has an endowment of goods, which he sells to both *Bhumihar* and labourer. The *Bhumihar* is the bigger customer thus more important for the merchant. The labourer has nothing but his labour power, which he sells to the *Bhumihar.* Whatever little he gets in the form of wages (both kind and cash) he purchases goods from the merchant. *Bhumihar* and *labourer* relationship can work in two ways:

(a) Both can act as price takers. Contracts and exchange relationship can be voluntarily determined (Basu, 1990); and
(b) *Bhumihar* acts as an extortionate monopolist and the merchant always sides with him as *Bhumihar's* relative importance for the merchant, in a triadic situation, outweighs that of the laborer.

The first framework does not exist in our study area and in the second, the worst sufferer is the agricultural labourer who is forced to undertake involuntary contracts/exchange relations to his perpetual disadvantage. In such coercive conditions of exchange and production, land tenure and concentration of land are bound to generate and exacerbate poverty due to the following specific characteristics or conditions:

(a) *Bhumihars'* monopoly (including institutional monopoly) over all critical input markets resulting in low productivity from underutilisation of principal resources (labour/land) and loss of potential gains in the total primary sector output;
(b) *Bhumihars* bidding for transfer of: landed property, irrigation rights, and common property resources resulting in inflationary prices with no increase in real output;
(c) Barriers to entry into: land, credit, irrigation and fertiliser markets, which inhibits landless agricultural labourer, marginal farmers, small farmers and even non-farm rural occupational people (carpenters, barbers, boatmen, fisherman, wood cutters, earth diggers, etc.) from purchasing farmland or title to any property; and
(d) A caste-based rigid and decadent social structure characterised by minority of big landowners (enjoying all privileges) and large sections of powerless poor and disadvantaged with a wide social gulf between them.

Bhumihar in our study hires labourfor a variety of requirements, i.e. farming and allied farming activities, accessing common property resources, as domestic servants and sometimes even servants for esteem only. Marginal and small farmers do not hire labouror they are incapable of hiring laboureven if they require it during peak farming operation like transplantation and harvesting. Engaging labour for livestock, poultry and other allied agricultural operation is almost non-existent among them. Due to illiteracy and very exorbitant search costs poor people are also incapable of accessing the credit, information and extension services' markets. Law of exclusion is enforced with Impunity by the *Bhumihar* in collaboration with official machinery. Net consequence is rural underdevelopment. This type of underdevelopment and consequent poverty thereof cannot be analysed in economic terms alone. Asides economic determinants other equally important factors are: (i) Social values and customs; and (ii) Inter-class relationships (covering power, social esteem, prestige, subservience and servility) associated with land tenure systems. There are also factors outside the land tenure system (both local and trans-local).

Poor people are invariably unable to produce for the market. Even if they produce for the market they are not in a position to sell on voluntary basis. Some among poor are aware about the existence of critical commodity markets but they are incapable of accessing them like the factor markets (even if control is granted) due to associated infirmities such as: illiteracy, search costs, transaction costs and last but not the least the social factors. For example, if a lower caste agricultural labourer (person living below officially defined poverty line) is given a high yielding *jersey* miltch cow under IRDP (a poverty alleviation strategy in operation for the last 23 years) and all required inputs (fodder, veterinary services, credit, feeds, cow sheds, etc.) he is capable of producing surplus milk. But he will be incapable of selling this surplus milk in his village or in adjoining villages because of social stigma attached to the milk of a miltch cow brought up by a lower caste Hindu (everybody in village is aware about the caste configuration and believes in them as a matter of *Karma*[8]). The alternative for the poor milk producer is to sell the milk in a distant market where nobody is aware about his antecedents. But this involves transaction costs and knowledge about markets and availability of safe milk carrying technology. All these are missing (a situation which Stiglitz calls *missing market*). The third option is provided by milk cooperative (self-organised processing and marketing union) on the *Anand Dairy Model* of Western India. This is also absent in the sampled village. The fourth option is the involuntary sale to the local milk contractors. This is the only option available. The milk contractor acts like a monopolist and is in a position to enforce involuntary exchange of surplus milk. What is true for surplus milk sale is true for all other forms of surplus disposal in rural Bihar, particularly perishable marketable surplus like fruits, vegetables, milk, and milk products.

The available secondary data on macro social-economic aggregates at district and block level amply support our results. For example, official estimates of rural poverty and land concentration are one of the highest in the country. Inter-district variations in the levels of living are also very acute and persisted over the years. Size and composition of the state domestic product and occupational distribution of workforce have undergone very little transformation. If the present agrarian power structure is not reformed rural poverty and social instability are bound to intensify further. The possible solutions are proposed in the following section.

VII

Conclusion

The main objective of the study was to explore and explain the causality among rural poverty, land concentration, and agrarian power.

Our hypothesis was: there is significant causal relationship between rural poverty (as dependent variable) and land concentration and agrarian power (as predictors).

The results of logistic regression employed in the present

study have confirmed the proposed relationship between dependent variable and the explanatory variables.

Normally a person possessing land (particularly big landowners) can afford a land use and cropping patterns, which are conducive for diversification of primary sector, i.e. along with cereals, they can produce cash crops Rare: milch cows, sheep, goats, buffalos, and poultry. All these need access to: water, credit and commodity markets. This diversification can be further propped by two critical inputs, i.e. control over and access resources/common property resources and different forms of state intervention in the name of rural development (extension services, institutional sources of finances, democratic decentralisation, different forms of participatory development, explicit/implicit subsidies, price support policies, procurement policies, social infrastructure, etc.). Since *Bhumihars* of Bihar own almost entire available land they control all possible sources of surplus generation. They have the potential resource base for generating growth. But by motivation they are rent seekers. Therefore, do not accumulate and invest. Poor people are not in position to accumulate because they have no resource-base or they lack agrarian power. The net result of this dichotomous situation is underdevelopment and poverty. This puts fortt two questions:

(a) Can the power structure, institutional obstacles and land-tenure systems, which these structures sustain, be reformed by the state intervention?

(b) Can the incidence of poverty be rapidly reduced if landless agricultural labourers, marginal and small farmers have control over and access to critical factor and commodity markets, resource endowments as food producing, stable income earning and labourusing assets?

The answer to above questions is yes. Let us focus on the first question:

1. As discussed in the previous section, in the study area the prevailing agrarian power and the institutions, which sustains it, breed rural underdevelopment. Despite immense possibilities and potentialities of achieving higher growth,

rural Bihar has lagged behind in almost all macro-indicators of growth and development. For poverty removal achieving higher growth is a critical requirement. Along with the reforms in the agrarian power structures there is need for major reforms in the size, quality and direction of state intervention. At present state interventions on various counts, retarded growth and have become major obstacles to poverty removal. Number of studies have suggested that rural markets are interlinked. Imperfections in one market are bound to affect the functioning of other markets. Studies have also established the importance of land as reliable source of surplus generation and social esteem in agrarian societies. In a way even the working of credit, irrigation, fertiliser and commodity markets is directly linked to the land market. Control over and access to overall markets is necessary for increasing the overall agricultural growth. Restructuring of these markets is thus warranted both from efficiency and equity considerations. The basic question is: 'can this be done through state intervention?'. This brings into focus the nature and quality of state intervention in a democratic society. Post-1947 economic history of India provides enough examples wherein anti-growth institutional set-ups and rigidities have been successfully reformed (e.g. democratic decentralization, through constitutional 73rd and 74th amendments, agrarian reforms in West Bengal, Kerala, and Jammu & Kashmir and recent economic reforms). There is no reason why it cannot be done in Bihar. The alternative is anarchy.

Thus, growth and distributive measures/institutional changes together are necessary for removing/reducing poverty in Bihar. Bihar subsists mainly on agriculture whose fortune fluctuates with the vagaries of nature. This is because irrigation exists only in a limited area and much of it is 'protective' in nature, rather than being aimed at production or growth. The poor are the worst victims of recurring floods in large parts of the state. Public investment in irrigation, flood control, drainage, rural electrification and generation of rural power supply are the inescapable preconditions for development. There is a need to take up an ambitious scheme of rural industrialisation also. Bihar has witnessed deterioration in the employment structure in recent years—the proportion of workers engaged in the primary sector has increased and that in the secondary sector has declined. This is really a matter of concern and therefore schemes of rural industrialisation and other schemes of diversification of the economy in rural and semi-urban areas are urgently needed.

2. The issue of agrarian reforms has been cast in the received literature in two senses–*narrow* and *broad*. As mentioned above, studies have also shown that ownership acts as an incentive for higher production. This provides an additional justification in the context of Bihar. In a narrow sense, land reforms are synonymous of a form of state intervention in land market. The land-tenure (defined as institutional arrangement pertaining to property rights and duties. Division of decision making are legally or customarily determined) is considered exploitative and breeding rural underdevelopment. The major objective of reforms is: redistribution of private land property rights and use; imposition of upper ceilings on land ownership; enacting tenurial laws to protect the interests of tenants/ share croppers and consolidation of holdings. The aim is to eliminate or remove barriers to entry to factor markets and provide peasants command over food thereby reducing poverty and inequality (El Ghonemy, 1990). In broader sense, land reforms are considered as a substitute for agrarian transformation/agrarian reform. This entails an understanding of underdevelopment and what is involved in the eradication of economic backwardness. Reforms generally include: reforms in both factor and commodity markets, land settlement programmes, land registration, rental controls, consolidation of fragmented holding, arresting parcellisation of holdings, tenancy reforms, farm management technique, common property resources, land/ irrigation augmenting techniques of production and appropriate rural development strategies. Thus, this goes beyond the changes in land tenure. It involves necessarily land market but is in no way land-centric. This in any case do not supplant each other. Joshi calls former as first stage and the latter as second stage of agrarian reforms (see Joshi, 1974). Joshi and many others (see El Ghonemy, 1990) rightly argue that to realise the goals of agrarian reforms (like one identified above) both the stages are of seminal importance. In many Indian states agrarian reforms were introduced

with great success and speed. But due to slackness at the second stage in sustaining gains from the first stage marginalisation of agricultural holding and land concentration have increased over the years in the absence of appropriate technology. Due to alternative employment sources of income, underdevelopment has persisted in these states (See Bhatt, 2000). But of this, argument is that land distribution alone cannot achieve the objective of providing command over food thereby alleviate poverty and reduce inequality. Increasing output or productivity of land/labour in the reformed sector demands more than the celebrated remark by Arthur Young *The magic of property turns sand into gold* (El Ghonemy, 1990).

NOTES*

*The authors are grateful to: Prof. D.N. Rao (Centre for Economic Studies and Planning, Jawaharlal Nehru University, New Delhi), Prof. Pulin B. Nayak (Delhi School of Economics, University of Delhi, Delhi), Dr Sabya Sachi (Department of Sociology, Jamia Millia Islamia, New Delhi) and Dr Shahid Ahmed (Department of Economics, Jamia Millia Islamia, New Delhi) for their incisive and valuable comments on an earlier draft of this paper. Usual disclaimers apply.

1. Etymological meaning of the term 'agrarian' is relating to or connected with landed property or pertaining to fields, or lands, or their tenure; especially relating to an equal or equitable division of lands; as the agrarian laws of Rome, which distributed the conquered and other public lands among citizens (Oxford Dictionary). According to the *International Encyclopedia of Sociology: Vol. I*, 'Agrarian societies are generally considered to be pre-industrial societies that employ ploughs and other farm equipment in the production of food. Agrarian economic systems comprise control of production, the ownership or control of production, and the distribution of food products. Agrarian systems vary in intensity. The more extensive systems are those in which inputs are few; the more intensive ones are those in which the level of inputs is high.' In the present study agrarian society is defined as a society, which not only derives its main sources of sustenance from the primary sector (agriculture proper, plus allied agricultural activities, forests, mining and quarrying)

but where agriculture is also way of life.

2. In India, various definitions of a village are in vogue. Villages as defined for the purposes of the census may not be the same as villages recognised by the revenue authorities. The revenue villages are territorial units, which include cultivable fields, fallow and uncultivable areas as well as such land as are devoted to residential purposes. We adopt Ashok Rudra's definition of an Indian village. Rudra says: 'we mean by a village a cluster of homesteads in close proximity to each other and usually separated from each other by open spaces. Such a village constitutes a social unit and it is this unit we call a locality. In the real world, however, there are exceptions. In some parts of India (e.g. Kerala) one can't distinguish any clusters of homesteads: they are found to be scattered over the countryside in a continuous stretch. In other areas it may happen that a village consists exclusively of upper caste landowning families and in such a case one can usually discover a nearby settlement of labourers, poor tenants, etc., possibly with a different census or revenue identification. In such a case these two settlements are to be taken together as constituting the smallest social unit. In certain other cases a very large census or revenue village may have several quarters or wards not all of which may constitute a single social unit. That is to say, there may be different localities each consisting of one or more of the quarters or wards' (Rudra, 1984).
3. Bihar (a state of Republic of India, located in the eastern region of the country and to the south of Nepal as a bordering state) has the highest incidence of rural poverty in the country.
4. For more details see Harris, 1992.
5. Dual Economy is characterised by a huge subsistence sector and a highly capital intensive modern sector. The two are distinguishable by presence of organisational, production and other types of asymmetries.
6. Reserve Bank of India and many studies have revealed that land is the most important asset in the rural areas followed by livestock, utensils, and farm equipment. Land's relative share in the distribution of rural assets is more than 70 per cent according to their estimates. It is because of this reason that we have introduced concentration of land as a important explanatory variable. Studies have also shown that there is a very significant positive correlation between higher values of

G_c of land and incidence of poverty (For details see Vaidyanathan, Bardhan, Minhas, Dandekar and Rath, El Ghonemy).

7. The Expert Group recommendations have been made by the committee headed by D.T. Lakadawala in 1994, which defined that 2400 cal is required for rural areas and 2200 cal is required for urban areas for not being in BPL.
8. See Haney M. Lewis (Indian print 1979) 'History of Economic Thought', Surjeet Publication, Delhi.

REFERENCES

Ahluwalia, M.S., 1978, 'Rural Poverty and Agricultural Performance in India,' *Journal of Development Studies*, 14, 298-323.

Amemiya, T., 1981, 'Qualitative Response Models: A Survey,' *Journal of Economic Literature*, 19, 1483-1536.

Ansty, V., 1952, *'The Economic Development of India,'* Fourth Edition, Longman, Green and Co. London.

Atwood, Donald W., 1984, 'Capital and the Transformation of Agrarian Class Systems: Sugar Production in India' published in (ed.) Meghnad Desai, S.H. Rudolph, & A. Rudra *'Agrarian Power and Agricultural Productivity in South Asia,'* Oxford University Press, Delhi, 1984.

Bailey, R. & Brake, M. (Eds), 1975, *'Radical Social Work,'* London: Edward Arnold.

Bardhan, P.K., 1984, *'Land, Labourand Rural Poverty,'* Columbia University Press, New York.

Bardhan, P. K., 1986, 'Poverty and Trickle-Down In Rural India: A Quantitative Analysis,' in *'Agricultural Change and Rural Poverty: Variations on a Theme'* By Dharam Narain, Ed. J.W. Mellor and G.M. Desai.

Basu, K., 1984, *'The Less Developed Economy: A Critique of Contemporary Theory,'* Oxford University Press, Delhi.

Basu, K., 1986, 'One kind of Power,' *Oxford Economic Papers*, Vol. 38.

Basu, K., 1990, *'Agrarian Structure and Under Development,'* Harwood Academic Publisher, London.

Bhaduri, A., 1973, 'A Study in Agricultural Backwardness under Semi-Feudalism,' *Economic Journal*, Vol. 83.

Bhatt, M.S., 2000, 'Land Distribution in Rural Jammu and Kashmir: An Inter-temporal Analysis,' published in *'Land Reforms in India Vol. 5 An Unfinished Agenda'* (Ed.) by B.K. Sinha & Pushpendra, Sage Publications, New Delhi.

Bhattacharya, N., D. Coondoo, P. Maiti, and R. Mukherjee, 1991, *'Poverty, Inequality and Prices in Rural India,'* New Delhi: Sage Publications.

Chakravarty, Sukhamoy, 1984, 'Power Structure and Agricultural Productivity' published in (ed.) Meghnad Desai, S.H. Rudolph, & A. Rudra *'Agrarian Power and Agricultural Productivity in South Asia,'* Oxford University Press, Delhi, 1984.

Chambers, Robert, 1983, *'Rural Development - Putting the Last First,'* Longman Group Limited, Harlow.

Chambers, Robert, 1992, 'Poverty in India: Concept Research in Reality' in *'Poverty in India—Research & Policy'* edited by Harriss, et. al. 1992, Oxford University Press.

Chaudhuri, B.B. (1984): 'Rural Power Structure and Agricultural Productivity in Eastern India, 1757-1947' published in (ed.) Meghnad Desai, S.H. Rudolph, & A. Rudra *'Agrarian Power and Agricultural Productivity in South Asia,'* Oxford University Press, Delhi, 1984.

Cohen, S., 1979, 'The Punitive City: Notes on the Dispersal of Social Control,' *Contemporary Crises*, 3: 339-63.

Corrigan, P. & Leonard, P., 1978, *'Social Work Practice under Capitalism,'* London: Macmillan.

Dandekar, V.M. and N. Rath, 1971, 'Poverty in India,' Indian School of Political Economy. Pune. First published in *Economic and Political Weekly*. Vol. 6 Nos. 1 & 2 and 9. January 1971. Bombay.

Deaton, Angus & Dreze, 2002, 'Computing Prices and Poverty Rates in India, 1999-2000,' Princeton University.

Desai, Meghnad, 1984, 'Power and Agrarian Relations: Some Concepts and Measurements' published in (ed.) Meghnad Desai, S.H. Rudolph, & A. Rudra *'Agrarian Power and Agricultural Productivity in South Asia,'* Oxford University Press, Delhi, 1984.

Desai, Meghnad, S.H. Rudolph, & A. Rudra, 1984, *'Agrarian Power and Agricultural Productivity in South Asia,'* Oxford University Press, Delhi.

Donzelot, J., 1979, *'The Policing of Families,'* London: Hutchinson.

Edwards, A., 1988, *'Regulation and Repression-The Study of Social Control,'* Sydney: Allen Unwin.

El Ghonemy, Mohammad Riad, 1990, *'The Political Economy of Rural Poverty: The Case for Land Reforms,'* Routledge, London.

Gaiha, Raghav, 1988, 'On Measuring Risk of Poverty in Rural India' in *'Rural Poverty in South-East Asia,'* Bardhan P.K. and T.N.

Srinivasan (Eds.), Oxford.

Government of India, 1991, '*Economic Survey*' published by Government of India.

Government of India, 1945, '*Famine Inquiry Commission, India, Final Report*,' Madras.

Government of India, 1960, '*70th Evaluation Report on Community Development and Allied Fields*,' PED, p. 104.

Government of India, 1960, '*Report of the Committee on the Distribution of Income and Levels of Living*,' Part I (Feb. 1964), Part II (July 1969), GOI, Planning Commission, New Delhi.

Government of India, 1969-1990: '*Fourth, Fifth, Sixth and Seventh Five Year Plans*,' 1969, 1974, 1980-85, 1985-90

Government of India, 1974, '*Perspective of Development: 1961-1976, Implications of Planning for Minimum Levels of Living, in Poverty and Income Distribution In India*,' Ed. Srinivasan and Bardhan, Statistical Publishing Society, Calcutta.

Government of India, 1978, '*Manual on IRDP*,' Ministry of Rural Development, Delhi.

Government of India, 1979, '*The Report of the Task Force on Projections of Minimum Needs and Effective Consumption Demand*,' Perspective Planning Division, Planning Commission, New Delhi.

Government of India, 1981, '*National Committee on the Development of Backward Areas: Report on General Issues*,' Planning Commission, p. 24.

Government of India, 1986, '*IRDP and Allied Programmes–A Manual*,' Department of Rural Development, Ministry of Agriculture, New Delhi.

Government of India, 1990, '*Improvements in the Quality of Life in Rural Areas*,' Country Paper On India, Presented in the Study Meeting at Korea Productivity Centre, Seoul, April 9-16, Department of Rural Development, Ministry of Agriculture.

Government of India, 1990, '*National Seminar on Agricultural Labour(Proceedings & Conclusions)*' Organized by the National Commission on Agricultural Labor, Ministry of Labor, Government of India, New Delhi, July 24.

Government of India, 1993, '*Report of the Expert Group on Estimation of Proportion and Number of Poor*,' Perspective Planning Division, Planning Commission, New Delhi, June.

Government of India, 1997a, '*Estimates of Poverty*,' Press Information Bureau (Press Release), New Delhi, March 11.

Government of India, 1997b, '*Approach Paper to the Ninth Five Year*

Plan (1997-2002),' Planning Commission, New Delhi.

Griffin, K.B., and Ghose, A.K. (1979): 'Growth and Impoverishment in the Rural Areas of Asia,' *World Development*, Vol. 7, No. 4/ 5.

Harris, John C., 1980, 'Contemporary Marxist Analysis of the Agrarian Question in India,' *Madras Institute of Development Studies* Working Paper No. 14 (Madras).

Harriss, B., S. Guhan, & R.H. Cassen, 1992, *'Poverty in India—Research & Policy,'* (ed.) Oxford University Press, Bombay.

Herring, Ronald J., 1984, 'Economic Consequences of Local Power Configurations in Rural South Asia' published in (ed.) Meghnad Desai, S.H. Rudolph, & A. Rudra *'Agrarian Power and Agricultural Productivity in South Asia,'* Oxford University Press, Delhi, 1984.

Jha, R., 2000, 'Reducing Poverty and Inequality in India: Has Liberalization Helped' *Discussion Paper 204, WIDER*, Helsinki.

Jodha. N.S., 1986, 'Poverty Debate in India: A Minority View,' *Economic and Political Weekly*, Special Number, November.

Joshi, P.C., 1974, 'Land Reform and Agrarian Change in India and Pakistan since 1947: II,' *The Journal of Peasant Studies*, Vol. 1, No.3., April 1974.

Kakwani, N. and Rao, S.K., 1990, 'Rural Poverty and Its Alleviation In India,' *Economic and Political Weekly*, March 31.

Kakwani, N. and Rao, S.K., 1992, 'Rural Poverty In India: 1973-86,' in *'Poverty In India—Data Base Issues,'* Kadekodi G.K. and G. V.S.N. Murthy (eds.), Vikas Publishing House, New Delhi-14.

Kerala Study, 1976, *'Poverty, Unemployment and Development Policy: A Case Study of Selected Issues with reference to Kerala,'* UNDESA, New York.

Kumar, Brajesh, 2002, *'Rural Poverty in Bihar – An Econometric Analysis,'* Mimeograph/Ph.D. Thesis, Department of Economics, Jamia Millia Islamia, New Delhi.

Mathur, S.C., 1985, 'Rural Poverty and Agricultural Performance In India,' *The Journal of Development Studies*, Vol. 21, No.3, pp. 422-28.

Mead, G.H., 1925, 'The Genesis of the Self and Social Control,' *International Journal of Ethics*, 35: 251-77.

Meier, R.F., 1982, 'Perspectives on the Concept of Social Control,' *Annual Review of Sociology*, 8: 35-55.

Minhas, B.S., 1974, 'Rural Poverty, Land Distribution and Development Strategy,' reprinted in *'Poverty and Income Distribution in India,'* T.N. Srinivasan and P.K. Bardhan (eds.)

Calcutta Statistical Publishing Society.

Minhas, et. al., 1988, 'Measurement of General Cost of Living in Urban India-AII India and Different States,' *Sarvekshana*, vol. XII, No. I, July, pp.1-23.

Minhas, et. al., 1989, 'Comparison of NSS And CSO Estimàtes of Private Consumption: Some Observations Based on 1983 Data,' *The Journal of Income and Wealth*, vol. 11, No. 1, Jan., pp. 7-24.

Minhas, et. al., 1990, 'Rural Cost of Living: 1970-71 to 1983: States and All India,' *The Indian Economic Review*, vol. XXV, No.1, pp. 75-104, January-June.

Minhas, et. al., 1991, 'Declining Incidence of Poverty In 1980s: Evidence VERSUS Artifacts,' *Economic and Political Weekly*, Vol. XXVI, Nos. 27.28, pp. 1673-1682, July 6-13.

Mundle, S., 1984, 'Land, Labourand Levels of Living in Rural Punjab,' in *'Poverty in Rural Asia,'* A.R. Khan and E. Lee (Eds.), ILO, ARTEP, Bangkok, pp. 81-106.

Narain, Dharam, 1979, 'Income Distribution, Redistributive Policies and Growth,' in *'Strategies on Indian Agriculture'* edited by Raj, Sen, Rao.

Nayyar, R., 1991, *'Rural Poverty in India – An Analysis of Inter-state Differences,'* Oxford University Press.

Nehru, J.L., 1963, 'Lok Sabha Address,' Dec. 13, 1963, in *'Constraints on Growth,'* P.N. Dhar, Oxford University Press, Delhi, 1990.

Palmer, Richard, Jones, and Kunal Sen, 2001, 'On India's Poverty Puzzels and Statistics of Poverty,' *Economic and Political Weekly*, January 20, 2001.

Pant, Devendra Kumar, 1997, 'Human Development, Demographic Transition and Economic Growth Linkage - An Econometric Analysis with India Data,' *NCAER Working Paper* Number 67.

Piven, F.F. and Cloward, R.A., 1972, *'Regulating the Poor – The functions of public welfare,'* London: Tavistock, 1972.

Prasad, P.H., 1975, 'Limits to Investment Planning' in A. Mitra (ed.), *'Economic Theory and Planning: Essays in Honor of A.K. Das Gupta'* Delhi: Oxford University Press.

Rajaraman, I., 1975, 'Poverty, Inequality and Economic Growth: Punjab 1960-61 to 1970-71,' *Journal of Development Studies*, Vol. 11, No. 4, July.

Rao, C.H.H., 1991, 'Rural Poverty and Industrialisation,' *Economic and Political Weekly*.

Rao, C.H.H. et. al., 1986, 'Infrastructural Development and Rural

Poverty in India: A Cross Sectional Analysis,' in *'Agricultural Change and Rural Poverty,'* Edited by John W. Mellor and G.M. Desai, Oxford University Press.

Ravallion, Martin, 2000, 'Food Prices, Real Wages and Rural Poverty: Interpreting the Time Series Evidence for India,' *Food Policy*, August 2000.

Ray, Debraj, 2000, *'Development Economics,'* Oxford University Press, Delhi.

Ross, E.A., 1901, *'Social Control,'* New York: Macmillan.

Rudra, Ashok, 1974, Minimum Level of Living 'A Statistical Examination,' in *'Poverty and Income Distribution in India,'* Srinivasan T.N. and Bardhan P.K., (Ed.) Statistical Society Calcutta.

Rudra, Ashok, 1984, 'Local Power and Farm-Level Decision-Making' published in (ed.) Meghnad Desai, S.H. Rudolph, & A. Rudra *'Agrarian Power and Agricultural Productivity in South Asia,'* Oxford University Press, Delhi, 1984.

Saith, A., 1981, 'Production, Prices and Poverty in Rural India,' *Journal of Development Studies*, Vol., 17, No.2, pp. 196-213.

Saith, A., 1990, 'Development Strategies and the Rural Poor,' *Journal of Peasant Studies*, Vol., 17, No.2, pp. 171-244.

Sawant, S., 1990, 'Incidence of Poverty in Rural India,' in *'Social Science Research and Problem of Poverty,'* Tarlok Singh (Ed.), Concept Publishing House, New Delhi 110059.

Sengupta, S. and Joshi, P.D., 1979, 'A Note on the Determination of Poverty Line Based on NSS 27th Round Data,' *Sarvekshana*, Vol. II, No. 1, July, 1979.

Sharma, Alakh, N., 1995, 'Political Economy of Poverty in Bihar,' *Economic and Political Weekly*, Vol. XXX, Nos. 41 and 42.

Srinivasan, 1981, published in (ed.) Meghnad Desai, S.H. Rudolph, & A. Rudra *'Agrarian Power and Agricultural Productivity in South Asia,'* Oxford University Press, Delhi, 1984.

Sukhatme, P.V., 1991, 'Relationship Between Malnutrition and Poverty,' in *'Social Science Research and Problem of Poverty,'* Tarlok Singh (ed.), Concept For Policy Research, New Delhi.

Sen, A.K., 1974, 'Poverty, Inequality and Unemployment: Some Conceptual Issues in Measurement,' in *'Poverty and Income Distribution in India,'* Srinivasan T.N. and Bardhan P.K., (Eds.), Statistical Publishing Society, Calcutta.

Sundaram, K. and Suresh D. Tendulkar, 1983, 'Poverty—Mid Term Appraisal,' *Economic and Political Weekly*, Vol. XIII, November 5-12, pp. 1928-35.

Sundaram, K. and Suresh D. Tendulkar, 2001, NAS-NSS Estimates of Private Consumption for Poverty Estimation, A Disaggregated Comparison for 1993-94,' *Economic and Political Weekly*, January 13, 2001.

Thakur, Jawahar, Manik, LB; Mahabub Hossain, AJ Anaiah, 2000, 'Rural Income Distribution and Poverty in Bihar – Insights from Village Studies,' *Economic and Political Weekly*, December 30, 2000.

Thorner, Daniel, 1973, '*The Agrarian Prospect in India*,' Allied Publishers Private Limited.

Vaidyanathan, A., 1974, 'Some Aspects of Inequalities in Living Standards in Rural India,' in '*Poverty and Income Distribution in India*,' T.N. Srinivasan and P.K. Bardhan (ed.), Statistical Publishing Society, Calcutta.

Walle, D. Van D. E., 1981, 'Population Growth and Poverty: Another Look at the Indian Time Series Data,' *Journal of Development Studies*, Vol. 21, No. 3, pp. 429-39, 1981.

TABLE 15.1

Sampling Design Information

Number of observations	200
Sum of weights	35.0
Number of strata	2 strata in the Sampling Design

CODE	*STRATA*	*PSU*	*LSU*	*OBS*	*P (strata)*	*FPC (f_h)*
1	1	2	6	100	0.579	0.100
2	2	2	6	100	0.428	0.133
Total	2	4	12	200	1.000	—

Remarks: P (strata_i): represents the share of the population which live in strata_i.

Note: These results were computed by using DAD 4.0 software.

TABLE 15.1a
Description of Vectors

Vectors	*Description*
Strata	Specifies the name of the variable (integer type) that contains stratum identifiers as in the present study it is Upper Ganga River Region or North Bihar plain and Lower Ganga River region or South Bihar plain of Bihar.
PSU	Specifies the name of the variable (integer type) that contains identifiers for the Primary Sampling Units, which is two villages from each strata, i.e. Bhavdevpur Got (Sitamarhi District) & Barasra (Siwan District) from Upper Ganga River Region and Sonahri (Gaya District) and Kanaudi (Gaya District) from Lower Ganga River Region carrying two distinct features of the state.
LSU	Specifies the name of the variable (integer type) that contains identifiers for the Last Sampling Units as in the present study these are small farmer (including share cropper and landless labor), medium farmers, and large farmers of village that comes out to be three from each village.
SW	Specifies the name of the variable for the Sampling Weights. Sampling weights are the inverse of the sampling rate. Roughly speaking, they equal the number of observations in the underlying population that are represented by each sample observation. Specifies the name of the variable for the Finite Population Correction factor.
FPC	With FPC, it derives an indicator fh for each observation h, which is then used to compute SD-corrected sampling errors. If the variable FCP is not specified, f_h=0 for all observations; When the variable specified has values <= 1, it is directly interpreted as a stratum sampling rate f_h =n_h/N_h, where n_h = number of PSUs sampled from the strata to which h belongs and N_h = total number of PSUs in the population belonging to stratum h. When the variable specified has values greater than or equal to n_h, it is interpreted as representing N_h; f_h is then set to n_h/N_h.

TABLE 15.2
Variable

Variable	*Variable Description*
Y	Computed from consumption expenditure survey, as referred above, coded as 0 for those who are APL and 1 for those who are BPL.
X1	Gini co-efficients of the ownership land holdings for each villages.
X2	Response to the question: 'Does land owned by the respondent or not?' Yes = 1 and No = 0
X3	Response to the question: 'Does respondent hire labourfor cultivation?' Yes = 1 and No = 0
X4	Response to the question: 'Does respondent has control over assured irrigation?' Yes = 1 and No = 0
X5	Response to the question: 'Does respondent use fertilizers/pesticides for cultivation?' Yes = 1 and No = 0
X6	Response to the question: 'Does respondent borrow credit for agriculture purposes?' Yes = 1 and No = 0
X7	Response to the question: 'Does respondent assure supply/availability of extension services?' Yes = 1 and No = 0
X8	Response to the question: 'Does respondent market access produce?' Yes = 1 and No = 0
X9	Response to the question: 'Does respondent get appropriate price for marketed surplus?' Yes = 1 and No = 0
X10	Response to the question: 'Does respondent sell vegetables?' Yes = 1 and No = 0
X11	Response to the question: 'Does respondent sell straw?' Yes = 1 and No = 0
X12	Response to the question: 'Does respondent sell manure?' Yes = 1 and No = 0
X13	Response to the question: 'Does respondent sell milk?' Yes = 1 and No = 0
Z1	Arithmetic average of response to the questions from X2 to X7. [Note: Here for No = 2 in lieu of '0' has been assigned]
Z2	Arithmetic average of response to the questions from X8 to X13. [Note: Here for No = 2 in lieu of '0' has been assigned]
AP	Arithmetic average of Z1 and Z2.

TABLE 15.3
Descriptive Statistics

Variable	*N*	*Minimum*	*Maximum*	*Mean*	*Std. Deviation*
Y	200	0	1	0.730	0.445
X1	200	0	1	0.925	0.264
X2	200	0	1	0.930	0.256
X3	200	0	1	0.680	0.468
X4	200	0	1	0.475	0.501
X5	200	0	1	0.435	0.497
X6	200	0	1	0.430	0.496
X7	200	0	1	0.275	0.448
X8	200	0	1	0.435	0.497
X9	200	0	1	0.250	0.434
X10	200	0	1	0.250	0.434
X11	200	0	1	0.670	0.471
X12	200	0	1	0.560	0.498
X13	200	0	1	0.925	0.264
AP	200	1.830	1.474	1.474	0.177

TABLE 15.4
Logistic Regression Results

	Dependent Variable = Y			
	Model 1		*Model 2*	
Variables	*Coefficient*	*Z Values*	*Coefficient*	*Wald*
Intercept	2.335	1.233 (0.2174)	-5.757	13.717 (0.000)
X1	4.333	2.482 (0.0131)	1.421	2.694 (0.101)
X2	–2.114	1.751 (0.0799)		
X3	0.565	0.675 (0.4997)		
X4	–0.824	0.934 (0.3498)		
X5	–0.724	1.111 (0.2664)		

	Dependent Variable = Y			
	Model 1		*Model 2*	
Variables	*Coefficient*	*Z Values*	*Coefficient*	*Wald*
X6	–0.135	0.345 (0.73)		
X7	0.168	0.433 (0.6652)		
X8	–0.091	0.162 (0.8711)		
X9	–0.295	0.415 (0.6776)		
X10	0.670	1.979 (0.0478)		
X11	0.670	1.979 (0.0478)		
X12	0.535	1.060 (0.2889)		
X13	–2.790	3.286 (0.001)		
AP			–4.158	14.297 (0.000)
Model Chi-Square (Sig.) [df]		33.983 (0.000) [3]		24.302 (0.000) [3]
Block Chi-Square (Sig.) [df]		33.983 (0.000) [3]		24.302 (0.000) [3]
% Correct Predictions		78.77		73.00
Mc-Fadden's R2		0.379		0.31

Note: The Wald statistics are distributed chi-square with 1 degree of freedom.

* Indicates that the coefficient is statistically significant at, at least, the 0.01 levels.

APPENDIX I

India Poverty Trends (1951–1997) Corrected for CPIAL Changes
(Poverty line = Rs. 49 per capita per month at Oct 73 – Jun 74 rural prices)
(For urban sector Rs. 57 per capita per month at 1973-74 prices)

NSS Round	*Survey period*	*Headcount index (India)*			*Headcount index (Bihar)*	
		Rural	*Urban*	*National*	*Rural*	*Urban*
13	Sep 57-May 58	55.16	47.75	53.84	65.36	60.7
14	Jul 58-Jun 59	53.26	44.76	51.75	66.22	58.63
15	Jul 59-Jun 60	50.89	49.17	50.58	62.19	61.56
16	Jul 60-Aug 61	45.4	44.65	45.27	47.34	48.13
17	Sep 61-Jul 62	47.2	43.55	46.54	56.86	46.14
18	Feb 63-Jan 64	48.53	44.83	47.85	54.96	52.26
19	Jul 64-Jun 65	53.66	48.78	52.75	59.79	55.03
20	Jul 65-Jun 66	57.6	52.9	56.71	67.51	62.88
21	Jul 66-Jun 67	64.3	52.24	62	80.31	67.85
22	Jul 67-Jun 68	63.67	52.91	61.6	77.08	62.36
23	Jul 68-Jun 69	59	49.29	57.11	67.53	53.15
24	Jul 69-Jun 70	57.61	47.16	55.56	66.02	53.42
25	Jul 70-Jun 71	54.84	44.98	52.88	67.29	52.55
27	Oct 72-Sep 73	55.36	45.67	53.37	69.19	52.61
28	Oct 73-Jun 74	55.72	47.96	54.1	69.54	57.35
32	Jul 77-Jun 78	50.6	40.5	48.36	66.21	51.9
38	Jan 83-Dec 83	45.31	35.65	43	69.94	50.32
42	Jul 86-Jun 87	38.81	34.29	37.69	56.45	42.78
43	Jul 87-Jun 88	39.23	36.2	38.47	58.57	52.94
44	Jul 88-Jun 89	39.06	36.6	38.44	—	—
45	Jul 89-Jun 90	34.3	33.4	34.07	58.57	42.29
46	Jul 90-Jun 91	36.43	32.76	35.49	58.29	41.13
47	Jul 91-Dec 91	37.42	33.23	36.34	—	—
48	Jan 92-Dec 92	43.47	33.73	40.93	67.81	46.32
50	Jul 93-Jun 94	36.66	30.51	35.04	63.51	39.72
51	Jul 94-Jun 95	39.75	33.5	38.4	—	—
52	Jul 95-Jun 96	37.46	28.04	35	—	—
53	Jan 97-Dec 97	35.69	29.99	34.4	—	—
55*	Jul 99-Jun 00	27.61	25.09	40.15	—	—
55**	Jul 99-Jun 00	24.49	23.22	36.1	—	—

Note: All poverty measures are expressed as percentage.
* 30 days recall period.
** 7 days recall period.

Source: Datta(1999), Jha(2000).

(Continued)

The vast majority of the rural poor in India are engaged in agriculture (including fishery and livestock) either as agricultural wage laborers or marginal farmers and self-employed. Data on 1993-94 states that almost 42 per cent of the rural poor fall into the most economically disadvantaged group of agricultural labor. More than half of this group consists of scheduled castes (SC) and scheduled tribes (ST). Hence SC/ST constitute more than half of the most vulnerable section of the rural poor. SC and ST are about 32 per cent of the rural population but account for more than 42 per cent of the poor. Hence, there is good rationale for the targeting of SC and ST. Even within the rural poor the case of women is particularly worrisome.

Chapter 16

State-led and Market-assisted Land Reforms
History, Theory, and Insight from the Philippines

Ugo Pica Ciamarra

Introduction

Land property rights have recently received increased attention as policy instruments that affect access to food. Links between land and food generally fall within a linear framework that starts with access to resources and proceeds casually through production, income generation, consumption decisions and nutritional status (Maxwell and Wiebe, 1998). An extensive economic literature, in fact, indicates that small farmers are more productive per unit of land than large ones (for example, Berry and Cline, 1979; Cornia, 1985) and that equality in land asset distribution fosters economic growth and development (for example, Alesina and Rodrick, 1994; Deininger and Squire, 1998). Despite this evidence, in several developing countries land distribution is severely skewed, as a consequence of non-economic forces and/or market and institutional imperfections and failures (Binswanger et al., 1995). It follows that reforms that involve intervention in the existing structure of land access are desirable both from an equity and an efficiency standpoint.[1]

Empirical and theoretical findings indicate that there exists a variety of complementary paths that can secure access to land for the rural poor (de Janvry, 2002). This paper focuses on the political economy of land reform, that is the establishment of new land property rights relationships. Among land reform practitioners, there are two contending positions on what constitutes the most appropriate land redistributive policy. Some scholars maintain that primarily the State has to redistribute the land (state-led reform); others argue that above all the market has to promote land reallocation (market-assisted reform). State-led land reform advocates – who are usually representatives of civil society and non-governmental organizations – contend that exogenous land transfers are particularly effective: 'There is a need to recognize that States have a central role in promoting land reform programs' (AKA[2], 2001, p.1; Rosset, 2001; Reyes, 1999). Market-driven land reform proponents – who are mainly members of international organisations, such as the World Bank that first pushed for market-assisted land reform programs in the second half of the 1990s – affirm that, under certain conditions, markets can endogenously lead to equal and efficient land asset distribution: 'The market can redistribute natural resources as substitute for (state-led) land reforms in countries where land ownership is particularly concentrated'[3] (Vogelsegang, 1998, p.16; Deininger, 1999). This paper shows that, under certain respects, the divergence between state-led and market-driven land reform is ill-conceived, and that complementarity exists between these two approaches to land reallocation.

Our arguments are developed in three stages. Section I provides the historical background and the conceptual bases of state-led and market-driven land reforms. It shows that these reforms originate in different historical contexts and respond to different challenges and, hence, they are not simply comparable. However, in the last few years state-led and market-assisted land reform proponents have been intensely disputing over the political economy of land redistribution. Section II analyses differences and similarities between these two approaches to land reallocation. It concludes that, apart from the obvious divergence in the coercive/voluntary land transfer mechanism, major differences refer to constraints in the functioning of the land market, to the area targeted for redistribution and number of beneficiaries, and partly to the role of private investors in the land acquisition process. But it also highlights that the practices of contemporary state-led and market-assisted land reforms are extensively overlapped, especially as they both rest upon the trilogy market/state/ civil society. Section III, on the basis of empirical evidences, argues that state-led and market-driven land reforms can be successful complements in securing fair access to land for the resource poor. In particular, it presents the 1988 Philippine agrarian reform program as a case in point. Section IV summarizes the main findings.

I

Historical and Economic Rationale of State-led and Market-Assisted Land Reforms

State-led land reforms consist of a central authority that dispossesses (or attempts to) large landowners from the land, and redistributes it to selected beneficiaries. On paper, landowners are compensated below market value so that the reform process includes a confiscatory component. Payments to landlords are made mostly in interest-bearing bonds spread over a period of years, with cash seldom exceeding 20 per cent of the fixed price of land. Beneficiaries either receive the land free of charge, or they have several years to repay it to the government, often benefiting from favorable interest rates. In theory, small farmers are provided with technical assistance and support services as well (Ladeijinsky, 1964; Raup, 1967).

State-led land reforms were high on the political agendas in the 1950s (in Asia and the Middle East) and in 1960s (in Latin America) especially in countries with high land property concentration, great social and economic inequality, abject rural poverty and widespread landlessness. Production was carried out in exploitative feudal *haciendas* and in large plantations, such as in Latin America and colonial Africa, or in landlord estates where oppressed tenants cultivated the land, such as in several Asian countries. Exploitative production relations in agriculture repeatedly ended up in rural rebellions and revolts (Barraclough, 1994). These conflicting situations, that Barraclough (1970) refers to as the 'agrarian problem,' as opposed to the 'agricultural development problem,' led several governments to legislate land reform programmes to legitimate their ruling by reducing inequality in access to land and, hence, mitigating rural unrest (Deininger, 1999; Grossman, 1994; Horowitz, 1993). Local authorities were frequently backed by foreign governments and international agencies, which were increasingly concerned about a perspective communist threat and intended to thwart rural people's protests (Dorner, 1992; Putzel, 1992).

In the 1950s and the 1960s state-led land reforms were thus directed at legitimating governments in power and averting socialist revolutions. They did not have any explicit economic aim, up to the point that commitment to reform faltered once social tensions had subsided. In effect, in those two decades the cornerstone to economic growth and development was input substitution industrialisation, and agricultural growth was primarily associated with technological change (Schultz, 1964). Yet, there is a pervasive attitude to evaluate state-led land reforms in terms of their economic outcome. Under this perspective, successful reforms were carried out in Japan and South Korea, under the auspices of US, and in Taiwan, under the Kuomintang. Organisational requirements of conducting such reforms were minimal, as they were implemented by independent foreign authorities and consisted of redistribution of agricultural estates to existing experienced tenants, without revolutionising the pattern of production (Dorner, 1992; Kawagoe, 1999).

In most cases, however, the economic performance of reforms has been disappointing. De Janvry (1981) maintains that in the 1960s Latin American land reforms ended up to be an instrument for promoting technological change in the non-reformed sector, rather than to make the poor rural dwellers better off. Otsuka (1993) contends that in Asia land redistribution did not have any significant impact on rural poverty; El Ghonemy (2001) asserts that African land reforms destroyed functional systems of collective land property rights in semi-arid regions. Results were unsatisfactory because of three specific difficulties. First, the number of beneficiaries and the percentage of arable land distributed were relatively low, at least with respect to the successful Asian experiences. Governments often legislated cosmetic reforms and the landowning class put up fierce resistance to expropriation. Second, on the assumption that the resource-poor farmers did not suffer any competitive disadvantage in the sphere of production, governmental investments in complementary infrastructure and delivery of support services were lacking. Yet, in situations characterised by incomplete contracting, changes in patterns of landownership lead to an increase in agricultural income as far as adequate provision is made for the supply of necessary inputs and mandatory services to land reform beneficiaries (for example, World Bank, 1975). Third, governments severely restricted land sale and rental markets and so contributed to reduce efficiency levels. For instance, if land cannot be bought and sold, it could not be used as collateral. Without access to credit market, beneficiaries may underinvest in their land, resort to distress sales and lead to effective reconcentration of landownership patterns[4] (Jonakin, 1996).

Following the disappointing experiences of the sixties, land reforms largely fell off the political agenda. In the 1970s agricultural development was primarily associated with the technology of the Green Revolution, with central role given to international institutions and the State; in the 1980s, in the attempt to 'get the prices right,' the role of governments was reduced and the economy liberalised under stabilisation and structural adjustment policies. De Janvry et al. (2001b) define this period as one of retrogression in rural development, but at the same time one of setting the context of new approaches to rural development in terms of market incentives and new roles for civil society. In the 1990s, in fact, the rural development agenda has been characterised by the market/ state/civil society trilogy, and the issue of access to land has returned full force in political debates. In particular, for the first time in history, in the neoclassical framework land reform has been regarded as a device for facilitating the functioning of rural markets, achieving greater efficiency in resource allocation, and equity in the distribution of the produce. With respect to the fifties and the sixties, however, the instrument proposed to secure equal access to land has changed drastically. Government directed one-time land redistribution is in fact substituted by non-coercive continuing mechanisms of adjustment in access to land. In particular, reference is made to market-assisted, market-driven, market-friendly or negotiated land reforms, to indicate strategies that intend to dynamize the demand for and the supply of land.

Market-assisted land reforms consist of beneficiaries, assisted by the community and local government, receiving a combination of grants and loans from the public and private sectors which they use to negotiate the purchase of the land from willing sellers and to set up viable farms. The grant must cover the overpricing of the land relative to its productive value plus the start-up and the net working capital costs for the first year. To be eligible beneficiaries, individuals are obliged to come up with a farm development plan, which has to be set up with the support of non-governmental organisations, farmers' associations and local governments and partly financed by private investors. Proponents of market-assisted land reform maintain that: (1) this approach reduces landlords' resistance to land transfer, as exchanges are voluntary and compensation 100 per cent in cash and at market value; (2) with respect to coercive expropriation based on cumbersome bureaucratic requirements, a decentralised and community-based voluntarily land transfer between willing sellers and buyers is more effective because of the involvement of a wide spectrum of rural actors in the process, both public and private; (3) as private investors are likely to finance only those rural dwellers able to set up a viable and sustainable farm, a lower threshold to farm efficiency is set (Deininger,

1999; 2001).

Market-assisted land reforms rest upon two major microeconomic evidences: (1) that there exists an inverse relation between farm size and output per unit of land; (2) that the land market is regressive for the resource-poor.

First, empirical analyses point at the existence of an inverse relation between farm size and output per hectare. This relation is often referred to as the 'official theory of agrarian reform' (FAO, 1993). Even though this indication dates back to the publication of the *Indian Farm Management Studies* in the 1950s, economists gave particular attention to the inverse relation in the 1970s and the 1980s (Berry and Cline, 1979; Bardhan, 1973; Barraclough, 1970; Bhalla and Roy, 1988; Carter, 1984; Cornia, 1985; Kutcher and Scandizzo, 1981). Essentially, the inverse relation rests upon imperfect substitutability between family and hired labour, because of supervision costs associated with wage labour (Hayami and Otsuka, 1993b). However, secure access to land also enhances opportunities to use resources (as family labour) that in many cases are underused (Deininger, 2001); it allows farmers to transact in markets where land can be used as collateral (Banjeree and Newman, 1994); it encourages lump-sum investments in both physical and human capital (Deininger et al., 2000); it has positive effects on nutrition level, both through enhanced income and direct access to calories intake (Burgess, 2000); and it protects against calamity, making it less severe exogenous shocks of nature (Berry, 1998).

Second, the market is not able to shift land to the resource poor. The price of land, in fact, exceeds the present discounted value of the income flow that can be produced from farming, as it is inflated by credit subsidies, by fiscal policies allowing the use of agriculture as a tax shelter, by the social value of the land, and by macroeconomic instability that encourages the use of land as an inflation hedge. But even in perfect market environments the resource-poor cannot access the land because of 'the fundamental financing problem of the poor' (Binswanger, 1987). The landless and near-landless individuals, whose incomes are at the margin of subsistence, cannot purchase land (using money borrowed at the market rate of interest) without curtailing their consumption below what they could earn in the labour market. In fact, at equilibrium the income increment for a unit of land would be exactly equal to the interest payment (Binswanger, 1987; Carter and Mesbah, 1993). Individuals without accumulated savings, therefore, should have to reduce their consumption below subsistence level to make principal payments on the purchased land. It follows that the relatively wealthy landowners are net buyers of land and the relatively small landholders are net sellers of land (Carter and Salgado, 2001).

On the basis of these considerations, market-assisted land reform programmes intend to secure access to land to all the rural dwellers by altering the performance of the rural markets so as not to discriminate against the rural poor, and in this way set up an effectively and continuously adjusting mechanism of placing resources efficiently and enhancing social equity. Pilot projects of market-assisted land reform have been implemented in Brazil, Colombia and South Africa. The evidence is very mixed. Deininger (1999) asserts that in Colombia beneficiaries, in order to set up a viable family farm, need between 30 per cent and 50 per cent of the land that had been necessary under earlier reform programs. This is so as under the current programme farmers acquire an entire 'productive package' that includes land, factor inputs, technical assistance and the like. Sauer (2001) contends that in Northeast Brazil people are complaining that the programme is driving up the land price, that it is failing to reduce poverty level and that potential beneficiaries are not even informed of the programme. Deininger (1999), on the other hand, asserts that in Brazil community-based implementation of the program is particularly rapid. Borras (2002a) maintains that the Brazilian market-assisted land reform if implemented nationwide would be much more expensive that the state-led implemented program. Lyne et al. (2000) presents evidence from the province of KwaZulu-Natal in South Africa that land grants from the government have so far performed disappointingly as to land transfer activities and agricultural production trend.

II

Divergence and Convergence and Convergence between State-Led and Market-Assisted Land Reforms

The evolution of land reform from state-led to market-driven is hardly surprising: it replicates the dynamics of the term 'reform' along the second half of last century. Educational reform denoted universal primary schooling, free at least for the poor; the redefinition encompasses financial stabilisation and recovery of costs from users. In developing countries government reform used to mean intervention to satisfy the basic needs of the whole population; it is now coming to mean liberalisation, regulation and legalisation of a number of markets. Fiscal reform indicated measures to increase horizontal and vertical equity; it now refers to lower tax rates and a shift towards indirect taxation. In brief, reform first indicates the removal of arbitrary privileges, and then efforts towards a better functioning of the market mechanism (Lipton, 1995).

Land reform is no exception: state-led land reform used to mean the redistribution of land property rights from the rich to the poor through the state apparatus; market-assisted land reform denotes equal access to land asset through the market mechanism in order to promote efficient resource allocation. It follows that market reform can be considered as the successor to redistributive reform, and one may argue that any association between state-led and market-assisted land reform risks to be merely speculative.

In recent times, however, disagreements have arisen among state-led reform advocates and market-assisted reform proponents, and countless debates have been held about the appropriate policies to promote equal access to land asset (for example, de Janvry et al., 2001; Ghimire, 2001; ICARRD, 2000). On the one hand, neoclassical economists are increasingly concerned with markets functioning and high quality institutions to trigger economic growth and development; under their perspective, market-assisted land reallocation is clearly efficiency-enhancing (Deininger, 1999; World Bank, n.d.). On the other hand, the diffusion of democracy and the explosion in number and quality of grassroots movements have given farmers bargaining power in the political arena, so as to exert pressure on governments to legislate state-led land reform programs. Poor rural dwellers and civil society are essentially concerned with equity and, as markets are often regressive for them, define market-assisted land reforms as 'questionable,' 'inequitable' and 'indecent' and question the usefulness and effectiveness of 'land market reform' programs (El Ghonemy, 2001, p. 106; KMP, 2000; Reyes, 1999; Rosset, 2001; Sauer, 2000; 2001).

These contrasting views not only rely on ideological and rational bases, but also upon a series of ambiguities. In effect, market-assisted reform proponents have never pushed that models of market-driven reform are the only way to secure equal access to land, but maintain that market reforms can produce genuine benefits where the political situation does not permit exogenous redistribution: 'negotiated land reform is a complement,. . . for other forms of gaining access to land' (Deininger, 1999, p. 666). But ambiguities subsist. First, state-led reform proponents often speak of 'land market reform' (see El Ghonemy, 2001; 2002), while advocates of market-assisted reform have always referred to 'market-assisted land reform.' In particular, the first refereed article on the subject titles 'negotiated land reform' (Deininger, 1999), to indicate the necessity of a broad-encompassing approach to development. Subsequent terms have been 'community-based,' 'community-managed,' 'market-friendly' and 'market-assisted' land reform and, in Brazil, 'rural poverty alleviation strateg.' Second, in a comprehensive survey of the World Bank's land policy, Deininger and Binswanger (1999, p. 267-268) assert that market-assisted land reform also 'aims to replace the confrontational atmosphere that has characterized land reforms with a more collabourative attitude,' and contend that 'by drawing on the private sector, nongovernmental organisations, and the community to develop, finance, and administer projects, the approach promises to overcome some of the informational imperfections that have plagued the implementations of land reform by government bureaucracies.' Third, in the first part of his seminal article on negotiated land reforms, Deininger (1999) lists and discusses on the presumed advantages of market-assisted land reforms vis-à-vis flaws and shortcomings of state-led reforms. Finally, in their work on 'Access to Land, Rural Poverty and Public Action,' de Janvry et al. (2001a, p. 1) affirm that large scale expropriative land reforms are generally not attuned to the contemporary political state of affairs. It is thus understandable that market-assisted and state-led land reforms can appear to be as substitute political instruments.

An in-depth analysis of these two land policies, however, shows that the divergence between state-led and market-assisted land reform is limited. First, market-assisted land reform makes sense only in circumscribed areas and, although the land transfer is price-driven, several of its components may well be elements of state-led reforms, in particular the extensive involvement of local actors in program implementation. Second, apart from the voluntary/coercive land transfer mechanism, the main distinctions refer to rules and regulations that affect the functioning of rural markets, to the quantification of the area targeted for redistribution and number of beneficiaries, and partly to the role of private investors in programme implementation. Third, as Section 3 will show, the market and the state can be also successful complements in securing equal access to land for the resource poor.

Target area, beneficiaries and market functioning

In history state-led large-scale expropriative land reforms are generally associated with entire countries and/or charismatic political leaders. For instance, reference is made to the successful Japanese and Taiwanese land reforms, or to Cárdenas and Allende as political leaders able to generate broad support and defeat opposing interests to land redistribution in Mexico and Chile respectively. Comprehensive state-led agrarian reforms are by construction large-scale, as they are usually implemented through laws and regulations (at least in non-socialist economies) whose applicability is all over the country. These laws typically indicate the landholding to be expropriated and redistributed, specify retention limit for landowners and their compensation package, quantify perspective beneficiaries and stipulate their land ceiling and payment schedule, indicate the timing and phasing of redistribution, etc.. In general, in order to avoid re-concentration of landholding, these laws also attenuate the bundle of rights for beneficiaries by setting up rules and regulations that restrict land use and transfer. Consequently, they affect the operation of the land market and the level of exchanges, with probable negative consequences on resource allocation (Brandão and Feder, 1995). A review of these policies, in fact, finds that they have rarely achieved their goals as in several instances farmers have departed from or bypassed the laws by inventing innovative labour and/or land contracts (Deininger and Binswanger, 1999; Hayami and Otsuka, 1993a; Hayami et al.,1990; Stiglitz, 1998).

Contrary to state-led land reforms, market-assisted land reforms are neither based on one-time national laws nor they obstruct the functioning of the land market; quite the opposite, they attempt to maintain access to land ownership continuously open for the rural poor by dynamising the demand/supply relationship. In general, the efficacy of market assisted reforms crucially depends on how severe the initial inequalities are (also those unrelated to economic contribution) vis-à-vis economic distortions. For instance, if the levels of schooling, health, research, communication and transport and other infrastructure are to some extent developed, market-assisted land reforms are likely to reduce inequality and trigger economic growth. But if the opposite holds, such as in almost every developing country, results of large-scale market reforms would be repeatedly disappointing as poor people are trapped in socioeconomic structures that prevent them from exploiting the potential of market incentives (for example, Lipton, 1995; World Bank, 2002). These situations constitute a *prima facie* case for Government intervention, suggesting that large-scale successful market-assisted reallocation may require more public spending (for example in infrastructure and cooperatives building) than state-led reform (Lipton, 1995).

On small scale and under peculiar circumstances, however, there is room for market-assisted reforms to work. To begin with, the following two exogenous conditions are to be satisfied. First, large tracts of land of arable potential, which are not fully exploited, unutilised or underutilised, are to be available in the market. Would the opposite hold, other redistributive policies are in order (e.g. labour market regulations). This condition is likely to be fulfilled in a region or a smaller area, devoted for example to extensive livestock grazing, and not in an entire country. It follows that, contrary to state-led reforms, modern and developed agricultural farms are likely to be *ex-ante* excluded from reallocation. Second, successful market-assisted reform requires an excess latent supply of land vis-à-vis the perspective demand. This is to avoid that reform just ends up in pumping up the land price, threatening to undermine any efficiency and equity outcome from the process. For instance, in pilot areas of Colombia the supply/demand ratio per unit of land is required to be at minimum 3. It follows that, contrary to state-led reforms, the perspective target area of market-assisted land reform is generally limited. Furthermore, as market-assisted models are voluntary, neither they point to explicit targets for land distribution that will be eventually achieved nor they quantify the perspective number of beneficiaries, neither they specify retention limits for landowners nor they indicate land ceilings for reform beneficiaries. Therefore, the agrarian structure that will be ultimately realised is *a priori* uncertain, as it depends on a series of variables, such as the potential supply of land, that can be only roughly estimated.

The role of local governments and civil society in land reform programmes

Section I showed that market-assisted land reform does not end up in granting loans to potential beneficiaries. Its implementation necessitates the extensive and common involvement of the local government, the community and private investors to alter the performance of the market in favor of the poor landless. In Colombia, for instance, the municipality has to set up a comprehensive and well-publicised land reform plan to identify potential sellers and buyers of land (Deininger, 2001); in Northeast Brazil the land to be transferred to the poor rural dwellers is selected by community-groups and only associations of peasants can assume financial obligations, which are a mutual responsibility of all farmers (Souza Filho et al., 1999).

In general, local administrators and community-based organisations are first to quantify the potential demand for and supply of land and to elabourate an area development plan, which takes into account the necessities of the perspective agrarian reform beneficiaries, as well as the needs of those unable to buy the land on the market. Measuring the latent demand for and supply of land is a challenging task. The potential demand is generally quantified by allowing selected beneficiaries to enter a list by registering, for example, at local public offices. Perspective supply may be at best estimated on the basis of underused and unutilised farms in determined ecologically suitable zones. Local actors are also to provide legal and technical assistance to farmers during land market transactions and to guide beneficiaries in the start-up phase to set up a viable productive farm. On paper, local actors have sociological, geographical and informative advantages and self-interest at providing these services with respect to central government institutions. Their extensive involvement in the reform process is thus considered efficiency-enhancing, as well as one of the original elements of market-assisted land reform programs (Deininger, 2001).

But grassroots strategy to development is not an exclusive trait of market-driven land reforms. Nowadays, in fact, there is a strong consensus over the advantage and the efficiency of local governments and communities vis-à-vis central authorities. In particular, in the last 15 years the growing diffusion of democracy have elicited processes of devolution and decentralization so that local governments are increasingly accountable in front of rural people, and willing to provide a growing percentage of public goods (Bardhan and Ghatak, 1999; Zhang et al., 2001). In their turn, accountable and transparent local and national governments, in which people have a real chance to participate, are associated with the explosion in number and quality of the organisation and political savvy of peasant groups and grassroots movements. Today farmers' organisations not only are the main supporters of state-led redistribution by exerting political pressures at local (for exammple, in Brazil and the Philippines) and international level (e.g. The International Farmers Movement *La Via Campesina*), but are also able to raise local resources and provide farmers with technical, financial and legal assistance[5] (Ghimire, 2001). It follows that a decentralised approach to land reform is likely to be a characteristic of contemporary state-led redistribution as well (Borras, 1999; Wilson, 1987). Under this aspect, therefore, state-led and market-assisted land reforms are clearly complement any policies.

Private investors financing land reform

Traditional state-led reform requires the State to carry out both the land acquisition and distribution and the supplying of support service components of the programme. Most recent experiments, such as that of the Philippines, are, however, attempting to attract private investors in supplying credit and production inputs to farmers. The typical tool is by way of contract-growing or contract-labour schemes, by which there is agreement to perform work but the farmer is not employed by the (agri-business) firm for whom he performs the work, although he is provided with factor inputs, cash advance and technical assistance. These arrangements are potentially profitable as small farmers are residual claimants to profits, the scope for economies of scale in agriculture is very limited (with the exception of few plantation crops), and the need to monitor and enforce labourers' effort on large-scale farms is particularly costly (or impossible). Empirical evidence suggests that, for contract-labour schemes to work, the government has to provide the necessary institutional framework upon which parties can structure contracts by share risks in light of incentive problems (FAO, 2001).

Market-assisted land reform programmes establish that private investors, together with community-based actors, have to contribute largely to programme implementation. Differently from state-led programs, however, market-assisted land reform does not distinguish between the land acquisition and distribution element and the delivery of support services component of the programme. Commercial banks, in fact, are to grant loans to the poor tillers for purchasing the land and other factor inputs on the market. Furthermore, as part of their self-interest in seeing the loan repaid, they provide technical assistance to beneficiaries and supervise their farming activities as well. Therefore, any financing from private investors ends up to partly fund the transfer of land. This is possibly the most innovative component of market-assisted land reform programmes. However, for commercial banks to finance land transfers, the extensive involvement of local governments, NGOs and farmers' associations is required, both in setting up an area development plan and agricultural productive projects, so as to reduce risk and uncertainty for potential private investors.

Two are the distinguishing characteristics with this mechanism vis-a-vis *tout-court* state-led redistribution. First, potential budget constraints of the government are fulfilled by private funds, so that the scope of reform may be as large as ever in state-led programems. Second, the commercial banks that grant the loans to purchase the land want farmers to acquire low-priced productive lands, and do not allow transactions at inflated prices. In this way the risk of farmers being exploited by wealthy and informed actors in the market is reduced to a minimum. Finally, as in traditional contract-labour schemes, banks and agri-business firms have incentives at providing technical assistance and monitoring farming activities of beneficiaries so as to avoid high rates of default. It follows that viable and efficient family farms are likely to be set up.

State-led and market-assisted land reforms: Summary

Our brief survey of state-led and market-assisted land reforms showed that, under some respects, debates over the appropriate policy to secure equal access to land are more cosmetic than real. In particular, there is evidence that, although historical and theoretical differences exist between these two approaches to land reallocation, their practices are to some extent overlapped.

First, the major difference between state-led and market-assisted land reform refers to the voluntary/coercive land transfer mechanism. The main convergence is that their successful implementation relies upon the extensive involvement of all rural actors in programme implementation, from farmers to local governments, from private investors to NGOs, to local communities. Second, if successful state-led land reforms have been implemented under peculiar political and economic circumstances, market-assisted land reform has very limited applicability as well. In particular, it requires two demanding conditions to be satisfied, i.e. a negative balance between the demand for and supply of land, and a somewhat developed institutional infrastructure. Its most distinguishing features are that it seeks implementation of continuous mechanism of adjustment in access to land as opposed to one time coercive state redistribution, and it requires the involvement of private investors in land transfer activities. Its main flaw is that it is *a priori* impossible to know what agrarian structure will be achieved after programme implementation, as its outcome depends on a number of variables that are at best roughly estimated, such as the potential supply of land and the trust of private investors in the program. Conversely, state-led reform programmes *a priori* indicate the area targeted for redistribution, identify retention limit for landowners and land ceiling for beneficiaries, and specify implementation schedule. However, they frequently constrain the operations of rural markets and coercive expropriation can often be hardly carried out because of fierce resistance from landowners, budget constraints, and lack of political commitment. In these cases negotiated land reallocation may provide a lower cost and quicker method to transfer resources to the asset poor.

A question remains open: what is the most appropriate land reallocative policy? How much farmers are willing to oppose market-assisted reforms and occupy idle and underused land illegally vis-à-vis opposition to expropriation from large landowners? Is it possible to reconcile landowners' and small farmers' interests and aspirations? Is it possible to merge state-led and market-assisted land reform programmes? Answers to these questions are idiosyncratic, as they rest upon the peculiar economic, social and cultural institutions of the country at hand. The following presents and comments on the contemporary Philippine land reform programme that is, at the same time, coercive state-led and free market-driven. This experience suggests that the two approaches to secure equal access to land for the resource poor can be jointly implemented on a large-scale base, with probably better outcome would they be carried out independently.

III

Expropliation and Market in Concert : Land Reform in the Philippines

Background

Land distribution in the Philippines has been traditionally skewed, as a result of Spanish colonisation (1565–1898), US dominion (1898–46) and the exclusionary agroexport growth promoted after the 1946 independence (Allen, 1938; Constantino, 1978; Ruiz, 1945; Willis, 1905). In 1988, 5 per cent of all families owned 83 percent of the arable land, with a Gini coefficient of 0.647 (Putzel, 1992). Since 1574 the Philippine history has been thus characterised by countless rural riots and revolts, largely negative reactions to exploitative labour and tenancy relationships, and by several agrarian laws, which intended to mitigate social tensions in rural areas (IBON, 1988; Kerkvliet, 1974; Monk, 1990). The most recent attempt to change the pattern of landownership has been the 1988

'Comprehensive Agrarian Reform Programme (CARP),' usually referred to as CARP, that it is still being implemented at present.

CARP has been legislated during the democratic Government of Corazon Aquino, voted president of the country in February 1986 after twenty years of Marcos' dictatorship. It is the first Philippine agrarian reform programme not entirely state-led, as grassroots peasants' movements and nongovernmental organisations exerted tremendous pressures on the government during the legislative process (Bulatao, 2000). As a result, CARP presents both conservative and progressive components (ROP, 1988). Conservative elements are the following: a variable land retention limit, a ten-year (then twenty-year) implementation schedule, a compensation formula that may price the land above the market value (Putzel, 1992), the deferred redistribution of commercial farms, a corporate stock-sharing scheme that can replace land expropriation and, finally, constraints on the transferability of land titles for a ten-year period. But CARP is also progressive, at least with respect to previous Philippine agrarian reform laws. First, it shifts from tenure regulations in rice and grain lands to land redistribution; second, it covers all public and private agricultural lands, that is over ten million hectares projected to benefit 3.9 million rural-based producers and workers. In January 1998 this target was lowered to less than 8 million hectares, with around 21 per cent of the presumed beneficiaries losing out with this reduction. Anyhow, this scope is well above the targets of the successful Japanese, Taiwanese and South Korean agrarian reform programmes (Hayami *et al.*, 1990). Finally, CARP offers a range of alternative schemes of land redistribution, both state-led and market-based.

The land acquisition and distribution component of the programme is administered by two departments. The Department of Environment and Natural Resources (DENR) is responsible for redistributing around 3.5 million hectares of public agricultural lands; the Department of Agrarian Reform (DAR) is in charge of acquiring and redistributing about 4.3 million hectares of private agricultural lands and some government-owned lands (in particular those managed by government financial institutions).[6] As of December 2000, 67 per cent of the target has been accomplished, with 70 per cent of the land distributed belonged to the public and government sector.[7] On the whole, CARP has achieved something substantial, as the Philippines ranks third in terms of percentage of arable land redistributed among those countries that carried out agrarian reforms after World War II.

The programme does not intend to simply distribute the land, but also to ensure that beneficiaries benefit from being owner-cultivators. It is, in fact, also concerned with the provision of support services to smallholders (e.g. irrigation facilities, credit, infrastructure, training, marketing and management assistance, support to cooperatives and farmers' organisations), so much that 27 per cent of all agrarian reform funds have been devoted to 'Programme Beneficiaries Development' so far.[8] The delivery of support services to farmers is managed by eight governmental agencies, the principal being the Land Bank of the Philippines (LBP) and the Department of Agriculture (DA).

Attempts to quantify the comprehensive effects of land redistribution and support services delivery to farmers beneficiaries have been scanty so far. The Philippine government, in fact, has been oriented towards measuring land reform accomplishment exclusively in terms of hectares distributed, disregarding the impact on target beneficiaries, on their income, technology and welfare (Morales, 1999; Reyes, 2000). Recently, however, some academic studies have indicated that in pilot areas the overall impact has been encouraging: not only beneficiaries are better off, but they have increased investments in human and physical capital, with positive prospects for future growth and development (Deininger et al., 1999, 2000; Riedinger and Kang, 2000).

Coercive and voluntary land transfer mechanisms

One of the most challenging issues of the Philippine land reform programme is the distribution of privately non-government owned land, as landlords are given endless legal and illegal chances to oppose expropriation, for example by court challenges or by bribing local officers. In 1998 the World Bank released a report titled 'Philippines Promoting Equitable Rural Growth' that advised the Philippine government to implement a market-assisted land reform, as 'more of the land transfer that has taken place is mainly of lands which have some form of government ownership or control related to it; virtually all of private lands – potentially the most contentious and costly component of the programme – remain to be acquired and distributed.' (World Bank, 1998, p.35). The World Bank proposal was backed by an offer of an initial US $ 15 million to be granted to target beneficiaries in selected pilot communities. This plan was meant to expedite completion of land acquisition target. The Philippine government refused the World Bank proposal, albeit in some areas of the country prospects for market-based reform appeared to exist, such as in the underutilised coconut plantations of Negros islands. The agrarian reform law, however, already offered a wide range of transfer mechanisms, including market transactions; namely it regulates operation land transfer (OLT), compulsory acquisition (CA), voluntary-offer-to-sell (VOS) and voluntary-land-transfer (VLT) (Adriano, 1992; Hayami et al., 1990; ROP, 1988).

Operation Land Transfer (OLT) (originally under the Marcos 1972 land reform program and later subsumed by CARP) covers tenanted rice and corn lands and consists of transferring ownership from landowners to tenant-tillers. Compulsory Acquisition (CA) consists of government expropriating private properties in non-rice non-corn areas and distributing them to selected beneficiaries. These arrangements are coercive and executed whether or not landlords cooperate with the program; landowners are paid via a staggered bonds-cash payment, with the cash portion not more than 30 per cent and the rest in bonds spread over ten years. The voluntary-offer-to-sell (VOS) scheme consists of landowners surrendering of their own volition their land to government for valuation and distribution. It is a scheme that intends to encourage landlords cooperation by giving them incentive when they voluntarily cooperate with the program; landowners are in fact entitled to an additional 5 per cent in cash portion of the payment (with a corresponding decrease of 5 per cent in the bonds payment). The voluntary-land-transfer (VLT) arrangement, also referred to as the Direct Payment Scheme, is a land transaction directly made between landlords and peasants under terms and conditions mutually agreed upon, and subject to government approval. Landowners are paid directly in cash or in kind by farmer-beneficiaries and the Government's role is minimal and merely facilitating. While OLT and CA represent coercive methods of land redistribu-tion, VOS and VLT schemes are voluntary.

Table 16.1 presents DAR land redistribution accomplishment (in hectares and percentages) in non-government private lands, that is around half of DAR achievement so far.[9] Classification is made according to administration and mode of acquisition.

The compulsory acquisition (CA) scheme has been the least utilized mode of acquisition as it accounts just for 12.5 per cent all of private land redistributed. At the other extreme, operation land transfer (OLT) explains 33 per cent of the accomplishment so far. Voluntary-land-transfer (VLT) and voluntary-offer-to-sell (VOS) make up 28.1 per cent and 26.4 per cent of all private land redistributed respectively.

The poor performance of CA is hardly unexpected. Historically, coercive widespread land redistribution has been carried under autocratic regime and not by democratic elected governments, such as in contemporary Philippines. In democratic settings, in fact, the process of land expropriation and distribution is lengthy and complex. Under CARP the basic steps are the following: *identification* of landholding potentially covered by the programme by municipal officers of the Department of Agrarian Reform; *land survey* by the Department of Agrarian Reform that establishes the suitability, productivity and tenurial characteristics of the land to be expropriated; *land valuation and compensation* by the Land Bank of the Philippines; *land titling and registration* by the Land

Registration Authority; *transfer of land titles to beneficiaries* by the Department of Agrarian Reform. All along this process landlords can resist expropriation by bribing local government officers, hiding property titles, and delay expropriation by making application for land conversion or stock-distribution option. Most of them, however, have been exercising court challenges, up to the point that in mid-2001 there were 16.000 cases pending before courts (*Business World*, 2001). The litigious process of settling disputes over the coverage of lands is, in fact, extremely time-consuming. Because of the legal requirement of due process, where the protagonists in a dispute over the coverage of a piece of land are given seemingly endless chances to contest the statement of each other, the settlement of such disputes often drag for months, if not years. As due process is an indispensable element of democracy, this seems to confirm the assumption of de Janvry et al. (2001a) that in contemporary democratic developing countries there is no ample room for large-scale expropriative models of land redistribution. It follows that market-assisted land reform may well provide a lower and more efficient method to secure equal access to land for the poor rural dwellers.

Operation land transfer (OLT), that covers tenanted rice and corn lands, has been the most utilised method of redistribution hitherto. Its decline in importance across the succeeding administrations is due to the reduction of tenanted areas. This result was expected too. The successful Asian land reform programmes, in fact, were implemented in tenanted areas where landlords were mainly absentees and production technology obsolete. In the Philippines, OLT has been largely executed in the old-settled island of Luzon, in irrigated lands with relatively favorable cropping conditions and where pressures from tenants were particularly high. OLT is relatively straightforward as all that is required is the transfer of the bundle of property rights to already cultivating farmers. The successful income transfer, however, has induced several agrarian reform beneficiaries to shift their status from actual tillers to semi-landlords, who hire in seasonal and permanent labourers. The law, in fact, prohibits beneficiaries to agree

TABLE 16.1
Non-government private land redistributed per political administration and mode of acquisition, 1972-2000 (hectares and percentages)

	Operation land transfer	*acquisition Compulsory*	*Voluntary offer to sell*	*Voluntary land transfer*	*Total*
Ferdinando Marcos *1972–1986*	15,061 (100%)	0 (0%)	0 (0%)	0 (0%)	15,061 (100%)
Corazon Aquino *1986–June 1992*	340,045 (79.4%)	13,482 (3.1%)	54,011 (12.6%)	20,732 (4.9%)	428,270 (100%)
Fidel Ramos *June 1992–June 1998*	141,620 (16.7%)	120,828 (14.3%)	255,341 (30.2%)	328,654 (38.8%)	846,443 (100%)
Joseph E. Estrada *June 1998–Dec.2000*	18,750 (8.7%)	47,685 (22.0%)	76,919 (35.5%)	73,340 (33.8%)	216,694 (100%)
G. Magapagal-Arroyo *Jan.2001–Dec.2001*	5,886 (8.1%)	15,472 (21.6%)	30,033 (41.9%)	20,372 (28.4%)	71,763 (100%)
Total	521,567 (33.0%)	195,506 (12.5%)	416,382 (26.4%)	443,176 (28.1%)	1,506,468 (100%)

Source: elaborated from DAR, Management and Information Service (2002)

upon sharecropping and leasing contracts and to sell out their land for a period of ten years. Therefore, even though OLT has reduced the duality in Philippine agricultural structure, it has created a new class of 'opportunistic' middlemen and moneylenders (Hayami *et al.*, 1990).

The non-coercive voluntary-offer-to-sell (VOS) and voluntary-land-transfer (VLT) arrangements have been widely used, as they account for 26.4 per cent and 28.1 per cent of all non-government private land redistributed so far.

The VOS scheme is somewhat ambiguous. In fact, even though it is voluntary, it can be effectively expropriative and redistributive when there is strong demand for land from highly autonomous peasant movements and grassroots organizations, often backed by committed government authorities (the so called 'sandwich strategy') (Borras, 1999). In these instances, landlords realise that resistance to land reform is futile, withdraw opposition and opt for a better compensation package under VOS. In other words, in the Philippine context this scheme looks able to dynamise the supply side of the land market. The land transfer is of course faster than under compulsory acquisition and redistribution, as several bureaucratic steps are bypassed. However, in occasions where VOS schemes are implemented, especially on a wide scale, without intervention from autonomous rural grassroots movements, chances are that this scheme is employed by corrupt government officials in connivance with landlords to manipulate the reform process and exploit public funds by jacking up prices of marginal lands (Borras, 2000). For instance, Putzel (1992) reports that DAR officials in Negros province purchased the 374-hectare Villasor estate at 20,217 Philippine pesos per hectare, that is 7.6 million pesos. This was an abandoned upland property formerly offered on the land market at 3 million pesos. Riedinger (1995) maintains that the most scandalous transaction under VOS was that of the 1,888-hectare Garchitorena estate in Camarine Sur, a hilly property largely unsuited to cultivation, that was valued over 33 million Philippine pesos, i.e. more than 33,222 pesos per hectare.

Voluntary-land-transfer: Amid land market and State redistribution

The most utilised land redistributive scheme – except for OLT – has been the voluntary-land-transfer arrangement, that accounts for around 28 per cent of all private land reallocation. This is partly surprising. The government, in fact, does not finance this kind of transactions and the resource poor farmers – who are typically rationed in the credit market and have no accumulated savings – have to find their own financial sources to pay the land directly to landowners. This scheme is, therefore, often associated with contract-growing or contract-labour schemes and, in rare cases, with the constitution of joint agri-business enterprises among beneficiaries and landowners. In any case, necessary condition is that farmers earn enough income to cover the annual instalments on the land purchase price. Past experiences show that economic agents are likely to agree upon one of the following agreements: (i) a simple buyer-seller agreement where parties commit to sell and buy a certain product for a given price (or at the prevailing market price at the time of the exchange); (ii) a buyer-seller agreement of type (i) in which the buyer commits to provide farmers also with physical and financial inputs for production purposes; (iii) a buyer-seller agreement of type (i) where the buyer provides farmers with physical and financial inputs, technical assistance and conducts a monitoring activity as well (FAO, 2001; SARC-TSARRD, 1998a).

VLT arrangements are particularly popular in plantation areas. For example, the North Cotabato and Bukidnon provinces in Mindanao – the currently most important expansion areas of agroexport fruits – have land reform accomplishment in private lands extremely skewed in favour of VLT. This is so as agreements have not been found on the distribution of non-land assets, and the government is not willing to destroy functional modern large-scale farms (Borras, 2002b). VLT is also common in regions outside the commercial plantation sector, and regardless of land size category. In these circumstances, however, beneficiaries may be relatives of the landowners and 'strawmen.' Hence, the partitioning of the landowner's properties among his heirs is merely facilitated by VLT, as cost for documentation, transfer taxes, surveys, and titling are all charged to agrarian reform funds (Borras, 2000). Finally, even in those cases where transfer is in favor of poor-landless, in rural Philippines pervasive traditional patron-client relations between landowners and tillers may well oblige beneficiaries to accept unfavorable terms of transfer, that prevent them from setting up viable family farms (Conroy Franco, 2000).

In conclusion, it appears that VLT is facilitating the transfer of large plantations and *haciendas*, that are generally unlikely to be easily expropriated and redistributed. However, there are doubts that in some cases transfers are merely cosmetic, as VLT can be used by landowners to evade and delay CARP implementation, and that poor farmers do not benefit from the land transfer, as the law does not stipulate that the terms of transfer are to be no less favorable than under compulsory acquisition. Further and independent analyses are highly desirable.

Is there any relation between voluntary land transfer mechanisms and market-assisted land reform programmes?

Market-assisted land reform moves towards the right the demand for land as selected beneficiaries are granted loan from public and private sources to acquire the land on the market and start farming activities; the supply curve is instead supposed to move towards the right in response to traditional fiscal and macroeconomic policies. Contrasts this with VLT. First, differently from market-assisted land reform, farmers are not granted public resources to acquire the land. Since rural markets are typically imperfect, one would expect the land market to be thin and highly segmented, the credit market ineffective, poor farmers unable to acquire the land and VLT ineffective. Second, in VLT the shift of the supply curve largely hinges on powerful grassroots movements exercising political pressures and on the threat of credible government expropriation for landowners, who thus resolve to offer their lands on the market in the hope of getting a better compensation package. In other words, in a market-assisted land-reform programme, landowners who are not willing to sell their estates are not compelled to yield, wherein under a joint compulsory-acquisition/voluntary-land-transfer approach the government can expropriate the land coercively. It looks then that in the Philippine context the VLT approach is able to dynamise the supply curve (through the 'sandwich strategy'), but the question remains open about its capacity of translating the demand for land. Yet, VLT accounts for 28.1 per cent of all non-government private land reallocated so far.

The demand for land has been supported by the extensive involvement of rural communities, non-governmental organisations, local administrations and private investors in program implementation (like in traditional market-assisted land-reform programme!), in particular through the enactment of the Local Government Code in 1991 and the Jeep (Joint Economic Enterprises for Productivity) Programme in 1999.

The Philippine Local Government Code of 1991 has devolved and decentralised functions and responsibilities from national to local governments in the fields of health, social welfare, agriculture, and social and environmental infrastructure. Regarding agriculture, it is widely acknowledged that in developing countries agricultural output (and income) is more responsive to institutional than to price variables (for example, Rao and Storm, 2003). In the Philippine context, local administrations are mainly to set up an area development plan, to provide farmers with support services and infrastructure building, and to encourage peasants to set up rural cooperatives in order to raise local funds and gain bargaining power in the market. They are also to make credit available to members of rural cooperatives for acquiring agricultural production inputs, pre- and post-harvest facilities and fixed assets (DAR, 2000; ROP, 1991).

The Joint Economic Enterprises for Productivity (Jeep) programme aims at attracting private investors in the countryside. In particular, the program rests upon a three-pronged strategies that consists of (i) building up marketing-matching mechanisms between farmers and agribusiness enterprises. These are fora where beneficiaries, leaders of farmers' organisations, agri-business enterprises and other private and public investors discuss the possibilities of doing business together and share relevant information, in this way reducing perspective transaction costs; (ii) setting up a network of government staff at the central, regional and provincial level responsible for training farmers about bargaining strategies and negotiation procedures, so that contracts agreed upon do not place resources only with the already wealthy; (iii) publishing and disseminating market and investment opportunities brochures, that include the area development plans developed by local communities and administrations, so as to reduce risk and uncertainty for actors investing in rural areas (DAR, 1999; SARC-TSARRD, 1998a).

In conclusion, on the one hand the 'sandwich strategy' has dynamised the supply of land while, on the other hand, the combined implementation of the Local Government Code and the Jeep programme has dynamised the demand for land. Jointly, they have partly encouraged the transfer of land to the rural poor on a voluntary market base. For instance, in the island of Mindanao, the Tagum Agricultural Development Corporation (TADECO) almost 4,000 hectares banana plantation has been redistributed to beneficiaries who leased back the land to the owner, which pays 5,000 Philippine pesos per hectare per year rent and hire them as permanent labourers. Del Monte agreed upon a voluntary transfer covering a pineapple plantation and simultaneously negotiated a long-term lease contract with the agrarian reform beneficiaries. Stanfilco (a division of Dole) agreed upon a voluntary transfer covering a banana plantation and at the same time agreed upon a long-term growers' contract with agrarian reform beneficiaries (Rodriguez, 2000).

Small-local investors are making business with agrarian reform beneficiaries as well. For instance, according to FAO field investigations, in 1993 the Philippines imported 30,000 metric tonne of peanuts, that is a crop highly suitable for its agro-climatic condition. As a result of simple market information dissemination that underlined the potential demand for this produce, a multi-purpose cooperative of agrarian reform beneficiaries in Region II, Luzon, obtained a bank loan and started planting peanuts in 15.5 hectare of its land. The return per hectare ranged between 27,000 and 32,000 Philippine pesos, well above the average 21,000 peso per hectare of the yellow corn previously grown. Given this positive return, the following season 50 hectare were planted at peanuts (TSARRD, 1995a; 1995b). Another FAO study presents and discusses the relevant features of two agreements between one feed milling enterprises and two multi-purpose cooperatives. The related cost-benefit analyses indicate that, because of these agreements, each cooperative has obtained a net benefit of roughly 3,00,000 Philippine pesos (SARC-TSARRD, 1998b).

Lessons from the 1988 Philippine agrarian reform programme

The Philippine state-led land-reform programem presents some aspects that resemble those of market-assisted land reform, as land reallocation can be carried out both through coercive and voluntary mechanisms. In particular, the voluntary-land-transfer scheme is entirely based on a market transaction between willing seller and buyers and it accounts for around 28 per cent of private non-government land distributed hitherto and, as in market-assisted land-reform pilot projects, local governments, farmers associations and private investors are extensively involved in programme implementation. The missing link between VLT and market-assisted programme is that Philippine agrarian reform beneficiaries are not financed by public authorities to acquire the land on the market.[10] The question is then: how is it that poor farmers find resources to acquire the land in the market? The answers are multiple. The Philippine government has been decentralising and devolving its functions and responsibilities, empowering local administrations and communities and, above all, setting up a bottom up development strategy able to attract private investors in the countryside. In this context, on the one hand agricultural productivity in small farms has mounted up and, on the other, landowners have found it convenient to sell their land to farmers and to agree upon contract-growing schemes. Finally, grassroots movements are particularly mature, the government still retains coercive confiscatory power and landowners, if not willing to sell their land voluntary, are compelled to transfer it because of compulsory acquisition and distribution (that is a state-led approach to land reallocation). With respect to simple market-assisted and state-led reforms, the joint state/market land redistributive policy of the Philippines has the following characteristics. First, it is likely not to encounter strong political opposition from the part of landowners; quite the opposite, plantation owners may have advantages in transferring their land to potentially efficient small farmers and set up contract-growing arrangements, because of reduction of free-riding behaviors and lack of scale economies in production. Second, a joint state/market approach has a cost-advantage with respect to both state-led and market-assisted land reform as it requires all the land transfer to be financed by private investors. In this way it reduces to a minimum rent-seeking activities from the part of government bureaucrats and land sellers. The administrative costs are, however, high and worth measuring and, at least on paper, the state should be always able to raise enough resources to finance hypothetical compulsory expropriations. Third, a joint state/market approach can be well large-scale as it allows self-selection of areas where market reforms are viable. Finally, this approach can always specify, through its compulsory component, the area to be expropriated and redistributed, giving the State the chance to better shape its economic and social policies.

Conclusion

Theoretical and empirical evidence supports the view that equal land asset distribution fosters social-equity and triggers efficiency in resource allocation. Among land reform practitioners, there are disagreements about the political economy of land reallocation, in particular about the effectiveness of coercive state-led vis-à-vis voluntary market-assisted redistribution. Neoclassical economists maintain that the market, by way of the right stimuli, is the most effective mechanism to transfer the land to the resource poor; civil society representatives assert that especially exogenous coercive reform can accomplish large-scale successful land redistribution. In theory, both reforms can do well, although they bear the risk, if not associated with high quality institutions, of placing resources not with the poor but with the powerful economic and political elite.

The analysis of this paper shows that debates about state-led and market-assisted land reform advocates are somewhat ill-conceived. First, these two approaches to land redistribution originate in different historical periods, respond to different pressures and aim at different objectives, political on the one hand, economic on the other. Second, major theoretical differences between state-led and market-assisted refer to the land transfer mechanism, to the area targeted for redistribution, to rules and regulations that constraint the functioning of the market in state-led redistributive programmes, and to private investors partly financing land reallocation in market-assisted reforms. Third, the contemporary approach to rural development, that rests upon the trilogy market/state/civil society, is attuned both to state-led and market-assisted land-reform programmes. In effect, processes of devolution and decentralisation of government functions and responsibilities, the widespread and pervasive diffusion of democracy, the growing capacity and ability of grassroots movements to demand for equity and justice, and the recognition that markets can contribute to place resources efficiently, are all elements that have to be considered and exploited in shaping both contemporary state-led and market-driven land reallocation policies.

Finally, the analysis of the 1988 Philippine agrarian reform experience showed that state-led and market-assisted land reform approaches to land reallocation can be successful complement policies. The Philippine agrarian reform programem is both coercive state-led and voluntary market-driven. Contrary to market-assisted land reform, it allows compulsory acquisition of privately owned land; side-by-side with market-assisted land reform, it stipulates that land transfer can be based on voluntary agreements among willing buyers and willing sellers. However, differently from pilot projects of market-driven reform in Brazil and Colombia, the Philippine program does not require that public institutions are to finance land market-exchanges. It is thus somewhat unexpected that the most used modes of land acquisition and distribution, except for tenanted rice and corn land, have been the voluntary-land-transfer (VLT) and voluntary offer to sell (VOS) mechanisms. This is so as in the democratic Philippines, on the one hand, vigorous grassroots movements are able to exert strong political and economic pressures on central and local authorities and, on the other hand, the government has decentralised its operating functions, devolved its duties and responsibilities to local authorities, and it has set up an institutional infrastructure that encourages private investors and groups of small farmers to enter into contract-growing or contract-labour agreements in the countryside. Above all, on the background there is the credible threat of the Government, backed by popular movements, to compulsory acquire the land in case landowners are not willing to sell it. It is this environment that has strongly contributed to the success of market transfer mechanisms, not only in underused and underutilised lands but also in large profitable commercial plantations. There are doubts, however, that several of the voluntary land transfers have been merely cosmetic.

The Philippine experience indicates that possibilities exist for the process of land acquisition and distribution to be successfully carried out under a joint state-led/market-assisted approach, challenging the disagreement between state-led and market-assisted land reform proponents. Of course, the Philippine programme is very innovative and worth monitoring carefully and subject to rigorous and independent scrutiny in order to extract lessons for better application and applications in other contexts.

NOTES

1. Note that a complete transfer of land ownership does not necessarily improve technical efficiency (Carter, 1984) but it eliminates agency costs (e.g. labour shirking) altogether.
2. In 2001 AKA, the 'German Permanent Working Group on Poverty Reduction – Helping People to Help Themselves,' held a conference on Agrarian Reforms to which over 100 representatives of civil society, popular movements, women organizations and international agencies took part.
3. This grouping is of course arbitrarily and makes sense as any attempt at classification. However, the recent electronic discussion on the World Bank's draft Policy Research Report 'Land Policy for Pro-Poor Development' (Dec. 30, 2002–Jan. 17, 2003) has indicated that disagreements among scholars exist even because of their institutional roles. See Kanbur (2001) for an in-depth categorisation of these two groups with reference to anti-poverty strategies.
4. Rawal (2000) argues that the functioning of rural markets is one of the main components of the successful state-led land reform in West Bengal.
5. For instance, in Brazil and the Philippines several hectares of land have been acquired and redistributed thanks to organised grassroots movements (Quitoriano,1999; Wolford, 2001).
6. For a detailed list of DAR and DENR tasks, see ROP (1998), Riedinger (1995) and Borras (2000, 2001).
7. Redistribution of public land is not straightforward in the Philippines. Several hectares of public lands, in fact, are under agricultural cultivation and in effective control of private elite, in spite of the absence of legal ownership titles. Countless cattle ranches, logging concessions and large plantations are located on government-owned lands (Borras, 1999).
8. Data from the Presidential Agrarian Reform Council, Quezon City, Philippines.
9. The other half mainly refers to private land property of government financial institutions.
10. The Philippine Senate has recently proposed that the farmer-beneficiary be allowed to borrow from the Land Bank of the Philippines up to 85 percent of the purchase price of the land as support for production activities, technology transfer and product marketing.

REFERENCES

Adriano, L.S., 1992, *A General Assessment of the Comprehensive Agrarian Reform Program*, typescript, College of Economics and Management, Los Baños, University of the Philippines.

AKA, Arbeitskreis Armutsbekämpfung, 2001, *The Bonn Statement on Access to Land*, International Conference on: Access to Land: Innovative Agrarian Reforms for Sustainability and Poverty Reduction, Bonn, Germany, 19 – 23 March.

Alesina, A. and Rodrik, D., 1994, The Political Economy of Growth: A Critical Review of the Literature, *The World Bank Economic Review* 8, 351-371.

Allen, J.S., 1938, Agrarian Tendencies in the Philippines, *Pacific Affairs*, 11 (1), 52-65.

Banerjee, A.V. and Newman, A.F., 1994, Poverty, Incentives, and Development, *American Economic Review* 84(2), 211-215.

Bardhan, P., 1973, Size, Productivity, and Returns to Scale: An Analysis of Farm-level Data in Indian Agriculture, *Journal of Political Economy*, 81(6), 1370-1386.

Bardhan, P. and Ghathak, M., 1999, *Inequality, Imperfections, and Collective Action Problems*, mimeo, University of California at Berkeley and University of Chicago.

Barraclough, S.L., 1994, The legacy of Latin American land reform, *NACLA Report on the Americas*, 28(3), 16-21.

Barraclough, S.L., 1970, Agricultural Policy and Land Reform, *Journal of Political Economy*, 78(4), 906-947.

Berry, R.A., 1998, *Agrarian Reform, Land Distribution, and Small-Farm Policy as Preventive of Humanitarian Emergencies*, Working Paper 3, Department of Economics, University of Toronto.

Berry, R.A. and W.R. Cline, 1979, *Agrarian Structure and Productivity in Developing Countries*, Baltimore and London, The Johns Hopkins University Press.

Bhalla, S.S. and Roy, P., 1988, Misspecification in Farm Productivity Analysis: The Role of Land Quality, *Oxford Economic Papers* 40, 55-73.

Binswanger, H.P., 1987, *Impact of government policies and legal provisions on land use, land value and agrarian structure: analytical framework, hypothesis and terms of reference*, mimeo, Washington D.C., World Bank.

Binswanger, H.P., K. Deininger and G. Feder, 1995, Power, Distortions, Revolt and Reform in Agricultural Land Relations in J. Behrman and T.N. Srinivasan (eds.), *Handbook of Development*

Economics, Volume III, Elsevier Science B.V..

Borras, S.M. Jr., 2002a, Towards a better understanding of the market-led agrarian reform in theory and practice: focusing on the Brazilian case, *Land Reform* 1, 33-50.

Borras, S.M. Jr., 2002b, *Stuck in the Mud: Land Reform Under the Macapagal-Arroyo Administration*, Political Brief, Institute for Popular Democracy, Manila.

Borras, S.M Jr., 2001, State-Society Relations in Land Reform Implementation in the Philippines, *Development and Change* 32(3), 531-561.

Borras, S.M. Jr., 2000, *The Philippine Agrarian Reform: Relatively Vibrant Land Redistribution amidst less-than-dynamic Agricultural Transformation*, paper delivered at the International Conference on Agrarian Reform and Rural Development (ICARRD), Tagaytay City, Philippines, December 5-8.

Borras, S.M. Jr., 1999, *The Bibingka Strategy in Land Reform Implementation – Autonomous Peasant Movements and State Reformists in the Philippines*, IPD, Institute for Popular Democracy, Philippines, Quezon City.

Brandão A.S.P. and Feder G., 1995, Regulatory policies and reform: the case of land markets, C. Frischtak (ed.), *Regulatory Policies and Reform: A Comparative Perspective*, Washington, The World Bank.

Bulatao, G. Jr., 2000, State-led Reform: Can the Momentum be Sustained?, *Lok Niti*, Journal of the Asian NGO Coalition for Agrarian Reform and Rural Development (ANGOC), 20/20.

Burgess, R., 2000, *Land distribution and Welfare in Rural China*, mimeo, Department and Economics and STICERD, London School of Economics.

Business World, 2001, Agrarian Reform Snags, Manila, Philippines, August 17.

Carter, M.R., 1984, Identification of the Inverse Relationship between Farm Size and Productivity: An Empirical Analysis of Peasant Agricultural Production, *Oxford Economic Papers* 36, 131-145.

Carter, M.R. and Salgado R., 2001, Land market Liberalization and the Agrarian Question in Latin America, in de Janvry, A., Gordillo, G., Platteau J.P. and Sadoulet, E. (eds.) *Access to Land, Rural Poverty, and Public Action*, Oxford, Oxford University Press.

Carter, M.R. and Mesbah D., 1993, Can Land Market Reform Mitigate the Exclusionary Aspects of Rapid Agro-Export Growth? *World Development* 21(7), 1085-1100.

Conroy Franco, J., 2000, *Campaigning for Democracy. Grassroots Citizenship Movements, Less-than-Democratic Elections, and Regime Transition in the Philippines*, Institute for Popular Democracy, Philippines, Quezon City.

Constantino, R., 1978, *The Philippines: A Past Revisited*, Foundation for Nationalist Studies, Philippines, Quezon City.

Cornia, G.A., 1985, Farm Size, Land Yields, and the Agricultural Production Function: An Analysis of Fifteen Developing Countries, *World Development*, 13:513-534.

DAR, Department of Agrarian Reform of the Government of the Philippines, 2000, *Primer on Credit Programs for ARBs and Small Farmers. A Guide to Accessing Credit*, Philippines, Quezon City.

DAR, Department of Agrarian Reform of the Government of the Philippines, 1999, Rules and Regulations Covering Joint Economic Enterprises for Productivity (JEEP) in Agrarian Reform Areas, *Administrative Order No. 2, Series of 1999, Manila, Philippines*, 1999.

Deininger, K., 2001, Negotiated Land Reform as One Way of Land Access: Experiences from Colombia, Brazil and South Africa, in de Janvry, A., Gordillo, G., Platteau J.P. and Sadoulet, E. (eds.) *Access to Land, Rural Poverty, and Public Action*, Oxford, Oxford University Press.

Deininger, K., 1999, Making Negotiated Land Reform Work: Initial Experience from Colombia, Brazil and South Africa, *World Development*, 27(4), 651-672.

Deininger, K., Olinto, P. and Maertens, M., 2000, *Redistribution, Investment, and Human Capital Accumulation: the Case of Agrarian Reform in the Philippines*, paper delivered at the Annual (World) Bank Conference on Development Economics, World Bank, Washington D.C., April.

Deininger, K., Lara, F. Jr., Maertens, M. and Quisumbing, A., 1999, *Agrarian Reform in the Philippines: Past Impact and Future Challenges*, paper delivered at the 'Global Development Network Conference,' Bonn, Germany, December.

Deininger, K. and Binswanger, H., 1999, The Evolution of the World Bank's Land Policy: Principles, Experience, and Future Challenges, *World Bank Research Observer*, 14(2), 247-276.

Deininger, K. and Squire, L., 1998, New Ways of Looking at Old Issues: Inequality and Growth», *Journal of Development Economics*, 57:259-287.

de Janvry, A., 2002, *Land Reforms in Latin America: The Lesson toward a Contemporary Agenda*, paper presented at the 'Regional

Workshop on Land,' organized by the World Bank, Pachuca, Mexico, May 19-22.

de Janvry, A., 1981, *The Agrarian Question and Reformism in Latin America*, Baltimore and London, The Johns Hopkins University Press.

de Janvry, A., Platteau, J.P., Gordillo G. and Sadoulet, E., 2001a, Access to Land and Land Policy Reforms, in de Janvry, A., Gordillo, G., Platteau J.P. and Sadoulet, E. (eds.) *Access to Land, Rural Poverty, and Public Action*, Oxford, Oxford University Press.

de Janvry, A., Murgay, R. and Sadoulet, E., 2001b, Rural Development and Rural Policy, *Handbook of Agricultural Economics*, Gardner B. and Rausser G., Netherlands, Elsevier.

Dorner, P., 1992, *Latin American Land Reforms in Theory and Practice. A Retrospective Analysis*, Madison, The University of Wisconsin Press.

El Ghonemy, M.R., 2002, The Land Market Approach to Rural Development, in Ramachandran, V.K., Swaminathan, M. (eds.), *Agrarian Studies. Essays on Agrarian Relations in Less-Developed Countries*, New Delhi, Tulika Books.

El Ghonemy M.R., 2001, Peasant's Pursuit of Outside Alliances and Legal Support in the Process of Land Reform, in Ghimire, K.B. (ed.), *Agrarian Reform and Peasant Livelihoods: The Social Dynamics of Rural Poverty in Developing Countries*, London, ITDG, and New York, UNRISD.

FAO, Food and Agricultural Organization of the United Nations, 2001, *Contract Farming. Partnerships for Growth* (by Eaton C. and Shepherd A.W.), FAO Agricultural Services Bulletin 145, Rome, FAO.

FAO, Food and Agricultural Organization of the United Nations, 1993, *Réforme Agraire et Ajustement Structurel en Afrique Subsaharienne: Controverses et Orientations*, Etude FAO Développement Economique et Social, 107, Rome, FAO.

Ghimire, K.B. (ed.), 2001, *Agrarian Reform and Peasant Livelihoods: The Social Dynamics of Rural Poverty in Developing Countries*, London, ITDG, and New York, UNRISD.

Grossman, H.I., 1994, Production, Appropriation, and Land Reform, *American Economic Review* 84(3), 705-712.

Hayami, Y. and Otsuka, K., 1993a, *Kasugpong* in the Philippines Rice Bowl: The Emergence of New Labour Institutions after Land Reform, in K. Hoff, A. Braverman, J.E. Stiglitz (eds.), *The Economics of Rural Organization: Theory, Practice, and Policy*, Oxford, Oxford University Press.

Hayami, Y. and Otsuka, K., 1993b, *The Economics of Contract Choice: An Agrarian Perspective*, Oxford, Clarendon Press.

Hayami, Y., Quisumbing, M.A.R. and Adriano, L.S., 1990, *Toward an Alternative Land Reform Paradigm, A Philippine Perspective*, Manila, Ateneo de Manila University Press.

Horowitz. A.W., 1993, Time Paths of Land Reform: A Theoretical Model of Reform Dynamics, *American Economic Review* 83(4), 1003-1010.

Ibon Primer Series, *Land Reform in the Philippines*, IBON Databank Phils Inc., Metro Manila, Philippines, 1988.

ICARRD, 2000, Proceedings of the International Conference on Agrarian Reform and Rural Development (ICARRD), Philippines, Tagaytay City, December 5-8.

Jonakin, J., 1996, The Impact of Structural Adjustment and Property Rights Conflicts on Nicaraguan Agrarian Reform Beneficiaries, *World Development*, 24(7):1179-1191.

Kanbur, R., 2001, Economic Policy, Distribution and Poverty: The Nature of Disagreements, *World Development*, 29 (6), 1083-1094.

Kawagoe, T., 1999, *Agricultural Land Reform in Post-war Japan: Experiences and Issues*, mimeo, The World Bank and Seikei University.

Kerkvliet, B.J., 1974, Land Reform in the Philippines Since the Marcos Coup, *Pacific Affairs*, 47(3):286-304.

KMP, Kilusang Magbubukid ng Pilipinas, 2000, *The World Bank's Market-Assisted Land Reform: Obstacle to Rural Justice*, mimeo, Manila, Peasant Movement of the Philippines.

Kutcher G.P and Scandizzo, P.L., 1981, *The agricultural economy of Northeast Brazil*, Washington D.C., World Bank.

Ladejinsky, W., 1964, Land Reform, L.J. Walinsky (ed.), *The Selected Papers of Wolf Ladejinsky. Agrarian Reform as Unfinished Business*, Oxford University Press, 1977.

Lipton, M., 1995, Market, Redistributive and Proto-Reform: Can Liberalization Help the Poor?, *Asian Development Review* 13(1), 1-35.

Lyne, M., Zille, P. and Graham D., 2000, *Financing the Market-Based Redistribution of Land to Disadvantaged Farmers and Farm Workers in South Africa: Recent Performance of the Land Reform Credit Facility*, mimeo, Land Tenure Center, University of Wisoncsin, Madison.

Maxwell, D., Wiebe, K., 1998, *Land Tenure and Food Security: A Review of Concepts, Evidence and Methods*, Research Paper no.129, Land Tenure Center, University of Wisconsin, Madison.

Monk, P.M., 1990, *Truth and Power. Robert S. Hardie and Land Reform Debates in the Philippines, 1950-1987*, Monash University, Centre for Southeast Asian Studies, Monash Paper N. 20, Victoria, Australia.

Morales H.R. Jr., 1999, *When Does Agrarian Reform Work for the Poor?*, paper delivered at the Manila Social Forum: The New Social Agenda for Central, East & Southeast Asia, Manila, Philippines, November.

Otsuka, K., 1993, Land Tenure and Rural Poverty, Quibria, M.G. (ed.), *Rural Poverty in Asia. Priority Issues and Policy Options*, Manila, Philippines, Asian Development Bank.

Putzel, J., 1992, *A Captive Land. The Politics of Agrarian Reform in the Philippines*, Ateneo de Manila University Press, Manila.

Quitoriano, E.L., 1999, *Agrarian Reform and Local Governance. A Study on DAR-LGU Convergence*, mimeo, GUAVE Dynamics Consulting Co., Philippines, Manila.

Rao, J.M., Storm, S., 2003, La globalizzazione dell'agricoltura nei paesi in via di sviluppo: regole, logiche e conseguenze, forthcoming in *La Questione Agraria*, No.2, 2003.

Raup, P.M., 1967, Land Reform and Agricultural Development, in Southworth, H.M. and Johnston, F.J. (eds.), *Agricultural Development and Economic Growth*, Ithaca and London, Cornell University Press,.

Rawal, V., 2000, Agrarian Reform and Land Markets: A Study of Land Transactions in Two Villages of West Bengal, *Economic Development and Cultural Change*, 49(3), 611-629.

Reyes, R.B. (2000) CARP Past the Deadline: Where's the Beef?, *MODE Research Papers*, 1(4), 7-56.

Reyes, B.R., 1999, *Market-Assisted Land Reform: An Indecent Proposal*, paper delivered at "The Global Forum on the Philippines. The Estrada Government amidst the Crisis: Can it Deliver its Promises to the Poor?", Utrecht, the Netherlands, April 23.

Riedinger, J.M., 1995, *Agrarian Reform in the Philippines. Democratic Transitions and Redistributive Reform*, Stanford University Press, California, Stanford.

Riedinger, J.M. and Kang, S., 2000, Back to the Land: Revisiting the Rationale for Agrarian Reform, *MODE Research Papers*, 1(4), 57-74, Philippines, Quezon City.

Rodriguez, J., 2000, Agrarian Reform in Commercial Farms. Designing an Appropriate Institutional Response, *MODE Research Paper*, 1(3), Philippines, Quezon City.

ROP, Republic of the Philippines, 1991, *RA7160: The Local Government*

Code of 1991, Philippines, Manila.

ROP, Republic of the Philippines, 1988, *Comprehensive Agrarian Reform Law of 1988, R.A. 6657*, Philippines, Manila.

Rosset, P., 2001, *Tides Shift on Agrarian Reform: New Movements Show the Why*, Food First, Institute for Food and Development.

Ruiz, L.T., 1945, Farm Tenancy and Cooperatives in the Philippines, *Far Eastern Quarterly*, 4(2), 163-169.

SARC-TSARRD, FAO Sustainable Agrarian Reform Communities – Technical Support to Agrarian Reform and Rural Development, 1998a, *Innovative Experience in Agribusiness Linkages for Agrarian Reform Beneficiaries*, Philippines, Manila.

SARC-TSARRD, FAO Sustainable Agrarian Reform Communities – Technical Support to Agrarian Reform and Rural Development, 1998b, *Production and Marketing Agreement between Blue Circle Farms Corporation and Two Farmers Cooperatives in the Philippines: A Project Experience*, Philippines, Manila.

Sauer, S., 2001, *A Proposta de 'Reforma Agrária de Mercado' do Banco Mundial No Brasil*, mimeo, Brasilia, Senado Federal, Brazil.

Sauer, S., 2000, Market Assisted Land Reform: Does it Works?, *Lok Niti*, Journal of the Asian NGO Coalition for Agrarian Reform and Rural Development (ANGOC), 20/20, 28.

Schultz, T., 1964, *Transforming Traditional Agriculture*, New Haven, Yale University Press.

Souza Filho, H.M., Buainain, A.M. and Magalhães, M.M., 1999, *Assessing the Selection of Market Assisted Agrarian Reform: The Case of Cèdula da Terra*, mimeo, IE/UNICAMP, Brazil.

Stiglitz, J.E., 1998, *Distribution, Efficiency and Voice: Designing the Second Generation of Reforms*, paper delivered at the Conference on Asset Distribution, Poverty, and Economic Growth, Brasilia, Brazil, 14 July.

TSARRD, FAO Technical Support to Agrarian Reform and Rural Development, 1998a, Agrarian Reform Beneficiaries Double Income: Isabela Farmers Meet "Big Business", *Agribusiness Bulletin, No. 4*, Philippines, Manila.

TSARRD, FAO Technical Support to Agrarian Reform and Rural Development, 1998b, *Experiences in Linking Agrarian Reform Beneficiaries' Organizations with Agribusiness Enterprises*, mimeo, Philippines, Manila.

Vogelsegang, F., 1998, Tierra, mercado y estado, in: *Perspectivas sobre mercados de tierras rurales en América Latina: informe técnico*, Washington, D.C. : Banco Interamericano de Desarrollo,

Departamento de Desarrollo Sostenible, División de Medio Ambiente, p. 14-29.

Willis, H.P., 1905, The Economic Situation in the Philippines, *Journal of Political Economy*, 13 (2), 145-172.

Wilson P.A., 1987, Regionalization and Decentralization in Nicaragua, *Latin American Perspectives* 53(14), 237-254.

Wolford, W., 2001, Case Study. Grassroots-Initiated Land Reform in Brazil: The Rural Landless Workers' Movement, in de Janvry, A., Gordillo, G., Platteau J.P. and Sadoulet, E. (eds.) *Access to Land, Rural Poverty, and Public Action*, Oxford, Oxford University Press.

World Bank (The), 2002, *Globalization, Growth and Poverty: Building and Inclusive World Economy*, World Bank, Washington D.C.; Oxford University Press, Oxford.

World Bank (The), 1998, *Philippines Promoting Equitable Rural Growth*, Report No. 17979-PH, Rural Development and Natural Resource Sector Unit, East Asia and the Pacific Region.

World Bank (The) (1975), *Land Reform: sector policy paper*, World Bank, Washington D.C.

World Bank (The) (n.d.), *The theory behind market-assisted land reform* (available at www.worldbank.org/landpolicy/).

Zhang, X., Fan, S., Zhang, L. and Huang J., 2001, *Local Governance and Public Goods Provision*, paper presented at the annual meeting of the American Economics, Chicago, August 5-8.

Chapter 17

People's Participation in Poverty Alleviation and Rural Development Programmes

A Case of Kerala's People's Plan Experience (PPP)

Asheref Illiyan & P.C. Jaffer

Introduction

Poverty alleviation has been one of the main objectives of planned economic development in India especially after Fifth Five Year Plan. The slogan of 'Garibi hatao' was adopted in 1971 with main emphasis on eradication of poverty. Government during the late 1970s and early 1980s started a number of poverty alleviation schemes. Unfortunately, none of these programmes could acheive desired result as poverty and food security still eludes the country.

Many studies have pointed out weaknesses of the poverty alleviation programmes such as excessive centralisation, corruption, mis-identification of beneficiaries, etc. Centralised approach of planning that we have been following has a few shortcomings: (a) Decisions are taken single-handedly by a few people (b) The projects are formulated without considering the local aspirations and the local resource availability and (c) Excessive bureaucratisation and the subsequent rule orientation just for the sake of the rules.

Indian Planning has encouraged departmentalism. It is just preparation of schemes of different nature by various departments. Such schemes do not have any interrelation. These plans are centralised and bureaucracy-oriented. Beneficiaries do not have a say in the plan process. Monitoring is not at all satisfactory. Many projects are proposed at the same time without considering the resource crunch.

A major solution to these problem is decentralisation and involvement of people in the formulation and implementation of these programmes. This has a few advantages. Only through a local process, we can prepare plans considering geographical factors and needs of the people. We can understand relatedness of various fields in a particular locality. Resources needed for local development can be mobilised locally. This can be through donations or voluntary participation. Local planning and implementation would ensure proper monitoring of schemes as well as reduction of leakage in the plan allocations.

A number of attempts have been made towards decentralisation, albeit on a small scale. However, 'a major reason for the failure of earlier efforts to decentralise planning process has been the absence of a popular representative administrative structure below the state level. Even though decentralisation was a national ideal, venerated in the directive principles of Constitution itself, the euphoria of Gram Swaraj did not survive the early 1960s and 1970s. Ashok Mehtha has chronicled the erosion of Panchayat Raj Institutions over 1960s and 1970s. These institutions were never endowed with real power or financial resources to enable serious development intervention. In reality, their scope was confined to mere civic duties, that too under the strict supervison of local bodies' (Isaac and Harilal, 1997).

In short, major reasons for the failure of decentralisation have been:

1. Lack of data needed for the planning at the local level;
2. Absence of the experts at the local level;
3. Inadequate powers to plan and implement various developmental schemes;
4. Lack of political will to devolve powers to the lower levels.

In order to give more power to local bodies, Government of India enacted Constitutional Amendment 1993 (Panchayat Raj Act) and Constitutional Amendment 1993 (Nagarapalika Bill). Almost all the states have conducted election to the local bodies. A Three-tier Panchayat Raj System came into existence in the Kerala on 2 October, 1995 following the enactment of Kerala Panchayat Act in the light of 73 rd and 74th constitutional amendments. At present there are 991 Gram Panchayats, 53 municipalities and 5 municipal corporations.

LDF Government led by CPI(M) gave a new direction to the decentralization of planning in Kerala. Kerala, which has many firsts to its credit, decided to launch Ninth Plan as peoples plan where people's involvement and participation was ensured at each stage of the plan.

What Does Peoples Participation and Decentralised Planning Mean?

Participatory planning, seen as a political process, involves exercise of power by people as decision makers. In India power of people is manifested mainly in (and often limited to) the right to exercise franchise and freedom of speech and action. However, existence of these basic rights is not adequate to empower people in decision-making, as long as political and bureacratic structures remain centralised. Therefore, suitable political environment is required to enable and ensure participation of people in decentralised planning. In the economic context, decentralised planning is often considered as a mechanism at the micro level to achieve development with wider dispersion of the benefits, especially among the weaker sections. 'Decentralisation' of the power from top to lower level functionaries of the political and bureaucratic structures is considered essential for effective planning and implementation of development programmes.

A number of features distinguish Kerala experiment with decentralised planning for similar, efforts in a few other states. To begin with, it was launched with a bold decision to earmark 35 to 40 per cent of plan funds for projects and programmes prepared by the local institutions. Further, this devolution was not predicted on the existence of capacity to plan and utilise these funds at the lower levels or their 'absorptive capacity'. Making this a prerequisite tends to postpone actual devolution indefinitely. Rather, the experiment chose to build that capacity in the act of doing or in the course of putting to use funds devolved. And finally, to ensure that lack of capacity did not result in large-scale wastage and leakages. Entire process of decentralised planning is technically called People's Plan Campaign. Ninth Plan was termed as People's Plan. The popular slogan was *'Ninth Plan, People's Plan'*.

Objectives of the People' Plan Campaign (PPP)

PPP had the following objectives.

(i) To ensure people's participation;
(ii) Inculcate a new development culture among the people – Develop hope, optimism, and direction in them;
(iii) Strengthen the Panchayats/municipalities as the units of self-government;
(iv) Effective implementation of those schemes that have been already handed over to the Panchayats.

According to Isaac and Harilal (1997), designed after the success of total literacy movement, the campaign seeks to motivate and bring together the following groups of people in every locality in the preparation of the Ninth Plan:

(i) Elected representatives;
(ii) Officials in various live departments;
(iii) Non-official experts;
(iv) Retired people;
(v) NGOs.

Against this backdrop, the present paper attempts to describe and assess:

1. Ways and means of peoples, participation;
2. Institutional mechanism for people's participation;
3. How people's participation does make a difference;
4. The physical achievements of the Ninth Plan.

Ways of People's Participation

The PPP (People's Plan Programme) ensures peoples participation through Gram Sabha, Development Seminars, NGOs, etc. PPP for Ninth Plan was carried out in five stages.

In the *first stage* the focus was on preparation of campaign materials and training resources persons. About 300 key resource persons selected by District Planning Board were trained for seven to ten days. These resource persons were to train district resource persons. There were around 6,000 key resource persons at a three-day camp. District key resource persons, in turn, trained around 30,000 local level resource persons at village level. Main tasks of local resource persons was to guide and facilitate discussions in Gram Sabha.

In the *second stage* special Gram Sabha is convened. The main task of Gram Sabha is to identify felt needs of the people and gaps in the local development. Gram Sabha discusses needs of a locality, available structure, possible resources and other demands.

To ensure maximum participation, Gram Sabhas were convened on holidays. Squads of volunteers visited households to explain the programme and request their participation in the meeting. Separate meetings of mass organisations were also held to ensure maximum participation. Various novel propaganda devices have been innovated by the panchayat themselves. 'It is estimated that around 3 million persons participated in these Gram Sabha/Ward conventions out of which women accounted for 27 per cent (*Economic Review*, Kerala State, 2000). Discussions in the Gram Sabha were organised in groups of 25–50, one for each development sector in addition to one group for SC/ST development and one for women development.

Discussion was carried out under 12 subjects or sectors: (1) Agriculture, Animal Husbandry and Allied Activities, (2) Industry, (3) Education, (4) Culture, (5) Transport, (6) Housing, (7) Women's Welfare, (8) SC/ST Welfare, (9) Cooperation, (10) Roads and Energy, and (11) Resource Mobilisation.

Major gains in the success of special Gram Sabha meetings

were: (1) The felt needs, their priorities and development perceptions of the people were listed, (2) A general awareness was created among various sections of people regarding the decentralisation programme and (3) the basic organisational structure of the campaign was laid.

Gram Sabha also selected representatives to Development Seminars of Panchayats and Municipal Council. These representatives were selected on the basis of the groups that had deliberated in the meeting. Two people were selected from each group. Of these, one had to be a female. On the basis of these demands local resource persons drafted the *Development report, which* was to be presented in the Development Seminar.

In the *third stage* Municipal/Panchayat Development seminars were held to discuss the problems identified at lower level. Discussion in Development Seminar was centered on the Panchayat/Municipal Development Report. Development reports were to be drafted on the basis (a) Consolidation of Gram Sabha Reports, (b) Reviewing of ongoing schemes, (c) collection of secondary data, (d) geographical study of the area, and (e) a brief survey of local history.

Development reports were supposed to offer an objective assessment of the resource potential and problems of each development sector with a historical perspective. On the basis of such an objective analysis and with explicit consideration of the problems identified by the Gram Sabha, a list of recommendations for action for each sector was to be drawn up. It is in this seminar that integrated solutions for the various problems identified by Gram Sabha/Ward convention were approved through discussion among peoples, representatives, officials and experts. Apart from the representatives selected by Gram Sabha, the seminar was also attended by all key officials of the area and invited experts from within and outside the locality.

Development Seminars at the end, constituted task forces of experts to prepare development projects for each development sector. Task force was entrusted with the responsibility of identifying, prioritising and preparing schemes coming under different sectors. Project contained objectives, cost-benefit analysis, time schedule and agencies for implementation mechanism for monitoring and expected benefits. An expert group then prepared a development plan based on reports of the task force. 'It has been estimated that around 5 lakh persons attended the development seminar' (*Economic Review*, 2000). Chairman of the task force was panchayat member, vice chairman a political dignitary, convenor an officer in the department concerned and joint convenor and members selected from among the participants of the seminar.

The *Fourth face* of the plan had been the actual formulation of the panchayat or municipal plan. Special meeting of the local bodies was convened for this purpose. They also the help of experts in preparing the final plan document. For finalising the plan, the panchayat had to make: (1) a clear assessment of their capacity to mobilise additional resources; (2) Evolve a development strategy on the basis of problems identified and resource potential of locality, prioritises and select projects to be implemented, and (3) Decide on monitoring mechanism.

On the basis of the above analysis, each panchayat was to prepare a plan document comprising eight chapters, viz., introduction, development strategy, resource mobilisation, sectoral programmes, integrated development, welfare of the SC/ST, women's development programmes and monitoring. projects were submitted to Block Level Expert Committee (BLEC), and Voluntary Technical Corps (VTC) (for examining their technical feasibility) which consisted of both public and experts.

Annual plans of higher tiers were prepared only after the Gram Panchayats had drafted their plans. This was to ensure that the plans of the various tiers are integrated and plans of the higher tiers are complementary to those of lower tiers. Block and district panchayat also organised seminars to discuss their draft plans.

In the *final stage:* A State level development congress was held where reports of State level task forces (with representatives from government departments) appointed by the Planning Board were integrated with the district development plans to prepare a State plan. Congress discussed Kerala's draft Ninth Plan.

Implementation

Once formulated, the next important stage was its proper implementation. A unique feature of the people's plan has been the way beneficiaries were identified and selected by the people themselves. One major problem with poverty alleviation programme has been wrong identification of beneficiaries. This flaw has been greatly removed in people's plan. Under the plan there are two types of projects. The first category is the individual projects – one that benefits individual beneficiaries and other one that of social projects.

Selection of the Individual Beneficiaries

It is inidentification of beneficiaries that the PPP had really ensured people's participation and complete transparency. For identification of the potential beneficiaries of each area Gram Sabha constituted Neighbourhood Committee or Ward level committee. Neighbourhood committee included around 25 households in a locality. There were 8–10 Neighbourhood committees in a ward. Chairman/Convenor 4 members had to be females.

For identification of beneficiaries preferences were given to: (1) Widows; (2) People Below Poverty line; (3) SCs/STs; (4) Handicapped; (5) Land Possession (for some specified projects such as irrigation projects in such project in order to be eligible for financial assistance from Panchayat the beneficiary should have at least half acre of land under his/her possession); (6) Families having Girl Child only; (7) unemployed persons in the family; and (8) Families with marriage aged girls, etc. Neighbourhood committees ranked each application on the basis of this weightage. The application after assigning weightages was presented in front of the Gram Sabha. Gram Sabha prioritisesd the list and prepared a general list. This list was presented to the Panchayat Board which prepared a general list for the panchayat as a whole.

Panchayat Board approved the projects and awarded money according to priorities set by the Development Seminar. A meeting of potential beneficiaries was called by Panchayat member/Board. At this meeting a *Beneficiary Committee* of the local people was formed to carry out work on their own avoiding contractors and intermediaries. In order to have more transparency in these projects details of the work like name, name of the convenor, materials used and its amount, etc., were displayed at the site.

Monitoring

Monitoring is as important as the planning or implementation. Monitoring was carried out throughout the implementation stage and after the completion of the projects. A panchayat member headed monitoring committee. Other members were nominated by the panchayat board among voters (people) and officers of the panchayat. The money allotted was made available only after getting a report of the monitoring committee. Thus PPP adopted social monitoring instead of official monitoring, which is always beset with corruption, leakages and delay.

Achievements

Local self Government institutions were given a role in *preparing plans for their own development* for the first time in Indian history.

PPP gives emphasis on utilising resources that can be mobilised locally. Donations, voluntary works, and beneficiary's share together constituted about 25 per cent of the total plan allocation. Because of this, people had a feeling that they themselves are planning and executing the projects. They considerd the projects as their own. This ensured their active involvement at all stages of the project.

Channelising the energy through mutual respect and informal relationships within the local society: Informal relationships in the local society were channellised into development activities. This has been another unique feature of people's plan. People come together irrespective of their caste, religion, regional affinities and differences. This has enhanced unity among the people.

Increased social monitoring for development activities: Social Auditing and Gram Sabha deliberations played an effective role. People kept strict vigil on the quality of work and proper utilisation of allotted fund. Besides the normal local fund departmental audit, a performance audit has also been initiated.

Transparency in selecting the beneficiary: This has been another advantage of the people's plan. Due care has been taken to ensure openness, transparency and accountability in plan implementation.

Reduced leakage and wastage: Even though leakages could not be contained completely, this had been reduced to the bare minimal level. Even if there is some leakage, this was made up by the additional contributions made by the locals.

Success in *creating awareness among the people* is marvellous.

Financial autonomy: Instead of getting Rs 3 or 5 lakh per annum, the Panchayats started getting Rs 20 lakh to one crore. This was made possible because 35–40 per cent of the plan allocation was routed through the local self-government institutions.

Participation of women: About 75 lakh women have come to public sphere as a result of peoples plan programme during the Ninth Plan period. Ten per cent of the total plan allocation is reserved for the women's welfare. 'JAGARANA SAMITI' has been constituted to deal with atrocities against women in rural areas under the aegis of the Gram Panchayat. There is also special women component plan under each local body. Kudumbashree projects and self-help groups were also started as part of the women empowerment programme. Women's participation had contributed in containing the menace of alcoholism. At a place where Gram Sabha is active, they even have the powers to decide whether to allow a liquor shop or not.

Yet another achievement of the programme is the utilisation of *the expertise of those people who are retired* from the service and sitting at home under the banner of voluntary participation.

PPP has been *well applauded nationally and internationally.* An *International Conference on Democratic Decentralisation held at Trivandrum,* was well attended by academicians, administrators, political leaders within the country and abroad. World Bank has approved a project on water supply scheme to be implemented through Panchayat with a financial support of about Rs 350 crore. Switzerland Agency for Development, an agency of the Government of Switzerland is currently providing financial support for strengthening the infrastructure for training and human resources development for the purpose of decentralised planning. A scheme for computerising the local bodies has been approved by the Planning Commission, Government of India. The Commission has allocated a special central assistance of Rs 31 crore. Financing agencies (like World Bank and Dutch Government) have put implementation through peoples programme as a precondition for financial assistance/loans as aid conditionality.

Special Emphasis on Marginalised People

Effective decentralisation is not merely a demand for representatives in the local bodies but of people at large. In this respect PPP makes special efforts to bring marginalised people of the society into the mainstream. Decentralisation of the Special Component Plan (SCP) and Tribal Sub-Plans (TSP) in 1997-98 resulted in an improvement in the allocation of the plan funds and project implementation. In the absence of effective beneficiary participation, the decentralisation of SCP and TSP tended to be increasingly bureaucratic. In the Ninth Five-Year Plan a decisive step was taken towards democratic decentralisation by devolving the planning of SCP and TSP to the local self-government institutions.

In the past it was left to each development department to determine appropriate schemes for the weaker sections in their areas as part of SCP and TSP. This practice led to considerable notional flow in calculation of the outlay for SCP and TSP. Instead of first allocation of funds to each department and letting the departments to earmark schemes and funds for weaker sections, now 11 per cent of the plan outlay is pooled

TABLE 17.1

Sl no	*Items*	*Unit*	*General*	*SCP*	*TSP*	*Total*
1.	Add area under cultivation	Acre	284939.55	20584.09	11258.18	315881.81
2.	Number of beneficiaries of seeds /fertiliser/pesticides	No	3268371	261554	42739	3572664
3.	Tillers	No	3765	443	223	4431
4.	No of cattles	No	177260	86792	10520	274572
5.	No of chicken distributed	No	1532559	310653	24305	1867517
6.	Cattle –sheds	No	62019	11570	1047	74636
7.	Sewing machines	No	36976	15764	732	53472
8.	No of persons trained	No	63761	19803	1353	84917
9.	Houses	No	189115	103040	14133	306288
10.	No of plots allotted	No	4305	10079	715	15099
11.	No of houses repaired	No	59874	51522	6634	118019
12.	No of toilets constructed	No	322666	80941	9567	413174
13.	House wiring	No	62002	41138	4577	107717
14.	No of wells	No	66306	19637	1648	87591
15.	No of water taps	No	24940	6432	1131	32503
16.	No of ponds distilled	No	26625	603	215	27443
17.	No of pump sets	No	52044	6300	867	59211
18.	No of roads	No	19623	3666	665	23954

19.	Length of roads	Km	13234.43	2540.21	1413.54	17188.18
20.	No of culverts	No	3566	314	130	4010
21.	No of bridges	No	14654	200	61	1725
22.	No. of cooperatives formed	No	3421	340	43	3804
23.	New Schols built (area)	M.sq	87720.95	1665.80	4163.09	93548.84
24.	Hospital buildings	M.sq	86512.96	1366.62	2142.06	90021.64
25.	Offices built(area)	M.sq	107035.36	3071.39	1693.33	111800.09
26.	Marketing complexes	M.sq	50329.60	5991.00	8.00	56328.60

Source: Economic Review, State Planing Board, Kerala, 2000

together and set aside for SCP and TSP. As a result, there has been a significant rise in the real funds available to SCP and TSP.

Democratic decentralisation of SCP/TSP creates opportunity for the weaker sections to directly participate in planning for their own well-being. If this opportunity is properly utilised, this could very well be a turning point to the development of the weaker sections of the state.

Whether Decentralisation Promotes Corruption or Checks Corruption?

There is always a apprehension that decentralisation may degenerate into decentralisation of corruption. The best check against such an eventuality is to ensure total transparency in the proceedings. This is a concept that has been held paramount in all transactions of People's Campaign. Thus for example all documents of beneficiary selection, such as verification of application forms, reports and minutes of meeting are all public documents. Even more importantly, all documents with respect to the works undertaken by local bodies through contractors, beneficiary committees or directly by itself including bills and vouchers, are public documents with access to any member of the public. Copies of these documents may be had on payment of a fee. Essential facts about any public works in common language has to be exhibited on notice board at the work site. *Right to information has been one of the key themes of the campaign.*

Selected Physical Achievements of Annual Plans of Local Bodies

In the Table 17.1 we present the physical achievement for certain selected items for the first three annual plans of 1997-98, 1998-99, 1999-2000. Data have been taken from the review report of the first three annul plans presented by each Gram Panchayt and municipality at block/municipal levels seminars as a part of the fourth year annual plan preparation. To this extent, data have been subject to public scrutiny and may be accepted with high degree of reliability.

From the Table 17.2 it is clear that when compared to the

TABLE 17.2

8th plan and 9th plan comparison- Physical achievements

	8th Plan	9th Plan (Ist three yrs)	4th yr.
Houses	2.7 lakhs	3.06	498499
Latrines	1.2 lakhs	4.13	442741
Other District Roads	1009 km	4873 km	
Village Roads	7991km	11863 km	
Houses for weaker sections (As part of SCP and TSP)	18023	117173	

Source: Economic Review, State Planing Board, Kerala 2000

physical achievements during the Eighth Plan the achievements of local bodies during Ninth Plan are encouraging, particularly in the social sectors. During the first and second year, 54,712 and 81,739 houses were built whose number doubled to 1,69,837 houses. During the third year, 3,06,288 houses were constructed. As against this all housing agencies of the state government had together constructed only 2,69,998 houses during the entire Eighth Plan.

Similarly, local bodies constructed 4,13,174 latrines during first three years as against 1.25 lakh latrines built during the Eighth Plan. During Eighth plan, 7,991 km and 1,009 km other district roads were constructed. Gram Panchayats and municipalities constructed 11,863 km of roads and block and district Panchayats 4,873 km of roads during first three years of PPP.

Likewise, the plinth area of additional facilities built in hospitals, schools and other public buildings during the past three years has outdone the achievements of the Eighth Plan. Avoiding duplication, on an average, 6 lakh families have benefited from the plan schemes and the gross area cultivated increased by 31,55,881 acres. In addition, there has been a visible improvement in vegetable and milk production.

Women and weaker sections have been main beneficiaries of decentralized planning. While achievement of the Eighth Plan was only 18,023 houses for weaker sections, 1,17,173 houses were built as part of the SCP and TSP during the first three years of the Nineth Plan. Women constitute majority of individual beneficiaries in local plans.

During the Nineth Plan 6.5 crore *employment* days were created (only in construction sector only).

Income generation: Most of the projects were integrated with local economy. For instance, in housing 40 per cent of Rs 1000 crore were wages. And 30 per cent locally available construction materials was used. It had multiplier effect.

Agricultural growth: Agriculture has grown at 3.82 per cent in 1998-99 as against 1.3 per cent of preceding 3 years. For example, the amount of milk collected by Milma (Cooperative Milk Society) increased from Rs 4.67 lakh litre in 1998-99 to

6.12 lakh litre in 1999-00 and to Rs 7.25 lakh litre in 2000-01

Industrial sector: New cooperative institutions numbering 3,804 were started and 84,917 people were given training for employment. Such a concept of massive training was beyond imagination during the previous plans. (84,917 people were given training for employment).

Drinking water: Approximately 33,000 taps were installed for the purpose of providing drinking water. Likewise 84,591 wells were dug. For the same purpose cleaning of 27,443 ponds were undertaken.

Limitations of the People's Plan

Although people's participation does ensure better allocation of resources, proper identification of beneficiaries and monitoring of projects, etc., yet, it is not free of limitations. Some of these are:

1. *Bureaucratic apathy:* This was the complaint heard most often during PPP. Officials who were oriented to system of rigid rule orientation and speed money from the contractors found it difficult to adjust to changed developmental culture. Though government was very careful in arranging training and orientation programmes, bureaucracy was not attuned to it. Till the time the concept was decided upon and implementation started, bureaucracy was not given either training or orientation;
2. Lack of expertise;
3. Allegations of nepotism/political favouratism from the panchayat board. In fact, board is given power to supersede priorities set by the *Development Seminar.* There are chances that this power may be misused;
4. Panchayat ruled by opposition parties had to face sometimes problems in getting projects approved by Block Level Experts. (BLEC). This happened because state government nominates BLEC;
5. *Corruption:* Though PPP had certain inbuilt checks and safeguards exceptions were there. It has been reported from some places that beneficiary committee just authorised local contractors to do work. This was done when convenor of beneficiary committee failed to face indifferent attitude of the bureaucrats. This led to corruption in some places. However,

whenever convenor had some guts to face this, he was successful in getting things done. In some Panchayats allegations were heard regarding wide spread corruption in purchasing and distributing goats, cows, etc. However, these allegations should not be given importance beyond a certain limit.

Conclusion

People's Plan Programme launched by Government of Kerala was indeed a major innovation carried out in this field so far. It has made a major impact on planning and rural development in the state. Enthusiasm generated among masses is a reflection of positive impact this new approach has made. There is increasing realisation that problems of people can best be addressed by ensuring their participation in planning for development. Now people are aware of technicalities of planning and implementation of various schemes.

Our analysis makes it clear that people's participation in rural development and poverty alleviation schemes makes significant difference in terms of better allocation of resources, completion of projects in time and space, formulating projects suitable to local resource endowment, both human and physical, proper identification of beneficiaries, proper monitoring and social audit, etc. This has generated a feeling of participation in developmental processes among people who were hitherto by-passed in the process of development. A new culture of participative development has developed. Of course this model is not free of limitations as common people who do not have any experience are asked to prepare complex plan document. These have to be looked aberrations that are bound to take place while the system moves into a new phase. It is to be noted that other states have to learn lessons and take inspirations from this unique experience. Kerala's experiment in decentralization could serve as a role model for other states.

REFERENCES

Anil Kurunthati, 1998, 'Vikasanathinu Janakeeya Mathrakakal'

(People's Model for Development), Madhyamam weekly, 12 June 1998 pp 14-16.

Biju. M.R., 1998, 'Panchayat Raj in Kerala: Problems and Prospects' Kurukshethra, Vol 46-7, April 1998 pp 68-71.

Chandrashekar C.P., 2000, 'Kerala: Development and Politics,' Frontline, 23, Oct , 2000, pp 107-108.

Economic Review, 2000, State Planning Board, Govt of Kerala.

Isaac, TMT & Harilal K.N., 1997, 'Planning for Empowerment: People's Campaign for decentralized planning in Kerala' *EPW* 4-11, Jan, pp 53-58.

Jose George, 1997, 'Panchayats and Participatory Planning in Kerala' IJPA, Vol , 43:1 , 1997 pp79-92.

Kumar Krishna R., 1996, 'A Kerala Initiative: The People's Campaign for the Ninth Plan,' Frontline, 23 Aug 1996 pp. 102-104

Kurup Balachandran, 1996, 'Development as People's drive, Indian Express (cochin 30 Aug, 1996).

Radhakrishnan C and Varghees T.A., 1992, 'People's Participation in Development Planning Constraints and Possibilities in the context of Kerala,' ISDA journal, Vol: No.4 Oct-Dec 1992, pp 281-292.

Ramachandran,V., 1992, 'Preparation Should have Preceded Implementation,' ISDA Journal Vol-ii. A. Oct-Dec,1992, pp 273-279.

Saji James, 2001, 'Janakeeya Aasoothranam Attimarikkapedumo' (Would People's Plan be Sabotaged), 'Malayalam' weekly 5, Jan, 2001, Vol. 4:35.

State Planning Board and Department of General Education, 1997, 'Aasoothranam Sahayi, Vidhyabhyasa Mekhala' (Planning Guide, Education Sector), State Planning Board and Department of General Education, Trivandrum.

State Planning Board, 1996, 'Power to the People, People's Plan – Ninth Plan,' Thiruvananthapuram, 1996.

State Plannning Board, 1996, 'People's Campaign for 9th Plan- An Approach paper,' Thiruvananthapuram.

State Plannning Board, 1997, 'Project Vilayuruthal Kaipusthakam' (Handbook for Project Evaluation), Kerala State Planning Board, Trivandrum.

Chapter 18

Nutrient Intake Outcome Measures and Productivity
Some Evidence from Primary School Children

R.L. Bhat and Kuldeep Raj Sharma

Introduction

The concept of food security has undergone lot of change during the last couple of decades. Availability and stability of food stocks in adequate measure, do not necessarily ensure food security. As such, a condition of hunger, starvation and undernutrition of a sizeable section of population co-exists with huge piles of food stocks. After attaining self sufficiency in food production during mid-70s, the general perception was that the adequate availability of food would automatically take care of problems of hunger and starvation and the food security will be ensured. However, it was soon realised that this security could not be attained and ensured in spite of public intervention in terms of Public distribution System (Radhakrishnan, 2002). Food security in rural areas and among the weaker sections could not be ensured, in spite of huge buffer stocks and the Public Distribution System.

Deficiency of aggregate effective demand for food in relation to its available supply is a cause of concern. There are reports of starvation deaths pouring in occasionally from different parts of the country. Such incidents make big news, but the problem of much more colossal nature with significant long term implications is that of a vast multitude of undernourished. It has been reported that there has taken place a decline in the demand for cereals in India during the last decade suggesting that the shift might have taken place in favour of non-cereal food items. One thing that has clearly come out is that there is a pronounced calories-protein malnutrition among a wide spectrum of Indian population, particularly in the younger age groups. Inadequacy of nutritional intake has long-term repercussions, not only on the proper physical growth of human body, but also on the development of the mental faculties. Inadequate nutritional intake during early years of life is, in particular, relevant in this context. Impact of food intake in terms of both its quantity and quality gets reflected in the nutritional attainments, like, the body weight, the height, arm circumference and the fat fold at biceps/triceps. These 'outcome measures' can also be assessed in terms of clinical signs of malnutrition, biochemical indicators and physical activity. However, the afore-mentioned four outcome measures have an advantage over other indicators, as the body measurements are sensitive to even minor level of malnutrition, whereas the biochemical and clinical indicators are useful only when the level of malnutrition is extreme.

One would have to make a distinction between chronically malnourished households and those which face such impoverished state in a transitory manner, like, off season, drought and during the inflationary conditions. It is the former, which is a cause of more concern. In such households, availability of food is insecure, patchy and so inadequate. Per capita availability of nutrients in these households is much lower than the recommended norms. It is in such a context, that the World Bank (1980) summarised, that the serious and extensive nutritional deficiencies in developing countries are caused by undernourishment and shortage of food and not by the imbalance between calories and proteins. Growth and development of children in developing countries is retarded due to lack of food and high prevalence of infections, which aggravates malnutrition (Rathor et al., 1975). Children, who live in those parts of the world, where there is a shortage of food and those, who have suffered the result of war and famine (disaster) reflect the stunting effects of insufficient food intake (Brown, 1980). In developing countries, growth retardation is common among pre-school as well as school age children. Undernutrition affects old and young, male and female, urban and rural dwellers and reduces their resistance to diseases and is a major cause of their deaths (World Development Report, 1992). Chronic undernutrition leads to a slowing in a child's state of growth. A chronically malnourished child will be short for his age (stunting) although he/she may be of otherwise normal proportion. An acute episode of severe undernutrition results in a loss of muscles and fats which are used to provide energy and the individual becomes thinner without significant effect upon height, i.e., wasting. Undernutrition, during childhood, may prevent an individual from attaining his/her genetically determined potential for height at maturity (Dashuman et al., 1996). Malnutrition, particularly in young children, exerts permanent adverse effects on their whole development–mental as well as physical (Giok et al., 1968). Well-nourished children are much more likely to be healthy, both physically and mentally, and are also more able to resist infectious diseases than undernourished children (Williams, 1996). Severe malnutrition, during the early years of life, impairs physical development. It results in the incidence of morbidity and mortality among the young and also poses a threat to their physical and mental development (Benjamin, 1990). The calories, proteins and other nutrient deficiencies are wide- spread throughout the developing world which results into deteriorating physical health and school performance (Wolfe and Behrman, 1987). In developing societies malnutrition or undernutrition creates, both short run and long run, health problems, which in turn interface with, the reading ability, capacity to work, behaviour and well -being of large segments of the population (Berg, 1981). It has been found that the children belonging to the same social class but different in nutritional status differ significantly in their school performance. (Singh et al., 1977). Many researchers have found, that, greater the reduction of weight, lesser is the mean IQ (see, for example, Bhat et al., 1973). Degree of malnutrition has its impact on the intellectual functioning of the children. (Singh et al., 1976). Poor health results in poor performance in the mental ability test and good health results in better performance, indicating positive correlation between health status and mental ability (Netesan and Devdass, 1981). It has also been argued, that effect of early malnutrition on later childhood shows a significant difference in anthropometric measure and a general impairment of intellectual abilities. (Hooring and Standifield, 1976). Thus, there cannot be two opinions that children need to be adequately fed if they are to be successful in warding off illness and performing well at school. (Cabak et al., 1965).

Undernourished children have a relatively deficient memory quotient, lower scores for abilities related to personal and current information, mental control, logical memory, digit span and associative learning (see, Aggarwal et al., 1995). Well nourished children, on the other hand, are heavier and taller than their undernourished counterparts. At the final testing the mean IQ of the undernourished group (70.86) differs from that of controlled well nourished group (93.48) by 22.62 points which is statistically significant (Stoch and Smythi, 1963). Moock and Leslie (1986) analysing data on the basis of the study of 350 primary school age children in Nepal, found that, of those children, who were enrolled in school, taller children tended to be in higher grade attainment than shorter children of the same age. Choudary and Rao (1984) found that the mean IQ of the children having lower anthropometric measurement was 84.6 points significantly lower than the IQ suggested for normal intelligence, i.e. 90 and above. Malnourished children had IQ 20 per cent lower than those of well nourished children (Correa, 1975).

In the present study, an attempt has been made to assess the nutritional intake of primary school children in the age group of 6–12 in Khour data, collected from 214 primary-school-going children on the basis of a stratified random sample.

Data have been collected from the respondents regarding their usual/normal daily food consumption, during the previous nonth, which has become the basis for estimating the intake of various nutrients. For the purpose of this study, 13 variables have been chosen to study and analyse the linkages between the nutritional intake and nutritional attainments and their effect on the productivity of the children. Five variables of nutritional intake used are: Calories (X1); Protein (X2); Calcium (X3); Vitamin-A (X4); and Iron (X5). Four outcome measure used are: weight (Y1); height (Y2); arm circumference (Y3); and fat fold IT biceps (Y4), of the respondent children. Number of sickness days in the preceding year (P) has been used as an indicator of health; and percentage of marks obtained in the last qualifying examination (X) as an indicator of the productivity of the respondent children. In the present study, the productivity of the children is measured in terms of their performance at school, which may depend on a number of factors like family income, education of parents, IQ various facilities at school, pre school education and such other variables. But there can be no doubt that a child cannot give out his/her best at school if he/she does not enjoy a good health status. Women's schooling is associated with better health and educational outcome of their children. How well a woman performs her task of rearing children depends mainly on her schooling. The mother's education is widely posited to affect positively her own and her children's health and nutrition in developing economies. Father's educational attainment level can be used as a proxy for the involvement and the commitment of the household towards the education of the child. As such, education level of the parents (Z1 for mother's educational level and Z2 for father's educational level) has been used as an indicator of the socio-economic environment of the child. Above list is certainly a less than exhaustive list of the variables that should be taken into consideration for such a study. However, aforementioned variables used provide a reasonable insight into the interrelationships among the variables like nutrient intake, outcome measures, health status and productivity.

Area Under Study

Khour Block is one of the 11 blocks of the Jammu district of Jammu & Kashmir state. The Block comprises 91 villages an 1 urban area and had an area of 96,811 acre with 34,294 acre as cultivated area. The total population of the Block in 2001 was 1,05,421, consisting of 55,588 males and 49,833 females resulting in a sex ration of 896 females for 1,000 males. The literacy rate in the Block was 68.33 per cent with 70.19 per cent for males and 58.02 per cent for females. As much as 99 per cent of population of the Block was Hindus. Maize and Bajra were very favourite grains in Kandi and hilly areas and were mainly consumed from September to May. Wheat, Rice and Pulses were consumed throughout the year. Vegetables were commonly used, while as meat and eggs were a luxury and in some houses, prohibited.

Characteristics of Sample Children

The present study is based on the data collected from 214 sample primary school children who were studying in Class II–VI and were aged between 6–12 years. The sample consisted of 101 females and 113 males; 156 belonged to non-SC/ST category while as the remaining 58 were from SC/ST category. The average level of mother's education of the sample children was 4.19 years while as that of father was 7.91 years. These children belonged to households with multiple economic activities. However, the main occupation of the father of 114 children was causal labour/private service and that of 21 was some business activity. All the sample households had some amount of agricultural land, but the size of the land holding for 147 was less than 2.5 acre; that for 60 households varied between 2.5 to 5 acre and there were only 7 households who had a landholding of more than 5 acre. As many as 178 respondents had nuclear families and only 36 lived in joint families. A study of the household per capita annual family income revealed that 89 families had a figure of less than Rs 2,500; 59 families had it in the range of Rs 2,500 to Rs 5,000 and the remaining 66 had a figure of Rs 5,000 to Rs 7,500.

Analysis of Results

The nutrient intake of the respondent children was estimated on the basis of their usual/normal food intake during the month preceding the collection of data. The estimation of the average intake of the five nutrients, viz., Calories; Protein; calcium; vitamin-A; and Iron along with the coefficients of variation are presented in Table 18.1, wherefrom

TABLE 18.1
Mean and Coefficient of Variation of Variables

Variable		*Mean*	*C.V.*
Calorie Intake (Kcl)	X1	1187.4	11.39
Protein Intake (mgm)	X2	35.2	9.32
Calcium Intake (mgm)	X3	452.2	26.53
Vitamin-A Intake (micgm)	X4	1425.6	22.39
Iron Intake (mgm)	X5	14.1	12.2
Weight (kgs)	Y1	23.1	22.47
Height (cms)	Y2	125.1	10.06
Arm Circumference (cms)	Y3	125.0	9.94
Fat Fold at Biceps (cms)	Y4	15.6	12.88
Mother's Education (yrs)	Z1	4.1	89.75
Father's Education (yrs)	Z2	7.9	43.04
Sickness Days (pre.year)	P	9.8	21.12
%age of Marks obtained	Q	61.4	12.72

it is clear that in comparison to the recommended daily intake (for children in the age group of 6–12) of various nutrients, the estimated values in this sample study, are much lower. This study, in fact, reveals that no sample respondent enjoyed the recommended level of 1,925 Calories or 41 gm of Protein or 2400 microgm of Vitamin-A or 22-48 ml gm of Iron. It was only in case of Calcium, that 24 children enjoyed an intake of more than the recommended 600 mgm a day. Table 18.1 shows that the sample children, on an average, were deficient in all the five nutrients used here. Furthermore, the distribution of nutrients across the sample children was skewed, indicating a severe state of undernutrition in case of a significant proportion of sample children. One could not find any significant variation in the nutrient intake across gender of the sample children. This shows that the overall nutritional availability in the sample households was so low that it didn't offer much of a chance in its uneven distribution among the male and female children.

As far as the various attainment measures are concerned, it has been found that there is again no significant variation across the gender as far as the 4 indicators of height, weight, arm circumference and fat fold at biceps are concerned. As is clear from Table 18.2, except for weight, there was not much of a variation in the outcome measures of the sample children.

TABLE 18.2

Mean and Coefficient of Variation of Outcome Measures

Variable	*Mean*			*Coefficient of Variation*		
	F	*M*	*T*	*F*	*M*	*T*
Weight (kgs)	23.1	23.1	23.1	23.34	21.56	22.47
Height (cms)	124.3	125.9	125.1	11.21	8.9	10.06
Arm (Circumference (cms)	125.1	124.9	125.0	10.12	9.8	9.94
Fat Fold (cms)	15.5	15.7	15.6	11.55	13.87	12.88

The impact of nutrient intake on the health status of the children has been assessed in terms of one morbidity indicator i.e. the number of sickness days during the last one year. The present study reveals that, on an average, a child was sick for about 10 days in a year–the sickness days here are understood in terms of confinement to bed. However, the distribution in the incidence of sickness was skewed as is indicated by a coefficient of variation of 21.12. The productivity of sample children measured in terms of the percentage of marks obtained in the previous annual examination. On an average,

TABLE 18.3
Correlation Matrix

	X1	*X2*	*X3*	*X4*	*X5*	*Y1*	*Y2*	*Y3*	*Y4*	*Z1*	*Z2*	*P*	*C*
X1	1.0												
X2	0.63	1.0											
X3	0.79	0.58	1.0										
X4	0.77	0.57	0.81	1.0									
X5	0.76	0.54	0.75	0.73	1.0								
Y1	0.45	0.23	0.24	0.25	0.39	1.0							
Y2	0.32	0.12	0.18	0.15	0.30	0.67	1.0						
Y3	0.37	0.14	0.23	0.23	0.37	0.81	0.81	1.0					
Y4	0.41	0.18	0.22	0.24	0.29	0.74	0.64	0.74	1.0				
Z1	0.28	0.15	0.29	0.24	0.29	0.08	0.10	0.08	0.02	1.0			
Z2	0.36	0.30	0.37	0.32	0.38	0.16	0.12	0.17	0.08	0.73	1.0		
P	–0.44	–0.32	–0.38	–0.39	–0.38	–0.16	–0.05	–0.12	–0.17	–0.26	1.0		
C	0.75	0.49	0.68	0.63	0.66	0.40	0.34	0.35	0.38	0.33	0.44	–0.54	1.

X1 = Calorie intake (kcal); X2 = Protein intake (mgs); X3 = Calcium intake (mgs)
X4 = Vitamin-A intake (micro gms); X5 = Iron intake (mgs)
Y1 = Weight in kgs; Y2 = Height in cms; Y3 = Arm Circumference in cms;
Y4 = Fat Fold at Biceps in cms; Z1 = Mother's Education Level;
Z2 = Father's Education Level; P = Sickness Days; Q = %age of Marks Obtained.

a child had obtained 61.4 per cent of marks with no significant variation between males and females. The study further reveals that, on an average, a sample child had mother's education of 4.1 years of successful schooling while as the corresponding figure for that of the father was 7.9 years. However, the distribution of mother's and father's education was highly skewed with the respective coefficients of variation being 89.75 and 43.04.

The coefficients of correlation among the 13 variables used in the present study have been presented in Table 18.3. A perusal of this Table shows that the five nutrient variables had a significant positive correlation among themselves, with the Calcium intake and Vitamin-A intake reporting a coefficient of correlation of as high as 0.81. The coefficients of correlation between the intake of Calcium and Calories; Calories and Vitamin-A, and that between calcium and Iron were above 0.75. The correlation coefficients among the four outcome measures were all positive and very high with the coefficient between the height and arm circumference and that between weight and arm circumference being more than 0.8. The coefficient of correlation of the sickness rate with the remaining 12 variables had the expected negative sign. This rate had a reasonable negative correlation with all the five sickness rate as a negative measure of health status and the percentage of marks secured, as a measure of productivity of a child is very good at –0.50. The mother's and father's education are also positively correlated with each other, as expected. Both the variables have a positive correlation with all the nutrient intake variables and outcome measures, a reasonable positive correlation with the productivity of a child and a negative correlation with the health of the child.

REFERENCES

Aggarwal, K.N., D.K. Aggarwal and S.K. Upadhyay, 1995, 'Impact of Chronic Under Nutrition on Higher Mental Functions in Indian Boys Aged 10-12,' *Acta Paediatrica*, Vol. 84, No. 7-12; Supp. Pp 1357.

Berg, A., 1981, 'Malnourished People–A Policy Review,' *Poverty and Basic Needs Series.*

Benjamin, S., 1990, 'Determinants of Nutrition and Health Status of Pre-School Children–An analysis of Longitudinal Data' *Economic Development and Cultural Change* Vol. 20, No. 3.

Bhat, Usha, S., P.M. Udhani, B.P. Shah, P.A. Naik and S.G. Eghuthachan, 1973, 'Nutritional Growth Faillure and Mental Development,' *Indian Pediatrics,* Vol-X, No. 11.

Brown, Ann. M., 1980, Nutrition: Food and You. Thomas Nelson Publishing House, Nigeria.

Cabak, V. and R. Najadanvic, 1965, 'Effect of Undernutrition in Early Life on Physical and Mental Development, *Archives of Disabled Childhood.* Vol. 40, pp 532-543.

Choudhary, Maya and K. Visweswara Rao, 1984, 'Association of Growth status and Mental Function in Pre-School Children' *The Indian Journal of Nutrition and Diettices.* Vol. 21, No. 1.

Correa, H., 1975, Economics of Human Resources. North-Holland Publishing Company, Amsterdam.

Dashuman, Theodore, D.E. Blocker and Nora Baker, 1996, Manual For Human Nutrition. Harwood Academic Publication.

Giok, Lauw Tjin, C.S. Rose, Pek Hien, Laing and P Gyorgy, 1968, 'A Study of the Influence of Early Malnutrition on Some Aspects of the Health of School Age Children' *The Journal of Vitaminology.* Vol. 14, Suppl.

Horring, G.C., 1976, Protein-Energy Malnutrition and Intellectual Abilities. The Hague/Paris: Mouton.

Moock, Peter, R. and Joanee, Lesled, 1986, 'Childhood Malnutrition and Schooling in the Terai Region of Nepal,' *Journal of Development economics,* Vol. 20, No. 1, pp 33-52.

Natesen, H. and R.P. Devdas, 1981, 'Measurement of Mental Abilities of Well-Nourished and Malnourished Children,' *Journal of Psychological Research* Vol. 25, No. 3, pp 121-124.

Radhakrishnan, R., 2002, Food and Nutrition Security in Kirit S Parikh and R Radhakrishnan (ed.), India Development report, Oxford.

Rathor, B.S., H.C. Mathur and S. Sexsena, 1975, 'Nutritional Antropometery of 1000 Children Dwelling in Slum Area of Jaipur Compared To that of 500 Children of the Elite,' *Indian Journal of Pediatrics.* Vol. 42, No 332, pp 264-276.

Singh, M.V., N.K. Anand, S. Gupta and D.C. Dingra, 1976, 'Intelligence in Relation to Degree of Malnutrition,' *Indian Journal of Clinical Psychology* Vol. 3, pp 117-120.

Singh, M.V., N.K. Anand, D.C. Dingra and S. Gupta, 1977, 'Schoolistic Performance in Relation to Protein Calorie Malnutrition,' *Indian Journal of Clinical Psychology.* Vol. 4, No 1, pp 15-18.

Stoch, M.B. and P.M. Smythe, 1963, 'Does Undernutrition During Infancy Inhibit brain Growth and Subsequent Intellectual development?' Archives of Disabled Childhood Vol. 38, No. 201, pp. 546-552.

Williams Sue Rodwell, 1996, Basic Nutrition and Diet *Therapy* (10th ed) Mosby Year Book Iic.

Wolfe, Barbara, L. and Jere, R. Behraman, 1987, 'Women's Schooling and Children's Health,' *Journal of Health Economics,* Vol. 6, No. 3, pp 239-254.

World Development Report, 1980, 'Nutritional Education' World Bank, Oxford University Press.

World Development Report, 1992, 'Nutrition' World Bank, Oxford University Press.

Chapter 19

Poverty Alleviation
Results of an Impact Assessment Study

K. Srinivasa Rao

Introduction

The Ministry of Rural Development (MRD), Government of India, through its various programmes, endeavours to reach out to the last and the most disadvantaged sections of the society through special employment generation programmes and productive assets through institutional credit and subsidy. Programmes of rural housing and area development, land reforms, drinking water supply and sanitation are specially designed to improve the quality of life in rural areas. In order to assess the impact of various programmes, the Ministry has been conducting a number of concurrent evaluation studies addressing questions relating to individual programmes, largely dealing with programme delivery and impact on the beneficiary. It is against this background that MRD had taken the initiative of conducting quick impact assessment studies in various less developed districts of the country. Districts and States are selected on the basis of relative level of development and performance of the programmes based on past evaluations.

MRD has assigned the Impact Assessment of Rural Development Programmes in Bahraich District of Uttar Pradesh to the Institute of Applied Manpower Research. The main objective of the Impact Assessment Studies was to assess the overall impact of the programmes on poverty alleviation. The specific objectives spelt out for the study were to:

- examine whether the guidelines on various programmes are being followed with reference to selection of beneficiaries, utilisation of funds allocated and transparency and involvement of people in programme implementation;
- examine the survival of assets created, in particular whether all the assets created under the schemes have survived, are in use and cost effective;
- assess the impact of the programmes on productivity and poverty alleviation and, in particular, whether the programmes have contributed in increasing/improving production, employment and living conditions of people below the poverty line. (The study was required to estimate the number of people who have crossed the poverty line after availing of the assistance under various programmes);
- examine the role and functioning of the Panchayati Raj Institutions (PRIs) in the implementation of the programmes.
- verify the assets created at the village level, quality of construction, maintenance of the common facilities created and infrastructure development assess whether the infrastructure development; under JRY, Water Supply, DPAP, DDP and IWDP have contributed in providing minimum basic services and overall improvement in the living conditions of the poor in the rural areas.

To attain the above objectives the study covered the goals enunciated in each of the programme guidelines and its actual implementation in the selected districts/blocks and villages and also the actual beneficiaries in the sampled households. It includes review of: the departmental records of the last 3 years from 1997-98 to 1999-2000, allocation and utilisation of funds under the programme, evaluation of performance of the programme on the basis of targets set and the achievements made in line with the national level norms, critical assessment of the number and quality of assets created, nature of expenditure incurred and their contribution to the generation of employment opportunities.

The study also covered evaluation of the relevance of sanctioned projects in terms of correspondence with local level priorities and degree of community participation, understanding the factors undermining programme performance including external compulsions influencing project selection and non-adherence to prescribed norms. An assessment of the process of beneficiary selection, processing of applications and credit disbursement including malpractices, if any, in the process of beneficiary-oriented scheme .

Other aspects covered under the study are critical evaluation of the sustainability of the activities including identification of critical factors, determining the same and development of case specific recommendations for improving the delivery system and overall impact of these programmes.

From each selected district, 4 blocks were selected, namely, Kaiserganj, Risia, Shivpur and Mihipurwa, based on the relative level of development. From each of the selected block 10 villages were selected on a random sampling basis and from each village 15 beneficiaries and 4 non-beneficiaries were selected for collection of detailed information. Thus, the sample size consisted of 40 villages, 600 beneficiaries and 160 non-beneficiaries in each district as per the guidelines given by the Ministry of Rural Development.

Self-Employment Programmes

Integrated Rural Development Programme (IRDP) has reached almost all the villages and its coverage has been good. Out of the total sample, 30.62 per cent were IRDP beneficiaries. Among these beneficiaries, the caste composition shows that 48.91 per cent were SC, 7.61 per cent ST, 25 per cent OBC and 18.48 per cent were others. And it is also worth noting that 30.43 per cent women got selected as beneficiaries under IRDP. In the Focus Group Discussion all the beneficiaries reported that they had to pay bribe for getting scheme approved; as a result, the desired objectives of the schemes could not be met. It was also reported that until some money was paid, the bank officials did not cooperate in getting the loan sanctioned. Almost the entire subsidy went as bribe. This is the main reason why the people are highly reluctant to take part in IRDP.

It was also noticed that majority of the beneficiaries under IRDP scheme were in primary sector followed by tertiary sectors. Most beneficiaries were satisfied with the level of financial assistance. Assets created were mainly livestock, goattery and piggery. In some cases some animals died. An attempt was made to provide insurance coverage for livestock of the beneficiaries, but so far they have not received any compensation from the insurance company. For nearly 69.57 per cent of the beneficiaries, assets were surviving and currently in use. It is interesting to note that the percentage retention of assets were relatively more in Kaiserganj and Risia as compared to Shivpur and Mihipurwa blocks. Scheme-wise retention of assets was observed in the case of buffalo herding, goat rearing, piggery and poultry. Average income from assets, ranges from Rs 368 to Rs 4,602. It varies not only from activity to activity but also block to block. Till the date of survey, 90 per cent of the beneficiaries were not paid the loan amount properly. Around 90 per cent beneficiaries of IRDP are defaulters in repayment of instalments. This is the main reason why the bankers are not willing to come forward to offer loans. In all such cases non-existence of enterprise is the reason cited by the cross section of people including Project Director, DRDA. Around 70 per cent beneficiaries reported that there was improvement in their economic condition after availing the IRDP scheme.

Regarding SGSY, the group formation is the main problem. A Focus Group Discussion was held with the beneficiaries, non-beneficiaries, elected representatives and officials at different levels. It was reported that due to poor coordination among the group members, the group formation under SGSY was very difficult. Target group was reluctant to work in the group because they felt that due to the fault of one member, all the other members in the group could be in serious trouble. Therefore, there is a need to evolve the group in a natural process rather than making a forcible attempt to form the group. It was also reported that the banks were not interested in providing credit to the group members as they had no obligation on the part of any agency. Attempt was also made to capture the perception of bankers. They stated that before providing credit to any group, bank ensures that the scheme is viable and the recovery factor is also taken into consideration. They also reported that if the amount disbursed is not recorded, the responsibility is fixed on them. Earlier experience shows that the record of recovery is very poor in the social sector schemes. It may also be noted that an insignificant percentage of beneficiaries under TRYSEM had made attempts to start self-employment in the study area. The programme however, was not effective.

The beneficiaries of SITRA are highly satisfied with the scheme. Of the total sample, 30 (5 per cent) benefited under this scheme. Caste wise data reveal that majority of the beneficiaries belonged to other backward castes (OBC), followed by others and scheduled castes. Only 2 SC women benefited under this scheme. As a whole, the status of only 26.67 per cent beneficiaries was uplifted from BPL to APL. The scheme has played positive role in increasing the incomes of the beneficiaries in the study areas. But due to merger of the scheme with SGSY the scheme is not in existence any longer. The scheme has positive impact on the beneficiaries and should be launched again, according to the opinion of a cross section of people.

At the district level the main problem is the lack of skilled trainers. The kind of vocation for which training has been imparted includes welding, carpentry, TV and radio repair, hand-pump repair, etc. The beneficiaries also received tool kits. It was observed that government functionaries took no follow-up action once the beneficiary started the enterprise.

Under DWCRA the beneficiaries were supposed to establish the self-help group and to start income generating activities. Unfortunately, no DWCRA beneficiary was covered in the survey. An attempt was also made to discuss the issues with the concerned BDOs; they have reported that due to non-existence of the scheme its impact could not be seen.

Regarding MWS, the economic status of beneficiaries had marginally increased. Beneficiaries received the full benefits of this scheme. Caste composition in the data shows that around 55 per cent SC, 26 per cent OBC, 16 per cent others and 3 per cent ST benefited under MWS. Except in the 'others' category, one woman in each caste benefited under MWS. physical sustainability was very high (90.32 per cent) under MWS projects. As many as 77.42 per cent beneficiaries reported that their economic condition has improved.

Under wage employment category, there are two programmes such as JRY and EAS/SRY. As already mentioned, in place of JRY, JGSY was introduced. EAS/SRY was not effective in the study area due to lack of awareness.

Caste composition of the beneficiaries shows that 44.52 per cent SC, 3.42 per cent ST, 34.25 per cent OBC and 19.18 per cent of others benefited under JRY. Female participation was highly insignificant. Works undertaken under JRY were mainly: approach roads, soil work, community hall construction, panchayat bhawan construction and bridge construction, etc. Regarding the performance of these works, no written records were available in the Gram Panchayat. Especially in case of approach roads there was lot of repetition because they were not permanent in nature and earlier no work was recorded. In focus group discussion, the villagers reported that most of the works carried out under JRY were decided by the Pradhan himself.

Regarding the creation of man-days of employment, there was no uniformity in the study area. Proper records were also not available as to when the work was performed and how many man-days of employment were created. It is also significant that the prescribed wage rates were not properly implemented in the study area. While participating in JRY, 63 per cent of the beneficiaries reported that their economic condition has improved. However, almost all the beneficiaries expressed their desire to work continuously under this scheme because it was highly effective. Gram Pradhan expressed that under JGSY, the number of man-days creation was less as compared to JRY, because the priority of works was different. This type of problem arises due to lack of awareness, as EAS was already there to provide a number of mandays. On the other hand, the impact of wage rates was there in infra-structurally poor blocks. But in infra-structurally developed blocks, Agriculture wage rates are favourable to the workers as compared to JRY wages, because in these blocks apart from wages, kind component (food) was also there.

Since 80 per cent Pradhans were illiterate, (and as such not aware of the accounting procedures), and were dependent on the village panchayat and development officer. Unfortunately, in Uttar Pradesh after the implementation of New Panchayat Raj Act the grassroot level functionaries of seven departments including tube-well operator form Jal Nigam were clubbed together and re-named as village panchayat and development officer. These people do not have exposure to the activities of rural development at grassroot level: Therefore, it is difficult for them to implement the schemes designed for the rural development. It is suggested that all of them be given orientation training followed by intensive training for successful implementation of rural development programmes. In addition to orientation programme and intensive training programme, sensitisation programme for one week may also be organised for them. Most Gram Panchayat officials do not maintain the assets creation records or other necessary records. Funds allocated to the district were effectively utilised and 63 per cent beneficiaries reported that the scheme was very useful and it had contributed in improving the economic conditions of the beneficiaries in general. And 95 per cent of the beneficiaries expressed their desire to work continuously under JRY. The scheme provided gainful employment in the hour of crisis and had a positive impact. Impact of the scheme was more positive on SC and OBC beneficiaries.

Indira Awaas Yojana (IAY)

Surveyed data as well as the Focus Group Discussions have proved that Indira Awaas Yojana is the only scheme which is considered to be highly successful in the entire district. The data reveal that 87.50 per cent women benefited under this scheme. Of this 49.26 per cent SC, 1.47 per cent ST, 26.47 per cent OBC and 10.29 per cent other caste groups benefited.

Even though the beneficiaries expressed some practical problems, their response to the significance of the scheme was very good. It was observed that Rs 400 to 4,500 were invested by the beneficiaries at the time of construction. So, the main problem is inadequate financial support. All the beneficiaries have reported that the assistance provided under the scheme is insufficient and it should be increased. Currently a sum of Rs. 20,000 is provided to the beneficiaries for constructing the house. Apart from the house, they have to construct sanitary toilet and smokeless Chullas. Majority of the beneficiaries expressed that it was not feasible to construct the sanitary toilet in all the cases along with the houses. It was also reported that because of the condition fixed for the scheme some needy persons are reluctant to take benefit of the scheme. It was also observed that: the number of houses allocated was far less than required. Only the influential persons were getting benefited under the scheme. It was reported that in certain cases households above poverty line were also benefitting by the scheme. Beneficiaries had to pay bribe to the Pradhan and government officials for getting assistance. In certain cases the constructed house was not being properly utilised for the residential purpose. Instead, it was being used for keeping animals and storage of grains, etc. It is interesting to note the quality of houses was very good because the beneficiaries themselves were involved in the construction process. It seems that no contractors were involved.

Welfare Programmes

The scheme was well received in the district. Caste composition of beneficiaries indicates that 30.88 per cent of SC, 1.47 per cent ST, 41.18 per cent OBC and 25 per cent others benefited. Ratio between male and female beneficiaries was 22.05 : 77.94. Among women beneficiaries, OBC women got more benefited, followed by SC and others. However, the beneficiaries of NOAPS and widow pension reported that the pension was received in an irregular manner.

Beneficiaries of NOAPS and widow pensioners reported that they had to face a lot of harassment in the hands of the bank personnel, the gram Pradhan and the Lekhpal. In certain cases the identification of the beneficiaries was improper and persons ineligible were selected as beneficiaries. However, in the absence of other social security measures, the beneficiaries were quite happy and content with whatever was given to them. They would like to continue to be benefited from the scheme.

The National Maternity Benefit Scheme also had a positive impact on the rural society in general and beneficiary women in particular. It was reported that in most of the cases the assistance was provided after 4-5 months of delivery, defeating the basic objective of the scheme.

Grass root level functionaries have reported that the current practice is that the case is prepared by them and forwarded to social welfare department for getting approval. Social welfare department releases the assistance. Due to tedious procedure plenty of time is consumed in processing of applications.

The analysis clearly indicates that three types of programmes like self-employment, wage employment and housing and welfare programmes are highly useful to the BPL families for improving their standard of living. Among the self-employment programmes, DWCRA, TRYSEM and GKY failed to reach the beneficiaries. On the other hand, schemes such as JGSY and SGSY were implemented recently. So far, no beneficiary received the benefit under SGSY in this district. But the study team made an attempt to collect information about JGSY and SGSY from the beneficiaries, elected representatives, grass root level functionaries and higher level officials. They also reported that employment creation, group formation, bankers willingness, marketing facilities, forward and backward linkages, awareness and mobilisation were the major factors for the success of the programmes. Though, it is early to comment on the impact of the above mentioned two programmes, it can be said that the objectives of the schemes were very good and will definitely help the poor masses.

Overall Impact

To assess the overall impact of the programmes changes in the household assets, income and expenditure pattern of the beneficiaries were taken into consideration.

Household Assets: According to the reports of beneficiaries in Mihipurwa, household assets of all caste groups increased after availing the benefits especially in case of durable goods and livestock assets in Risia, SC and OBC caste beneficiaries' assets improved. In Kaiserganj only others caste groups assets improved after availing the benefits. This shows that marginal improvement had taken place on durable assets in Mihipurwa, Risia and Kaiserganj. No improvement was observed on durable assets in Shivpur.

Household Income and Expenditure: Data related to in income and expenditure reveal that, average income was marginally higher (1.02 per cent) than average expenditure. On the other hand, among the studied blocks, Shivpur and Mihipurwa block's average incomes were higher than the average expenditures of the same blocks as compared to Kaiserganj and Risia blocks. But the caste-wise data show that SC's average incomes were higher than the average expenditure in all the studied blocks. In the case of OBCs, except in Mihipurwa, the average income was higher than the average expenditure in the remaining blocks. As a whole, the per cent increase in average income was highly favourable to OBCs as compared to SCs.

Indebtedness: Among sample beneficiaries 60 per cent of them did not report whether they had debt or not. According to reported beneficiaries' data, 8.50 per cent of Scheduled Caste, 0.33 per cent of STs, 4.17 per cent of OBCs and 2.50 per cent of others had fallen in the debt trap. Except for the others caste group, the remaining caste groups were highly indebted in Kaiserganj and Risia blocks as compared to Shivpur and Mihipurwa blocks.

Change in Life Style: According to non-beneficiaries' perception, 46.25 per cent beneficiaries' life had changed after they benefited under these programmes. Change was observed in all the sample blocks except Kaiserganj. In Shivpur and Risia the change of life was observed among 62.50 per cent beneficiaries. And 42.50 per cent change was observed in Mihipurwa.

Economic Status: Though, around 7 per cent of the beneficiaries did not respond, 15.50 per cent beneficiaries reported that their economic status had improved. In other words, only 15.50 per cent beneficiaries were uplifted from below poverty level to above poverty level. More than 70 per cent beneficiaries remained below poverty line in the study area. Caste-wise data reveals that around 7 per cent of SCs and around 7 per cent of OBCs economic status has improved from BPL to APL and one per cent ST beneficiaries also improved their economic status. Block-wise figures show that Kaiserganj and Risia block's status of improvement was higher than Shivpur and Mihipurwa . Risia was the highest beneficiary and Shivpur got lowest impact among the studied villages.

Findings

One of the major findings of the present study is that the IRDP along with its allied programmes presented a matrix of multiple programmes without desired linkages. These were implemented as separate programmes without realising the overall objective of generating sustainable incomes. The average investment per family remained at sub-critical levels, too inadequate to generate income of Rs 2000 per family per month as it was expected to do. Consequently viable project could not be undertaken to provide adequate incomes on a sustained basis. Management of the enterprise, delivery of credit from banks, overcrowding in certain selected activities and exclusion of the poor from community decision making were some of the problems encountered in the implementation of this programme. Rising indebtedness of IRDP beneficiaries is another finding. In some cases beneficiaries had to borrow money at much higher interest rates in order to repay the IRDP loan to avoid legal action. This has raised serious doubts about the viability of the projects in generating adequate incomes for the beneficiary to cross the poverty line and to repay the loan.

Presently, under SGSY formation of SHGs took considerable time and has been one of the prime reasons for less than expected performance under the scheme in 1999-2000.

The study also shows that under JRY the employment generated per person was too inadequate to bring about any meaningful increase in the earnings of the beneficiaries. On an average, 10-15 days of employment generated under the programme in a year could not make any significant impact on the income levels of the beneficiaries. Achievements are much below the targets for employment generation in the rural areas. The rural poor perceived this programme as an asset building programme rather than as a wage-employment programme. Hence the entire focus was on creation of assets. It was also observed that the projects were executed by contractors who sometimes hired outside labourers at lower wages. By effective intervention in the labour market, the wage-employment programme was expected to exert upward pressure on the market wages. Although this happened in a few cases, the success was limited due to insufficient man-days generated by the programmes. There have also been instances of differential wages paid to male and female workers. Despite all its shortcomings the programme did succeed in creating durable community assets in rural areas. Villagers generally appeared to have liked the idea of building up rural infrastructure especially when the assets were directly relevant to the community such as school building. Further, the programme led to empowerment of panchayats as the funds were placed at their disposal along with the power to get the works executed through line departments. However, unless technical officials are also transferred to the panchayats along with funds and functions, the dependence on bureaucracy will continue and it will not be in a the interest of effective implementation of anti-poverty programmes.

Implementation of Indira Awaas Yojana is not free of problems such as insufficiency of fund allocated for construction of dwelling units, poor quality of construction, involvement of contractors and middlemen and wrong selection of beneficiaries. Despite all these limitations, IAY is a well-accepted scheme in the rural areas primarily because of the direct ownership of assets by the beneficiary under the scheme. However, it was found that there are several pressure groups working in the rural areas to avail of the subsidy under IAY. Under the existing system, the DRDAs/Zila Parishads make allocations and fix targets for the number of houses to be constructed panchayat-wise. Given the large number of potential beneficiaries awaiting the allotment of a free house, in several gram panchayats it would be possible to cover only very few households each year. This obviously leads to local pressure in allotment of housing units. Considering the various problems encountered in the field in implementation of IAY, the scope and coverage of rural housing have been widened recently.

Implementation of NSAP is also fraught with problems as the programme was being implemented by a large number of agencies which raise coordination issues. By and large, it was seen that the norms prescribed under the programme were being followed. However, the criteria of identifying destitutes were not clear and different states follow different norms. On the whole, the programmes are reported to have been well targeted. It was felt that there is need for creating awareness about the programme. It was also seen that wherever Gram Sabhas were well in place and met regularly, information dissemination was very effective. The procedure of registration involves production of several proofs and certificates which makes it very cumbersome. Most of the NMBS beneficiaries are reported to have received the benefits after the delivery. Need to create awareness about the scheme has been brought out by the studies. Procedures under the scheme need to be simplified and made more transparent to enable the target groups to derive the intended benefits.

However, the study reveals that the reach and coverage of the programmes were poor. Guidelines were not followed in case of selection of beneficiaries. It also shows that even the improvement was not much in the beneficiary families.

Lessons from the Survey

On the strength of the survey results, we believe a holistic approach is needed to implement the various programmes at the grassroot level and to tackle issues ranging from socio-economic to local level administration. In spite of continuous efforts made by the government, chronic problems are rampant in the studied villages. It also reveals that the required infrastructure facilities are not availabe in the desired quantity and quality in this district. If at all some facilities are existing their working condition is very poor. For example, drinking water facility is being provided for all the villages but the quality of water is poor and supply inadequate . Almost same is the case of electricity and schools. The present study also suggests that people are aware of discrepancies in the implementation of ongoing rural development programmes.

At present, local level administration lacks transparency and accountability. Though, gram panchayat officials know all about the maintenance of records, accounts, maintenance of assets, social audit, etc., the problem lies in lack of supervision and lack of power to control the gram panchayat Pradhan. This is one of the major loopholes in the existing system. According to present norms, only the awareness of the people will be the solution to the perfect implementation of the rural development programmes.

Level of awareness of the local population, presence of local administrative bodies like Panchayats, commitment of implementing agencies at various levels from the village to the block and district levels are important factors that make all the difference between success and failure.

Presence of middleman, contractors, corrupt officials and local vested interest (who deflect the benefit under the programme from the target population to line their own pockets) is a major stumbling block which has to be overcome in order to improve the success rate of the anti-poverty programmes.

Proper identification of the target population, viz. population below the poverty line (BPL) is in itself a major task which seems to have not been rigorously adhered to.

Absence of a system of proper maintenance of records at the local level results in arbitrary selection and renders monitoring difficult.

The findings of the survey results underline the importance of building the local Panchayati Raj Institutions (PRIs) which alone can act as an effective delivery mechanism because it will ensure people's participation at various stages of implementation and transparency. PRIs can play an important role in improving the efficiency and effectiveness of the schemes and reducing leakages.

Anti-poverty programmes being aimed at the most disadvantaged group with low income and low level of literacy, need for a locally effective delivery system is of critical importance. Assistance has to reach at the door step of the beneficiary. Such a functicn can be best performed only by the local panchayats. The Gram Sabha can play a key role in the selection of beneficiaries which is being done in certain States like Kerala and Punjab.

Although most of the anti-poverty programmes have been in vogue for several years, there is still lack of information about their scope and content and sometimes even their existence.

Formation of Village Development Committees, with participation by the poor, should be empowered to implement the schemes. Intensive awareness generation campaigns have to be launched to disseminate information on the programmes and their benefits.

Also, in villages where literacy rate is satisfactory, bill boards can be displayed at prominent locations to reach the message to the people. Formation of beneficiary groups would go a long way in sustaining the programmes.

Most of the elected representatives are illiterate and there is a need to launch a special programme to make them literate so that their effective participation in the programme implementation is ensured at the grass root level.

Intensive training programme needs to be designed for the Pradhan and elected representatives for making them aware about the rules and regulations and their implications, if not followed properly.

As far as the role of women Pradhans is concerned, in some cases their husbands or sons were performing the duties of the Pradhan as a proxy. Though this is the initial phase of decentralised governance it was observed that these women Pradhans were keen to learn new practices. They have been participating in the Gram Sabha meetings as wells meeting at the higher level, as and when called by the high level functionaries. They are feeling empowered and in time to come more and more females are likely to come forward to participate in the election as well as other affairs of the village.

In most of the surveyed villages all the committees were reported to be in existence but none were found for physical verification. An attempt should be made to make the committees more viable.

The presence of empowered local bodies like panchayats, an effective interventionist NGOs' movement and people's participation at the grassroot level constitute the bull-work for the success of the anti-poverty programmes.

Poverty Alleviation Programmes that are Region-specific will benefit more. It is a known fact that at present the implementation process is taking too much time to reach the beneficiaries. Benefits are also not reaching in time. In the process the poor person has to spend a lot of money.

It is a known fact that majority of the BPL families are from downtrodden communities. The present study has shown that though Scheduled Castes and Other Backward Communities have started improving their quality of life with the help of poverty alleviation programmes over the period, still there is a long way to go in raising these people above poverty level on a sustainable basis.

Chapter 20

Poverty Alleviation in Orissa

M. Altaf Khan

When planned efforts for development were initiated in 1951, Orissa was a classical example of a totally underdeveloped economy – 'a severe resources constraint, low per capita income, mass poverty, chronic unemployment, very low level of technology and poor economic organisation. The usual vicious circle of poverty causes low productivity which perpetuated itself. This implies a circular constellation of forces tending to act and react upon one another in such a way as to keep Orissa in a state of poverty.'[1] In addition, this high incidence of poverty can also be attributed to the natural calamities such as floods, droughts and cyclones which occur regularly in Orissa. Cyclones have in recent years become a regular feature. In 1972, Orissa was hit by cyclone that affected the coastal districts. In 1973 floods brought great damages in Balasore and Mayurbhanj district. In 1974-75 a drought of long duration descended on the state. According to Government reports about 12 million people in 1823 villages were affected by drought. In 1979 a tornado destroyed the village Puruna-Bandha Goda. In 1980 a heavy flood brought great damages in Rayagada district. Hundreds of people were washed away in floodwater. In 1982 and in 1985 floods and cyclones occurred. Again in 1990 heavy flood occurred in South Orissa and hundreds of families suffered a great loss of lives and assets. Orissa is a riverine state, so it quite impossible to prevent flood completely.

A super cyclone swept throughout the state on 29 October, 1999. It soon become evident that it was a national calamity, causing damages and 1.5 crore people of Orissa were affected. A series of natural calamities not only make the state backward but create and perpetuate unemployment, wastage, and poverty. These are the overall factors which are responsible for generating poverty in Orissa.

According to National Sample Survey Organisation's Report the percentage of people living below poverty line (BPL) in the country has come down to 26 per cent in 2000 from 36 per cent in 1993. Among the states, Orissa has a dubious distinction of having the highest proportion at 47.15 per cent of its population living under BPL – Scheduled Tribe and Schedule Caste constitutes 22.21 per cent and 16.20 per cent of the total population of the state respectively. Article 46 of the Indian constitution requires the state and the Union Governments to promote their educational and economical interests and protect them from social injustice and exploitation.'[2]

Poverty Eradication Programmes

A number of tribal development programmes have been launched by the government and other agencies for poverty alleviation and economic upliftment of the poor Tribals of Orissa. Major poverty eradication programmes of Orissa particularly for Tribal areas are:

Tribal Sub-Plan

It was launched in the Fifth Plan period with the objective of improving socio-economic conditions of the tribal population, strengthening of infrastructure in tribal areas, protecting the tribals against exploitation and promoting then interest through legal and administrative support. Under this plan 44.7 per cent of the geographical area of Orissa was identified and declared as scheduled tribe area covering as many as 62 tribal communities including 12 primitive tribal groups. In these tribal areas, developmental programmes are being implemented through 21 Integrated Tribal Development Agencies (ITDA) and 17 micro projects. In 1997-98, the flow of funds to ITDA was Rs 576.62 crore from the state plan. In addition to Rs 134.14 crore from central plan, Rs 37.88 crores from special central assistance was sponsored.

Modified Area Development Approach (MADA)

MADA aims at development of tribal falling outside the ITDA areas. About 5.67 lakh tribals in 46 pockets covering parts of 47 blocks of 17 districts are covered under MADA programme. During 1997-98 an amount of Rs 2.36 crore was spent covering 3,759 tribal beneficiaries. An outlay of Rs 2.66 crore was provided for the year 1998-99 under special central assistance scheme for tribals economic development.

Cluster Approach

Cluster Approach has been adopted since the seventh plan for the development of contiguous areas having 5000 population and where 50 per cent or more tribals live. Till 1999 more than 14 pockets comprising parts of 13 blocks in 10 districts with 52,793 tribals had been covered under cluster approach. During the year 1997-98 an amount of Rs 18.13 lakh was spent. In 2000 the proposed outlay, worked out as Rs 20.45 lakh under special central assistance for eradication of poverty of tribal areas of Orissa which includes Kashipur block of Rayagada district.

Orissa Tribal Development Project (OTDP)

This is the most important project. This project was launched in 1988-89 with the joint assistance of international funds for agriculture development, Government of India and state government, for the all round development of Tribals of Kasipur Block of Rayagada district. A sum of Rs 59.41 crore was spent in this area for overall development of tribals.

Causes of Starvation in Kashipur

In our field tours to Kashipur block, we found following reasons for mounting poverty leading to starvation deaths:

(i) It was found that most of the benefits of the welfare schemes were harvested by vested interests. In many cases the works/ projects could not start because of quarrels between contractors. There are several instances of misappropriation in works done under calamity Relief Fund (CRF) and food for work (FFW) programmes in 2000-01. The beneficiaries were misidentified,

(ii) That there is no positive correlation between the requirements of tribals and welfare Schemes of the government. According to the local tribals no project had been launched for them to generate income regularly. Hence they are bound to do the unproductive activity: mortgage of crops and land.

Failures of programmes and policies are due to lack of: awareness, interest by the officials, coordination among beneficiaries, the authorities and the local politicians.

Combating Poverty

Combating poverty is not an easy task. To eradicate poverty the BPL group should gain the strength in generating income to feed themselves without liquidating the earning source. Effective management is a key to the success of all plans and programmes. Mismanagement squanders our resources, creates chaos and endangers our well-being. So management is the only mantra to implement the projects of the government through a team of talented, motivated and devoted officers.

There is a need for a trained talented team which can secure better results in eradicating poverty. A Tailor Made Management Programme (TMP) is to be spread and the training facilities to be given to the trainers . The trainee will also work (i) As Coordinator to Coordinate the BPL beneficiaries with the officials; (ii) Create the awareness and motivation among the beneficiaries to act in accordance to the proposed project of poverty eradication programme of the Government; (iii) follow up and coordination with financing or funding agencies to provide timely credit as well as to guide and convince loanees for repayments of loans since further financing of the projects depends on recovery of finance. The proposed TMP has three important areas of training. These are: *(A) Awareness programme (B) Coordination Programme (C)*

Credit for self-help programme.

The Awareness Programme aims at breeding entrepreneurship qualities among the BPL groups This can be launched by imparting training to the local school teacher or NGOs who are having aptitude to serve the society. The school infrastructure will be used for awareness programmes, conducted in evening or on holidays. The objective is to create interest among the BPL group to fight against poverty, through business knowledge, awareness about nature's gift and their commercial utilization of their knowledge and labour. Above all some dreams should be developed in their heart so that they will work systematically and work for the project's success and for their own success. This programme should be developed in vernacular language and their own people should impart it. Therefore local school teachers, NGOs officials and the school is the best combination for launching the Awareness Programme in Tribal areas.

There is a need for coordinating activities. Co-ordination is the essence of management. The failure of the programmes is due to lack of coordination between targeted beneficiaries and the official machinery. In order to develop a perfect co-ordination, orientation programme for block level officials should be organised on regular basis. Values and holism are two sides of the coin for poverty eradication programmes. Values should imparted by higher officials so that it can reach to bottom levels office assistants who are involved in poverty eradication programmes and projects of the centre and State Governments. Otherwise it cannot achieve the holistic objectives.

There is an urgent need of supplying credit without interest if possible or with very little interest, which should be linked with income, profit or surplus to stop hunger and starvation deaths. Credit creates entitlement of resources, which can be used for further resource creation.

Conclusion

Orissa is a land of prosperity and peace, but it still remains an enigma to the economists and philosophers. It is the only state in the country which is endowed with all bounties of nature. It has a long coastal line and rich minerals. In addition to this it has many beautiful and scenic spots dotted by historical monuments which can be developed as a heritage and eco - friendly tourist spots. The beauty of this state is that it has peaceful, comparatively cheaper and disciplined labour yet the state is seething in poverty. So, there is a need of TMP, mixing three important elements such as Awareness Programme, Coordination Programme and Credit Programme systematically. It should be based on requirements of a block because the requirements vary from block to block. Knowledge is a power. Let us share it in the shape of information through Tailor-made Management Programme for combating poverty. No poor, No hunger, No violence' is our kaleema. To achieve this noble purpose, there is a need for setting up a centre for poverty eradication programme where TMP for poverty eradication programmes will develop. A state level and district level centres are required to conduct overall studies of poverty problems of various states of India. Because the poverty problems are quite different from state to state and district to district. Therefore some coordination of all these should be made at a state as well as district level. These centres will cater the different needs like Awareness programme, Coordination programme and credit programme.

NOTES

1. Tripathy, P.C., 'Interface Between Infrastructure and Economic Development,' *The Orissa Journal of Commerce*, vol. XXI No. 1, 1997, Page 9.
2. *Economic Survey of Orissa*, 1998-99, Page 20.

Index